OXFORD STUDIES IN
SOCIAL AND CULTURAL ANTHROPOLOGY

Editorial Board

NATIONALISM AND HYBRIDITY IN MONGOLIA

OXFORD STUDIES IN SOCIAL AND CULTURAL ANTHROPOLOGY

Oxford Studies in Social and Cultural Anthropology represents the work of authors, new and established, which will set the criteria of excellence in ethnographic description and innovation in analysis. The series serves as an essential source of information about the world and the discipline.

NATIONALISM AND HYBRIDITY IN MONGOLIA

URADYN E. BULAG

CLARENDON PRESS · OXFORD
1998

Oxford University Press, Great Clarendon Street, Oxford OX2 6DP
Oxford New York
Athens Auckland Bangkok Bogota Bombay
Buenos Aires Calcutta Cape Town Dar es Salaam
Delhi Florence Hong Kong Istanbul Karachi
Kuala Lumpur Madras Madrid Melbourne
Mexico City Nairobi Paris Singapore
Taipei Tokyo Toronto Warsaw

and associated companies in
Berlin Ibadan

Oxford is a trade mark of Oxford University Press

Published in the United States
by Oxford University Press Inc., New York

British Library Cataloguing in Publication Data
Data available

Library of Congress Cataloging in Publication Data
Data available

ISBN 0–19–823357–4

1 3 5 7 9 10 8 6 4 2

Typeset by Pure Tech India Limited, Pondicherry
Printed in Great Britain
on acid-free paper by
Bookcraft (Bath) Ltd.
Midsomer Norton, Somerset

FOREWORD

Caroline Humphrey
Reader in Asian Anthropology, University of Cambridge

For the past fifty years studies of Mongolian society and culture have been dominated by three paradigms. This is not the place to describe them in detail, but to put Bulag's work in context let me characterize them briefly. One strand has been dominated by the historical geographical work of Owen Lattimore and his theory of the frontier zone. Mongolia and Manchuria were such zones, where over thousands of years waves of Russian and Chinese settlers created and re-created their own economic ways of life in a constantly changing relation with native pastoralists. A completely different view has been provided by orientalist scholars, predominantly German, Russian, Japanese, and British. Here the interest was in Mongolian culture and political history, which was approached almost entirely through manuscripts. The focus was on accurate recording and there was a tendency to abstain from overt theorization of any kind. The third, Marxist, perspective has been almost diametrically opposed to the second, since it brought in general theories of social evolution and class relations, setting aside the cultural insights to be obtained from Mongolian manuscripts as relevant only to the aristocracy and religious élite. In the context of these scholarly traditions, Bulag's book is a highly original achievement. It is the first monograph to investigate in a coherent way a series of a questions addressed separately earlier, and to attempt to go beyond what, with no disrespect, we can see as the scattered, haphazard offerings of 'Mongolian Studies'. Bulag addresses the political place occupied by Mongolia and Mongolians among the other peoples of Inner Asia, the relation to this of historically changing Mongolian culture, and the issues of class and ethnic categorization addressed by the Marxists.

It has been extraordinarily difficult to create an anthropology of Mongolia in the twentieth century. One reason is quite simple. For decades anthropologists and ethnographers were allowed only limited access to 'the field', and short visits outside the major cities were always carried out under conditions of supervision. This was the case in all three major Mongolian-culture regions: the Mongolian People's Republic, Buryatia in the USSR (Russia), and Inner Mongolia in China. I myself, as someone who worked under these conditions, have no resentments on this score: if a country wishes to preserve itself from anthropologists' instrusions, it has a right to do so. Furthermore, such a policy is part of how that society or polity constitutes itself, and no doubt, from that perspective, anthropological interpretations designed almost entirely to interest an academic audience in the West appear at best irrelevant and at worst impertinent meddling. However, there is another, perhaps deeper reason why anthropology has been so difficult in these regions. It is that the twentieth century has seen great tragedies in Inner Asia, such as the virtual elimination of Buddhist institutions, the purges, killing and imprisonment of all kinds of enemies of the state regimes, and the systematic persecution of certain ethnic groups. These events were 'local', but at the same time they were implicated in broad inter-national political relations. Here, it is not just that information about such matters has been systematically occluded, but that anthropologists had, until recently, difficulty in working out anthropological ways of thinking about them. Anthropology's subject matter being what 'really happens' in social relationships and cultural discourse, when the conditions are those of realistic fear this is exactly what people hide or have little wish to remember about the past. Bulag's book sheds light on this troubled area of history and its implications for the present. His book details the enormous amount of debate in Mongolia over Mongolian history, identity, and nationhood, something outsiders might take for granted, but over which there is clearly much internal contestation. His argument is that the Mongols are facing a choice between a purist, racialized nationalism and a more open, adaptive nationalism accepting of diversity, hybridity, and multi-culturalism.

The significance of Bulag's work is that it bravely and comprehen-sively takes on the important questions which arose in Mongolia at a turning-point in history, the early 1990s, when new forms of government and national symbols were in the making. Who are we as a people? What are our basic values, *vis-à-vis* those of our neighbours in Russia and China? The book addresses these large questions anthropologically, i.e. with close attention to the minutiae of what people did and said at the time of the field-work, to social situations, and to the specifically cultural formulations of the issues. At the same time, Bulag has a wide grasp of Inner Asian history and an original perspective on it. Furthermore, Bulag's anthropology is informed by the recent debates on reflexivity and the politics of writing, so his text stands throughout as a consciously situated and intentionally partial text, determined by his own position as an Inner Mongolian writing about Mongolia.

Again to put this book in the context of existing work on Mongolia, we can compare it with Jagchid and Hyer's *Mongolia's Culture and Society*, which is probably the major study of date. Jagchid and Hyer's book is valuable as a compendious survey of the social, cultural, economic, and political history of the Mongols up to the early twentieth century, with an additional short chapter on the socialist period. However, it situates its materials neither in relation to historical propositions and arguments, nor in relation to the authors' stance as writers (Jagchid is an Inner Mongolian, a refugee from the communists in China). Bulag, on the other hand, does not ignore his own situation in the social relations he encountered in Mongolia, nor the way this influenced his understanding. He grasps the nettle—which stung bitterly, as I know—of having been judged 'not a real Mongol' and 'a Chinese hybrid' (*erliiz*) while he was in the field. Indeed, it was acknowledging this 'interstitial identity' (in the words of Homi Bhabha) that gave him many of his insights, while his sense that he was, after all, also a Mongol gave him an inalienable, almost moral, baseline, empowering him not to hide behind objectivity but to write as a Mongol for other Mongols.

Bulag's book is an important contribution to the growing number of works by indigenous anthropologists. In this context, readers may like to know more about him than he tells us in the book itself. Bulag was born as the son of a quite ordinary Mongolian family (his father is a Mongolian herbal medical practitioner and his mother is a dressmaker) in the Ordos region of Inner Mongolia. Brought up in a desert oasis, he received education in Chinese, as there was no Mongolian-language teaching in 1972 when he went to school. Undergoing numerous humiliations as a member of a national minority, Bulag however excelled at schools in the commune and prefecture centres and then at university in Hohhot. In 1986, despite having achieved the highest marks, he was 'sent down to the countryside' after graduation. Bulag then taught in a rural secondary school, but determined somehow to escape that life. He focused on perfecting his English language, and he took a job as an interpreter for a wool factory when an opening came up. This enabled him to act as research assistant to the anthropologist and ethnomusicologist, Carole Pegg, when she was collecting data in Inner Mongolia. At the same time, Bulag was gathering materials about the cult of Chinggis Khan, hoping to introduce Mongolian culture to a wider world.

Meanwhile Urgunge Onon and I started up the Mongolia and Inner Asia Studies Unit at the University of Cambridge and we were looking for young Mongolian scholars to invite. Carole mentioned Bulag's name. In January 1989 he came to England on a short visit and his abilities immediately impressed, for he was given a scholarship by Corpus Christi College, Cambridge. Thereafter, with all the difficulties and loneliness of being the first Mongolian in the University, he flourished.

This is a brave book because it deals with certain issues (nationalism of various kinds, cultural stereotypes of purity, nutrition, and sexuality) that are sensitive and on which Mongols do not agree. Furthermore, in the post-socialist turmoil these matters can seem to change quite rapidly. Nevertheless, I believe that Bulag has been able to probe centrally important aspects of Mongolian society, politics, and culture. Mongols are caught between a Soviet-dominated past and a Chinese threatened future. Now we have a book on nation-building in these circumstances. Bulag's sophisticated conclusion analyses a situation that can be found elsewhere in the world, that of an economically disadvantaged core 'guarding against its own peripheries'. However, he sees his main contribution as problematizing the idea of Mongolia as a homogeneous place and people. His message is that Mongolia needs unity through acknowledging diversity. With this book Mongolia should now enter the voluminous literature on nations and nationalism, and readers will have access not to just another case-study survey but to the unique insights of a Mongol who is both an insider and an outsider.

ACKNOWLEDGEMENTS

This book is based on a year of field-work in Mongolia 1991–2, which led to a Ph.D. thesis submitted to the University of Cambridge in 1993. My gratitude goes first to Mongols in Ulaanbaatar, Hentii, and Dornod. Some of the ideas were first conceived in my discussions with scholars in my host institution, the International Association for Mongolian Studies: Sh. Bira, D. Tsolmon, E. Puntsag, and others. Gantogtoh, a linguist, and Badamnyam, a professional translator, have been particularly helpful in guiding me to understand many aspects of the Buriat life.

As many will testify, thesis writing is a lone business, but I was particularly blessed with a most knowledgeable supervisor, Caroline Humphrey. Despite her overwhelming load of academic commitments, she gave unstintingly of her time to discuss every aspect of the thesis. Throughout the research, she helped me crystallize many of the main ideas. She not only encouraged me to publish the thesis for a wider access, but read the entire finished manuscript and made many incisive comments and suggestions. It is a great honour that she agreed to writing a foreword for this book.

Carole Pegg deserves my special gratitude, for this work would not have been possible if she had not introduced me to Cambridge in the first place. Throughout my research in Cambridge, she has been supportive and followed my progress. She also read the completed manuscript and offered her gift of knowledge on diverse Mongolian cultures.

I owe numerous debts to many friends for commenting on the thesis or manuscript. It was particularly gratifying that one of my thesis examiners, the late Professor Ernest Gellner, made detailed comments on the thesis, which proved extremely useful in revising it into the present book. Wurlig Borchigud and Edward Kaplan helped by reading the whole thesis and suggesting specific changes. Solonggowa Borzigin, A. Hurelbaatar, Pan Jiao, Jerry Jirimutu, Almaz Khan, Stephan Muller, and Chuluu Wu read parts of the thesis or manuscript and offered many insightful suggestions and criticisms. I also acknowledge the helpful comments of anonymous reviewers in the process of submitting the work for publication.

My debt for institutional and financial support of research in this project is to Corpus Christi College, Cambridge, which provided me with a research scholarship and supported my M.Phil. and Ph.D. studies in social anthropology from 1989 to 1992. The rewriting was completed during my non-stipendiary research fellowship at the same college (1995–8), and whilst holding a Leverhulme Trust fellowship (1995–8) and an Isaac Newton Trust grant (1995–9). I am also grateful to the Mongolia and Inner Asia Studies Unit, Cambridge, for providing a useful 'Mongolian' environment where I could test many of my ideas.

Finally, I would like to thank my wife, Lan Mei, for accompanying me on my field-work trip, putting up with many discomforts, and enthusiastically supporting my research.

This book records a tremendous change that is taking place in Mongolia, and it is to the benefit of the Mongols that I devote this work. I hope that they may find some interest in my reflections. However, none of the people or institutions mentioned above should be held responsible for the interpretations and errors in this book, which are all my own.

Notes on Sources

I have used a number of illustrations from Mongolian artists. As Mongolia is not party to either the Berne Convention or the Universal Copyright Convention, and their artworks are not subject to copyrights, I can only offer my thanks to the artists for their witty and interesting art that I reproduce here.

Since Mongolian newspapers are short, and the individual newspaper articles that I refer to are very easy to locate, I have omitted page numbers of quotes from them.

CONTENTS

LIST OF FIGURES

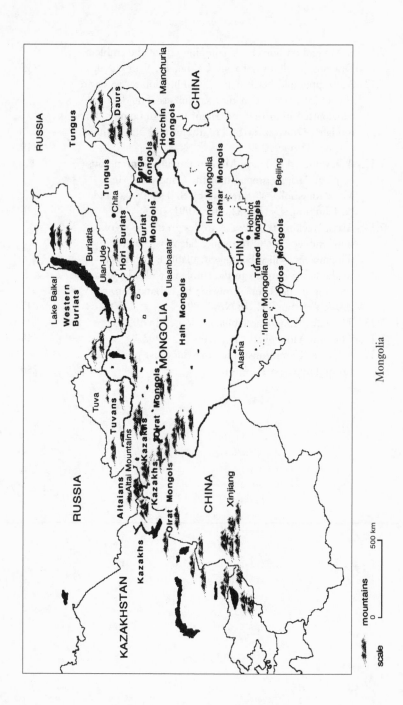

Mongolia

1

Introduction: Situating Hybridity

This book is an attempt to study contemporary nationalism in Mongolia and its implications for Mongols who are dispersed widely in neighbouring countries. Let me begin by briefly outlining my treatment of this issue as an introduction and guide-line to the book. I begin by examining socialist modernization, which shaped a strong Halh 'nation'—that is, the predominant Mongol 'ethnic' group in Mongolia, which is often claimed to be conterminous with Mongolia.

This book examines Mongolian nationalism in the context of the three main populations of Mongols in different nation-states: the Buryat Mongols in Russia, the Halh Mongols in the Mongolian People's Republic (now called Mongolia), and the Inner Mongols in China. In the pre-socialist period relations between them were constructed mainly symbolically, through politically significant marriage alliances. This was beneficial to the ruling élites, which needed external legitimacy to enable them to hold on to power. However, this system, although it continued to some extent in the socialist period, is no longer workable in the present (post 1989) nationalist period. Domestic politics in Mongolia has developed the negative category of *erliiz*, a concept of 'half-breed' or 'hybrid' now applied to people as well as animals, and conceived not only as a biological category but also as a cultural one.

Denouncing pan-Mongolism—that is, a sentiment that all Mongols should have wider links—Halh-centric nationalism frightens people with the spectre of the imminent swallowing up of Mongolia by China. This generally held anxiety is cultivated by the ex-Communists to maintain their leading position. The Mongolian People's Revolutionary Party (MPRP) has assumed the role of guardian of national independence, formerly exercised by the Russians; in this context I examine the fierce debate over national emblems and symbols which pitted democrats and ex-Communists against one another.

Finally, I propose a new approach to understanding Mongolian nationalism, investigating the way in which the nation is conceived as a unique combination of fraternity and femininity (not sorority). The contemporary nation, conceiving its culture as feminine, can be seen as a modern endogamous 'tribe', which departs from earlier exogamous practices. However, since cultural, biological, and economic endogamy cannot be sustained, this must remain a political ideal, in dialectical conflict with other, mainly economic, processes. What this situation generates in society is a post-socialist 'hybridity', the production of excluded and despised categories of people. I believe that this may have considerable implications for the study of nationalism in other post-socialist countries.

The question naturally arises as to how I came to this conclusion. It is central to the way anthropology is done these days that one should contextualize one's role in the ethnographical world, which inevitably affects one's understanding of the society concerned. I am no exception; indeed, I should say that my experiences in Mongolia had a direct bearing on my choice of theme and the content of this book.

An Erliiz[1] *Anthropologist and Greater Mongolia*

The theme of the book is directly related to my personal relations with Mongolia, a reflection of my own ethnic identity as a Mongol from China. I was born into a Mongol family and brought up in a pastoral area, but subsequently received a formal education in Chinese. I have become personally sensitive to nationalism and ethnicity. My idea of ethnicity was originally a primordialist one like that of many of my compatriots; I dreamed of going to Mongolia, the Mecca of many Inner Mongols, if not all.

What is Inner Mongolian ethnicity? Different people may have different perceptions of this. It is a large topic that needs to be dealt with separately, and here I address only some ideas which I believe are also held by many in Inner Mongolia. It comprises a sense of loss and a refusal to identify with a Chinese state that is largely perceived to be alien. The division of Inner and Outer Mongolia was very much an arbitrary one created by the Manchu who established the Qing Dynasty (1644–1911),[2] the very institutionalized terminology indicating separate

---

[1] Half-breed or hybrid; this is a concept that I discuss extensively.

[2] The Manchus subjugated the Mongols between 1640 and 1691. Initially the Mongols viewed Manchu rule less as a subjugation than as a military and kinship alliance, but the Manchu's total identification with the Han Chinese towards the end of the dynasty sounded a knell for their political relationship. For a Mongolian perspective on the Manchu–Chinese rule of Mongolia, see Sanjdorj (1980).

administration. Mongols would, however, conceptualize the two in body language: as *Övör* (bosom) Mongol and *Ar* (back) Mongol (for a detailed discussion, see Chapter 6).

For many Mongols in Inner Mongolia, the existence of an independent Mongolia[3] has always been a reference point by which to measure their own progress and struggle or competition with the Chinese. The long genealogy of Mongolia's communism, paradoxically, boosted the Mongols in Inner Mongolia to counteract the Chinese, enabling them to claim that Mongols are not as 'primitive' as the Chinese claim them to be. In fact, in terms of communism, the Mongols say that the Chinese should recognize that they are junior to the Mongols, for the Mongolian Communist revolution succeeded in 1921, thereby becoming the second oldest Communist regime after the former Soviet Union. This challenges the hegemonic notion that the Mongols in Inner Mongolia should look up to Chinese culture and civilization as the only legitimate source for progress. For many, until 1990, there had been a burning desire to communicate with Mongols in Mongolia for cultural and kinship, if not political, purposes. It was a deeply held conviction that, although two Mongol populations are accommodated in two different states, their kinship and cultural ties should nevertheless be everlasting. Inner Mongolian ethnic identification with Mongolia is thus a refutation of the assimilationist ideology of the modern nation-state, in which everybody, regardless of ethnic background, should look to a political centre in loyalty and affiliation. Contemporary Inner Mongolian ethnicity is therefore not so much oriented towards establishing a nation-state of its own, as bewildered that somehow Inner Mongols have been left out of the mainstream Mongol world. This sense of incompleteness leads them to idealize Mongolia as a paradise where Mongols live in happiness, where genuine Mongolian culture is developed without restriction, and Mongols can walk shoulder to shoulder with any nation in the world. The

---

[3] For Mongols in Inner Mongolia, Mongolia has been independent since 1911. In reality, the proclaimed independence was soon reduced to an autonomous status under the suzerainty of China, in 1915. In 1921, with the help of the Soviet Red Army, Mongolian socialist-nationalists set up a People's Government and in 1924 declared the Mongolian People's Republic (MPR). The MPR was not an independent country, however; the Soviet Union continued to recognize Chinese suzerainty over the MPR until 1946, when Mongolia's sovereignty was reluctantly recognized by the Nationalist Government of China. This recognition did not amount to genuine independence; the Soviet Union controlled almost every sphere of Mongolian society until 1990, when the democratic revolution in Mongolia finally made it a *de facto* independent country. For the new Mongolian view of the nature of Mongolia's sovereignty, see Baabar (1996).

sense of being neglected, and forgotten, and the frustration from not
being able to prosper as a nation in a predominantly Chinese environment, even though it is their homeland, has created a sense of being
separate as a diaspora. This feeling became especially strong after the
genocidal repression of the Cultural Revolution,[4] and the long period of
being incommunicado with the Mongols of Mongolia, Buryatia, and
elsewhere for almost three decades since the mid-1960s.

Notions of diaspora of course apply to people dispersed from their
homeland, living in exile, either voluntarily or by force. According to the
editors of *Public Culture* (1989), 'diasporas always leave a trail of collective memory about another place and time and create new maps of desire
and attachment' (quoted in Aug 1993: 5). The feeling of diasporism of
Mongols in Inner Mongolia, in their own homeland, is extraordinary,
but it is perhaps a logical consequence of the development of the nation-
state. As China now claims that Inner Mongolia is an inalienable part of
China, and has swamped it with Han Chinese migrants, the landscape of
Inner Mongolia has fundamentally altered. As they lose confidence in
their ability to keep Inner Mongolia as their homeland, Mongols in Inner
Mongolia have shifted their focus to the other half of the geo-body (to
use the term of Winichakul 1994) that seems to them successful. Mongols in Inner Mongolia are increasingly defining themselves in diasporic
terms, reminiscent of a process elsewhere in nation-states where minorities are uprooted to make space for homogeneity (see Tölölyan 1991).
What this situation creates is not only a loss of interest in the homeland,
but also a call to ethnic kindred elsewhere.

In August 1990, I was able to visit Mongolia, and I did so as a pilgrim
on the occasion of the celebration of the 750th anniversary of the *Secret
History of the Mongols* (hereinafter *Secret History*), the most important
indigenous Mongolian historical source.[5] I had expected to experience a
common Mongolian bond and solidarity from the Mongols there, just as
I was filled with such an emotion. However, my naïvety was soon dashed.
There in Mongolia, for the first time I realized I was not a 'Mongol', but
an 'Inner Mongol' and a citizen of China. Worse still, I was sometimes
regarded as Chinese. Clearly the Mongols in Mongolia did not share my

---

[4]   There are a few works in English concerning the persecution of the Mongols during the
Cultural Revolution: Hyer and Heaton (1968), Jankowiak (1988), Sneath (1994), Woody
(1993). The full-scale violence against the Mongols during the Cultural Revolution has
recently been recorded and published by Tu Men and Zhu (1995).
[5]   Three English versions of the *Secret History* are now available: Cleaves (1982), Igor de
Rachewiltz (1971–84), and Onon (1990).

vision. This puzzled me and many other Mongols from Inner Mongolia who had undergone similar experiences. Mongols in China seldom think in terms of citizenship or international relations that Mongols in Mongolia take for granted. That I was surprised by these politicized multiple identities was probably due to the lack of a citizenship notion in China. China is still a country that constructs itself along majority–minority lines (see Gladney 1994). In such a society, the most immediate concept that is meaningful to me is that of Mongolian nationality (*menggu zu* in Chinese, *mongol ündesten* in Mongolian), rather than of Chinese citizen (*gongmin*). Van Amersfoort (1995) suggests that such an organization by nationality is characteristic of states with ethnic stratification and a cultural division of labour. 'The concept of citizenship contains a notion of fundamental equality that runs counter to the experience of ethnic groups that are hierarchically included in the nation' (1995: 166). I have now discovered that I am an Inner Mongol; at the same time, I am both Chinese and Mongol, a being betwixt and between.

My second visit to Mongolia (April 1991–April 1992) coincided with the political liberalization that took place in Mongolia and the rest of the socialist world. At the same time, border exchanges and communications between three Mongolias (Buryatia, Mongolia, and Inner Mongolia) became frequent. This provided a unique opportunity to examine the Halh Mongolian attitude towards these other Mongols. The discrimination, or rejection, I had encountered was not an isolated case. It was part of a more general rejection by Mongolia of Mongols from outside Mongolia. And this rejection is very often expressed in terms of purity: Mongols in Mongolia are represented as pure or genuine Mongols, while those outside are neither. It is interesting to note that this notion of purity is also held by the Mongols from Inner Mongolia; the pressure for assimilation in China forces them to idealize the purity of Mongolia, not only ethnically, but in terms of culture, the environment, etc. However, their notion of purity is somewhat different from that perceived of Mongols in Mongolia. The Inner Mongols' admiration for the purity of Mongolia is a wish to align themselves with it, whereas the Mongols of Mongolia's emphasis on their own purity betrays the fact that they wish to dissociate themselves from Mongols from outside.

I will not talk much about this Inner Mongolian perception of the purity of Mongolia, but will discuss how the Mongols' *exclusive* type of purity came to be so. While I recognize its roots in international relations—Mongolia's paranoid fear of China—I suggest that it is also the new interaction of Mongols from different countries that has lent weight to the theme of 'pure Mongolness'. This is seen in a number of key symbols and preoccupations, such as virgin soil, animals, dung, milk, heart, mind, ancientness, and 'originalness'. All of these concepts separate the people and the country from the invasion of pan-Mongolism (that is, the aspiration of the other diaspora Mongols to unity), perceived now by many Halh Mongols as 'dirty', 'ambiguous', but also 'ambitious'.

My position as an anthropologist, neither native nor outsider, is a difficult one. At first I did not know how to be true to what anthropology required of me: that is, how to balance an objective attitude with my emotional subjectivity. Anthropological notions of 'purity' and 'danger' offer me some relief. I feel, perhaps, that I have a few words to say about this peculiar phenomenon in Mongolia.

The politics of field-work poses a difficulty for every anthropologist, but it varies according to circumstances. In Mongolia, a foreign anthropologist normally represents prestige and power; he or she is an outsider, and the insiders are eager to tell him or her stories, to boast about their culture. In the case of isolated people, they may beg foreign anthropologists to introduce their culture to the world; they therefore co-operate and, indeed, willingly offer as much information as possible. Foreign anthropologists are often entrusted by natives with the role of cultural brokers. However, native anthropologists do not enjoy this privilege, though they have others. Inside Mongolia, their work is seldom done on their own initiative; they are sent through bureaucratic channels, use standard surveys, and have access to local statistics, etc. Especially in the socialist period, native anthropologists conducted research projects which were part of a larger scheme to transform society, to identify either feudal elements or progressive people's culture, the latter to be reinjected into the newly constructed national culture. I enjoyed none of these advantages, though there were sympathetic Mongols, especially in rural areas, who treated me as a member of the Mongol diaspora who had not forgotten his roots.[6] In other places, especially in cities, I enjoyed a cocktail combining suspicion and friendship, depending on how personal relationships developed. My identity as a Mongol from China, currently studying in the West, but researching Mongolian politics, was certainly

---

[6] With such people, my identity, which is connected with Ordos (a term related to the more familiar English terms Urdu and Horde), a 'tribe' burdened with a symbolic association with the cult of Chinggis Khan and with a historic mission to guard his legendary shrine (*ongon*) and spirit (*süld*), was helpful. For the cult of Chinggis Khan in Ordos, see Andrews (1981), Jamtsarano (1961), Lattimore (1941), Sainjirgal and Sharaldai (1983), Serruys (1971).

puzzling to many people. I sometimes had to play several roles, in order to get along, depending on circumstances.

I have briefly discussed the distinction between the foreign anthropologist and the native anthropologist. Clearly, I do not belong to either category. But I could be both. My prior knowledge of my own Ordos Mongol culture convinced me that what was going on in Mongolia was just like 'us' Ordos Mongols. I could sometimes conceptualize the discrimination against me in a simple, yet famous proverb: *Mongol Mongoldoo muu*—'Mongols are bad to each other'. So what's the big deal? The long separation of Mongols in Mongolia and China, and the subsequent new 'national' cultures built around the Soviet and Chinese models respectively, did not necessarily obliterate the basic Mongolness in me and in Mongols in Mongolia. It was my conviction that what united me and the Mongols in Mongolia was a common culture, a 'supra-Mongol' culture that had its roots in pastoralism and history, that transcended tribal and now nation-state boundaries. Clearly, there were new things that I had to adapt to, but that adaptation was certainly no greater than that required of a total stranger. However, it was in this context that, like many native anthropologists, I was blind to many aspects which might seem strange to foreigners. I did not feel very different from the Mongols, a fact which pleased me as a Mongol, yet worried me as an anthropologist. It was only after the realization that they felt different from me, that I seriously questioned my own naïve, but I plead genuine, assumption that I was no different from them. This led me to question why I was received so ambiguously. The experience reminded me of the division between Eastern and Western Mongols in Inner Mongolia,[7] which is psychological and cultural, and now very often institutionalized in job allocation in the local governments of various levels. The extension of this scenario to the relationship between Inner and Outer Mongolia (now called Mongolia) certainly needs some consideration.

I have already remarked that I was regarded as an *erliiz* in the sense that I was excluded because I was not an 'insider'. The geographical distance between Ordos and central Mongolia allowed me to feign ignorance, in order to enable Mongols in Mongolia to tell me something.

---

[7] The root of the present East–West division in Inner Mongolia, in my view, largely lies in the decades of Japanese administration of the eastern part of Inner Mongolia until 1945. However, western Inner Mongols would often invoke the historical precedence of the Horchin (Eastern Mongols) allying with the Manchu in the seventeenth century.

This field-work was an interaction, and my struggle was to understand that relationship. In this sense, the book is embued with my own assumptions, which I indulge in calling a 'Mongolian perspective'. Although I personally resented the treatment I received, paradoxically I respect the Mongols' choice to exclude me. So I do not suggest that pan-Mongolism is better than Halh-centrism, or the other way round; they are two modes of thought, but clearly both have to be moderated in this hostile geo-political world: pan-Mongolists to understand their exclusion from Mongolia, and Halh-centrists to respect the feeling of Mongols outside Mongolia for their ethnic roots.

This study is also about how 'pure' Mongols look at me, a 'hybrid' Mongol. Anthropologists, as criticized by Rosaldo (1993), often take the position that their own culture is invisible, and thereby ethnography becomes a one-way traffic, an objective description of a culture. The usual stance is for ethnographers to position themselves as students receiving an education from the people they study. Although such a stance looks humble and laudable, the very notion of objective, educated-type writing ignores human interaction; thus it unconsciously occupies the moral high ground. In my case, I could hardly afford this. In fact, I myself became an object of the Mongols' enquiry, putting myself in a position, clearly visible to them. Therefore, my field-work was very much 'a recurring conflict of interests, an agonistic drama resulting in mutual respect, complicity in a productive balance of power' (Clifford 1988: 76).

This suggests that I have gone beyond the traditional role of the anthropologist, of objectively recording and analysing my field data or experiences. I am not detached, I am emotionally involved, and further-more have an axe to grind. Perhaps anthropology does not require 'objectivity' any longer. Although such an attitude is stressed, it is no longer a binding principle, at least not since such influential works as Jean-Paul Dumont's *The Headman and I* (1978) and Clifford and Mar-cus's *Writing Culture* (1986). Dumont effectively reveals the paradox of 'involved sympathy' and 'disciplined detachment' which underlies the pretext of objectivity. Field-work experience for Dumont involves being encultured and acculturated by the people one lives with, and also bringing changes to the society one studies. Dumont champions a subjectivist understanding by echoing Mead: 'There is no such thing as an unbiased report upon any social situation. An unbiased report is, from the stand-point of its relevance to the ethos, no report at all; it is comparable to a colour-blind man reporting on a sunset' (quoted in Dumont 1978: 13).

Perhaps the most important shift in anthropological writing since Clifford and Marcus (1986) is the collapse of the notion of representation of others by scholars—in this case, by anthropologists. While anthropologists increasingly question their standpoint from which to view the world, they have to occupy a new strategic ground 'centre stage' of a fiction, as it were. '[O]ne cannot occupy, unambiguously, a bounded cultural world from which to journey out and analyse other cultures. Human ways of life increasingly influence, dominate, parody, translate, and subvert one another. Cultural analysis is always enmeshed in global movements of difference and power' (Clifford and Marcus 1986: 22).

These theoretical realignments have effectively removed the distinction between a native anthropologist and a foreign anthropologist. At least the native anthropologist's moral ground of subjectivity is recognized and becomes less of a disadvantage, if not an advantage. Therefore, I, as a half-native anthropologist cannot, do not, and will not represent Mongolian culture; rather, I conduct a cultural analysis involving power relations and discourse, and do so through my personal experience, however trivial it may be. And here, my own experience of being included and excluded puts me in the centre of this drama. Narayan (1993), in a recent penetrating discussion of 'native' anthropologists, suggests that 'objectivity' is no longer the marker distinguishing the native from the foreign anthropologist. A native anthropologist must identify his or her own location in the society being studied, rather than claim complete representation. Personal location in the society will ultimately dislodge the monolithic whole, but will also reveal one's hybrid or multi-cultural identity. In her scheme of 'enactment of hybridity' Narayan asserts that 'objectivity must be replaced by an involvement that is unabashedly subjective as it interacts with and invites other subjectivities to take a place in anthropological productions. Knowledge, in this scheme, is not transcendental, but situated, negotiated, and part of an ongoing process. This process spans personal, professional, and cultural domains' (1993: 682). Clearly this also implies that we must accept Rosaldo's point, that just as the social analyst is a positioned subject, not a blank slate, 'the objects of social analysis are also analysing subjects whose perceptions must be taken nearly as seriously as "we" take our own' (Rosaldo 1993: 207).

The shift in emphasis from objectivity to subjectivity thus opens avenues for a native or hybrid anthropologist like me, as subjective perception becomes legitimate. The analysis of my own predicament, however, poses yet another dilemma. That is, the experience is my own.

I cannot generalize. Although I claim to be a Mongol from Inner Mongolia, I cannot possibly be a complete example of that people or culture. This registration of caution concerning my own unrepresent-ativeness, is counterbalanced, however, by the perceptions of Mongols who view me as somehow an example of that culture. My own identifica-tion that I am a Mongol, ignoring political boundaries, is also a move beyond 'cultural difference' studies to a kind of political advocacy. Native anthropologists studying their societies may produce texts similar to the autobiographical writing produced by Black America:

[A]utobiography (at least in its most potent forms) is predicated on a moral vision, on a vibrant relation between a sense of self and a community, on a retrospective or prophetic appeal to a community of spirit, be it religious or social, or on...a feel for moral tradition....What thus seem initially to be individualistic autobiographical searchings turn out to be revelations of tradi-tions, recollections of disseminated identities and of the divine sparks from the breaking of the vessels. These are a modern version of the Pythagorean arts of memory: retrospection to gain a vision for the future. In so becoming, the searches also turn out to be powerful critiques of several contemporary rhetorics of domination. (Fischer 1986: 197–8)

However, although I recognize my subjectivity and move towards pol-itical advocacy, I have also been led to recognize through my anthro-pological training not to confuse myself with 'them'. The gist of my text is therefore essentially different from what Jameson (1986) calls the 'national allegory' characteristic of all Third World texts.[8] My stance and position, as stated earlier (see Narayan's point) are what give me ground for political advocacy (I will discuss this in Chapter 8).

The period in which I did my field-work (1991–2) was not stable; rather, Mongolia was in a transitional historical stage that was shocking the whole nation. The society and economy were changing rapidly, making it very difficult to grasp the real situation. This is one reason why I have written comparatively little here about social categories such as 'class'. The sudden change of ideology often confused people, and there were different opinions. The hysterical nationalist sentiment or democratic fervour must have stabilized considerably by now. This book is therefore largely a historical study of Mongolia in 1990–2. Although I hope the anomalies recorded here are short-term phenomena, I am of the

---

[8] Many scholars (e.g. Ahmad 1992, Sprinker 1993) rightly criticize Jameson for essen-tializing the Third World notion in non-Western literature, thus catering to the superiority of the First World.

impression that my general conclusion is still valid up to 1995–6. It is ironic, indeed, that while as an anthropologist I hope my conclusion is right, as a Mongol, I wish only to overturn it. Whatever I reveal and criticize is meant to contribute to a genuine bright future for Mongolia and to improved inter-Mongol relations, but without upsetting current nation-state arrangements. The message I want to convey is, now, not just to professionals, but also to my Mongol people, who live in different countries.

Below I present a brief historical overview of Mongolia to contextualize my discussion of contemporary Mongolian nationalism and ethnicity. More details of the history will be mentioned in later chapters.

Historical Overview

Mongolia, located in the heart of Inner Asia, is landlocked between Russia to the north and China to the east, west, and south (see map). With a total area of 1,566,500 sq. km, in 1990 Mongolia had a population of only 2.1 million, one of the lowest population densities in the world. Mongolia is the only country where Mongols constitute a majority of the population. Other Mongols are scattered in many parts of China—for example, Inner Mongolia, Xinjiang, Höhnuur, etc.—as well as different areas of Russia (Buryatia, Irkusk, Chita, and Volga regions).

Having been part of Central Asian nomadic states at different times since the third century B C, Mongols emerged as a distinct group between the eleventh and twelfth centuries. Under the leadership of Temüjin (Chinggis Khan), a powerful nomadic state was built in 1206, establishing the first *Mongol Uls* (Mongol nation), which gave its name to current Mongolia. Mongols ruled China for about a century, and Russia for over two centuries, before the gradual disintegration of the Mongol Empire.[9] Mongols in Mongolia proper—that is, north of the Great Wall of China—split into three main groups: the Oirat (later known as Western Mongols), the Mongol (later known as Eastern Mongols), and the Horchin (later incorporated into the Eastern Mongols). In the fifteenth century, the Eastern Mongols were united under Batmönh Dayan Khan, who became ruler in 1479. He divided his subjects into six Tümen:[10]

[9] For the history of the period see Morgan (1987) and Endicott-West (1989).

[10] A Tümen was a military unit of 10,000 men, or myriarchy. The six Tümen divisions of the Mongols should not be read literally as six 'ten thousand men', but as six Khanates.

Tsahar, Halh, and Urianghai in the left wing, and Ordos, Tümed, and Yongshebu in the right wing. The Khanship fell on the Tsahar Tümen, the deputy Khanship, or Jinong, on the Ordos Tümen. In the seventeenth century, various Mongol groups were brought under control, one after another, by the Qing Dynasty, except for the 'Buryat' and 'Kalmyk', who came under the rule of the advancing Russian Empire. By the late seventeenth century, the present major geo-political divisions were more or less fixed: Mongols under the Manchu were divided into Inner Mongolia and Outer Mongolia, while those under the Russians became known as Buryats and Kalmyks. Outer Mongolia, based on the Halh Tümen, unlike Inner Mongolia, was only indirectly ruled by the Qing Dynasty. As significant as the colonial administration of Mongolia, Mongols in both Inner Mongolia and Outer Mongolia had been converted to Tibetan Buddhism; their religious nobility gradually outweighed the Chinggisid aristocracy in political and moral authority. At the approach of Tsarist Russia, Mongolia was no longer a backwater on the frontier of the Qing Dynasty, but a contesting ground between it and Russia.

In 1911, the collapse of the Qing Dynasty made it possible for Outer Mongolia to gain independence. A theocratic state was proclaimed, with the religious leader the eighth Jebtsundamba Hutag (also known as Bogd Gegeen)[11] as its monarch (Khan). The majority of the Inner Mongolian banners declared allegiance to the Bogd Khan; in the Bogd Khan Government, Buryats and Inner Mongolian intellectuals and princes played prominent roles. Bogd Khan Mongolia (1911–21) was short-lived, however. In 1915, as a result of the Kyakhta tripartite conference, Outer Mongolia became an autonomous state under Chinese suzerainty. Taken over first by Chinese troops in 1919, then by the remnants of the Russian White Guards in 1920, Mongolia won independence from China in 1921 with the assistance of the Soviet Red Army. In 1924, Outer Mongolia was able to declare itself the Mongolian People's Republic (MPR), the second Communist state to be founded after the Soviet Union. The Buryats once again played an important role, controlling various government ministries such as information, education, finances, and ideologies, only to be eliminated when their agenda of helping Mongolia clashed with that of the Soviets.

---

[11] The paramount Mongolian Buddhist leader. The first and second incarnations were Mongols from the lineage of Chinggis Khan, but the subsequent reincarnations were all Tibetans. For recent Mongolian re-evaluation of the Bogd Khan, see Humphrey (1994).

This part of modern Mongolian history has been contested. As far as China is concerned, Mongolia had always been part of China, a claim that often flabbergasted Mongols. While China[12] claims that Mongolia became independent only in 1946, when the Kuomingtang (KMT, the Nationalist Party of China) government recognized it, Mongolia insists that 1921 marked the day of independence,[13] a claim supported by most Western writings. The discrepancy between the two accounts lies in the difference between *de facto* independence and *de jure* independence. Or, as Bhabha (1990) would say, what matters is the way in which Mongolia chooses to construct its collective memories, how it narrates itself into pride and glory. However, the Mongols' denial of the Soviet colonization of Mongolia seems more a strategic narration, as the former Soviet Union was considered to be the best guarantor of its independence from China. Nevertheless, the unsavoury conduct of the Soviet Union in Mongolia pushed the Mongols to question this general friendship. When national sovereignty came to outweigh friendship, Mongol dissidents started to reveal the negative aspects of the Sovietization of Mongolia (Baabar 1990). With the collapse of the Soviet Union, Mongols are now able to assess realistically their country's relations with the Soviet Union. A number of Mongolian scholars have started to challenge the myths of the People's Republic (see Baabar 1996, Dashpurev and Soni 1992, Battogtoh 1991). The Soviet Union, according to them, always kept Mongolia as a strategic buffer zone. It is now known that the Soviet Union signed a bilateral agreement with China in 1923 confirming the status of Mongolia as part of China, and that the Soviet Union promised to return Mongolia to China once a Communist revolution succeeded in China (see Elleman 1994).

Mongolian independence from China was established by a huge internal sacrifice, by a process of complete transformation from what is diagnosed as a feudal society to a socialist one. Consolidation of a socialist system meant eradication of 'feudal elements'. In late 1923 and early 1924, in a nation-wide reshuffle of local administration, most of the aristocrats and lamas were dismissed. In 1928, Mongolia embarked on an ambitious plan to confiscate the properties of nobles and transfer them to *ard* (commoners, that is, proletarians), an attempt that triggered an uprising that had to be put down by Soviet and Mongolian armies. An

---

[12] China's official position is that Mongolia, prior to 1946, had always been part of China (see Yu 1994).

[13] The Mongolian capital Urga (Ulaanbaatar) was liberated in July 1921. Since then, 11 July has been marked as Mongolia's national day.

estimated 10 per cent of Mongolia's population fled Mongolia into Xinjiang and Inner Mongolia. The instability in Mongolia was exacerbated by the Japanese advance into Inner Mongolia and the Japanese-sponsored pan-Mongolian movement in the 1930s. The establishment of Manchukuo and the promised deliverance of an independent Mongolian state by the Japanese, intermingled with Japanese expansionism and Buddhist Shambala, or paradise, now espoused by the exiled ninth Panchen Lama, fuelled the imagination of the beleaguered Mongolian Buddhists and others that combining forces with them would enable them to escape from the evil of Communist oppression. In the name of safeguarding Mongolia, a Red Terror, echoing the great purge in the Soviet Union, swept across Mongolia in the late 1930s, eliminating the monks and almost the entire adult male population of Barga, Buryat, Tsahar and Chinese; they became double victims, both of Communist ideology and by being accused of collaborating with the Japanese (see Dashpurev and Soni 1992).

The purge was followed by a war in 1939 between Manchukuo and Mongolia (see Coox 1985, Moses 1967). A Mongolian–Soviet army jointly repulsed the Japanese–Mongolian troops. In this war, Mongols on both sides of the border were pitted against each other, supporting the Soviet Union and Japan respectively. According to Moses (1967), this war finalized the permanent separation of Mongolia and Inner Mongolia. The Soviet–Mongolian victory over the Japanese–Mongolian forces marked the further 'iron friendship' between the MPR and the USSR, which has been glorified as a guarantor of Mongolia's independence.[14]

In a post-Second World War settlement between victorious superpowers, Stalin negotiated Mongolia's sovereignty with the UK and the USA at the Yalta Conference in February 1945. The Chinese Nationalist Government's recognition of the independence of Mongolia came after a plebiscite in Mongolia conducted under UN auspices in October 1945, in which the Mongols voted unanimously for independence.

The establishment of this *de jure* nation-state hinged on the understanding that the MPR would permanently renounce Inner Mongolia. Inner Mongolia subsequently became an autonomous region of China in 1947. Still embracing the Communist notion of brotherhood, the newly

---

[14] The 'iron friendship' is symbolized in a huge statue dedicated to the heroic Soviet people on the mountain of Bogd Uul, dominating the city of Ulaanbaatar. As part of a wedding ritual, new couples would go up to pay homage to the statue, so as to enshrine the friendship.

founded People's Republic of China (PRC) recognized the MPR's independence. However, the initial honeymoon between the MPR, USSR, and PRC was overshadowed by the desire of Mao Zedong to return Mongolia to China, based on the 1923 and 1924 Soviet–Chinese treaties, for China's Communist revolution was now completed.[15] In the early 1950s, Mao asked Stalin to return Mongolia to China (in return for full Chinese participation in the Korean War), but Stalin refused (Milivojevic 1991*b*: 19). In a bizarre competition between the Soviet Union and China to control Mongolia, both sides extended huge aid to Mongolia, which led to the rapid development of infrastructure in Mongolia. China's desire to have Mongolia back, notwithstanding its diplomatic recognition of the sovereignty of Mongolia, prompted Mongolia to seek more protection from the Soviet Union. In the light of the subsequent rift between the Soviet Union and China, in 1966 Mongolia finally invited Soviet troops back to be stationed in Mongolia.[16]

On 27 October 1961, the MPR was admitted to UN membership. In 1962 Mongolia joined the Council for Mutual Economic Assistance (CMEA), or Comecon. From then on, Mongolian national plans were co-ordinated with those of the USSR and CMEA (Comecon) countries, which extended technical assistance. This marked the rapid economic development of Mongolia from a mono-cultural livestock-breeding country to an agrarian-industrial economy. In parallel with this change, Mongolia underwent rapid urbanization: 85 per cent of the population now live in urban settlements. The basic structural weaknesses of the Mongolian economy were exposed when the CMEA structure broke down after the late 1980s.

[15] According to Elleman (1994), the Chinese Communist Party (CCP) was the enthusiastic supporter of the autonomy of Mongolia in the early 1920s: 'the CCP actively helped the USSR retain the terms of the 1915 unequal treaty, which merely continued Outer Mongolia's position as a Russian protectorate. But much to the later displeasure of the CCP, this state of affairs endured well beyond the 1949 Communist revolution, as the USSR refused to reopen talks with the CCP on Outer Mongolia's status. For this reason, Outer Mongolia remained little more than a Soviet puppet state from 1924 through until the late 1980s, immediately prior to the demise of the USSR' (1994: 109).

[16] Milivojevic (1991*b*: 19–20) succinctly records the hostility between the MPR and PRC as follows: 'Thereafter, and especially during and after the so-called Cultural Revolution (1966–69) in China, Sino-Mongolian relations were to be even worse than those of its two neighbours towards each other. In 1969, when Mongolia's embassy in Beijing was attacked by a mob of Red Guards, Tsedenbal freely confessed—to an American journalist—that he hated the Han Chinese even more than did the Russians. Such racial hatred was fully reciprocated by the Chinese, who unleashed a Great Han campaign against the Mongols of IMAR [Inner Mongolian Autonomous Region] during the Cultural Revolution.'

The Mongolia of this period has been evaluated variously by scholars in the West. Lattimore (1962, 1987) marvelled at the miraculous change taking place in Mongolia, calling Mongolia a 'leading state in the world' (1987). Murphy (1966) and Rupen (1964, 1979), by contrast, strongly emphasized the colonial features of the MPR.

Mongolian nationalism during the socialist period was characterized by a tension between a desire for development towards a Soviet-oriented civilization and the wish to develop a national culture. The traditional identity was being transformed into the concept of a socialist 'new Mongol'. This was occasionally resisted by intellectuals, yet without the force that might undermine the 'iron friendship'.[17]

This change of identity, which had its background in the difficult relations with the Chinese, lent the Mongols the political and nationalist enthusiasm to deny themselves their oriental identity, and instead strive to be a 'Western' nation. During this period Mongolia's culture was archaeologically 'proved' to be much related to that of Soviet Central Asia, the Caucasus, and the Near East (Sanders 1987: 4–5).

The overt reliance on the Soviet Union produced a drama that created an essentialized identity for Mongolia, which could be seen only in opposition to China. While a *rapprochement* between China and the Soviet Union was negotiated from the late 1970s, with China's insistence that withdrawal of Soviet troops be one of the crucial pre-conditions, Mongolia understood that a peace between the two might be at its expense. In order to keep Soviet troops in Mongolia, the Mongolian government attempted to provoke China by expelling about eight thousand Chinese residents from 1979 to 1983 (see Sanders 1987: 148–53; Bonavia 1983). In a series of purges in 1983, Samplin Jalan Aajav, Mongolia's second most important leader, was sacked on the pretext of being a Chinese half-breed (*erliiz*).

Mongolian political and economic reforms started in 1984, when Gorbachev took over power in the Soviet Union. Yu. Tsedenbal,[18] the then Mongolian president, was removed from his post and replaced by

---

[17] Rupen (1979) commented on the content of the new identity which he saw actually as an elimination of the identity of the Mongols: 'The most important elements of that identity had been the Buddhist religion (in a Tibetan, lamaist version); the nomadic livestock herding of most Mongols outside the church; the Turkic (*sic*) language of the Mongols, unrelated to Chinese or Russian; their literature, which was largely folkloric and epic in form and content; and their history, which could be summed up in the name of Chinggis Khan and in the idea of pan-Mongolism' (1979: 68).

[18] Tsedenbal (1916–91) was Mongolian premier in 1952–75 and president in 1974–84.

the reform-minded Batmönh. Slowly Mongolia followed the path of *perestroika* (*öörchlen baiguulalt*) and *glasnost* (*il tod*). In 1986 the MPR and the PRC resumed diplomatic relations. The 100,000-strong Soviet troops began to withdraw from Mongolia in 1987, and were gone by 1992. Diplomatic relations were established with the United States in 1987. Gorbachev's visit to China in May 1989 formally ended the Sino-Soviet dispute, and in December 1989 relations between Mongolia and China were normalized. A more independent-minded Mongolia began to emerge from the shadow of its two neighbours.

Facing the aftermath of the collapse of the CMEA, the Mongolian leadership undertook major reforms to restructure the centrally planned economy into a market-oriented economy. Mongolia joined the Group of 77 in June 1989, and sought to join the Asian Development Bank. The USSR antagonized Mongolia by demanding payment of a debt of £10 billion (9.7 billion roubles).

Echoing the Eastern European pro-democracy revolution, and impatient at the inability of the Mongolian People's Revolutionary Party (MPRP) to carry out major political and economic reforms, opposition movements appeared in late 1989. In December 1989 the first public rally was held, followed by the formation of the Mongolian Democratic Union (MDU). On 18 February 1990, the Mongolian Democratic Party (MDP), the country's first opposition party, was established out of the MDU. On 7–9 March, ten members of the MDU/MDP started a hunger strike in the central square in Ulaanbaatar demanding the resignation of the Politburo. At an extraordinary plenary meeting of the MPRP Central Committee on 12–14 March all the members and candidate members of the Politburo and all secretaries of the Party Central Committee resigned, and the MPRP relinquished its monopoly of power as enshrined in the Constitution, thus paving ways for further democracy in Mongolia. It is worth pointing that this was done without bloodshed, which gave Mongols immense pride.

On 29 July 1990 the first ever multi-party general election was held, contested by six parties: the Mongolian People's Revolutionary Party (MPRP), the Mongolian Democratic Party (MDP), the Mongolian Social-Democratic Party (MSDP), the Mongolian Free Labour Party (MFLP), the Mongolian National Progressive Party (MNPP), and the Mongolian Green Party (MGP). The MPRP won 357 of the 430 seats in the People's Great Hural (Congress) and 31 of the 50 seats in the State Small Hural (SSH). P. Ochirbat (MPRP) was elected president; Gonchigdorj, leader of the Social Democratic Party, became vice-president and leader of the SSH. A coalition government was formed, headed by Byambasüren (MPRP).

In January 1992, a new Constitution was finally adopted, the country's name was changed to simply *Mongol Uls* (Mongolia), and the old state flag and emblem were changed. The Congress and the SSH were amalgamated, and now there is only one standing parliament, consisting of seventy-six seats. In the second general election in July 1992, the MPRP once again became the majority in the Parliament, taking seventy-one seats. After this event, the small parties united and formed a Mongolian National Democratic Party (MNDP).[19] Dramatically, P. Ochirbat ran for the presidency, representing the opposition rather than the MPRP. On 6 June 1993, he was re-elected president of Mongolia.

The whole recent period has been marked by strong Mongolian nationalism. With the withdrawal of Soviet troops, Mongolia feels particularly vulnerable. China still represents a threat, which may one day materialize, and Mongolia's small under-funded army (about 50,000) is no match for the several million-strong Chinese army. Consequently, Mongolia has started to loosen her ties with the former USSR (now Russia) and pursue a non-aligned foreign policy, with greater stress on relations with the nations of the Asia–Pacific region. This is a reorientation of Mongolia's historical and political identity.

The Mongols have begun to eulogize their traditions and culture. This 'Mongolizing' process has been rapid and wide-ranging, covering all aspects of Mongolian cultural, political, and economic life. Since 1990, the Mongols have re-evaluated the historical role of Chinggis Khan and accepted him as Mongolian hero, identity-giver, and nation-founder.[20] Buddhism and the classical script,[21] denounced previously, have been revived and are now encouraged as major ingredients of the new Mongolian nationalism (see Campi 1991). Shamanism, which was once thought to have disappeared long ago as the most authentic Mongolian religion, began to be 'performed' in theatres, very much like the theatrical neo-shamanism in post-socialist Siberia. The collectivized pastoral economic system is now regarded as alien and not fitting to the Mongolian

---

[19] For details of political development in Mongolia in this period, see Milivojevic 1991*b*, Heaton 1992, and Batbayar 1993.

[20] Almaz Khan (1995) discusses the process whereby Chinggis Khan has been transformed from an imperial ancestor to an ethnic hero in Inner Mongolia.

[21] See Juergensmeyer (1993: 115–24) for a discussion of Mongolia's religious nationalism. The plan to use the classical script as the official script from 1994 now appears to have been permanently postponed (see Grivelet 1995).

situation, and Mongols have started to return to traditional Mongolian herding practices.

Mongols are facing a massive work of restructuring, geared to creating a market economy. The new government (1990–2) began a privatization programme as its major economic restructuring strategy. However, their efforts were hampered by lack of experience and misunderstanding, and this has resulted in a chaotic situation. Privatization and the centrally controlled economy have also become the focus of ideological struggle. With its fragile infrastructure, its landlocked isolation, and 'three external shocks',[22] notwithstanding its rich natural resources and Western economic aid, Mongolia is experiencing a severe economic recession, which underlies many of its current social problems. Normalization of relations with China and freedom of travel and democracy have opened the doors of Mongolia. Large numbers of Mongols now travel to North America, Europe, China, and other Asian countries to do business, and vice versa. It is against this general background of profound political, economic, and international change that I shall discuss the question of nationalism and identity in Mongolia.

Below I present a brief sketch of two Buryat *sums*[23] to which I travelled, in order to give a picture of what rural life was like in 1990–2 and a context for my observations about nationalism and identity. I have chosen Dashbalbar and Dadal because in subsequent chapters I return to these Buryats in order to make various points about Mongolian attitudes to people now classed as different from themselves.

Buryats and Hamnigans of Dashbalbar and Dadal *Sums*

Dashbalbar *sum* and Dadal *sum* are in Dornod and Hentii provinces respectively. Buryat Mongols came to the region from Siberia in 1918–20 during the Russian Civil War. Dashbalbar has a population of about two and half thousand, of whom about two-thirds live in the *sum* centre. The great majority of the population is Aga Buryat.[24] There are only

---

[22] The three external shocks referred to are the termination of Soviet aid in 1991, the collapse of trading relations with the CMEA in 1991, and the exodus of senior technical advisers from the Soviet Union (see Griffin 1995).

[23] *Sum* is the subdivision of an *aimag* (province). Earlier, it was below a banner (*hoshuu*), a subdivision under an *aimag*. Banners, with their military and feudal connotations, were abolished by the MPR in 1931.

[24] The Aga Buryat were originally a part of the Hori Buryat, but they moved to the Aga region, from which they take their name.

some twenty families of Halh or other ethnic groups. Many people here know their clan names. The population in Dadal is around two thousand, mainly Hori Buryat intermixed with Hamnigan[25] and Halh Mongols. The Buryat clan names here are being forgotten. People can hardly speak their dialect, while the Dashbalbar Buryat are almost pure Buryat speakers.

In summer 1991 I decided to see how the national holiday was celebrated in Dashbalbar. Earlier, a medium-size Russian-made plane would fly from the capital to the *aimag* centre, and a smaller, 'green' plane would go from the *aimag* to the *sum* centre. But from 1991, the *aimag–sum* air link stopped as there was no petrol, and there was only a minibus going once a week. Neighbours and friends were fighting over twenty-odd seats.

Dashbalbar is known as the most conservative Buryat *sum* in Mongolia.[26] As soon as I arrived, my *tomilolt* (permit) was examined by a brigade leader. He threatened me, holding my collar, and said that he could not understand what was going on, why a foreigner was allowed to travel so freely. He questioned me, 'Who knows you are not a Chinese spy?' It turned out that he was not popular locally; I was received royally by the people, and established good friendships. In the words of Badamnyam, my guide, I was an envoy from Ordos. He said that in 1910 the first Buryat scholar, Jamtsarano, had visited Ordos and written an article about the cult of Chinggis Khan (Jamtsarano 1961); now, eighty years later, the first Ordos man had come to visit the Buryats—this was a symbolic exchange.

The *sum* was dominated by a collective (*negdel*) which had (1991–2) one pastoral production brigade, eight milking stations (*ferm*), a hundred small settlements (*suur*), and one technical auxiliary brigade. Seventy per cent of the people worked in pastoral production. A ten-year boarding-school here accepts pupils from neighbouring *sum*s, where they have only seven- or eight-year schools.

The Buryats in the *sum* centre live in wooden or brick houses. In winter, however, some families would erect *ger* (yurts), which they think

---

[25] Hamnigans are a group of Mongolized Tungus. They came to Mongolia along with the Buryats. See Janhunen 1990, 1991, and Shelear and Stuart 1989 for Hamnigans in Inner Mongolia. Janhunen (1996) has also touched on Hamnigans in Russia, Mongolia, and China.

[26] My decision to go there caused a sensation. Halh friends told me that the Buryats there were drunkards and rough; they fought, often using knives. I was not allowed to visit the countryside without an official permit (*tomilolt*) from the work unit; every hotel required this paper.

warmer than a wooden house. Away from the centre, all herdsmen live in *ger*. Every family had a sewing machine, and many had motor cycles, which could no longer be ridden because of the oil shortage.

Dashbalbar represents a centre of Buryat culture in Mongolia. There is a museum, almost comparable to the provincial museum. The local cultural club won a medal in the national singing and dancing competition in 1990. The members also visited Ulan Ude in 1990, where they gave a performance. Bold, a friendly local sage, was dismayed to tell me that the ignorant Buryats in Ulan Ude in Buryatia did not know he was wearing a traditional Buryat gown, but asked him what kind of gown it was.

Significantly enough, when I was in Dashbalbar, Central TV engineers arrived to set up a link to receive national TV programmes. Earlier the local people had TV, but they received only Russian programmes. It was not until July 1991 that Mongolian TV covered the entire country. The curious and delighted people were glued to the screens watching the national *naadam*[27] in Ulaanbaatar, which they were seeing for the first time. They thus neglected the local *sum naadam*, frustrating the organizers and my ethnographic hopes.

There were five political parties in Dashbalbar: the MPRP, MSDP, MDP, MNPP, and a religious party. I did not see any activity of the MSDP, though the chairman was the newly elected *sum* leader. The MPRP chairman was a young man of intelligence, active in privatization. The young leader of the MDP was the vice-leader of the *sum*; but he was mainly interested in doing business. The leader of the religious party was an elderly language teacher, often drunk.

Religious activity was perhaps the most salient local activity in Dashbalbar. The *oboo* (ritual cairn) worship was revived in 1990. The local religious party boasted 100 members, more than any other party (the MNPP had only four members!). Once every two weeks a tour to the Ugtum monastery was organized. Ugtum monastery, once the largest monastery in north Mongolia, known as Mongolia's Utai,[28] was reduced to rubble in the 1930s. There was an elderly Halh lama, who had been a novice lama (*bandi*) at the monastery sixty years previously. He shouldered the responsibility of training two disciples.

---

[27] *Naadam* is the summer sports festival in which wrestling, horse-racing, and archery are contested. (See Kabzinska-Stawarz (1987) for an anthropological study of the 'Three Games of the Men'.)

[28] Utai is a famous Buddhist monastery in Shanxi province, China, once frequently visited by Mongol pilgrims.

Apart from Buddhism, the people of Dashbalbar have some shaman-ism,[29] which started to re-emerge recently. During my stay, a shaman arrived one night without warning the *sum* people, and left on the same night to conduct a ritual nearby. I chased him to the neighbouring Bayan-uul state farm (which is one day's drive west of Dashbalbar) on a truck together with several of his relatives. Despite my request and the pleas of the relatives, his elderly sister was vehemently opposed to my participa-tion in the ritual. She said she did not trust any outsider from Ulaanbaa-tar, for her experience convinced her that a *darga*[30] (leader, hence oppressor) from the capital would only persecute her shaman brother. My Inner Mongolian identity was not able to persuade her either.

Dashbalbar in 1991 was on the verge of privatization. By the time of my arrival, the *negdel* had distributed seven sheep to each household. These sheep were soon consumed, and people were discussing what was the best way to privatize yet avoid catastrophic meat consumption, as little flour and rice were available. The local *horshoo* (co-operative shop) was frantic in organizing input of goods from Ulaanbaatar. Its manager, Baasanjav, swore he would stop drinking and would devote himself to organizing goods to enrich the life of the local people. The sight of his truck would delight the villagers. But the local shop had too little to sell. When I tried to buy several cassettes, the shop assistant said that she would not sell them to an outsider.

Alongside the collective, the Dashbalbar Buryats have a household-based subsistence economy centred on the productive activities of the nuclear or three-generation stem family. Each family has one or two milch cows pastured in the immediate vicinity. Women milk them and churn the milk into butter or cream. The main diet is meat, milk products, and flour, supplemented by *mangir*, a kind of wild garlic. Sometimes, local officials went to Mardai (Erdes Hot) for things unavail-able in the local *horshoo*; this was a secret, Russian-owned, uranium mine town, which once had about ten thousand Russian workers. There, the Buryats bartered with their butter and meat, through channels mutually agreed at the local official level.

---

[29] Shamanism was generally stronger among Buryats than among Halh. This is because Buddhism was introduced to Buryatia relatively later than Mongolia. For a detailed discus-sion of Buryat Buddhism and shamanism, see Snelling (1993) and Humphrey (1983).

[30] *Darga* (chief, head, or governor) is derived from the verb *darah*, to press. There are a number of terms denoting a leader: *joloodogch*, *udirdagch*, *tolgoilogch*, *darga*, and *noyan*, etc. While the first three are notably modern inventions, and *nomen actoris*, the latter two are traditional political nomenclature. See Aikman (1983) for an analysis of Mongolian political terminology.

Mardai mine was established in 1981 by an intergovernmental agreement, and the mine began shipments of uranium ore to the Soviet Union in 1988 (Worden and Savada 1991: p. xxxv). The town remained secret until late 1989, when the government revealed its existence. But since it was in the territory of Dashbalbar (four hours away from the *sum* centre by truck), the Russians would send some 'luxuries'. On 11 July 1991, the national holiday, the director and chief engineers from Mardai came to give the local Buryats a gift of two TV sets and some sports facilities.

Mardai was criticized by the Democratic leaders, and became a symbol of Russian colonial exploitation of Mongolia. In Mardai there is a railway link to the Russian railway, which is not marked on maps (likewise the town). It was used to transport uranium directly from Mardai to Russia, bypassing Mongol towns/authorities. In 1991 the Russians began to return to Russia, reluctantly. Twice I went to the town and collected *moil*, a kind of berry for making jam. The place was half-deserted. We were chased away by angry Russian residents. One Buryat said that in the past, if they had gone there uninvited, they would have been shot. No bird could fly over Mardai! Russians in Mardai were said to work at night and rest in the daytime. Buryats (usually officials) could come by special invitation from the Mardai administration, to shop; without this, no Mongols could walk in the town, let alone shop, even in summer 1991. Some Buryats said that the place was once beautiful, but was now filled by Mongols from Choibalsang city (capital of Dornod *aimag*); one pointed out several former criminals. The Buryats would like it to be a Russian town, so that they could benefit from exchange relations. Mongol control of the town would mean destruction, they said. In fact, people from Choibalsang, Dashbalbar, and Bayandung came to dismantle the houses and take away the logs. In Dashbalbar people were even using railway sleepers to build wooden houses. In the suburbs of Choibalsang the Soviet barracks were vandalized; wires, wood, and everything useful was taken away by the Mongols. Choibalsang, like many Mongol towns, had a severe housing shortage.

Political liberalization made visits between Buryats in Russia, Mongolia and Inner Mongolia possible. People crossed the border fairly frequently.[31] Such visits and trading liberalization led to the seasonal

---

[31] I met three visitors from Chita (a Russian town). In Bayan-uul state farm two Buryats from Chita came to negotiate to open a shop and import local pastoral products to Russia. Perenlei, the retired leader of the *negdel*, visited his aunt in Shinehen in Inner Mongolia in late 1990, followed by return visits. An Inner Mongolian Buryat and Barga business delegation visited Choibalsang city in summer of 1991.

opening of several land ports along the Sino-Mongolian border. I had
the impression that, although politically, Buryats in this region are
subject to Choibalsang and Ulaanbaatar, in kinship and economic
terms they are oriented towards Chita and other regions. They were
keen to visit Chita and Inner Mongolia, and asked me to write them
letters of invitation. From Dashbalbar, Ulaanbaatar is far away.

Dadal was similar to Dashbalbar in many respects. The Dadal Buryats
are also pastoralists who live in wooden houses of Russian type (while the
Halh and Hamnigan generally live in *ger*). Buryats there were relatively
wealthier than the Halh. Buryat households were usually nuclear
families, though there were also a few families headed by older women
whose husbands had not survived the purges of the 1930s. Some middle-
aged couples lived with their grandchildren while the parents worked in
the cities. Hamnigans seemed to have complex residential compounds.
For example, in one compound, I found four households, all relatives.

Hamnigans are not officially recognized as a separate *yastan* (ethnic
group), but are called Buryat. Both Buryats and Hamnigans object to
this, and some told me that they want the state to review their case.
Tserendorj, a local teacher, told me that when he insisted on being
registered as a Hamnigan, he was scolded for showing nationalism.
The first Hamnigan population census was made in 1989 along with
the general population census. The total population of the Hamnigan in
Mongolia was about 450 individuals.[32] However, this figure did not
appear in any record. In the *sum* marriage registration records and elsewhere Hamnigans are labelled as Buryat. So, for the moment it is
impossible to distinguish the Buryat from the Hamnigan without carrying out a major investigation. It is interesting to note that Hamnigans,
despite being called Buryats by Mongols, are denied this ethnonym by
'pure' Buryats.

Dadal has a famous sanatorium (*gurvan nuurin suvilal*). It is separate
from the main *sum* centre and under the direct control of the Health
Ministry. It is located near three small lakes, the mud of the lakes being
used for medicinal purposes. The locals said that in the middle lake a
small knoll sometimes emerged during drought; this was said by some to
be the famous Deluun Boldog, the place where the young Temüjin
played, as recorded in the *Secret History*. Immediately ashore is a gigantic

---

[32] According to Janhunen (1996), there are altogether no more than 2,000 Hamnigan
individuals in Russia, Mongolia, and China. In none of these countries are Hamnigans
recognized as a separate ethnic group.

statue of Chinggis Khan made in 1962, when the Mongols celebrated the 800th anniversary of his birth.[33] It was promptly denounced by the Soviets as reflecting nationalism. On the north-western hill is an *oboo* with a tablet marking it as the birthplace of Chinggis Khan. However, it is not at all clear whether this was really his birthplace. The place was chosen only in the 1920s by Jamian Gung, the then president of the Mongolian History Committee.[34] The immediate surroundings of the *sum* bear various names appearing in the *Secret History*, but legends about them are told by a Hamnigan, who was a late comer, rather than by the local Halh. In fact, people here do not feel particularly attached to the place as of symbolic importance. The hill with the *oboo* was not called Burhan Haldun (famous in the *Secret History*) but Bayan Horloo. Thus it seems that historical associations were conferred on it from outside. In 1992, before my departure from Mongolia, I learnt that the state had decided to build a mausoleum in every *sum* of Hentii *aimag* to commemorate the 830th anniversary of the birth of Chinggis Khan.[35]

In February 1992, I made a second brief visit to Dadal. There was little transportation between Ünderhaan (the capital of Hentii) and Dadal, only a truck going once a week. The atmosphere was totally different from my first jubilant visit in 1990. Now the local men went out into the forest nearby to hunt for deer horns. Several approached me asking me to smuggle them to Inner Mongolia where they could sell for better prices than on the Ulaanbaatar black market. This deer-horn hunting caused concern at the local ecology protection centre. Tsend, the local Green Party chairman, moved to live on the steppe with his sister's family, where he could monitor the hunting.

In this book I discuss mainly three groups: the Halh as the dominant group, now conterminous with Mongolia; the Inner Mongols; and the Buryat Mongols in Mongolia, the latter two identifying with Inner Mongolia in China and Buryatia in Russia. In Chapter 3, I also discuss some other minorities in Mongolia such as the Oirats and Kazakhs. Since Inner Mongols do not form a residential group in Mongolia, but are largely dispersed and few in number (it is not known how many there are), it is difficult to write an ethnography, but I have devoted Chapter 6

---

[33] For this episode, see Heissig (1966) and Ishjamts (1990).

[34] The Mongolian History Committee (*Sudar Bichgiin Hüreeleng*), founded in 1921, was the predecessor of the MPR Academy of Sciences, which opened in May 1961.

[35] It is significant that Mongols attempted to erect a mausoleum in every *sum* in Hentii to mark permanently the association of the whole region with Chinggis Khan. I believe the plan has not been carried out so far.

to them. Throughout the book, I explore and analyse the Halh Mongols' attitudes to these non-Halh groups. The findings of the various chapters will be discussed in the concluding chapter in relation to contemporary theories of nationalism, diaspora, and hybridity.

2

The Creation of Ethnicity and Nationalism in Twentieth-Century Mongolia

Introduction

I start this chapter by briefly defining two concepts that will be used throughout the book: nationalism and ethnicity. Theories of nationalism (Gellner 1983, 1987; Hobsbawm 1983, 1990, 1992; Anderson 1983) tend to converge on one point: that nationalism is a modern phenomenon and, as defined by Gellner (1983: 1), 'primarily a principle which holds that the political and national unit should be congruent', a definition shared by Hobsbawm (1990: 9). There are several ways to attain this, and the newly emergent nationalists, by emphasizing language, race, or certain selected cultural elements, 'cleanse' the state of those people and things now regarded as unwanted, either driving them out or absorbing and assimilating them. Nationalism in one state, embodied in a chosen people, may be particularly harsh towards other, disadvantaged groups. Such groups have either to imagine belonging to the dominant group, or to accept feeling different. Nationalism, by way of these two parallel processes, tends to create homogeneous cultures. This definition would fit the Halh-centric Mongolian nationalism that I discuss in this book. The identity that is meaningful in this context is national identity, rather than ethnic identity, or ethnicity, which I regard, following Hobsbawm, as something that is taken for granted and considered inherent in being an individual in a society. In this sense, I take Mongols as an *ethnie*, as defined by Smith (1992: 50), a unit of population with six characterizing features: a common proper name, myths of common ancestry, historical memories, distinctive elements of culture, association with a given territory, and a sense of social solidarity. My own ethnicity, as discussed in Chapter 1, satisfies all six of these criteria. Hobsbawm goes too far, however, in emphasizing the non-political aspect of ethnicity (1990). Ethnicity itself, as Epstein (1978: p. x) would argue, is a political phenomenon; it may develop into nationalism, but not always. Anthony

Smith (1986) asserts that most modern nationalist or ethnic discourse assumes a previous base of *ethnie*. He agrees that nationalism as an ideology is a modern phenomenon, but he argues: 'the "modern nation" in practice incorporates several features of pre-modern *ethnie* and owes much to a general model of ethnicity which has survived in many areas until the dawn of the "modern era" ' (1986: 18). Thus, according to this view, there is nationalism based on the Mongolian *ethnie* in various parts of Mongol history, but it was strengthened in the twentieth century.

It is my view, therefore, that the explanation of Mongolian nationalism today, in both its inclusive (Greater Mongolian) and exclusive (Halh-centric) forms, should be sought mainly in the socio-political trans-formations of the socialist period. I also suggest that Greater Mongolian nationalism is based on a thirteenth-century Mongolian state built by Chinggis Khan, and Halh-centric nationalism builds on a sixteenth-century tribal division which was later strengthened by the Manchu. In later sections and chapters I will discuss these two forms of national/ ethnic sentiment, and analyse how they clash with each other in the modern nation-state era, when such concepts as political loyalty, sover-eignty, national boundary, etc. play an overriding role.

Socialist revolution has always been accompanied by ethnic struggles, as one aim of Marxism-Leninism was to liberate colonial peoples from the yoke imposed by imperialist nations (see Connor 1984). For people like the Mongols, though, socialism itself was a modernization which negated the necessity of a bourgeois nationalist stage, and passed directly to strengthening the 'fraternal' relationships of different peoples on the basis of class solidarity, a historical process that was called 'by-passing capitalism' (Shirendyv 1968). This led to the institution of a centrally planned economic system in which everyone was forced to participate. However, we are often led to believe that socialism as a profound positive ideal has not been able to conquer the existing nationalist movements. Reform-minded Soviet anthropologists, while denouncing many of the practices of Soviet nationality policy, continue to embrace that view: 'The dramatic heritage of the Tsarist "prison-house of nations" and the failure of true socialism in the USSR merely enhanced the phenomenon of "ethnic revival" further' (Tishkov 1989: 200). The question is whether it is the 'failure of true socialism' that is to blame. I argue that modernization/socialism, or indeed the nature of the real socialist organ-ization (doctrinal, practical, or perhaps strategic), is intrinsic in creating nationalism and 'ethnic revival'. I will be arguing this point by going *back* into Mongol history.

It was perhaps the very diagnosis of the national relationship, virtually as a class relationship, and the ideal of Marxism in its universal authority to remould human kind, that intensified nationalism. Although Leninists attempted to alienate the capitalist world to provide a haven of nations without class differences, nevertheless, the administrative division of liberated colonial peoples along ethnic lines was hierarchized from union republics to autonomous republics, the different peoples being identified according to the Marxist paradigm of historical evolutionism: *plemya* (tribe), *narodnost* (people), and *natsiya* (nation) (Eidlitz Kuoljok 1985). It created a sense of differential value which was similar to that of the different values ('upper'/'lower', etc.) in a class system.

Mongolia, peculiar in its modern history as the most loyal satellite state of the former Soviet Union, copied many Soviet practices. A 'working' class had to be created to provide a legitimating excuse to wage revolution. Then a multinational structure was invented. This practice not only transformed the fundamental nature of Mongolian internal social organization, it also gave rise to many other unexpected consequences. In this chapter I examine the historical, social, and economic background to the emergence of nationalism and ethnic consciousness of the Mongols.

Building a 'Socialist Mongolian Nation' and the Vocabulary of Ethnicity

The manifestation of ethnicity and the creation of ethnic consciousness are in fact inherent in the socialist nation-building process. I shall make this argument in several stages, beginning with the fact that after the socialist period ethnicity was rampant. After many years of denial of any nationality problem in Mongolia, in 1990, there emerged a number of ethnic organizations aimed at reviving their cultures: the Buryat Association, the Dürbet Association, the Kazakh National Salvation Front, etc. In 1990, a Buryat politician demanded that a Buryat national district be built to unite all the Buryats, arguing that the Buryats are a separate nationality (*ündesten*) and that they should be granted their own territory.[1] The 'ethnic' factor was surging into the Mongolian political system. The Congress in 1990, after a democratic election, boasted of

---

[1] The Buryats in Dashbalbar and Dadal and many other Buryats did not share his view, though, insisting that the Buryats are Mongol.

TABLE 2.1. *Nationalities in Mongolia*

Nationalities	1918	1963	1969	1979	1989
Total pop.	647,504	1,017,158	1,188,271	1,594,386	2,043,954
Mongolian citizens					
@ Halh	492,000	775,527	911,079	1,235,806	1,610,424
§ Kazakh		47,735	62,812	84,305	120,506
* Dürbet	39,000	31,323	34,725	45,053	55,208
@ Buryat		29,523	29,772	29,802	35,444
* Bayat		19,891	25,479	31,053	39,233
@ Dariganga		18,587	20,603	24,564	29,040
§ Urianghai		14,399	15,662	18,957	21,325
* Zahchin	5,000	13,140	15,057	19,475	22,998
* Darhat		8,836	10,174	10,716	14,757
* Torguut		6,028	7,119	8,617	10,050
* Ööld	3,000	5,614	6,876	8,857	9,188
* Hoton	100	2,872	4,056	4,380	6,076
* Myangat	2,000	2,712	3,222	4,173	4,760
@ Barga		2,345	2,305	1,999	2,130
@ Uzemchin		2,072	2,127	2,030	2,086
@ Harchin		828	1,026	639	101
@ Tsahar		195	114	193	44
* Hotgoid				4,869	202
§ Uzbek		150	361	318	331
@ Horchin		119	108	152	83
§ Tuva					2,153
Russian	5,000		1,433	196	140
Chinese	100,000		725	344	247
Others	500	36,262	6,323	2,479	748
Foreign citizens			27,113		
USSR citizens				49,223	54,450
PRC citizens				5,448	1,421
Others (East Europeans)				735	809

Notes:
I have organized the nationalities into categories. @ represents 'Eastern Mongols',
* 'Western Mongols', and § 'Turkic peoples'. This is only for the initial guidance of
readers, since the nature of these categories is being debated in Mongolia now.
The 1918 data collected by M. Maiskii and the 1963 data are to be found in Ch. Nyambuu
(1976: 11 and 65). The 1969, 1979, and 1989 data are unpublished data from the State
Statistics Office.

its diverse ethnic composition: Halh 333, Kazakh 15, Buryat, 15, Dürbet 15, Bayat 14, Dariganga 10, Zahchin, 7, Urianghai 5, Ööld 3, Darhat 2, Torguud 2, and Barga 1. Furthermore, the Congress established a standing committee on the nationality question (Maidar 1990: 25).

There are challenges and counter-challenges as to whether such groups in Mongolia (see Table 2.1) are *ündesten* ('nationalities', literally, root-group). Many, like the Tuvans and Urianghai, say that they are *ündesten*, and reject the term *yastan* (literally, bone-group). However, there are also some who are against differentiation among Mongol groups and say that in Mongolia there are only two nationalities: Mongol and Kazakh. Differentiation of Mongol groups into nationalities is thought to be detrimental to the national interest. The terminology question related to nationality was discussed extensively during the session ratifying the new Constitution in the Second National Congress, November 1991 to January 1992. Eventually it was agreed that there are two nationalities (*ündesten*): the Mongol *Ündesten* and Kazakh *Ündesten*. As in Africa, politicians rejected the term equivalent to tribe (*yastan*) and used instead a term more like ethnic group (*ündesten*) (Gulliver 1969).

The terms *yastan* and *ündesten*, as we have seen above, are not just labels, but imply a political status. I will argue below that in the early socialist-period process of destroying the clergy and the *hamjilga* relationship (see below), many different subgroups were granted various levels of administrative autonomy and their own territories. In the 1930s a special term came to designate the status of such Mongol groups: *yastan*, which is derived from *yas* (bone), with the suffix *tan*. It can be translated as 'bone-group'. The term did not exist among the Halh Mongols. It was the prominent Buryat intellectual Jamtsarano ([1934] 1979) who first used it in his ethnography. But in fact, the term existed among the Buryats in the late nineteenth century. The Buryats as a whole were referred to as a *yastan*, as opposed to other non-Buryat groups in Russia (Tserenhand 1987).

The Mongols translated the whole range of Russian terms for the historical stages of ethnic communities as follows:

Russian	Mongolian	English
rod	*obog*	clan
plemya	*aimag*	tribe
narodnost	*yastan*	nationality
natsiya	*ündesten*	nation

Tribe (*aimag*), according to Sambuu, is based on the union of clans (*obog*s). An arcane Marxist explanation goes as follows: the appearance of the commodity form destroyed the *obog* system, and the dismantling of *aimag* created the conditions for the emergence of *yastan* (Sambuu 1983: 6). The *yastan* is a social group in feudal society; it is a unity of territory, language, and culture. *Ündesten* (nation) appears on the base of *yastan* when the market economy is developed in a capitalist society (Sambuu 1983: 129–30). Gungaadash (1986) suggests, on the other hand, that the main Mongol group in the eleventh to twelfth centuries was a *yastan*, which established the *Hamag Mongol Uls* (All Mongol Nation or State). This Mongol *yastan* included many *obog*s and *aimag*s. Meanwhile, there were many other *yastan*s of Mongol origin (*ugsaa*), and they all became one *ündesten* in the socialist period. The socialist Mongol *Ündesten* was based on the Halh Mongols, surrounded by other *yastan*s of Mongol origin and non-Mongol *yastan*s. Halh is the dominant *yastan* of the socialist Mongol *Ündesten* (Gungaadash 1986: 177–84).

In political terms, the *yastan* and *ündesten* are not equal, although the words are often written together denoting nationality, or the components of the socialist Mongolian nation. The term *yastan* has strong feudal implications: small *yastan*s are expected to perish in capitalist or socialist society. The term *ündesten* has a much more 'progressive' implication, and thus today all groups want to be classified as *ündesten*, as they feel this provides the true sense of a nationality. I will explain the symbolism of *yas* and *ündes* later.

This official translation of the Russian terms does not really reflect Mongolian, or perhaps even Russian, reality. Soviet ethnologists coined some other terms that had also been translated and used in Mongolia, adding further confusion. The Soviet ethnologists' interest was, however, strictly in line with socialist evolutionary development: the more backward peoples would have to be upgraded, so as to merge with more progressive nationalities to become a Soviet nation. This is called 'ethnic process', an important social engineering project in Soviet ethnology. Mongolian ethnologists followed this theory closely, and attempted to chart a Mongolian 'ethnic process'.

We may distinguish two periods regarding the study of the nationality question in Mongolian ethnography (*ugsaatnii zui*). In the 1960s, ethnographers were interested in the particularity of ethnic origins (*garal ugsaa*) and the material and spiritual culture of some *yastan*s. In the 1970s they began to assess 'ethnic processes', the formation of the socialist united Mongol *Ündesten* (Badamhatan 1982).

Let us discuss briefly some terminology. Bromley, a prominent Soviet ethnographer, put forward a notion which he called 'ethnos' (1974). In his opinion, *ethnos* is an elemental ethnic community; the most numerous and economically complete *ethnos*es will form nationalities during the capitalist period of history.

What is interesting is that *ethnos* is translated as *ugsaatan* in Mongolian. It is said that the ancient Mongol *obog* and *aimag* together form an *ugsaatan*, which has a basically biological definition and continues to exist in all times. This differentiates the Mongol view of *ugsaatan* from Bromley's *ethnos*. Badamhatan, a pre-eminent Mongolian ethnologist elaborates:

Ündesten was formed at an historical stage, when capitalist society destroyed feudal society, in particular. *Ugsaatan* [on the other hand] formed a unified descent group from the feudal period, and persisted throughout the development of society under the names of *aimag* and *yastan*. In the socialist period, as a result of social development and of changes in the culture and economy of *yastan* and *ugsaatan*, their consolidation forms a new ethnic unit, and further develops into socialist *ündesten*. (Badamhatan 1982: 9)

According to this theory, the *yastan*s formed in the feudal period should no longer be called such in the socialist period, but rather *ugsaatanii büleg* (ethnic group). The ethnic process, or the realization of the Mongol *Ündesten*, or new ethnic unit, is achieved by the smaller *yastan*s renouncing their own identities and adopting another, larger one. For example, in 1956 there were twenty-three *yastan*s, while in the 1969 population census, the number had dropped to ten. They have merged into what Badamhatan calls 'the socio-political unit of the socialist Mongolian *Ündesten*, which is based on the language, literature, and culture of Halh, the core group (*büleg*) of the Mongol *Ündesten*' (1982: 10). In this process, the Halh has become a symbolic central 'root' of all Mongols, and small *yastan*s have become feudalist 'bones' waiting to be recycled into fine socialist materials to support the growth of socialist Mongolian 'root'.

A socialist nation is a new ethnic unit, consisting of all the elements in the country, including the biologically defined *ugsaatan*. It too was regarded as something of a biological unity, for closer national integration is always measured by the degree of inter-ethnic marriage (Badamhatan 1982). In accordance with such ideas, state-controlled population movements from one area to another were designed not only to help even out population density but to achieve an ethnic homogeneity. Thus the socialist Mongolian nation was to be a new biological and cultural unity. This understanding excludes foreign Mongols. Following this logic, one may argue that the Chinese nation is a 'biological' union of all the groups of people under this political canopy; thus a Mongol in China is inevitably a Chinese, in the sense not only of a perceived political loyalty or identity but also of biological unity. I will discuss in detail this biological connotation in later chapters.

As is clear, the biological and cultural ethnic core of the Mongol nation is now Halh, the 'dominant' nationality in Mongolia. Halh is generally accepted as conterminous with Mongol in Mongolia, where the Halh constitute the majority. This idea that Halh equals 'proper Mongol' is further facilitated by the adoption of the Halh dialect as the standard language enshrined in the Cyrillic Mongolian script adopted in the 1940s. To receive an education is to become Halh-ized, which is equal to 'Mongolized'.

The nation building in Mongolia based on the majority Halh is not unique to Mongolia. The majority–minority dichotomy seems, nevertheless, something peculiar to the kind of nation-state which is supposed to be based on a group that constitutes the majority population within the delineated boundary. The convenient identification of a majority group with the state looks natural only in the decolonization process; as Spivak (1992: 105) argues, 'One of the gifts of the logic of decolonization is parliamentary democracy.' However, 'the majority' itself needs to be problematized, as it is also a social construction. In recent years, the seemingly natural monolithic Han Chinese majority has been challenged by both internal subgroups and scholars (Friedman 1995; Gladney 1991, 1994). Gladney writes that the Han were imagined by Sun Yat-sen as a majority for a strategic purpose, as 'a symbolic metaphorical opposition to the Manchu and all "foreigners" against whom the vast majority of people in China would easily rally' (1994: 98–9). 'Majorities by extension, become denaturalized, homogenized, and essentialized as "same"' (1994: 103).[2]

---

[2] In Japan, even the widely believed to be homogeneous uni-racial Japanese society cannot stand rigorous scrutiny. Kosaku Yoshino (1992) argues that the 'Japanese race' is an invented category. 'The Japanese historically formed an image of themselves as a "racially" distinct and homogenous people. Despite this myth, the Japanese, like all other peoples, are the product of a long period of mixture' (1992: 25). This homogeneous notion seems to have emerged largely for political reasons, through their interaction or confrontation with the West, as a means to contrast the difference along the line of homogeneous versus heterogeneous so as to highlight the uniqueness of the Japanese. Dominguez (1986), in her penetrating study of Creole identity in Louisiana, revealed that Creole has been trans-

A majority is not just a matter of numerical supremacy. It has the clearly ideological connotation of signifying the right track on which the people is advancing. Likewise, the mainstream majority is by extension, a standardization, against which all others are to be measured. It is the destiny towards which everything and everybody must strive. As in the case of coloured Creoles striving for whitening (see n. 2), non-Halh Mongols strive to emulate the Halh; for to be a Halh is to be not only a better Mongol, but a better human being, one step closer to socialist humanhood. By equating Halh with genuine Mongol, thus establishing hierarchical ethnic status, Mongolia has unwittingly created criteria to judge who is more Mongol, who is less.

This state-constructed ethnic identity creates the conditions for people to manipulate identities. Interestingly, 'Mongol' is not regarded as an official ethnic term, and one cannot register oneself as a Mongol in the internal passport. One would be punished for hiding one's identity, a crime in a socialist country where the Party wants to monitor everything. But Halh is an ethnic identity accessible to everyone in Mongolia. Thus there is difficulty in identifying the 'real' ethnic identity, because one usually has two identities, for example, either Dariganga or Halh, or even Dariganga Halh. A Darhat is a Halh in the city, but a Darhat when he goes back to his home village.

The pressure to become Halh is probably more evident in the identity of the second generation. Dugarsüren is a middle-aged Barga in Hentii. His mother is Barga; his father is a Buryat. According to the local practice, he said, a child of two different *yastan*s usually chooses the mother's *yastan* identity. His wife is a Buryat, and they have four children. They are all studying in Ulaanbaatar. They are registered as Halh. He tried to persuade them to register as Buryat, but none listened.

formed from a term which signifies 'local birth and foreign parentage' (1986: 122), a classification which gave rise to the socio-political tension between French and American. Towards the second half of the nineteenth century, with the upsurge of black or coloured political participation, 'rivalry between white Creoles and white Americans in the meantime lost momentum. Both groups increasingly perceived the entire coloured population as a common enemy, and temporarily subordinated the Creole/American opposition for the sake of fighting together for white supremacy' (1986: 136). This movement, for strategic reasons, transformed the 'antebellum system of racial classification in Louisiana, which was ternary (white/coloured/negro), into a binary one (white/negro)' (1986: 137). The reclassification immediately led to cleansing to make the classification congruent with reality. Blood became a dominant index to demarcate the racial categories equating purity with superiority and impurity with inferiority. In the strange reconfiguration of majority and minority in Louisiana, according to Dominguez, majorities become 'White by Definition'.

I met a Christian Mongol lady in Hentii.[3] Her father is a Buryat, but the daughter said he is not a *jinhin* (genuine) Buryat, as he is Hamnigan, and her mother is a Halh. She herself is a Halh. She explained that she did not know the Buryat dialect and customs, and that her father is not a real Buryat, so why should she be a Buryat? She further explained that one is not born a Buryat or a Halh. To be a Halh means one is a proper citizen, a real Mongol, and to be Buryat means to be peripheral. In Dadal, the majority of children of Halh and Buryat unions have chosen to be Halh. Particularly interesting is one family: the parents are both Buryat, and they have six children, of whom two born before 1977 are registered as Buryat, while the four younger ones are Halh. The pressure to become Halh became stronger from the late 1970s as I will explain below.[4]

'I am *jinhin* (genuine) Halh!' This is a phrase often bandied about. Could *jinhin* mean that the Halh are also asserting their genuineness as opposed to those assimilated? Being *jinhin* Halh certainly gives one pride, for it is the dominant *ethnos*; the identity of Mongol is closely linked to the Halh. On the other hand, people in Mongolia do not say to each other: *Bi jinhin Mongol hün* (I am a genuine Mongol). This is probably a matter of context, as one may argue that all are officially Mongols. However, my enquiry would be valid in so far as there are at least some people who are citizens of Mongolia who fall outside the category of Mongol, like the Kazakhs, Russians, and Chinese. Mongolia is a country defined on the basis of nationality, rather than culture. As it is the country of the Mongols, created by Mongols and for Mongols, to engage in a discourse of Mongolness within Mongolia has become meaningless, despite the existence of a significant number of non-Mongol citizens. Such a context has created a generic reference, *bid Mongolchuud*, or 'we Mongols'. This generalization or co-terminating of the majority of the citizens with the Mongol state is in fact a suppression of the identity of its minorities. However, Mongol is too large a concept, and too unrefined, so that to assert one's genuine Mongol identity, one must be Halh, and still more, *jinhin* Halh. The pronouncement of being an authentic Mongol then becomes meaningful in a wider context, between *jinhin* Halh and non-Halh Mongols both inside and outside Mongolia

[3] Christian evangelical movements are now prevalent in Mongolia. There seem to be some conflicts between Buddhists and Christians.

[4] Pegg (1998) observes that during the 1960s, schoolchildren of all groups in Mongolia except for the Buryats and Kazakhs were taught that they were Halh, and only recently have they become aware of their differing histories, cultural and political heroes, and performing arts.

who do not share the view that to be a Mongol is to be a Halh, or not to be a Halh is to be not Mongol or less Mongol.

On this view the ethnic process in Mongolia is a hierarchical development; smaller units are to be absorbed into bigger ones, and the latter will merge into Halh; thus a direct 'bypassing' into Halh nationhood is possible. But whatever the case, everybody will eventually become Halh, the Mongol of Mongols. The implication of this 'Halh equals Mongol' is that to become Halh is to be transformed from non-Mongol to Mongol, and from less Mongol to genuine Mongol. The symbolic biological connotations of Halh-ism, which have interesting political implications, are discussed later.

Separating Religion from the State

The seemingly complex 'ethnic process' described above becomes easily comprehensible in a historical context. After the Qing Dynasty proposed a new policy to open the Mongolian frontier in 1902, the Mongolian nationalist reaction mostly concerned a perceived threat to 'religion and root' (*shashin ündes*) by the Chinese, a concern so strong that it was largely responsible for emergence of the independence movement in Mongolia in 1911. After the 1911 revolution, characteristic of a colonial society, in which almost everything was dictated by foreign powers, Mongolia became a focus of disputes between the Russians and the Chinese. The Chinese Republic's claim over the sovereignty of Mongolia and its subsequent occupation of Mongolia in 1919 gave rise to another tide of Mongolian anti-Chinese nationalism. Even then, the Mongols were still thinking of themselves versus Chinese, rather than as part of a world revolution. The Mongolian revolutionaries were concerned to save merely 'religion and root', both of which were felt to be threatened by the Chinese military occupiers and, later, by White Russians.

Mongolia 'benefited' from a diagnosis by the Soviet revolutionaries that it was a colonial country; and it had to be 'liberated'. In Russia, the visiting Mongol revolutionaries were told by Lenin that Mongol society was a feudal society (Dorj 1961). Lenin advised them that the revolution should not be merely against the foreign oppressors, but also against the feudal lords and religion (Brown and Onon 1976). This Soviet emphasis on the class nature of Mongol society ultimately cost the lives of the main leaders of the Mongol revolution soon after. And significantly, a lama was later blamed for poisoning Sühbaatar, who was posthumously claimed to be the father of the new republic. Religion was made the enemy of the revolution.[5]

The revolution in Mongolia was to a great extent a Russian Red Army[6] operation directed by the Comintern. It was expedient for the Comintern, which held the Leninist atheist view of religion, to separate the entire religious organization from the masses. Mongolia at that time was a land of nomads, with about 113,000 lamas (the total population at that time was just over half a million). Furthermore, the lamaist organization was in control of about 150,000 people (Friters 1949: 39) in the form of what is known as the *hamjilga* relationship (usually translated as serfdom but in fact closer to a patron–client relationship) between the religious professionals and their attached laity.[7] The *hamjilga* relationship established between herders and black (lay) nobles, or with yellow (religious) nobles, was said by the Soviets to be exploitative, and hence a class relationship. This justified a separation of the monks and the nobles from the ordinary people. The separation meant major administrative reorganization. To achieve this end, we find, interestingly, that the Comintern resorted to bribery: offering 'self-determination' to various groups in return for breaking with the black and yellow feudal lords. Meanwhile, Party cells were set up in all the separated and newly established banners (*hoshuu*) by 1925 (Ichinnorov 1990). Territorial administrative change and tax exemption for many small groups were instituted in 1922.

According to Connor (1984), the fundamental characteristic of Marxist–Leninist nationality policies was a primary concern with nation building. For this purpose, strategic importance was attached to obtaining the support of minorities (1984: 38). In Mongolia, a 'Regulation for Establishing New Territorial Administration' was ratified, with the aim 'to establish self-determination over land and regions.'

In the first few years of the revolution, repeated meetings convened by the party and state took [various peoples] into consideration and issued clear instructions and resolutions about promoting the life, culture and education of the Urianghai frontier people; the Hoton, Darhat and Urianghai were liberated from the *hamjilga* of Dürbet Zorigt Wang and the Jebtsundamba Hutagt. This was a

---

[5] The Mongols today believe that this is a fabrication, and Sühbaatar was actually murdered by the Soviets.

[6] The Soviet Red Army did not leave until 1925.

[7] The lay clients of the religious patrons were called *shavinar*, i.e. disciples, while the clients of the nobility were *hamjilga* (serfs). Both relations are generally called *hamjilga*. For Mongol treatment of such social relations, see Natsagdorj 1972, Gongor 1978.

great step taken to grant political equal rights among the *yastan*s. (Badamhatan 1980: 17)

These administrative measures were clearly established in ethnic terms. And the ethnic relationship was at the same time a class relationship, defined against the feudal patrons such as Dürbet Zorigt Wang and the Jebtsundamba Hutagt. What is significant here is that in their proclaimed equality-building process, the Communists had actually reproduced inequality. The Party programme in 1925 read:

Completely wipe out the discrimination between Halh and other national small *aimags*[8] in the MPR, in particular get rid of the discrimination shown by the Halh against other national, small and weak *aimags*; respect the people's genuine freedom and the rights of the other national, small and weak *aimags* without discrimination.

The trouble with this 'ethnic' hierarchization is that, at the time, the majority Halh were not economically dominant, and in fact were the poorest group in Mongolia. The tax exemption extended to the small *aimags* just after the revolution, in the belief that the Halh was a large, oppressor nation, was guided by a mistaken notion that minorities were necessarily oppressed and the majority necessarily oppressors.

The separation of religion from the state was also justified by the Party and Government's vision of Mongolian national policy and its role of 'defending and protecting the territory (*gazar nutag*) and roots (*ündes yazguur*)' (Dashtseveg 1976: 28–9). They argued that religion was detrimental to the national interest, and indeed the very survival of the Mongols. The religious organization was accused of not teaching the Mongolian language.

Two different approaches to the question of Mongol society and religion were to mark what are known as the rightist and leftist deviations from 1925 to 1932. The rightists, notably represented by the Buryat Jamtsarano, argued that religious personnel should not be labelled as a separate class *vis-à-vis* the laity. He envisaged a reform of Buddhism, and held that Buddhism was not in principle contradictory to Communism. Jamtsarano argued:

Seeing that the basic aims of our Party and of Buddhism are both the welfare of the people, there is no conflict between the two of them . . . It is a special case that in Russia religion is the opium of the people. What our Lord Buddha taught cannot be equated with aggressive religions like Mohammedanism and Chris-

---

[8] *Aimag* meant both a province and a people in the past.

tianity, and though the Communist Party rejects religion and priesthood, this has nothing to do with our Buddhist faith. Our party wants to see the Buddhist faith flourishing in a pure form, and approves of lamas who stay in their monasteries, reciting the scriptures and faithfully observing their vows. (Quoted in Bawden 1968: 286)

What was needed was straightforward economic development, eliminating the unequal elements within the religious structure. The lamas were divided into three categories: the high lamas, the middle lamas, and the lower lamas. The herds of the feudals were distributed to the poor herders and the lower lama class.

However, from 1928, Stalin's second 'leftist' revolution spread to Mongolia. A Comintern delegation was sent to Mongolia to implement Stalin's anti-religious and collectivization policies (Moses 1977: 188–9). No sooner had the 'lower class' people begun to taste the benefits of the revolution than the Communists started to collectivize the livestock of the herdsmen. Forceful collectivization, and the physical destruction of religion and 'feudalism' in the late 1920s, began to push the lamas and herdsmen into a common defence against the Communists. A widespread uprising occurred between 1930 and 1932 (see Bawden 1968, Rupen 1964, Baabar 1996, for details).

This actually produced a centripetal force against the Communist regime, compelling the lamas and religiously minded herdsmen to look beyond the borders for support. An unprecedented 'ethnic' feature crept in, as the rebellion concentrated mostly in the western Mongolian region. For example, the lamas in Ulaangom used the expression 'the duty of all the Derbet [Dürbet] people' (Bawden 1968: 318). In the east, outside support, both real and mythical, was conveniently provided by the Panchen Lama, the Tibetan religious leader, and the Japan-sponsored pan-Mongolist movement. Ultimately, we shall see the Communists relentlessly destroying some communities like the Buryats and Barga who were tempted by these movements dominated by religious leaders.

By destroying this link between religion and Mongol social groups, and by exploiting the differences between groups and separating them, the Communists helped create not only 'class'[9] but also ethnicity. These were used expediently for the destruction of religion and feudalism.

---

[9] There is no doubt that class existed in pre-revolutionary Mongolia, if class is understood in terms of rich and poor, powerful and weak. The Manchus helped to maintain the hereditary élites. However, this relationship was far from antagonistic, as defined by Communist ideology. The relationship was rather symbiotic, or similar to a patron–client relationship.

Thus Buddhism became an enemy of the revolution, and pan-Mongolism detrimental to the Communist-controlled young republic. Subsequent history saw the production and reproduction of a potent myth based on the joint Soviet–Mongolian military operation at Nomonhan in 1939 against the joint Japanese–Inner Mongolian invasion. The destruction of the Buddhist sanga and the equation of pan-Mongolism with the imperialist Japanese invasion, and the celebration of Soviet–Mongol brotherhood, have been the most pervasive ingredients in the newly shaped Mongolian national identity.

Buddhism was one of the most important agents tying diverse Mongol groups into a coherent Mongolian culture with a sense of nationhood. The reason the lamas played so large a role in the early revolutionary process was that they were recruited from all 'classes' and all groups. Lamas were perhaps the only group that could move between administrative boundaries. Their mobility thus anticipated modern social mobility which fosters a common identity. The development of Soviet–Mongolian socialist nationalism directly encounters Buddhist and other forms of pan-Mongolism.

Revolution in a Feudal Country?

Revolution in a country like Mongolia was already an embarrassment to the Marxist theory of socialist revolution. Mongolia had no intellectuals, no urban proletariat, no industrial élite, no powerful military caste, and not even a really strong nobility. How was it that such a people could wage a nationalist revolution, if we agree that the 1911 and 1921 revolutions were both initially nationalistic? The Mongols were divided and ruled by the Manchus and Russians, and the structure of society was indeed what Gellner (1983) calls 'agrarian'. Agrarian societies, by his definition, are based on a fairly stable technology and are endowed with a clear structure. High culture is monopolized by a small, better-endowed élite. Gellner finds no homogenization process within such societies. So there is no nationalism there. The Mongolian case is clearly an exception. To refute Gellner's theory would involve my becoming embroiled in the debate between modernist and primordialist camps, the first represented by Ernest Gellner and Benedict Anderson, the second by Anthony Smith. I will confine myself to insisting that the social condition for waging nationalist revolution early this century was that the Mongols were a people who had a unified culture.

The unified culture of the Mongols rested on the following specific characteristics. There was a literary language, which enabled all the Mongol groups to communicate; there was a common pastoral mode of production, with only slight regional differences. Most importantly, Buddhism was able to cut across administrative boundaries, thus creating a single dominant culture that culminated in the sharp decline of the localized noble powers, so much so that it was lamas who led the revolution which declared independence from the Manchu state.

Perhaps it is not the division of labour that creates cohesion, as Gellner maintains, but the union of the mundane and the sacred. For this reason it was wrong, in my opinion, for the Communists to assert that the lamas formed a class. The lamas were not a class, as I use the term. They came from all walks of life; it was accepted that each family should send at least one son to a monastery. This network created a strong and lasting union, guaranteeing cohesion and interdependence between the sanga and the people, quite different from the Communist picture, whereby the Buddhist lamas poisoned the minds of the people and exploited them relentlessly (although it is true that the *hamjilga* relationship did generate a flow of wealth from clients to patrons).

Egalitarianism, which Gellner claims to be a feature only of industrial society, was in fact typical of the pastoral Mongols.[10] High culture was not monopolized by a few, but accessible to every man through the temple; meanwhile, everyone was familiar with pastoral production and the vast array of customs and rituals associated with it (except for the extremely few high lamas, who devoted themselves to studies). Livestock herding was the sole livelihood of the nomads. Material provisions like food, clothing, tents, and utensils and transportation were shared by all Mongols, including nobles and high lamas. Those who did not share this way of life were the Chinese and Russian traders; they indeed did exploit the Mongols indiscriminately, to such an extent that the lamas and the nobles could not form a 'class' solidarity with the Chinese Manchu, and in the end rose up to struggle for independence (Sanjdorj 1980). Whatever the social inequalities (which are bound to exist even in an 'egalitarian' Western industrial society), as a national principle, Mongol egalitarianism is an explicit expression of 'Mongolness', embedded in the

---

[10] Gellner in his later writings admits that egalitarianism is not restricted to industrial society. One other area in which it flourishes is, precisely, nomadic societies. See his discussion of the 'nomadism debate' in his *State and Society in Soviet Thought* (1988: 92–114).

centuries-old patterns of pastoral production. In such a society, one should not be too surprised to find To Wang, a late nineteenth-century Halh prince, teaching fellow herders how to look after animals, how to kill animals, or why not to give food to a dog in the evening, as otherwise it will sleep soundly and neglect its duty of vigilance against wolves (Natsagdorj 1968).

Anyone could rise in the sanga. The *hamjilga* relationship between ordinary people and nobles was limited to the performance of certain duties,[11] and was such that ordinary people could become very rich, and a prince could become a pauper if he did not handle his business properly. Economically, the vagaries of pastoralism (rapid growth and occasional disaster in livestock numbers) allowed for such eventualities. Socially, this was possible in a situation where the traditional clan society had declined and been replaced by the universal efficacy of Buddhism, and where the various Mongol groups had found a mode of coexistence which gradually eroded group differences.

I have argued against Gellner's theory largely in terms of cultural conditions. These conditions enable Mongols of various groups to imagine a community of Mongols transcending their immediate communities. Prasenjit Duara, in his criticism of the idea that nationalist thinking is a modern mentality, argues thus:

The manner in which we have conceptualized political identities is fundamentally problematic. In privileging modern society as the only social form capable of generating political awareness, Gellner and Anderson regard national identity as a distinctive mode of consciousness: the nation as a whole imagining itself to be the unified subject of history....[The] error...lies in the general postulate of a cohesive subjectivity.

Individuals and groups in both modern and agrarian societies identify simultaneously with several communities that are all imagined; these identifications are historically changeable, and often conflict internally and with each other. (1993: 8)

Nationalism in Mongolia earlier this century was 'imagined', but it was nevertheless predicated on another 'imagined community', the historical existence of the thirteenth–fourteenth-century Mongol state. This is a different idea of community from the 'common culture', union of secular and sacred, etc. This state arguably involved something

---

[11] Duties usually included dung collection, looking after animals, and occasional domestic assistance, post-relay, etc. They were not so arduous by the standard of agricultural societies like the Chinese.

like an 'ethnic' or 'national' principle at its core. Although it became a vast multi-ethnic empire, the expression used to describe it at its foundation in 1206, *Mongol Uls* (Mongol nation, Mongol state), conveyed the idea of ethnicity as providing the identity of the state. The *Mongol Uls* was in fact a revival of an earlier, much smaller, and shorter-lived polity named *Hamag Mongol* (All Mongol) which, at least according to the *Secret History*, arose around the leadership of Khutula Khan, an ancestor of Chinggis. During the period of the Mongol state, various concepts of Mongol ethnicity gained currency (*Mongol obogtan*, *Mongol yazguurtan*, *Mongol ugsaatan*, and *Mongol tuurgatan*[12]), all of which denote just one common ethnicity—Mongol.

It would be a mistake to suggest that there was no concept of a Mongol nation in the period of empire (thirteenth–fourteenth centuries). The base for this ethnic awareness, or perhaps consciousness, was the perennial conflict between the nomads and the sedentary peoples. The division was deeply entrenched. The Mongol rulers delineated four hierarchical nations within the Yuan Dynasty.[13] Mongols, by virtue of being the masters and rulers of the dynasty, were the most respectable. Moreover, the Mongols institutionalized the division of separate peoples, endowing them with cosmic substance. For example, during the Yuan period there were 'five coloured peoples and four foreigners' (*tavan öngö dörvön hari*). The colour symbolism used was related to the notion of five elements, denoting spirits of the year, directions, or planets. In this scheme, the Mongols were blue, Chinese red, Tibetans black, Uygurs yellow, and Koreans white. Logically, the other four peoples were the 'four foreigners' to the Mongol rulers (see Tserinpilov 1996). It is clear that the Mongols at the time held the notion that one's national identity was cosmologically fixed; trespassing ethnic boundaries was therefore prohibited. What is particularly interesting is the fact that, unlike other nomadic invaders of China, who promoted integration into Chinese culture, Mongol rulers prohibited Mongols from learning from Chinese culture, and also forbade the Chinese learning Mongolian customs. As Serruys (1987) wrote, based on a historical survey, the Chinese aspired to learn Mongolian, wear Mongolian dresses, and bear Mongolian names, so as to have access to privileges otherwise barred to them. However,

---

[12] These terms could be translated as, literally, person of Mongol clan, person of Mongol origin, person of Mongol race, and person of Mongol felt-walled tents.

[13] Menggu Ren or Mongol (Mongols), Semu Ren or Shar Nödtön (coloured-eyed people), Han Ren or Hyatad (people in north China, including Kitans, Jurchens, and Chinese), Nan Ren or Niyangad (Chinese in south China).

Mongol emperors promulgated repeated edicts to ban such natural integration. Consequently, after almost a hundred years, when Mongol rule was overthrown, Mongols were far from entangled with the Han, and most of them were able to retreat to the north of the Great Wall of China. The succeeding Ming emperor also, averting 'barbarian' customs the Hans had learned, announced laws to cleanse Chinese culture of any Mongol influences (Serruys 1987). The Ming also rebuilt the Great Wall in order to keep the Mongols out of China (see Waldron 1990). After the Mongols were conquered by the Manchu, they were kept separate from the Chinese; the two were not allowed to communicate without the consent of the Manchu emperor.

Thus, the Mongol *ethnie* is not only a construction of the Mongols themselves, but result of constant interaction with alien, sedentary nations like the Chinese. Furthermore, that identity was consolidated by the Manchu, who needed Mongol support to maintain their rule in China and Inner Asia.

I admit that it is an exaggeration to suggest that national consciousness existed at all times in Mongol history. Mongol nationalism, as reflected in wanting to build a country only for Mongols, is a relatively recent phenomenon, and was at least partly a response to nationalist movements in Europe and Asia. The point I wish to make here is that such ideologies cannot be entirely divorced from a concrete Mongolian historical past. Present Mongolian nationalism of various hues not only addresses the idea of the Mongol state, but also employs the same vocabulary as its pre-modern predecessor. It is my view that without the historical existence of the early Mongol state, more recent forms of Mongol nationalism would be barely conceivable. Hroch (1993) rightly points out: 'Nation-building was never a mere project of ambitious or narcissistic intellectuals, and ideas could not flow through Europe by their own inspirational force. Intellectuals can "invent" national communities only if certain objective preconditions for the formation of a nation already exist. Karl Deutsch long ago remarked that for national consciousness to arise, there must be something for it to become conscious of' (1993: 4). Hroch particularly mentions three irreplaceable features that play an important role in the nation-building process: '(i) a "memory" of some common past, treated as a "destiny" of the group—or at least of its core constituents; (ii) a destiny of linguistic or cultural ties enabling a higher degree of social communication within the group than beyond it; (iii) a conception of the equality of all members of the group organised as a civil society' (1993: 5). Similarly Duara has argued:

The idea of a single, radical break in self-consciousness is hard to sustain because it effectively denies history. By stressing the multiplicity of identities that is correlative with the varieties of histories... the nation [may] be understood through different contested narratives both historically and within the framework of the new nation–state system. (1993: 25)

We have seen that these crucial histories existed for the Mongols, and now we shall discuss the working out of nationalism in the socialist state.

Modern Mongolian 'Tribalism'

In previous sections I have argued that the Communists in Mongolia, guided by their ideology of destroying the old and building a new socialist relationship, have unwittingly created ethnicity. The ethnic process towards a Mongol nation is a process of assimilation of various groups into the majority Halh. But despite this Halh-equals-Mongol ethnic process, the actual road has never been easy. Many of the subsequent problems of nationalism and ethnicity were caused by Yu. Tsedenbal, a Dürbet who dominated Mongolian politics from 1952 to 1984. Tsedenbal was a 'de-nationalized man', in the sense that he was not interested in Mongolian nationalism, but advocated closer integration with the Soviet Union.

In the 1940s, Mongolian economic development faced a great difficulty because of the disastrous effect of the first attempt at collectivization in the 1930s and the liquidation of the wealthier social elements. It was realized by some that it would take a long time to build socialism without seeking help from other countries. The best way out, they thought, was to abandon the idea of national independence and join the Soviet Union. Tsedenbal, who had become the Party secretary, engineered an application that Mongolia be incorporated into the Soviet Union, but neither the Soviet Union, nor Choibalsang, the then Mongolian prime minister, accepted this application.[14] Tsedenbal changed his tactics in the 1960s, now aiming to 'rely on the powerful technical base of the Soviet Union and build socialism in Mongolia', or to 'integrate with the Soviet Union in all aspects'. This policy is now named Tsedenbalism: that is, allowing the fate of Mongolia to rest economically

---

[14] Choibalsang was generally known as Mongolia's Stalin because of his role in the purges of the 1930s. However, because he was insistent on an independent Mongolia, he is now regarded as a patriot, and his statue in front of the State University still stands.

and politically on the USSR. It is now said that Mongolia was turned into an economic colony of other socialist countries (Zardihan and Chuluunbaatar 1991: 66–7).

The subsequent decades were characteristic of the cold war period, although Mongolia's enemies were not merely the capitalists but also Communist China. The uneasy Sino-Soviet relations in the 1960s played a crucial role in creating a special mentality and national identity in Mongolia. This conflict, according to Milivojevic (1991*a*), benefited the MPR as a whole in economic and social terms. The Mongolian People's Army was totally dependent on the Soviet Union for manpower training, armaments, military equipment, and technical assistance (1991*a*: 142). The integration was not an ordinary one, for the army itself was formed on Russian territory, and was trained and led by Russian generals. The Mongolian People's Revolutionary Party was said to be controlled directly by the Soviet Embassy in Mongolia.

A new ideology then developed in Mongolia: 'patriotism' and 'internationalism'. Internationalism meant not just proletariat internationalist goodwill, but had a practical purpose: namely, relying on the Soviet Union for economic development as well as military protection from the Chinese threat. To be patriotic, then, meant going all out to engage in production, thus guaranteeing an internationalist division of labour, crucial for the security of the country. The group process in this economic interaction was the creation of a socialist Mongolian nation (*ündesten*), based on 'iron friendship' with the Soviet Union, and a culture 'socialist in content and national in form'.

In opposition to the patriotism and internationalism sponsored by the Soviet Union and Tsedenbal, there appeared a new phenomenon, 'nationalism' or 'chauvinism' (*ündserheh üzel*). Essentially it referred to any nationalist sentiment expressed against the USSR and other Soviet-block countries; it was dubbed *ündestnii aminch yavchuu üzel* or *ündestnii yavchuural* (selfish narrow-minded nationalism). Interestingly, these words would not be used to express nationalism against the Chinese. Mongolian nationalism against the Chinese was considered legitimate, against the Soviets not. In parallel with this 'nationalism' was *nutgarah üzel*, or localism. Nationalism and localism sometimes overlapped in the understanding of Mongolian ideologues. A resolution issued by the Central Committee of the MPRP in 1978 contained a clear definition of this:

To inspire a nationalistic tendency and embrace unreasonable localism is an especially persistent phenomenon entangled in thoughts harmful to our society, which is improper in political policy. Although the concrete conditions for brewing all sorts of contradictions in relationships in our country have long been destroyed, we should not think that there is no possibility of showing nationalist tendencies. *To distinguish by* nutag *and* omog [obog] *(locality and clan) is in the nature of one side of nationalism.* (Norovsambuu and Dashjamts 1988: 57, emphasis mine)

The Party had to admit that localism, or regionalism, was still a serious problem in Mongolian public relationships. After all the euphoria of the declaration of the birth of a socialist Mongolian *Ündesten* by 1960, marked by the Third Constitution, in a letter distributed to all the Party members in 1976, the Party Central Committee noted:

In recent times, there are cases of people drinking alcohol together only with people from the same *aimag* or *sum*, spreading narrow localism by distinguishing *nutag* differences... taking advantage of this, some elements of loose consciousness crack themselves up arrogantly, and utter politically unhealthy and unprincipled words. (ibid.: 57–8)

This was the target for attack from the MPRP. The more the MPRP attacked, the stronger the phenomenon became. In 1986, Batmönh (himself a Bayat), the then Mongolian president, reported to the Central Committee plenary meeting: 'It is proper to organize a powerful struggle everywhere against all sorts of phenomena contradictory to the socialist way of life, in particular, localism' (Batmönh 1986: 52).

Several terms were employed to refer to different levels of localism: *aimagchlah, hoshuuchlah, jalgachlah,* or localism at province, banner, and 'trench' or village level. All this was called *nutgarah üzel,* which was not differentiated, as we see above, from *ündserheh üzel* (chauvinism). A more fashionable term was *yasarhah üzel,* specifically referring to the sentiment of *yastan*s. People who stirred up discord between *yastan*s were *yas hayah*[15] (literally, throwing bones), and those who thought along this line were *yasharhagch.*

The extensive struggle against the above mentioned three 'isms'— namely, *ündserheh üzel* (nationalism or chauvinism), *nutgarah üzel* (localism), and *yasharhah üzel* (ethnic nationalism)—indicates the desire of MPRP ideologues to achieve success on three fronts: integration of Mongolia with the Soviet Union, mutual accommodation of people of different regions, and assimilation of various Mongolian 'ethnic groups'

---

[15] The full phrase is *hoyor nohoin hoorondo yas hayah,* 'throwing bones between two dogs', to stir up discord. This connection with the *yastan* suggests that people think along ethnic lines, ethnic exclusion, etc.

into the Halh nation. It also demonstrates, however, the difficulty of carrying out this social engineering project.

Socialist 'Feudal' Structure and Problems of Social Cohesion

Modern society, according to Gellner (1983, 1987), is marked by egalitarianism, which is generated by mobility. The division of labour is the driving force, for modern industrial production needs its labour force to be uniformly trained. Gellner's idea is that egalitarianism creates national cohesion, hence national identity and culture. But we see little social cohesion in industrialized modern Mongolia, where literacy is claimed to be 100 per cent and the majority of the population are engaged in industrial production or services. How can we explain this?

We may find that the factors necessary for creating Gellnerian egalitarianism are curiously lacking in contemporary Mongolia. There is a division of labour, and communication is extensive. But the communication between regions is vertical rather than horizontal. Each region has little direct contact with any other, their contact being largely mediated through a higher level of administration. This creates a pyramidal structure which is not very different from that of Gellner's agrarian model. In pre-revolutionary Mongolia the Manchu had prohibited movement between the banners in order to maintain social control (which, I argued earlier, nevertheless did not prevent the formation of a unitary and relatively egalitarian culture).

It appears that twentieth-century socialism has created something like feudalism. Potter and Potter (1990) and Potter (1993) have found that in China a caste-like social stratification structure was created during the Maoist period, separating the peasants and urban residents. This is a kind of 'bureaucratic feudalism that is reminiscent of European serfdom' (Potter 1993: 168). In Mongolia, it is also true that urban and rural masses have been created, although urban and rural mobility is easier than in China. But what is striking is that each *sum* had no direct link with any other *sum*, and communication of whatever kind had to be conducted via the provincial centre. Similarly, inter-provincial communication is via the capital. Humphrey (1983) describes a similar structure for Buryatia, and indeed the Soviet Union was probably the model for the Mongols. Such a structure creates a horizontal isolation, typical of a 'feudal agrarian' structure.

In essence, such an urban–rural relationship in Mongolia is largely a modern creation. After the brutal removal of the 'feudal' (black and yellow) classes, the state wanted to create a different kind of class system. The *ard*, the poor lay herders, were the equivalent of the proletariat, but in ideological terms they were still short of being such in that they still owned some private animals. Rapid industrialization in the 1960s began to change the national economy, which had been based on livestock breeding, and gave rise to a different class: a real, working-class proletariat (*ajilchin*) in a land without a capitalist class. Initially the proletariat's relationship with the *ard* herders was an alliance. But along with the dream of driving toward communism, the *ard* class became increasingly less sound ideologically, as it denoted a background other than industrial. This occurred when the national economy began to move away from animal husbandry toward heavy industry and exploitation of mineral resources (marked by the emergence of such industrial cities as Darhan and Erdenet in the 1970s). Urban workers (*ajilchin*) became a higher, more progressive class than the herders (*ard*). Thus, we find a change of class relations from the earlier model (the oppressor feudal class versus the revolutionary *ard*) to the backward *ard* class versus the progressive *ajilchin* working class. This ideological upgrading led to repeated campaigns against Mongolian customs, tradition, culture, and even the nomadic way of life, which were labelled as 'feudal remnants' contrary to the socialist way of life. Shirendyv writes:

Once the *ajilchin* class came into existence, the union between the *ajilchin* class and *hödölmörchin* (labouring) *ard* class strengthened, forming the political base of the people's (*ard*) democratic state. Thanks to this union, the people's government gradually transferred from the peculiar revolutionary dictatorship of the *hödölmörchin ard* to the dictatorship of the *ajilchin*. This dictatorship was able to build the base of socialism in this country by relying on the internationalist union and multi-sided brotherly co-operation established with the socialist peoples. (Shirendyv 1972: 27)

It is evident that the urban working class was perceived as more related to the 'brotherly' Soviet people than the rural herders. We can perhaps further formulate the Mongolian social structure in an encompassing hierarchy. The lower 'feudal' structure is actually the 'internal colony' of the higher order. The hierarchical relation can be seen as follows: Soviet Union—Ulaanbaatar—rural Mongolia. The economic basis of this hierarchy was the process whereby resources went from rural Mongolia to Ulaanbaatar, where they were semi-processed and then exported to the Soviet Union. Finally, finished products flowed back to Mongolia at a much higher price. So in modern 'industrial' Mongolia, there was not a single machine-building factory of any type; there was not even a paper factory (even today). Every item needed for industrial operation was imported from the Soviet Union or some East European countries. The relationship was such that the external centre was always the provider of technology, the subordinate depending on this external supply. This phenomenon is called *belenchileh*—that is, waiting for the supply from above—which kills all initiatives from below. It is perhaps characteristic of all socialist countries.

Verdery (1991, 1992, 1993) argues that the socialist economy is a supply-constrained economy. The state is the supplier, and the province is the demander, rather than the other way round. She explains that this kind of structure gives rise to a hoarding habit on the part of the lower order, as with a company which argued that if the state had supplied more, they would have been able to produce more. This bargaining mentality and the entire economic structure creates fierce competition which is best organized along ethnic lines. Verdery demonstrates that this is possible even in a country like Romania, where the state structure is not feudal. The socialist economy is always in a state of supply shortage, hence the need to procure more from the centre fosters 'acquisitionship' as opposed to capitalist salesmanship. This feature has persisted in the post-socialist period (see also Humphrey 1991). The non-Romanians were blamed for taking away the wealth of the country. An ethnic conflict then followed. While much of her argument is valid for the Mongolian case, we have to take account of the socialist 'feudal' hierarchy.

Verdery overemphasizes the bargaining power of the lower order and underestimates that of the upper order. In fact, the running of the entire socialist economy is guaranteed by direct control from the centre to curb the bargaining power of the lower order. We thus see the direct involvement of Soviet Russians in all strata of Mongol society; almost all the ministers had Russian advisers, and there were a large number of Russian technicians in almost every factory.[16]

In an effort to curb 'localism', officials from one province were assigned to work in places other than their own home towns. This practice went against the hoarding principle, caused clashes with local

[16] Most of them departed in 1991–2, leaving the Mongol technicians severely crippled in handling Soviet machinery.

interests, giving the impression that the centre was sending an outsider to exploit the locals. In the predominantly Buryat *sum* Dashbalbar, for example, until 1990, all the successive *sum* administrative leaders were non-local, and above all, non-Buryat. This caused bitter resentment from local leaders. On the other hand, some people welcomed outside leaders because they did not have local networks and were more honest. In the 1980s the Politburo twice criticized a Buryat *sum*, Dadal, for showing *ündserheh üzel*, or 'nationalism'. It turned out that the *sum* leader assigned from above was a Darhat, a non-local person; the local people could not get along with him, so they drove him away. Such strong 'localism' or 'nationalism' has led to a notion called *darga togtohgüi* (leader cannot settle down).

The collapse of the Communist monopoly of power in 1990 suddenly revealed the vulnerability of this central controlling system. In the Kazakh-populated Bayan Ölgii *aimag*, as a result of the democratic election in 1990, Mongol officials, once assigned by the state, were removed from the party, youth league, and *sum*, and almost all the posts in Bayan Ölgii were given to Kazakhs. This seems not to be an isolated incident. Nor is it only a matter of ethnic strains. It is reported that all the Övörhangai cadres dispatched to work in Sühbaatar, Dornogobi, and Selenge *aimag*s were driven back to Övörhangai *aimag* in 1990 (Byambadorj 1991). In this latter case, the conflict was amongst the Halh themselves.

In the Manchu period it was not so much the Manchus as Buddhism and the common culture of pastoralism that created unity. In the Soviet period these were replaced by the Communist (MPRP) Party as a unifying principle, but the MPRP's struggle against chauvinism of various hues was only partly successful. Today we see local rejection not just of non-local people but also of 'urban class' cadres.

Conditions for Fostering Nationalism: Economic Disintegration

Once this centrally controlled economy (here I mean the central control from Moscow over the Mongolian economy and the central control by the urban over the rural economy) collapsed, two things happened. The Mongolian economy, despite the enthusiasm of the government, was not able to sever the relationship with the Russian economy. Within Mongolia, the centre has little to offer the rural areas, thus calling into question the efficacy of the central government.

The economic crisis of the early 1990s was accompanied by the opening up of the borders. Anticipating its effects on the discourse on race (see Chapter 5), let us first focus on Ulaanbaatar. Commodities in Mongolia were traded by individuals, who started to take advantage of the enormous price differences in China. Bartered items on sale in Ulaanbaatar from the Soviet Union, Eastern Europe, and North Korea were cheap and luxurious. These items were bought up by Mongols, visiting Chinese, and Inner Mongols, who exported them to China at doubled or tripled prices and came back financially much stronger. Meanwhile, we find Mongolia becoming weaker in its ability to obtain goods to barter, as the entire system had collapsed. As a result, goods available in Mongolia became even scarcer than before. The high demand pushed up the prices. Even such domestic products as carpets were not sufficient to meet demand. Demand from tourists and export to China and perhaps the Soviet Union (now Russia) should in theory have stimulated economic growth, but it was hampered by the entire economic restructuring, as well as the collapse of the infrastructure. The power stations in Ulaanbaatar are so old that they stop functioning from time to time. With the shortage of oil, the entire production and transportation system came almost to a halt in the early 1990s.

During this period, Mongolian Customs began to restrict the types of items that could be taken out of the country. It did not allow any imported goods to be exported, and violations incurred legal penalties. From late 1991, even Mongolia-made products were restricted: a foreigner was allowed to take out one carpet, a Mongol two carpets. By the end of 1991, no foreigner was allowed to take out a single carpet, and by the time I left Mongolia in April 1992, even a Mongol citizen was not allowed to take out carpets. The restricted items extended to children's clothes. On the other hand, foreigners were allowed to take in anything they wanted. Chinese and Inner Mongols who visited Mongolia began to complain that the things they bought were not allowed out. The Customs and Mongolian TV began to unmask alleged offences. They constantly publicized the confiscation of 'illegal' items 'smuggled' out by the cunning and bad 'Chinese' (including Inner Mongols) and a few irresponsible Mongols, thus spreading anti-Chinese sentiment (see Fig. 2.1).

Frequently Inner Mongolians appealed to the Mongolian Customs officers using Mongolian language and other tactics, but to no avail. However, in due course, they found ingenious ways to get around the problem: for example, a Chinese would rely on an Inner Mongolian, and

FIGURE 2.1. Poverty-stricken Mongols crossing Mongolian borders to do petty trading, in order to get through the current economic crisis. From Tsenddoo 1994: 52.

an Inner Mongolian would in turn 'cultivate' a Mongolian citizen, each appealing to some common identity and interest. Together, they would bribe the Mongolian Customs, thus effectively evading the state regulations and at the same time creating cross-border ties and relationships. This is typical of the post-socialist 'mafia' phenomenon.

This 'I can buy yours but you cannot buy mine' mentality is peculiar to an unbalanced economy that cannot sustain growth. It is a rationale based on scarcity of resources. It would be useful to push this argument a bit further. Mongolia itself has, in this sense, become a scarce and precious good, that everybody is drooling for. A sense of uniqueness, something induplicable, has been fostered, that leads to a Mongolian nationalism based on notions of purity and danger that I will discuss in later chapters.

Tamara Dragadze (1993) writes, with regard to the economy and nationalism in the former Soviet Union, that what the Soviet system created is a friction between the centre and the regions, which are ethnicized in terms of territory, politics, culture, and economy. The appropriation of regional economic resources and their redistribution is 'exploitation' of the region from the centre. She suggests that we should 'distinguish between the economic urgency of regionalism (which is what people are doing), the universe of discourse of ethnicized regionalism (which is what people are saying) and constitutional regionalism (what people are dreaming of)' (1993: 80–1).

The peculiar Mongolian, three-layer, centre–periphery relationship, as discussed above, makes the Mongolian economy particularly vulnerable. While the urban class was closely related to the Soviet industry, the rural Mongols were left marginalized. The urban centre used administrative ordering to procure the livestock necessary to supply the Mongol meat factory for export and to feed urban dwellers. The fixing of herders in such a position was indeed a result of marginalization of livestock production and of surrendering the *ard* dictatorship to *ajilchin* dictatorship.

The prestige attached to urbanity has been a great incentive in drawing rural population to the cities, leading to rapid urbanization in Mongolia. One way to get into cities was through education. Almost all higher education institutions were concentrated in either Ulaanbaatar or, even better, in the former Soviet Union or the socialist bloc countries. Another way was to establish and maintain kinship networks, either real or fictive. *Huurai* (dry) or fictive kinship was common between urbanites and country herders, the latter depending on their fictive kinsmen in the cities to gain access to urban luxuries, medical services, and other things otherwise unavailable in the countryside. The countryside not only lost its natural attraction, but was deemed as belonging to the past and backward, a production base, the flow of wealth going to cities and abroad.

The Soviet 'exploitation' of Mongolia was vividly described by J. Pürev (1990) in an open letter to Gorbachev. He pointed out with outrage that animals (2.5–3 million a year) exported to the Soviet Union were bought at well below the world price and even four to five times less than the Soviet market price. Many of Mongolia's natural resources, like uranium, gold, silver, wolfram, and copper, were actually looted during the socialist period without leaving any documentation (for example, Mardai as mentioned in Chapter 1). He urged Gorbachev to reconsider the allegation that Mongolia was indebted to the USSR by ten billion roubles[17] (see Fig. 2.2).

---

[17] Some scholars would emphasize, perhaps echoing the Russian claim, that the Soviets (Russians) were subsidizing Mongolia at a rate of US$400 per capita per annum up through

Д. ОДГИЙВ зурав

FIGURE 2.2. The Soviet Union exchanging Leninism for Mongolian sovereignty, land, livestock, and treasures. Drawing by D. Odgiiv, *Ündesnii Devshil*, 17 Apr. 1991.

Similarly, the central exploitation of the herders also met resentment in the countryside. In Dashbalbar, the *sum* accountant told me that all the good lambs were taken to the meat factory in Choibalsang (to be exported to the Soviet Union and Bulgaria), thus destroying the entire herd structure, which needs a good balance of animals of different ages. In return, the people of the *sum* received little. He saw no reason why the *sum* should continue the contract, now that almost nothing was coming down from the centre.

1990 (Goldstein and Beall 1994: 96). These two claims may be reconciled, perhaps, by saying that the Soviet (Russian) right (subsidizing) hand did not know what its left (cheating) hand was up to (I am grateful to Edward H. Kaplan for drawing my attention to this point). This is also the case in China. While the Tibetans and other ethnic minorities accuse the Chinese government of exploiting the natural resources of the minority regions, the Chinese government would always point out that subsidizing the minority regional economies is a big burden (see Friedman 1995).

Herdsmen's attempts to withhold their animals from the urban centres developed to such an extent that in Ulaanbaatar a food ration system had to be adopted in 1991. Each urban resident was entitled to only 90 grams of meat per day. In desperation, the government decided to import meat from Inner Mongolia at a price of two US dollars per kilo. Herdsmen were outraged at this decision. Some told me that the stupid government did not even think of giving that money to the Mongolian herdsmen, who would be thrilled to have half of it. Besides, herdsmen thought that such a decision would bring shame on them, by implying that they could not or would not produce meat for the nation. As a compromise, the government freed meat prices and allowed herdsmen to sell their live-stock in Ulaanbaatar.

Thus the uneasy urban and rural relationship was exacerbated by the economic crisis; when the urban centre could not supply commodities to the rural areas, a gap appeared. In the early 1990s, rural herders were already self-reliant. Therefore many urban people chose to go back to the countryside, where they could have sufficient food and shelter. The privatization of collective property which started in 1991 has greatly benefited the *negdel* (collective) members. Those who did not have a share of the original stock in the collectives and late comers or outsiders have had to go back to their original collectives to claim their share. Many who had migrated to the cities returned to their home collective, digging into dusty record books to establish their claims. But they were often rejected by the herders. There seemed to be a lot of quarrels in Dash-balbar in August 1991. The collective members quarrelled over who had worked harder and thus contributed more; at the same time, the common economic interest united them against the outside intruders. Since 1992, the old collectives have been transformed into joint-stock companies.

The flow of urban population to the countryside of the 1990s is a reversal of the earlier trend of movement of rural populations to a few cities. Ironically, urbanites are now most enthusiastic to cultivate *huurai* or fictive kinship with rural herders. The countryside now represents not only a source of wealth, but also the source of 'genuine' Mongol culture, which is best kept there. In this context people are discovering what the Mongols call 'rural power' or *hödööni sabdag* (literally, rural god), which now provides an alternative to the earlier urban-centred 'progress', bring-ing down the ill-constructed socialist Mongol urban–rural hierarchy.

We thus see that the division of labour in Mongolia is not elaborate enough to make the urban–rural relationship a symbiotic one. What is happening now is a reversion to *ard* (rural herders) dictatorship, particularly irritating to *ajilchin* (workers and urbanites) dictatorship. It is rural power that makes the horse a symbol of the Mongol nation, the backbone of the country, the feeder and carrier (see Chapter 7).

Humphrey (1991) reports that in the Russian Republic, Buryat local enterprises have become politically stronger and economically more autonomous units; during the period of *perestroika* they began acting like petty feudal polities as redistributive domains. Some even issued their own currency to regulate the circulation of goods, jealously guarding against any outflow of local wealth. At the same time, these enterprises have been creating, often by barter, their own 'horizontal' economic links to their own advantage.

This is the road now being taken by the Mongol rural areas: an age-old one of looking horizontally toward the outside world (see Khazanov 1984). As the economic power of the centre weakens, Mongolian border regions quickly demand access to foreign countries directly, rather than via the centre, as was previously the case. Localism, as previously attacked time and again by the central authority, is now a reality, thanks to democratization. However, this localism is not an 'inward-looking' isolation, but a reappropriation of power in the hands of the locals to run their own economic activities. 'Isolation' is not possible, because Mongol rural areas have no industry to enable them to form an economically autonomous polity. Their geographical proximity to the outside fosters an outward-looking tendency.

While the capital city has been boiling with quarrels and disputes, Mongols in rural areas have been reluctant to come to Ulaanbaatar, and indeed, the transportation has become hardly available because of the oil shortage. It makes more economic sense to cross the border into China, where people can buy a cheaper and richer variety of goods, than to go to Ulaanbaatar or *aimag* centres. These cross-border visits are often facilitated by kinsmen or Mongols living in Xinjiang or Inner Mongolia. It is repeatedly reported that thousands of Mongols cross the border, without regard to regulations, and 'ransack' the Inner Mongolian border towns and their shops. The same is reported from Buryatia.[18] Economic fragmentation and the desire to establish economic links with economically better-endowed kinsmen across the borders meets the desire of the Mongols in China and Russia, who are either eager to help their kinsmen or hope for access to cheap resources. The Buryats in Dornod *aimag* were so interested in doing business in Inner Mongolia that many of the

---

[18] Balzhan Zhimbiev, personal communication, 1993.

leaders frequently crossed the border for trade negotiations. They also crossed the border into Russia and carried out a lot of trade there.

What is significant is that, during this process, a strong trans-national 'ethnic' interest has been aroused. Contacts with their kinsmen across borders have raised ethnic consciousness, which is otherwise losing ground in the wider, more politically defined Halh-equals-Mongol hegemony. The Buryats in Dashbalbar told me that they were ashamed to meet their relatives from Shinehen in Inner Mongolia. Although they are the best Buryat speakers in Mongolia, they feel they have lost much of the Buryat cultural flavour. They express a desire to make further contacts with their kinsmen, and to do so, they need to purify their dialect. They are now much interested in their own roots, and many sigh: 'We are no longer pure Buryat, and yet we cannot speak good Halh, either. Who are we?' Their economic interest and also cultural interest in their kinsmen in China and Russia has curiously put them in a triangle, which ignores political boundaries and maps the world in a more group-based way. This is a manifestation of what I call 'non-political Greater Mongolian sentiment', which cuts across present state boundaries. By virtue of their 'immigrant' status, many non-Halh groups in the border areas have an overt interest in their kinsmen. Their élites in Ulaanbaatar are therefore articulate about this sentiment in their pan-Mongolian approach to the delicate questions of Mongols outside Mongolia and their relations with Mongolia, which contrasts strikingly with the more inward-looking Halh approach.

In 1991 Bayan Ölgii *aimag* decided that the province would not take flour from the Mongolian government, but would barter for the necessities directly from Xinjiang (China) and Kazakhstan. They said that they would not give the Mongolian government any meat, wool, cashmere, skin, leather, or other raw materials; instead, these would be used to exchange goods with Kazakhstan and Xinjiang. This plan was actually said to have been approved by the national government. The *aimag* leaders started to arrange business with the two foreign regions and negotiated 15 thousand tons of flour from Kazakhstan. But by the beginning of December 1991, only 160 tons had arrived, and the *aimag* population had virtually nothing left to eat. The Mongolian government decided to alter their agreement and provide a fixed amount of flour to the *aimag*, guaranteeing 4–5 kilos per person per month for the residents. This was an enticement tactic, which sacrificed the interests of the neighbouring Hovd *aimag*, where each person had only one kilo of flour per month (Hahaar 1992).

Thus, in Mongolia, to some extent, the centre appeases, the periphery 'blackmails'. This is possible in a Mongolia surrounded by an outside world (this time, interestingly, the 'outside world' for the rural Mongols has become the Mongols in China and Russia, for the Kazakhs, the Kazakhs in Xinjiang and Kazakhstan) (Bulag 1994). The largely Communist-controlled centre sees this outward-looking tendency as essentially undermining its power and sovereignty.[19]

In order to curb rural localism, the new Mongolian Constitution, which is a brain-child of a largely Communist-dominated parliament,[20] stipulates 'The Livestock of the country shall be the national wealth and protected by the State', despite the fact that it also gives recognition to private ownership. This statement has no legal, but only emotional, significance. It also stipulates local rule by appointment from above, rather than by democratic elections among local people. The consequence of this latter stipulation is summarized in a recent study of local governance in Mongolia: 'Presently, the *hural* is granted little power *vis-à-vis* the governor, who is supposed to represent the state and to report directly to the higher level. Concerning some local issues, the authority of the *hural* is limited to comment on the governor's action' (Enkhbat and Odgaard 1996: 172).

Conclusion

In this chapter I have argued that seemingly homogeneous Mongolia has numerous 'ethnic' and social problems, many of which are directly related to the socialist experiment of creating a socialist Mongolian nation. The overemphasis on the Halh and the adoption of the Soviet classification of Mongol groups into 'ethnic groups' furthered, and indeed perhaps institutionalized, ethnicity. This is not to deny that

---

[19] It is curious to note that the Communists in power portrayed themselves as defenders of Mongolian sovereignty. Briefly, the democrats presided over the destruction of the socialist control system, yet were initially unable to provide a convincing framework as an alternative for social change. The democratic forces came under heavy criticism from all over the country, despite their ideals of freedom and democracy. The Communists (MPRP) had been able, in this milieu, to transform themselves to regain power as nation-defenders, catering to the nationalist sentiment that erupted in 1990; it is to their advantage to repeat the narrative of crisis of independence. However, the Communists did not live up to their promise of improving Mongolia's economy. In the general elections held in the summer of 1996, the Democratic Union of Coalition defeated the former Communist Party—MPRP—and won the government seat.

[20] The MPRP occupied 357 of the 430 seats in the People's Great Hural (Congress).

Mongols had group identities in the past: indeed, 'tribalism' was endemic, but it operated within a Mongol framework. The perpetuation of this 'tribalism', endowing it with modern concepts of class, ethnic hierarchy, and national identity, has greatly upset the fabric of Mongolian identity.

The destruction of certain so-called feudal elements very often alienated some Mongols. We may now identify an interesting pattern: in the early 1930s, the destruction of Buddhism created a centrifugal tendency, pushing Buddhist Mongols to the peripheries where some Buddhist sanctuary might be found. The persecution of the aristocracy frightened off Inner Mongolian nationalist leaders such as Prince Demchugdonrub from uniting with the MPR; he could not but ally with the Japanese for delivering some support.

The institutionalization of Halh identity as the most authentic Mongol one and as constituting the 'Whites' of Mongolia is also something unacceptable to many non-Halh Mongols. So far, I have not systematically explored the creation of this identity; but it is safe to suggest that nationalism, embodied in the Halh and the idea that it is the 'core nation' (see Chapter 3), defined furthermore on the basis of anti-Chinese imperialism, is hegemonic, in the sense that the role of other Mongols in the creation of the Mongol state has been overridden. The guardianship of the Halh also peripheralizes other Mongol groups, who are subjected to assimilation by shedding their non-Halh cultural properties and learning the Halh mode of speech. What this creates is not so much a material problem as a psychological one of identity. Nevertheless, such a socialist Mongolian nation has been relatively successful, largely through the state as a means of organizing economic wealth.

Socialist Mongolia built itself on the basis of an organic geo-body *vis-à-vis* other foreign geo-bodies. Since a nation is defined thereby, Mongols in foreign nation-states are designated non-Mongols, that is, as not officially belonging to the socialist Mongolian nation, but to other nations, such as the Chinese nation. I will discuss this in later chapters. But let me say in passing that the discrimination against the Mongols in China is based on both this notion of nation-state and the confrontation between the two states.

Today, with the collapse of the state as organizer of economic wealth, and despite the appeal of Mongolian nationalism, we also find an outward-looking tendency among Mongols. Mongolia is a large territory, but it cannot contain its small number of 'nomads'. Is this a historical tendency or a policy failure? Mongols may not perceive the problem in this way; one Mongol diplomat told me in early 1993 that only two Chinese residents had abandoned their Mongol passports and become Chinese citizens and that no real Mongol would betray the motherland. I do not say that the Mongols are abandoning Mongolia; instead, there is a force that is prying open the artificially created Mongolian border and connecting the Mongols right at the borders with adjacent Mongol-inhabited areas now under the jurisdiction of China and Russia. We may call this tendency a Greater Mongolia sentiment, but not 'pan-Mongolism'.

Greater Mongolia is a concept which may be compared with that of Greater China. Edward Friedman (1995) writes convincingly that the Chinese on the periphery of China, especially those in the south, look towards the Chinese diaspora for economic growth stimulants, and perhaps even democratic inspiration, instead of looking to the north or to the government in Beijing. The Communist government is based on the myth of 'the Han', which is very much a northern tradition. The Han nation is defined by the government as a unilineal, northern-based, anti-imperialist national identity. Friedman also contrasts this Han Chinese nationalism with Greater China sentiment. His intention is, however, to show that the furthering of the latter movement might lead to the demise of communism in China and the building of democracy. In my view, he overemphasizes the 'splittist' tendency of southern China. In the Mongolian case, non-Halh Mongols may be compared to the southern Chinese. My concept of Greater Mongolia is a cultural concept of identity, overriding the present nation-state boundary, yet without political implications. This is different from the earlier pan-Mongolian idea, stemming from the pan-Buddhist opposition to communism and the goal of political unification of all Mongols in one single country. It is something more economically and culturally oriented, legitimating all kinds of interactions, with perhaps a primordial appeal. However, as Greater Mongolia often reminds people of earlier pan-Mongolism, and is thought to be incompatible with the existing convention of so-called internationalism, and surely with the MPR (or Mongolia) as a political entity, we thus see in the centre of the country the emergence of another wave of rhetoric (see Bulag and Humphrey 1996). In the context of a centre economically disadvantaged in relation to the peripheries, we now see the birth of a kind of Mongolian nationalism, closely connected with Halh-ness, which pits independence and all the other most glorious appeals of nationalism against relations with non-Halh Mongols from outside Mongolia. But in the meantime, Greater Mongolia cultural sentiment is something that has to be reckoned with. Because much of the cultural content of this Greater Mongolia cultural identity overlaps with the more narrowly defined Halh, things like Chinggis Khan, Buddhism, Mongolian script, and others are used by all sides to argue for greater inclusion in the limited space of Mongolness.

3

Ethno-politics in Mongolia

Introduction

Mongolia is now embroiled in a myriad social problems, one of which is the issue of national integration. I have suggested that socialism in Mongolia has not been able to foster a homogeneous nationality; consequently, in a time of market economy and freedom, various groups openly desire to express their ethnicity.

Contemporary Mongolia is a multi-ethnic state. The population includes several ethnic groups of Mongolian origin and several of Turkic origin, as well as some Russians and Chinese. Tables 3.1 and 3.2 record the numbers of so called 'nationalities' and their distribution in Mongolia. As we can see, some nationalities have declined in numbers, and some have *disappeared*, not by elimination, but due to the special character of the 'ethnic process' in Mongolia which I have discussed in Chapter 2. This book will not deal in detail with the numerous small groups listed in the tables.[1] Instead, it attempts to answer one large question. Until the mid-twentieth century, Mongols of various affiliations recognized each other as Mongols, albeit differentiating boundaries with each other. Such a concept of Mongol was indeed Greater Mongolian in orientation, which overrode the minor subgroups in the country and included the Mongols living outside. Today this is no longer so. The Mongol people are divided among themselves, and a process of exclusion and redefinition of identities is under way. A hierarchization of Mongolian groups has emerged, delineating which is more Mongol, which is less Mongol, or which group should no longer be regarded as Mongol.

---

[1] Western study of Mongolian ethnicity is limited; see Szynkiewicz (1986, 1987*a*, 1988) and Pegg (1991, 1998). For ethnographic studies by Mongolian scholars, see Jamtsarano (1934), Rinchen (1979), and Badamhatan (1987). Jamtsarano (1934), in what was probably the first ethnographic survey of Mongolia, recorded the following groups: Darhat and Urianghai of Lake Hövsgöl, Dürbet, Hoton, Bayat, Ööld, Myangat, Zahchin, Torguut, Hoshut, Tsahar, Dariganga, Altai Urianghai, Kazakh, and Hamnigan, in addition to the

A small joke prevalent in Mongolia may give a foretaste of the Mongols' own perception of their internal relations.

Once upon a time, in Hell, there was a cauldron surrounded by noisy demons. Water was boiling in the cauldron and people were struggling to get out of it, only to be pushed in by demons with forks. When asked what it was all about, it was said that they were cooking the Jews who had committed sins in their previous births. Since the Jews helped each other to get out of this torture, it required numerous demons to struggle hard to keep them in there. There was another cauldron guarded by two to three demons who raised their forks only once in a while. Apparently, the Germans were being boiled there, but since they occasionally helped their own relatives, they still had to be guarded. There was a third cauldron, but no demons on guard; only the water was boiling, as if there was nobody inside. Well, in fact, the Mongols were being boiled. Since the Mongols always pulled each other down when they struggled to climb out, nobody had yet succeeded, so there was no need to keep an eye on them! (Adapted from Baabar 1990: 28)

The joke feeds on the earlier notion that the nomadic warriors had much internal tribalist animosity. The seemingly intense ethnicity in what was previously thought to be homogeneous Mongolia, which I discuss below, is not tribalism, nor just an inter-Mongol relational phenomenon, but operates in a much wider international context. In this chapter I discuss four different styles of ethnicity in Mongolia: Halh, Oirat, Buryat, and Kazakh. Each group emphasizes different aspects, but, with the exception of the Kazakh, who are notably a non-Mongol minority, two very broad approaches to Mongolness emerge. This is rather similar to the debates among the Tatars and Chuvash about their ethnogenesis, studied by Shnirelman (1996). Shnirelman points out that the Tatars are faced with a choice between emphasizing their indigeneity, based on a claim to the Bulgar, or emphasizing their non-indigeneity, by claiming an ancestral link with the Golden Horde. Despite the popularity (or perhaps authenticity) of the latter choice, political expediency determines that 'the Bulgar version of the Kazan Tatar ethnogenesis has better prospects in modern Tatarstan than does the Golden Horde/Nogay version, because it legitimates the contemporary territory of the Tatar Republic' (1996: 59). Shnirelman concedes, however, that 'the existence of a sub-

majority group, Halh. Subsequent Mongolian statistics would add some additional groups like Uzemchin, Barga, Sönit, Horchin, Harchin, etc. These latter groups (including Tsahar) came from Inner Mongolia after 1911, when many Inner Mongolian banners declared allegiance to Mongolia, and in 1945 when Soviet–Mongolian troops occupied Inner Mongolia.

TABLE 3.1. *Nationalities Distribution by Aimag (1969)*

Nationalities	Ulaanbaatar	Selenge	Töv	Hovd	Uvs	Ömnögobi	Sukhbaatar	Zavhan	Hövsgöl	Arhangai
Halh	217,239	35,565	58,412	16,103	11,396	26,310	15,537	67,864	60,892	70,751
Kazakh	3,238	720	640	6,429	307	14	20	7	17	34
Dürbet	5,456	898	583	2,307	22,406	7	14	27	65	24
Buryat	7,181	1,547	1,220	8	19	18	85	16	862	19
Bayat	2,499	179	78	113	22,123	2	3	25	32	12
Dariganga	970		27	15	16	5	18,197	1	3	6
Urianghai	1,919	7	262	3,311	111		12	2	3,240	9
Zahchin	1,614	609	146	12,440	48	3	5	32	52	7
Darhat	448	346	120	25	6	14	12	4	9,184	16
Torguut	1,246	158	38	5,401	23	23	5	4	24	10
Ööld	843	133	48	4,366	60	4	2	6	15	1,200
Hoton	619	133	11	10	3,391	1			2	
Myangat	376	9	34	2,539	132			5	1	
Barga	208	38	250	9	12		1	2	3	1
Uzemchin	127	19	7				4		3	
Harchin	36	8	5				369		3	3
Tsahar	74	6	6	2	1		2		1	
Hotgoid		16					1			
Uzbek	32	26	9	166	11	4	2	10	15	3
Horchin	59	15	4	9	1		1			2
Others	470	123	102	429	26	2	715	2,412	133	3

TABLE 3.1. (contd.)

Nationalities	Dundgobi	Övörhangai	Erdenet	Darhan	Bayan Ölgii	Bayanhongor	Bulgan	Gobi-Altai	Dorno-Gobi	Dornod	Hentii
Halh	29,555	66,175		15,256	252	52,152	36,228	47,186	29,176	24,672	30,358
Kazakh	20	27		215	48,086	18	14	81	342	70	2,513
Dürbet	20	18		632	1,873	44	16	37	202	58	44
Buryat	25	25		718	4	7	836	8	170	11,068	5,936
Bayat	4	6		249	20	2	4	13	67	26	20
Dariganga	16			79	1				152	953	155
Urianghai	11	11		158	5,846	4	4	4	97	28	24
Zahchin	3	17		172	18	6	2	33	67	34	12
Darhat	7	18		53		16	7	11	41	15	6
Torguut	10	9		88	29	21	10	8	32	17	7
Ööld	5	10		96	33	8	6	8	22	10	4
Hoton	1			2	3				2	6	
Myangat	7	9		43	6		1	8	16	2	2
Barga	4			29		3			7	1,715	40
Uzemchin		2		2			1		5	1,593	7
Harchin	906				2		1		22	41	2
Tsahar				3	1					8	1
Hotgoid											
Uzbek	2			3	48	5	3	2	4	7	9
Horchin	6			2	2				4	3	
Others	5	3		17	1,729	2	17	2	26	31	70

Source: unpublished statistics from the State Statistical Office, Mongolia.

Table 3.2. *Nationalities Distribution by Aimag (1989)*

Nationalities	Ulaanbaatar	Selenge	Töv	Hovd	Uvs	Ömnögobi	Sukhbaatar	Zavhan	Hövsgöl	Arhangai
Halh	481,663	73,591	94,773	20,397	13,706	42,267	25,874	88,120	84,179	82,752
Kazakh	9,005	3,229	2,167	12,814	950	18	9	68	24	90
Dürbet	8,208	2,214	727	3,609	33,941	30	26	99	53	61
Buryat	7,186	992	590	20	52	22	67	10	780	8
Bayat	5,177	707	317	227	29,672	21	19	81	64	40
Dariganga	1,727	69	36	15	3	4	24,521	1	13	4
Urianghai	2,445	1,768	420	5,403	74	21	7	8	3,215	19
Zahchin	2,692	857	160	17,228	63	33	9	37	20	21
Darhat	520	322	92	23	8	1	11	17	12,991	14
Torguut	1,071	458	90	6,703	22	4	9	6	5	14
Ööld	1,341	146	61	5,622	46	4		13	6	1,427
Hoton	131	558	45	23	5,007	1		3	1	4
Myangat	615	106	33	3,517	113	2	2	9	2	9
Barga	193	6	24	2	2	3	8			
Uzemchin	106	11	5	1	1		253			
Harchin	44	3	6	3			5		2	
Tsahar	30	2	3				1			
Hotgoid	32	7	18	2	1				101	
Uzbek	20	19	2	187	2		9	11		
Horchin	55	1								
Tuva	74	631	1	239	7			1	1	1

TABLE 3.2. (contd.)

Nationalities	Dundgobi	Övörhangai	Erdenet	Darhan	Bayan Ölgii	Bayanhongor	Bulgan	Gobi-Altai	Dorno-Gobi	Dornod	Hentii
Halh	49,183	96,138	41,281	67,580	393	74,455	51,071	62,340	53,682	49,588	57,391
Kazakh	3	65	1,336	3,116	82,750	9	8	98	872	220	3,655
Dürbet	4	62	991	2,528	1,382	32	56	81	345	551	208
Buryat	4	44	383	856	4	4	511	1	212	16,654	7,044
Bayat	25	31	393	1,377	63	3	122	58	332	319	185
Dariganga	3	18	27	80	3	1	1	4	225	1,932	354
Urianghai	1	18	433	845	5,100	7	18	13	86	120	1,304
Zahchin	9	19	339	926	66	8	11	80	129	240	51
Darhat	1	4	162	150	1	2	56	4	41	313	24
Torguut	1	10	79	493	16	2	4	36	39	169	801
Ööld	1	29	101	235	28	6	17	22	17	38	28
Hoton		4	81	123	11			5	28	49	2
Myangat	1	7	96	107	11			16	28	73	13
Barga	8	4	1	11	1	1	5		6	1,825	30
Uzemchin	1			2					1	1,697	8
Harchin	12	2		3	1			1	1	16	3
Tsahar	6									2	
Hotgoid		8	11	6			1		1	2	1
Uzbek		2	31	29	19					2	9
Horchin					1					21	10
Tuva	6	6	59	71	737			2	1	8	314

Source: unpublished statistics from the State Statistical Office, Mongolia.

stantial Tatar diaspora will fuel the latter version for a considerable period of time' (ibid.).

The earlier suppression of non-Halh Mongolian identities is now crumbling. But the strategy of the claims for separate identities on the part of non-Halh Mongol groups is not to assert non-Mongolness, but to challenge Halh hegemony. They aim to establish a direct route to Mongolness, not via Halh, but through historical links to Chinggis Khan, the unifier and identity-giver of Mongols. This new process is a reverse of the socialist ethnic process ideology, which, in its typical evolutionary scheme, privileged the numerical majority and a future orientation. In the post-socialist period, the location of moral authority has changed, and is seen as lying in the 'deep past' (Humphrey 1992*a*). This change of time-frame clearly makes the Halh-based socialist Mongolian identity untenable, but it does not undermine overall Mongolian identity or even the unity of Mongolia. The process entails making every Mongol group equal, rather than unequal, on the hierarchical ladder in the new Mongolian state. To make everybody a Mongol, then, the criteria of inclusion and exclusion have had to be changed. We are now seeing a unique phenomenon: the expansion of the defining frame of Mongolness even beyond Chinggis Khan and his unilineal royalty, making Mongols a diversified unit. This unity in diversity in Mongolia is clearly observable in the field of music and art, where different 'ethnic' styles, previously suppressed, are now being revived and are flourishing[2] (see Pegg 1998).

The Halh: From Marginality to Centrality

I have argued that in the discourse of socialist ethnicity, the Halh have an advantageous position; indeed, all other groups in Mongolia have to be defined *vis-à-vis* the Halh. This has given rise to, or strengthened, a notion that Halh are the quintessential Mongols. That this is so is largely based on the fact that the greater part of present-day Mongolian territory overlaps with what is historically known as 'Halh-land' (*Halh Oron*, *Halh Tümen*, or *Halh Uls*). The majority of the inhabitants of this land are known by the ethnonym Halh. I am not here discussing the historical creation of this Halh identity, but rather

---

[2] Humphrey and Onon write that the Daur Mongols use groves of trees called *duwalang* as a metaphor for their diverse social groups (1996: 98).

how Mongolian scholars define the Halh. I argue that, like other groups in Mongolia, the Halh have also been subjected to the Soviet-style ethnogenesis discourse. A highly influential theory put forward by Gongor (1970) traced the Halh genesis back to well before the thirteenth century, on the evidence that the word *Halh* appeared twice in the *Secret History*. The crucial question is whether *Halh* was a generic term for a cluster of Mongolian tribes and clans inhabiting the region which corresponds roughly to today's Mongolia. The meticulousness paid to the ancientness of the Halh by Halh historians is interesting.

The importance of the ethnonym Halh, Mongolian scholars suggest, lies in its symbolic meaning of 'support' or 'shield'. The present-day Mongolian territory constitutes the ancestral land of all the Mongols and, according to their interpretation of the Mongolian inheritance rule, the last son of the Khan should inherit the homeland. The youngest son is connected to the hearth (*golomt*), while older sons go out to found new units. The symbolic notion of hearth indicates genealogical continuity and centrality (*gol*) (the hearth is physically located at the centre of the yurt); hence the youngest son becomes the lord (*ejen*) of the ancestral yurt. The Mongol homeland ruled by Tolui was then called *Goliin Uls* (core or central nation), as mentioned in the *Secret History* (section 269).

Gongor (1970: 138) seems to suggest that Halh were the principal group which inhabited the Mongol homeland; he not only did not delineate the geographical boundary of this *Goliin Uls*, but excluded other Mongols who might have lived in the region as well. According to Rashid al-Din, the famous thirteenth–fourteenth-century Persian historian, after Tömör Khan was enthroned, succeeding his grandfather Khubilai Khan, he gave his elder brother Kamala Chin Wang the northern half of his empire.

To his elder brother Kamala he gave a full share of the property inherited from their father, and he sent him to Qara-Qorum [Karakorum], which is the region of the yurts and ordos of Chingiz-Khan. He placed the armies of that region under his command, and he administers all the countries of Qara-Qorum, the Chinas, the Shiba'uchi, the Onon and Kelüren, the Kem-Kemch'üt, the Selenge and Qayaliq as far as the region of the Qirqiz, and the great ghoruq of Chingiz-Khan, which they call Burqan-Qaldun and where the great Ordos of Chingiz-Khan are still situated. These latter are guarded by Kamala. There are four great ordos and five others there, nine in all, and no one is admitted to them. They have made portraits of them there and constantly burn perfumes and incense. Kamala too has built himself a temple there. (Boyle 1971: 321–2)

Okada (1993) comments that the four great Ordos of Chinggis Khan served by Prince Kamala titled Chin Wang was the origin of the later Chinggis Khan shrine tended by Chinggisid princes titled Jinong of the Ordos Tümen. 'Only the shrine's location had moved from the Kerülen in Outer Mongolia to the Yellow River Bend in Inner Mongolia' (Okada 1993: 189). Ordos was only one of the Mongol groups that once lived in the heart of the Mongol homeland. It is safe to say that the Mongol homeland was once the 'homeland' of most of the Mongols of Chinggis Khan, who have been dispersed all over Eurasia. However, the majority still live in Mongolia and Inner Mongolia; these two used to constitute what was then called *Goliin Uls*.

In the view of Halh historians, after the Yuan Dynasty, Mongolia was divided into two parts: Eastern Mongolia, which was also called Halh, and Western Mongolia, which was called Oirat. This classification is basically wrong, for it is merely a repetition of the Mongolian aristocratic historiography which regards those Mongol groups directly under the Chinggisids as 'Mongol', and the main contender for supremacy, the Oirat, as an alien force. Almost all history books published in the MPR took this line. But this historiography ignores an important Mongol group, the Horchin, which is numerically the largest group in present-day Inner Mongolia. A clearer picture may be the following: after the Yuan Dynasty, Mongols in Mongolia proper were split into three political groups: Oirat, Mongol, and Horchin. The basis for this classification is that the Oirat were non-Chinggisid-ruled Mongols, the 'Mongol' were Chinggisid-ruled Mongols, and the Horchin were Mongols ruled by Chinggis Khan's brother, Hasar. To use 'Mongol' to designate one particular group is a historical idiosyncrasy. The Oirat were later recognized as a Mongol group, and were named Western Mongol (*baruun Mongol*) according to their geographical location, and the 'Mongol' were correspondingly called Eastern Mongol (*züün Mongol*). However, the Horchin have been almost totally ignored until recently.

This is not the place to explore the ethnic origin of the Halh, but it is not far-fetched to suggest that the Halh were only one of the six myriarchies (Tümen) of the Eastern Mongols, further divided into two wings: Tsahar, Halh, and Urianghai in the eastern (left) wing (*züün gar*); Ordos, Tümed, and Yongshiebu in the western (right) wing (*baruun gar*).

Okada has an interesting explanation for the origin of these six Tümens, or myriarchies:

The Caqar [Tsahar] Myriarchy derived its origin from the personal fief of Qubilai Khan which he had received from his elder brother Möngke Khan in the province of Shensi, and was dedicated to the memories of the brothers' mother, Sorqagtani Begi of the Kereyid. The Qalqa [Halh] Myriarchy went back in origin to the five elite corps commanded by Muqali of the Jalayir and his descendants. The Uriangqan Myriarchy had its origin in the Uriangqan tribesmen who were assigned with the duty of guarding the tomb of Chinggis Khan in the Kentei Mountains. The Ordos Myriarchy kept up the tradition of serving the soul of Chinggis Khan that went back to the time when Qubilai Khan in 1292 created his grandson Kamala Chin Wang and enfeoffed the latter in the Four Great Ordos of Chinggis Khan on the Kerülen. Ever since that time the tribal chief of the Ordos bore the title of Jinong and acted as the head priest in the cult of Chinggis Khan. The Tümed Myriarchy had developed from the Turkic Önggüd Kingdom in the Yinshan Mountains. The Yöngsiyebu Myriarchy derived its origin from the fief of Prince Göden, a son of Ögedei Khan, in Kansu. (Okada 1989: 262–3)

There have been attempts among Halh historians to equate Eastern Mongol with Halh (Natsagdorj 1962). Gongor himself is oscillating between this idea of generalized Halh-equals-Eastern Mongol and the idea of Halh as one of the six Tümens of Eastern Mongolia. Interestingly, Gongor claims that amongst those on the eastern wing, the Halh were the central (*töv*) or core (*gol*) Tümen. It would take great imagination to reach such a conclusion, for in all the Mongol historical chronicles, the Tsahar Tümen was regarded as the central Tümen of the eastern wing. As noted above, the Tsahar Tümen was the personal fief of Khubilai Khan. Okada notes elsewhere that Manduul Khan, who sat on the Mongol throne in 1475, was 'the earliest Mongol chief known to have actually headed the Caqar Myriarchy' (Okada 1991: 156). Mongol Great Khans since then had always personally commanded the Tsahar Tümen, so much so that the last Mongol Great Khan, Ligden (died in 1634), became so localized that he was called a Khan of the Tsahar.

It is interesting to note that Okada identified the Halh as the army of Muqali (Muhalai), one of Chinggis Khan's four *hülüg* (steeds)—that is, most trusted war marshals. In 1218 Chinggis gave Muhalai the title Guo Wang (prince of the state) for his meritorious service and put him in charge of ten thousand men of the left wing, ruling a land from the Onon River to the Hingan Mountain (Onon 1990: 114). Muhalai was of an ancient tribe called Jalair. The Halh ruled by the Jalair nobles enjoyed

autonomy until the sixteenth century, when Batmönh Dayan Khan sent
two of his eleven sons to rule them directly. This was accomplished not
without difficulty. Initially Dayan Khan sent Gerbold to rule the seven
Halh *otog*s (clans), but the latter met with strong hostility from the Jalair
nobles. Gerbold was expelled by the Halh, so Dayan Khan sent Gerbold's younger brother, Gersenz, to conquer the Jalair nobles, which he
succeeded in doing. He stayed on and became the first Chinggisid ruler
of the Halh (Gongor 1970: 172). Gersenz subsequently assumed the title
Jalair Taij, or prince of the Jalair, according to a seventeenth-century
Mongolian chronicle *Altan Tovch* (Lubsandanjin 1990: 187).

The seven *otog*s of the Halh noted above were only part of the Halh,
which comprised 12 *otog*s, divided into Ar Halh (or northern Halh),
which had seven *otog*s, and Övör Halh (or southern Halh), which had five
*otog*s. The present-day Halh descend from the Ar Halh only. The Halh
at the time lived a nomadic life along the banks of the Halh River, which
is now the eastern border of Mongolia. The five Halh groups east of the
river were called Övör Halh, and those west of the river Ar Halh. The
Övör Halh were given to Alchibold, the sixth son of Dayan Khan. As
we have noted, the ideological foundation for claiming that the Halh are
the core of Mongols is based on Mongolian historians' interpretation of
the Mongolian tradition of the youngest son inheriting family property.
According to this scheme, they contend that in the sixteenth century
Batmönh Dayan Khan gave the Halh Tümen to his 'youngest' son,
Gersenz. This claim is dubious in light of the above discussion; that
even the northern part of the Halh was given to Gersenz is only
'accidental'.

However, what all Mongol historical chronicles consistently record is
that the Halh were an important group of the eastern wing, and did
support Batmönh Dayan Khan in conquering not only the three Tümens
of the western wing, but also the Oirat. Thus the Halh were duly praised
for contributing to Batmönh Dayan Khan's historic cause to reunify the
entire Mongols. Therefore, the celebrated song of praise (*magtaal*) to the
Halh describes the role and position of the Halh amongst the six
Tümens, as all six had similar praise songs. For example, the praise
song to the Tsahar Tümen listed at the beginning of the three eastern
wing groups reads:

> You are the blade of the striking sword,
> you are the sides of the rattling helmet.
> Tsahar Tümen.

This is followed by a piece to the Halh Tümen:

> Living in Hangai mountain
> you are the guards (watching for) those returning,
> You are the support to the hot life (of the Khan).
> Halh Tümen.[3]

(Damdinsüren 1982: 635, my translation)

These lines indicate that the Halh were not the central tribe, but a supporting one which provided protection to Batmönh Dayan Khan against the western wing as well as the Oirat Mongols, hence *Halh* (shield, flank). But this praise song is often taken by Halh historians to prove the centrality of the Halh.

In post-socialist Mongolia, the notion of the 'centrality of Halh' has gained further ground among Halh historians. This is no longer pure history, but arguments based on symbolic ideas and spurious etymologies of Halh. Bayasgalang (1991), in an article entitled 'Mongol Hearth—the Halh-centrist Notion', put forward several propositions. First, the building of Erdene Zuu Monastery was an attempt to make it the symbol of the political-religious dual system of the entire Mongol people (*Hamag Mongol*). Second, the significance of the establishment of Ih Hüree (that is, the residence of Jebtsundamba Hutagt, the highest Buddhist leader in Halh Mongolia) lies in the fact that it was 'the residence of the youngest son who had been requested by Mongol Great Khans to keep the fire and guard the hearth, and (it signified) that the Halh Tümen of the Eastern Mongols, for generation after generation, had become the symbol of the (Mongolian) state and the pillar for Mongolian independence'. Recently, Badral (1994) came up with a new definition of Halh by following the call of Gongor, who suggested that when studying the meaning of Halh, one should 'pay attention to the concrete historical reasons that it has become a term referring specifically to the core of the Mongol race (*ugsaatan*)'.[4] By linking *Halh* to *Halhai*, the latter term being an exclamation

---

[3] A different version is provided by Gongor (1970: 138), which reads in translation: 'Living in the Hangai Mountain, | You become a shield against the invading enemies (*harid daisand chinu halh bolson*), | You become the support to the hot life...'

[4] Gongor's claim that the Halh are the 'core' Mongols is also based on an allegedly classical document *Altan Devter* by Sh. Damdin written in Tibetan. Apparently it contains the phrase *Mongol orni töv bolson Halhin oron* (the Halh-land that has become the centre of Mongolia) (1970: 148). The acclaimed classicalness (*tulguur bichig*) of this source, however, turned out to be a twentieth-century production, written between 1919 and 1931 (1970: 165), when the Halh-based nation-state was already taking shape. Gongor and other modern Mongolian historians' influence in Mongolia is impressive.

expressed on touching something hot or fire, and by making the phon-
etical manipulation that *hal* equals *gal* (fire), Badral defines the Hahl
thus: 'The Halh Mongols have been protecting the fire hearth (*gal
golomt*) of the Mongolian race and centre of the original Mongol land.'

In addition to alleging that Halh is the core of the Mongols, some Halh
scholars and artists now try to appropriate Mongol Khans as 'Halh
Khans', giving them a distinct 'Halh' ethnic identity. Inspired by a vastly
popular film made in the 1980s based on Academician Sh. Natsagdorj's
novel *Manduhai*, in which he depicted the heroic role of Batmönh Dayan
Khan's wife, Manduhai Sechen Khatun, in reuniting the Mongols in the
sixteenth century, a popular song appeared in Mongolia in 1992, making
her 'ethnic identity' explicit and artistic:

> Golden seat of your ancestors,
> Ai Manduhai, you rose to defend it.
> Valuing peace between them,
> You united all Mongols.
> The broad mind of Öölün mother,
> You took as heritage and your deeds flourished.
> Wise Manduhai, ai Manduhai!
>
> Golden crown of the Lord Khan,
> Ai Manduhai, you rose to defend it.
> Enduring your love of Hasar's descendent,
> You united all Mongols.
> Your ancestor Temüjin's state seal,
> You embraced, and you made the state flourish.
> Wise Manduhai, ai Manduhai!
>
> *Golden lineage of the Halh people*,
> Manduhai, you loved and raised.
> Uniting your splintered state,
> You made everyone happy.
> Lord Chinggis' state flag,
> You raised, and you were immortalized.
> Wise Manduhai, ai Manduhai!
>
> (cited in Pegg 1998, emphasis mine)

The above are very much historians' and artists' visions of Halhness,
based on a strongly narcissistic view, delimiting the boundary of the
Halh in such a way as to exclude other Mongol groups, yet at the same
time embrace them, thus obliterating their historical role. I suggest that
this transition from marginality to centrality is a recent phenomenon,

when the isolation of Halh-land became not a drawback but a geo-political advantage, as Mongols started to wage a nationalist revolution at the beginning of this century. As is general in nationalist projects, which tend to project present notions back to the distant past, Halh historians and scholars have attempted to invent a history presenting the Halh as the most important group of Mongols from the inception of the Mongol nation.

The symbolic position now held by the Halh makes them tacitly recognized by all other Mongols as the core of Mongols. Other Mongols believe that they have kinship ties with the Halh, and that they also originated in that region. The modern Halh nationalist discourse would reverse this, denying such umbilical relations; rather *they* are the indi-genous Mongols, while Mongols elsewhere are semi-Mongols. They are thus creating a mythical notion of 'Mongol', according to which only they qualify. The justification of the Halh as the only true 'Mongols', with the genetic quality typical of 'the Mongol', is found in the writings of such Mongolian scholars as Jügder (1987) and Gongor (1970). They claim that the three-river region (the drainage area of the Onon, Herlen, and Tuul) is the ancestral land of the Halh, the 'indigenous' (*uuguul*)[5] Mongols, while the rest of the Mongols are merely 'Mongol-speaking people' (*Mongol helten*). Jügder writes that the Halh were the only original ethnic group in the three-river region. They were the earlier *nirun* (backbone) indigenous Mongols, as against the *darligin* (slave) Mongols,[6] mainly Mongol speakers.

[5] I guess *uuguul* (*uugal* in classical Mongolian spelling) could have its etymological origin in the term *uul* meaning 'original' or *uugan* (*augan*), eldest son, or first-born, and ultimately to *aug-a*, which means great, mighty, or powerful, etc. I deduce that to be original or indigenous means to be great or powerful.

[6] According to Rashid al-din, the Mongols were divided into two major groups, *Nirun* and *Darligin*. The word *Nirun* is explained as 'backbone'. According to the *Secret History*, Chinggis Khan's female ancestor Alan Goa, after the death of her husband, gave birth to three more sons. She said that a shining yellow man came in from the smoke hole at night, rubbed her back, and impregnated her. Therefore, the descendants of the three sons have been known as *Nirun* Mongols—i.e. born from Alan Goa's pure backbone, hence pure Mongols. Other Mongols are called *Darligin*. Rashid did not explain the meaning of *Darligin*. Gongor (1970) suggests that *Nirun* and *Darligin* are two tribes. He puts *Darligin* into the category of *bool* (slaves), apparently mistaking the etymology of *Darligin* (*Dar-* means oppress). Thus, the *Darligin* are the oppressed, or slave, people of the aristocratic *Nirun* Mongols. Irinchen (1984), an Inner Mongolian historian, however, interprets *Darligin* as 'people on the steppe', and the *Nirun* as 'people on the hill.' (*Nirun* can also mean the crest or spine of a hill/mountain.) He points out that *Nirun* Mongols and *Darligin* Mongols intermarried. In fact, the Kiyad clan and Nigus clan described by Rashid as the ancestors of the Mongols were *Nirun* and *Darligin* Mongols respectively. These two Mongol groups together were called *Hamag Mongol* (Entire Mongolia).

The creation of the 'pure' and 'indigenous' Halh is, in my view, both a modern version of Mongol nationalism and a deliberate reconstruction at the behest of the Soviet overlord, who did not want to see a link between all Mongol groups. The Russians undermined the Mongolness of the Buryats and created a Buryat 'national' identity. In the 1920s, the Mongol script was forbidden in Buryatia. An 'official' Buryat language was created, removing Mongolian vocabulary wherever possible, and the standard dialect was changed from the Selenge dialect, the dialect closest to spoken Halh Mongolian, to the Hori dialect. 'This involved a systematic shift of pronunciation away from Mongol, and was difficult for many groups of Buryats to understand' (Humphrey 1990: 293). 'By the 1950s . . . archaeologists were "revealing" that the Western Buryats were not really Mongolian at all but originally a Turkic people, subsequently Mongolized. This process culminated in the breakup and renaming of the Buryat–Mongol ASSR' (1990: 294). In 1958, the Buryat–Mongol ASSR was stripped of the word 'Mongol'; thus a new nationality was finally born, devoid of any link with the Mongols. If the Buryats are now a separate people, so must be the Halh. The purpose was, I argue, to hinder people of the same cultural or ethnic background communicating with one another. Winrow (1992: 102) notes a similar Soviet approach in Central Asia:

The Soviet authorities in 1924 had endeavoured to fashion these [Turkic] nations in part by deliberately magnifying the differences in the various Turkish dialects of these peoples. The aim was to counter the spread of one common Turkic language by artificially creating ostensibly separate and spoken languages for each nation. Phonetic distinctions were stressed and each 'language' infused with Russian vocabulary. The switch from Arabic to the Latin script and then in the late 1930s to the Cyrillic alphabet, facilitated this process.

In Mongolia, the Soviet Union equally disapproved of links between Mongolia and Inner Mongolia. The classical script was changed to the Cyrillic script, based on the Halh dialect. The role of the Halh Cyrillic script as the official script in Mongolia has facilitated the process whereby all other non-Halh Mongols and other groups in Mongolia have to become Halh-speakers in order to become proper citizens, but it also cuts the linguistic affinity with the rest of the Mongol-speaking populations in Inner Mongolia, who continue to use the classical script.

The Halh do not just compare themselves with the other Mongols, but also with all Mongoloid peoples. They say that the Mongolian plateau is the cradle of the Mongoloid 'race' (*töröhtön*), if not of all mankind. This latter claim is supported by a curious argument: palaeontological discoveries in the Gobi region in Mongolia (skeletons of prehistorical animals, dinosaurs, dinosaur eggs, crocodiles, turtles, and lizards) suggest that the earliest animals were 'Mongol', and early human beings naturally arose in this environment. The existence in this region, until early this century, of the wild horse (Przewalski's horse)—*tahi*—is also symbolically important, as it is believed to be the ancestor of the Mongolian horse. Genetic science is further appropriated by the Halh Mongols to claim that they are the direct descendants of the earliest Mongoloid humans. According to Batsuur (1987), the Tf^{Dchi} gene characteristic of the Mongol race has its maximum frequency among the population in Mongolia. It is about ten times lower in other populations. Among the Mongol population, he further claimed, the transferrent locus D allele has its ancestral origin in Central Asia or Mongolia.[7] The scientific interest in Mongolian human biology has developed into the hysterical claim that true Mongols possess special organisms immune to the HIV virus (Nomin 1992), which is unfortunately finding its way into Mongolian populations.

These claims amount to a proclamation that the Halh Mongols are a rare human species. Following popular logic, a thing is valued if it is rare; so they should be valued and protected. Most interestingly, Mongols have appropriated as positive the body mark known as the 'Mongolian spot', invented by European scientists with the clear purpose of marking the racial supremacy of Caucasians. Kevin Stuart (1996) suggests that although the phenomenon has been present and known for centuries, the coining of the appellation 'Mongolian spot' by Baelz, a German professor, in 1885, has since aroused zealous medical interest in searching for

---

[7] The biological claims associated with the idea of 'true Mongol' by contemporary Mongol scholars were in fact refuted as early as 1958. A joint Czechoslovak–Mongolian Archaeological Expedition to the MPR in 1958, which focused on the Halh in central Mongolia, the bastion of the 'true Mongols', revealed the racial diversity of the population in the region. The conclusion of the anthropological report is particularly interesting and is worth quoting at length:

This preliminary study showed first of all that the Khalkha [Halh] nationality does not represent one racial type as was generally accepted, but several sharply defined types.

Secondly even this restricted material discloses the enormous promiscuity of the present Mongolian population, so that our generally accepted views and ideas on the most Mongolian and purest elements among 'true Mongols' within the yellow race dissolve into thin air. Against what was to be expected, the true Mongol may not be considered a typical prototype for Mongoloids. This typicalness of the Mongolian race has been taken over apparently by other Asiatic tribes and nations, perhaps by the Tunguses....

Thirdly, on evaluation of types of the Khalkha population we may reach the following preliminary grouping of types: 10% ancient and sibirid elements, 30% classical Khalkha–Mongol types, 50% universal Mongol types and finally in 10–15% we may find 'Indian' types among the Khalkha population with a number of variations. (Vlcek 1965: 350)

the darkly pigmented skin patches among various populations for their possible intimations of 'Mongolian descent'. This racial connotation persists in the late twentieth century, when European medical science still insists on a strong link between Mongolian spots and race and mental retardation (Stuart 1996: 60–5). This particularly perverse Western 'scientific' knowledge has certainly convinced the Halh Mongols of the validity of the racial characteristic of the Mongolian spot, but for them it serves a different purpose. For Halh Mongols it does not denote an evolutionary ladder, but a distinction of a racial type. Just as some Europeans would contend that the lack of the Mongolian spot designates 'pure', uncontaminated Caucasian race, especially among the blond with blue eyes, current Mongolian folk biology holds that the Mongolian spot is the external bearer of the single Mongolian 'gene', distinct from other Mongols. They dub the spot *Mongol tolbo* (Mongolian spot) or *höh tolbo* (blue spot), and regard it as sacred, and heaven-designated, the key trait for determining who is Mongol.[8] The dilution of the 'gene' by foreign stock would erase the mark, thus obliterating the Mongolness. People having only a Mongolian cultural bearing (that is, language, mentality), but devoid of the Mongolian 'gene', are not regarded as pure Mongols.

However, the Mongolian blue spot, which is known in the West also as 'Mongol Salute' is not monopolized by the Mongols or Mongoloids. Illingworth (1987: 104) gives a very interesting summary of the spread of this 'Mongolian pigmentation':

It is almost universal in coloured children, common in Eskimos, and occurs in up to 5 per cent of Caucasian children. The French termed the pigmented areas 'tâches bleuatres'. It is said that a missionary first described it in 1745. In Japan the pigmentation was thought to be made by the God Kami-Sama, who presides over child birth, or else was due to the back of the fetus rubbing against the placenta. It was viewed in Iraq villages as a sign of Allah's favour.

Naturally, then, not just Mongols are interested in this spot; for Japanese and Koreans, the high incidence of this spot in their newborns symbolizes a genetic ancestral link to the Mongols, rather than the Chinese (see Saha and Tay 1992). Ironically, it is a known fact that the

---

[8] Erdenebileg (1994) has made an interesting list of Mongols' associations with 'blue': 'Mongolia is a land of blue skies, and the "blue heaven above" was the most sacred thing for them. Fatally wounded Mongolian warriors only utter the words, "Oh! The Blue Sky" as their final call. The Mongolians revere blue colour, they are born with a blue birth-mark and they present a blue sash as the most respected and sacred gift to their guests.'

Mongolian spot is found in only 90 per cent of new-born Halh Mongols; this is almost 10 per cent less than its incidence among Japanese newborns, which is 99.5 per cent (Vlcek 1965: 315–16). How are we to reconcile this discrepancy? Kevin Stuart was told by a Mongol that 'even Mongol intellectuals deliberately avoid questioning the scientific validity of the spot as a symbol of being Mongol, despite the knowledge that the "*Mongol tolbo*" is shared by other peoples' (Stuart 1996: 65).

This nostalgia for 'Mongolness' is a compelling force in today's Mongolian social popular thought. It is a concern for preserving the race and the breed, an acute awareness of the potential danger of losing independence, resulting in the extinction of the Mongol 'race'. I will discuss two interesting aspects of this concern in Chapters 4 and 5.

The Buryats: Pan-Mongolism and Marginalization

The Buryats, a people who have been largely outside mainstream Mongolian history, have nevertheless contributed greatly to modern Mongolian history. More recently, they have been marginalized inside Mongolia. This change symbolizes the shift of the ethnic power balance in Mongolia and, more significantly, charts the fate of a people who have located themselves both inside and outside the main group.

The participation of the Buryats in Mongolian politics in the early twentieth century marks the advent of nationalism and pan-Mongolism. Several hundred years of life under the Russians was important, for it had given the Buryats an opportunity to acquire some aspects of Russian or European culture. More importantly, it is perhaps proper to say that under the influence of nineteenth-century Russian nationalism, the Buryats were the first Mongols to become modern nationalists. At the turn of the twentieth century, both the ordinary herdsmen and the leadership were increasingly dissatisfied with the Russians. With the proclamation of the Stolypin reforms in 1902, clashes between Buryat herdsmen and Russian peasants over land were common in this part of the world. An emphasis on Mongolness fundamentally changed the Buryat political horizon. A series of mass emigrations of Buryats took place, in 1904 and 1917–22. Some Buryats fled to northern Mongolia, others to the Inner Mongolian Barga[9] region. Buryat political and intellectual leaders

[9] Barga is a Mongolian group in the Hülünbuir region of Inner Mongolia. The Barga is affiliated to the Buryat in kinship.

abandoned their hope of greater representation in the Russian government; instead, they looked to Mongolia, where the Mongolian way of life could be maintained and their political aspirations could be expressed. However, their pan-Mongolism was a curious mixture of many elements:

The Pan-Mongolism espoused by the Buryats was double-edged: as an anti-Russian weapon and a Buryat expression of separatism, a threat that the Buryats would leave the Russian Empire and join a Greater Mongolia, it promised much to the Halhs. But Buryats could also be valuable in extending Russian influence, and Russian imperialists, advocates of annexation of Mongolia, were also Pan-Mongolists. (Rupen 1964: 85)

In early 1919, the Buryats called for the formation of a pan-Mongolian state organized on a federal basis in which four *aimags* (Inner Mongolia, Outer Mongolia, Barga, and Buryatia) would enjoy broad autonomous power under a central government. A government was established by the half-Russian, half-Buryat Semenov, known as the Daur Government.[10] The Bogd Khan's attitude to the pan-Mongolian government was ambivalent; he and Mongolia were trapped by the 1915 Tripartite Treaty, which guaranteed the autonomy of Outer Mongolia under Chinese suzerainty. Pan-Mongolism essentially meant obliterating the treaty, and fundamentally obliterating the existing border, which would be a potential hazard. As a result, this pan-Mongolian movement received no support, and in the end killed both itself and Outer Mongolian 'autonomy'.

The retreating White military leader Baron Ungern von Sternberg moved into Mongolia through its eastern border in 1920, with the aim of establishing a Central Asian Empire. His army was strengthened by the Buryats recruited on the way to Urga (Ulaanbaatar). As soon as he moved into Urga, Ungern ordered all the Russian Buryats to 'join the army within three days; those who don't come will be arrested'. Almost all the Buryats in Urga were recruited by Ungern (Battogtoh 1991: 44). Baron Ungern turned Mongolia into an anti-Soviet base. This anti-Russian, anti-Chinese stance temporarily obtained the support of Bogd Khan, who used Ungern to get rid of the Chinese. Émigré Buryats, escaping from Russian oppression and turmoil, also turned to Ungern for help. They obtained arms from him, and turned on the Russians in the border villages for revenge. They used the hands of Ungern to attempt to exterminate the Bolsheviks and their sympathizers.

---

[10] Dauria is in Russian Siberia, see Bulag and Humphrey (1996).

In fact, Ungern's Central Asian Empire was fought for mainly by Buryats. In this sense the Mongolian revolution in 1921 against the Whites was ironically largely against the Buryats. The proportion of Russians in Ungern's army was small, and unimportant, according to Alioshin (1941). The role played by the Buryats during this period proved lethal to them consequently.

After the victory of the Bolsheviks, and the growth of Comintern control of the Far East, the Buryat leaders severed relations with Semenov's failed pan-Mongolist movement. They came under the wing of the Comintern, and continued to carry out their pan-Mongol policies. The chief Buryat figure in this period was Elbegdorj Rinchino. 'By his own account, he was planning to deliver Outer Mongolia to the Soviet Union in return for both more favourable treatment of the Buryats and the advancement of Pan-Mongolism' (Murphy 1966: 24).

The value of the Buryats in building Mongolia was nevertheless appreciated by the Halh Mongol leaders. Danzan requested the Russians in 1921 to allow the Buryats living in north Mongolia to become Mongolian citizens (Battogtoh 1991: 66). On 5 September 1924, Mongolia and the Soviet Union signed an agreement giving the Buryats the right to dual citizenship. At the first Congress of the Mongolian government on 18 November, the 4,316 families with a total population of 16,093 who had settled in Mongolia were finally ratified as citizens of the Mongolian People's Republic. In March 1926, another 927 households (3,656 individuals) were granted Mongolian citizenship (Badarchi 1994). However, their dual citizenship soon proved a useful device whereby they could be extradited to the Soviet Union later.

Some Buryats, from the very beginning, had followed the policy of the Comintern, basically trying to accelerate the revolutionary process, to strike at the lamas, and to go over to communes as soon as possible. They wished to achieve pan-Mongolism, but this was not supported by the Russians who dominated the Communist Party in Siberia. In 1925, the ruling Buryat National Committee was abolished in Buryatia. All of its members came to Mongolia and became Mongolian citizens. They were followed by many families. By September, there were about two thousand Buryats in Ulaanbaatar (Battogtoh 1991: 125–6). The majority of these highly qualified Buryats began holding government posts and working in the secret police as instructors and translators. This Buryat 'episode' of modern Mongolian history ended in 1928, when the 'struggle' over the Buryat 'Rightist Deviation' was declared a victory. Almost all Buryat leaders were sacked from their posts and expelled from

Mongolia by 1932. Their Mongolian citizenship was annulled (Murphy 1966: 105).

The Japanese intention to occupy Mongolia by the end of 1930 spelt trouble for Buryats in Mongolia. In the notorious 'Lhumbo case' in 1933, a prelude to the major assault on the Buryats later, from 1937 to 1939, twenty Buryat 'traitors' were purged (Bawden 1968: 338). A recently published source (Tod 1991) suggests that 317 people were prosecuted at that time; among them were 251 Buryats. Of these, 126 were repatriated to the USSR.

Choibalsang's report to the third plenary session of the MPRP Central Committee held in October 1937 signalled an all-out assault on lamas, Buryats, Bargas, and Chinese in Mongolia. The impending threat of the Japanese invasion of Mongolia gave Choibalsang an excellent chance to get rid of his 'enemies'. Then head of the Interior Ministry, he accused particularly the Buryats of espionage connections with the Japanese against Mongolia:

About the Buryats: the Japanese have been seeking agents among them just like among the lamas; as far as they are concerned, I am not referring to the entire Buryats, I should not say so. The Buryats are Mongols like us. But I am making the connection on the basis that persons should nevertheless be examined. In general, if you ask who are the Buryats residing in Mongolia, some of them are followers of the White generals like Semenov and Ungern. They were expelled by the people of the Soviet Union who are our inseparable warm-hearted and devoted friends, who have always been helping us with our cause. If (you) ask who headed the Daur government, it's the Buryats and the leading Japanese agent, General Semenov; if (you) ask who attempted to annex Mongolia to that government, it's Buryats like Sampilun and Tseveen Jamtsarano; and if (you) ask who directed the task of Japanese espionage until recent days, it's still the Buryats, namely, Elbegdorj Rinchino, Jamtsarano, Tsogt Badamjav, Galun Galjutov and others. (Choibalsang 1951: 485–7)

The consequence of this devastating purge still lingers on among the Buryats. Buryats told me that almost all men over 18 years old were killed. In both Dashbalbar and Dadal only about a dozen men returned home from prison, while the rest 'disappeared'. Some said that many Buryats were sent to Russian concentration camps and exterminated there. For decades, Dashbalbar and Dadal Buryats have been requesting their relatives in Ulaanbaatar, especially those few in high positions, to find out the whereabouts of the dead, and have been demanding full rehabilitation from the state. The charge that Buryats were traitors and Japanese spies, etc., was not dropped entirely until recently. Only in the last few years have Buryat politicians in Ulaanbaatar, using their newly attained positions, been able to discover full information about the purge in the Interior Ministry archives. In fact, they were also tracing their own fathers or grandfathers. In late 1991 I was given the figures of 2,663 Buryats from Hentii *aimag* and 2,705 from Dornod *aimag* liquidated in the purges. In addition, a large number of Buryats from other parts of Mongolia were exterminated, although the exact figure is unavailable to me.

The purge of the Buryats has left a deep scar on the mind of later generations. Dashin Byambasüren, prime minister of Mongolia from 1990 to 1992, who is a Buryat, reportedly told the Congress in 1992 that he could never forget that so many Buryat people (*zon*) had been liquidated in Mongolia. His remark, in the capacity of prime minister, fuelled an already sensitive issue. The angry Halh rebuked him by pointing out that it was the Halh who suffered most. A rosary-rolling poet O. Dashbalbar, despite being a Dariganga, has become a staunch Halh-centrist, in his struggle against the Buryats. In one of the eight charges against Byambasüren in his open letter to him in 1995, Dashbalbar accused Byambasüren of causing ethnic strife by emphasizing the Buryat suffering in the 1930s, without paying due attention to the tremendous loss to the Halh. It is interesting to note Dashbalbar's distinction of Buryats from 'Mongol' in his final advice to the former premier of Mongolia: 'Therefore, I put my hope on you, trusting you would sow the seed of harmony between the Buryat and Mongol *zon* (peoples)' (Dashbalbar 1995). The push for rehabilitation of the Buryats appears to be not only a matter of compensation for a crime committed by the Mongolian state against its own citizens, but has also resulted in the Buryats being targeted by a Halh leader representing the Mongolian national interest. Some Buryats would like to see the purge constituted as ethnocide. This line of argument is of course unacceptable to the Halh, who would point out that the majority of monks also perished in the thirties, during the same campaign by Choibalsang. The Buryats would say that the nature of the two purges was different; it was Choibalsang, and hence the Halh, in their opinion, who committed this atrocity against the Buryats. Badarchi (1994), a Buryat professor, voiced strong opposition to the Halh attempt to commemorate the hundredth anniversary of Choibalsang's birth in 1995, pointing out that such action would be an insult to the thousands of genocide victims and their descendants and relatives; moreover, it would 'drive towards ethnic split among the Mongolian people'.

The historical political relationships among the Buryat Mongols, Halh Mongols, Russians, and Manchus have put the Buryats in a rather disadvantageous position *vis-à-vis* the Halh. The Halh Mongols have never been able to accept the Buryats emotionally. This is reflected in the ridiculing of the very name 'Buryat'. There are two main explanations from the Halh. First, the term comes from the Russian word *Brat*, meaning brother. When the Russians came, they called the Siberian people 'brothers', hence 'Buryats'—brothers of the Russians—and they are loyal to them rather than to the Mongols. Or the word originated from *burih*, 'to desert' or 'to go in the wrong direction against the trend', implying that Buryats are traitors, not loyal to the Mongols.

After the 'Buryat episode' came the 'Dürbet episode' of Mongolian history (represented by Tsedenbal) between the 1940s and the 1980s. The dominance of the Dürbet and Halh Mongols categorically barred the political promotion of the Buryats. But some Buryats have managed to achieve much in culture and science. In the socialist decades, the political loyalty of both Buryatia and Mongolia to the Soviet Union considerably eased the relation between the Buryats and the Halh Mongols.[11] Interestingly, the Buryat image in Ulaanbaatar is of being intellectuals. They obtain better education than the Halh; the majority are white-collar workers. According to many Buryats, about 80 per cent of advanced Mongolian intellectuals are Buryats. Although this (probably exaggerated) achievement is more the result of individual effort than a collective conspiracy, it has contributed to the sudden resurgence of the second episode of Buryat prominence in Mongolian history.

The first democratic movement, started in late 1989, was led by Zorig and Bat-üül, both Buryats (Zorig's father is Buryat, his mother Russian). Zorig became the general co-ordinator of the Mongolian Democratic Union, the first popular mass movement organization. Bat-üül was elected chairman of the Democratic Party, which grew out of the Union. The general election in 1990 elected D. Byambasüren prime minister of Mongolia, again a Buryat.

This conspicuous Buryat presence in the Mongolian political arena is reminiscent of the Buryat dominance in the 1920s, and once again it has given rise to mistrust by the Halh. The revolutionary or democratic

---

[11] It is said that Tsedenbal had a Buryat girl-friend, but was told it would be politically naïve to marry her, so he finally married a Russian wife. The importance of the Western Mongols is also said to have encouraged Choibalsang to have an affair with a Dürbet girl. As I will argue in Chapter 5, such intrigues through marriage reveal something very fundamental in Mongolian politics.

movement in the 1990s has been in one way or another dominated by non-Halh, or *erliiz* (half-breeds); this is certainly part of the explanation for the rise of the social movement calling for 'pure blood'. In 1991 a campaign started, denouncing the Buryats, who were labelled 'Russian immigrants' *(Orosiin tsagaachid)* or 'motherlandless people' (*eh oronguichuud*). Because Byambasüren, although an MPRP member, adopted many policies proposed by other parties, he was opposed by both some Halh and his own Party. Byambasüren was consequently accused of being a traitor to the MPRP. On the other hand, because Bat-üül and Zorig compromised in the negotiation with the MPRP (the chief negotiator was Byambasüren) in early 1990, and participated in the reformed MPRP-dominated government, they were also seen as traitors to democracy, by promoting 'Buryatism'.

The National Progressive Party and the Democratic Party had been talking of unification in 1991. This was regarded as a plot, not for the purpose of democracy but to make it a party of Buryats and non-Halh people. Ganbold, the leader of the National Progressive Party, who is also the first deputy prime minister, is Bat-üül's second cousin. He is a *hurliiz*;[12] that is, his grandfather was Chinese. Byambasüren, too, is rumoured to have a kinship relation with Bat-üül (related to Bat-üül's mother). More importantly, the Byambasüren government, although a Communist-dominated government, adopted Ganbold's privatization scheme, one which is generally thought to have been untimely. Unfortunately, the Mongolian bank in 1991 lost about 80 million US dollars through improper banking management, which was suspected to have been the fault of Bat-üül and Ganbold, who played bank computers when drunk. However, in 1991 Byambasüren seemed to be still supporting Ganbold, who had become the most unpopular leader in Mongolia. This gave an excellent chance for other anti-Buryat forces to attack the Buryats, as well as the democratic forces.

The Buryat leaders have been constantly harassed. The government newspaper *Ardiin Erhe* reported in 1991 that Zorig pissed through his office window in a drunken state, thus desecrating the sacred government building, while *Ünen*, the newspaper of the MPRP, published accusations that Bat-üül beat somebody who was charging him with a criminal offence. Consequently, Zorig had to resign from his post, and Bat-üül failed to be elected chairman of the Democratic Party early in 1992. Zorig was not discouraged. He founded a new party, the Republican

[12] A *hurliiz* is an offspring of an *erliiz* (see Ch. 5 for detailed discussions).

Party. This party soon united with the Free Labour Party, the chairman of which, Döl, is said to be half-Buryat.

Meanwhile, Byambasüren was also building his power base by promoting Buryats to key positions. In August 1991, Byambasüren sacked the entire leadership of the TV and Radio, and replaced them with pro-government people. The general director of the Mongolian Radio and TV, the director of Radio, the Television director D. Jargal, the director of TV programmes G. Zoljargal, and TV art director B. Jargal are all said to be Buryats (Batbayar 1992).

Attacks on Byambasüren also come from within his own MPRP. M. Zenee, a Sinologist and a member of the Central Committee of the MPRP angrily wrote (1992): 'There is no need to hide that Byambasüren in reality is the originator of the Mongolian National Progressive Party and founder of the Mongolian Renaissance Party; he connives with the leaders of the Mongolian Democratic Party, and he wants to annihilate the political potential of the MPRP.' Byambasüren's progressive, democratic, Buryat, minority, and Chinese-'half-breed' government failed to get re-elected in 1992. We have identified that all the new government leaders were now Halh. The new prime minister and the leader of the reformed single parliament were both Halh. Buryats once again have suffered a setback. Perhaps unsurprisingly, D. Byambasüren founded the World Mongolian Congress in 1993, in an effort to establish cultural and economic links with Mongols throughout the world. The Congress, however, has aroused sustained suspicion and hostility from both the Chinese and the Mongolian security services.

What do these events mean to ordinary Buryats in Mongolia? Buryat history, a proud one, and their association with the Buryat ASSR in Russia, have made Buryats in Mongolia aware that, apart from Mongolian culture, they have another root that is Buryat. However, to them, Buryatness is part of Mongolness. In 1990, a Buryat Cultural Heritage Association was established, which was the first ethnic cultural association to emerge in Mongolia. Tsogtbaatar, a member of the association in Dashbalbar told me that it is not a political association: 'We intend to unite all the Buryats in the world. We announced it through the Mongolian News Agency. Buryats in Australia, Japan, America, wherever they are, can contact us. Here there is a need to emphasize the Halh participation in the movement. If only the Buryats are doing this, those Halh may become suspicious and jealous; in fact, it is the job of the Halh to organize such work, but what can I say? We are not attempting secession, only trying to revive the tradition and old cultures, and to regain the lost pastoral technology, and relearn the classical Mongolian script.'

Buryats in Mongolia are dismayed to find that their brothers across the border have become so Russified that they have lost their language. Buryats in Mongolia have taken on the task of reminding their brothers of their heritage, that they are Mongolian.[13] In 1992, with the demise of the Soviet Union, the official Soviet–Mongolian friendship society collapsed; new societies have been established, amongst which is the Mongolian–Buryat Society founded by Buryats in Mongolia aiming for closer cultural ties with their kinsmen across the borders.

The Buryats are bitter that they are denied their own heroes. They claim that Sühbaatar (the revolutionary hero and founding father of the MPR) was Buryat, not Halh. This claim immediately touched off a debate. The Halh resolutely maintain that Sühbaatar was pure Halh. This fight over Sühbaatar's ethnic identity is significant; it is a question of how much the Buryat have contributed to Mongolian history, whether they are loyal patriots or not. The strong assertion of their Mongolness on the part of the Buryats and the attack on their Buryatness on the part of the Halh mark the character of this 'ethnic' relationship in present-day Mongolia.

Despite strong Buryat participation in Mongolian politics, few ordinary Buryat people want to be leaders in Mongolia. According to Gantogtoh, a Buryat linguist, this should be explained in terms of Mongolian kinship consciousness. That is, the Mongols respect the mother's side— that is, *nagatsnar*. Chinggis Khan's wife, who was his mother's brother's daughter, is said to have been a Buryat, and an old Mongolian tradition determines that the *nagatsnar* would never *tör barih* (control the state power). Instead, the *nagatsnar* should supervise the welfare of the *zeener* (daughter's or sister's sons) and should contribute to the state and support it. It is with this in mind that Buryat intellectuals came to Mongolia to promote the cause of the Mongols. When I asked some ethnically conscious Buryats in Dashbalbar about their reaction to the draft Constitution item that only the Halh are entitled to the presidency, they agreed that a Buryat should not be the Mongolian president; this would cause ethnic conflict. After all, this land belongs to the Halh. They should be grateful to the Halh. But, they say, they have a duty to supervise the *zeener*, the Halh.

---

[13] Hamayon (forthcoming) analyses the surprisingly un-Mongol characteristics of Buryat nationalism in Buryatia.

Who are the Real Mongols? Settling an Old Score between the Oirats and the Halh

Despite his 'contribution' to Mongolian internationalism, the late Mongolian leader Tsedenbal retained significant links with his own Dürbet Mongols, so he was in fact an overtly 'tribalized man'. There are reasons to believe that his leadership strongly sharpened ethnic consciousness in Mongolia. Tsedenbal was not able to cut his own roots. He maintained extensive contacts with his own Dürbet kinsmen in Uvs *aimag* and with the Oirat Mongolian groups of which the Dürbet is one.

It is useful to put contemporary Mongolian ethnicity in a historical perspective. In Mongolia, the Oirat do not exist as a collective ethnic group. They have been fragmented into various subgroups which are known as 'nationalities' (*yastan*): Bayat, Dürbet, Zahchin, Myangat, Ööld, Sartuul, Torgut, Urianghai, Hotgoit, Montsogo, etc. They are concentrated in the five provinces of western Mongolia: Bayan Ölgii, Gobi-Altai, Zavhan, Uvs, and Hovd.[14] All of these groups know consciously that they are Oirat. The significance of the collective Oirat identity lies in its opposition to the Halh in particular.

Oirats have at different historical stages played an extremely important role in Mongolia. Four major historical stages may be discerned: the Mongol Empire (thirteenth to fourteenth centuries), the Oirat hegemony (fifteenth to sixteenth centuries), the Jungar Khanate (seventeenth to eighteenth centuries), and modern Mongolia (twentieth century). All these have been taken up by contemporary scholars in order to delineate the relationship between the Oirats and the Halh in today's Mongolia.

The dispute between Arigbuh and Khubilai in the thirteenth century is significant. The Oirats were subjects of Arigbuh, who was one of the younger brothers of Khubilai, the founding emperor of the Mongol Yuan Dynasty. The dispute ended in the defeat of Arigbuh and the consolidation of Mongol rule in China (for this story, see Rossabi 1988). This conflict, however, had a lasting influence upon the Oirat Mongols, who took upon themselves the role of defenders of Mongol interests, stalwart opponents of foreign rule or foreign influences. Thus a split reappeared immediately after the fall of the Yuan Dynasty, when Mongolia divided into three, the Oirat, the Mongols, and the Horchin.

---

[14] For the Mongolian analysis of the ethnic process in western Mongolia, see Norovsambuu *et al.* (1989).

In the fifteenth century, soon after the fall of the Mongol Yuan Dynasty, leaders of the Oirats challenged the Chinggisid rule of post-Yuan Mongolian society. And for over a century, all of Mongolia was conquered and unified by the Oirats. Indeed, during the Oirat hegemony, the Mongols collectively showed signs of vitality and repeatedly carried out warfare against the Chinese Ming Dynasty. However, the Oirat rule was largely unacceptable to the Chinggisids, who thought it legitimate only for them to rule the Mongols. The counter-conquest of the Oirats by the Chinggisid Mongols, led by Batmönh Dayan Khan with the assistance of his wife Manduhai Sechen Khatun, in the sixteenth century was so important in the minds of the legitimacy-conscious Chinggisid Mongols that they now trace their genealogy to Batmönh Dayan Khan. His re-establishment of the Chinggisid rule of Mongolia gained such a symbolic significance that it was as if it was a rebirth of the Mongol nation, secondary only to the founding of *Mongol Uls* by Chinggis Khan in 1206.

In the seventeenth century, the Oirat Mongols thrived under Galdan, who temporarily established a Jungar Khanate. In the wake of Manchu expansion, the Oirats briefly allied with the Halh, the only eastern Mongolian group still unconquered by the Manchu. However, this alliance broke down when the Oirat Mongols attempted to conquer the Halh, resulting in the latter's mass submission to the Manchus. A combined Halh–Manchu operation was eventually able to crush the Oirat Mongols, massacring about 80 per cent of a population which numbered around 600,000. Nevertheless, the Oirat continued to resist the Manchus, producing heroes like Amursanaa, who was later appropriated by contemporary Mongolian historians as the quintessential symbol of collective Mongolian resistance to the Manchu state in 1756–7 (see Kaplonski 1993). Early this century, Ja Lama, a mendicant lama from the Volga region, disguised himself as the reincarnation of Amursanaa and co-ordinated the Oirat Mongolian revolution with that of the Halh. It is arguable that he was responsible for the union of Oirat or Western Mongols with independent Outer Mongolia (see Gaunt 1993).

The Oirats gained prominence in Mongolia from 1940 to 1990. Their main representative was Tsedenbal, who succeeded Marshal Choibalsang in 1952 and became Mongolia's paramount leader. It is not clear whether he was backed by the Soviets precisely because he was a Dürbet. Many Halh would insist that the Russians deliberately carried out a divide-and-rule policy. In 1944, he and some Soviet-educated Mongol intellectuals proposed joining Mongolia to the USSR, to the anger of Choibalsang. This was not an isolated incident. In 1944, Tuva, once a part of Outer Mongolia, which was made independent of Mongolia in 1922, 'voluntarily' joined the Soviet Union.[15] Tsedenbal failed, but he certainly promoted Oirats in Mongolia; he also took over the task of carrying out the Soviet policy of 'internationalism'.

To implement his policies more effectively, Tsedenbal turned to his own Dürbet kinsmen in Uvs *aimag* or to other Oirat Mongolian groups. In the eyes of the Halh, he became the paramount Mongolian leader not because of his ability, but because the Russians employed him in the age-old stratagem of 'using the barbarian to check the barbarian'. After his downfall he was revealed to have begun his career as a KGB agent while studying in the Soviet Union.[16] Tsedenbal put himself in opposition to the Halh (but not all Halh). It is now clear that the famous 'anti-party clique' arraigned by Tsedenbal in the early 1960s—Loohuuz, Nyambuu, Surmaajav, Lhamjav, Sambuu, Dashnamjil, and Gungaajav—were all Halh from Sühbaatar and Gobi-Altai *aimag*s. Following their downfall, it became an unwritten law that Sühbaatar and Gobi-Altai Halh be barred from political promotion. Subsequently, people from two *aimag*s (Uvs and Dornogobi) dominated the highest political levels. There was a clear division of labour: the Uvs Dürbets were the majority in the Politburo, and the Dornogobi Halh in the Council of Ministers (see Chapter 5). This, according to many Mongols, began to make people conscious of their ethnic affiliation (*yastan*), especially at higher political levels. Tsedenbal put people from Uvs *aimag* not only in the Politburo but also in other upper and middle echelons, creating an ideological, economic, political, and bureaucratic stronghold. In turn, the Dürbets relied on him for promotion and better positions in society. In 1990, immediately after the democratic movement began in Mongolia, the Tsedenbal faction, mostly Oirats (the prime minister who succeeded Tsedenbal in 1984 was Batmönh, a Bayat, a subgroup of the Oirats), were removed

---

[15] It is widely circulated that the Tuvan prime minister was beaten up by Choibalsang for joining the Soviet Union. These stories, which may well be factual, give credit to Choibalsang, who is still regarded as a patriot, despite the fact that he carried out the Stalinist policy of liquidating hundreds of thousands of intellectuals, Buryat Mongols, Barga Mongols, and Chinese, as well as monks in the 1930s (see Dashpurev and Soni 1992). It is important to note that he is a Halh. For a Tuvan view of Tuva joining the Soviet Union in 1944, see Mongush (1993).

[16] Popular Halh dismay was caused by the fact that he married a highly domineering Russian woman, and because he ceded the region of his birthplace in western Mongolia to the Soviet Union.

from high office. To some extent one may say that the 1990 revolution was a revolution against the Soviet domination of Mongolia and their agents in Mongolia: that is, the Oirat Mongols. The Halh Mongolian nationalists charged the Tsedenbal faction with selling the interest of Mongolia to the Soviet Union. This is not a small charge, and it triggered a debate between the Oirats and the Halh, rekindling the old animosity. The following common sayings are more than a game, and more like a political struggle (see Chapter 5 for a detailed discussion of the role of rumours and sayings, etc., in Mongolian political life).

Halh: *Dürved hün hün bish*;
        (A Dürbet is not a human being;)
        Dürven shiir mah bish.
        (The four small legs of an animal are not meat.)

Dürbet: *Dürven höl maliin tulguur;*
        (The four legs are pillars of an animal;)
        Dürved hün töriin tulguur.
        (The Dürbets are pillars of the state.)

This is a controversy about who are real Mongols. Many prominent scholars from both sides became involved, each side accusing the other of having brought down the Mongol Empire. The Halh accuse the Oirats of destroying the Halh or Mongol heartland in the seventeenth century, thus weakening the Mongols in the period of Manchu ascendance, so that they could not organize effective resistance and finally had to submit. The Oirats, on the other hand, attribute the responsibility for the fall to the Halh to their hero ancestors, principally Khubilai Khan and Öndör Gegeen, the first Living Buddha of the Halh (that is, Jebtsundamba). In 1260 Khubilai Khan moved the capital of the Mongol Empire from Karakorum in present-day Mongolia to Shangdu and later to Beijing in present-day China (Shangdu is in Inner Mongolia). Öndör Gegeen and the Halh princes submitted to the Manchu in 1691. The Oirats acclaim Arigbuh, the legally elected Mongol Khan, as a true Mongol, thus accusing the Halh (in this case their leader, Khubilai Khan) of having been attracted to Chinese civilization. Ch. Dalai, a prominent Oirat historian, remarks angrily: 'But the two years of 1260 and 1691 are the historical years when Mongolian independence was sold, and it is futile to try to rehabilitate them. If attempts were made to rehabilitate them, then it would be against the heroic and rightful Mongolian state' (Dalai 1991*a*: 19).

To illustrate Halh resentment of Oirat domination of the Halh, let me provide an extract from a poem by Choinom, a deceased Halh poet, which has been recently published (Narangerel 1990). He now enjoys the image of a Halh martyr who died in opposing the cruel Communist regime. The poem contains some extremely anti-Tsedenbal lines associating Tsedenbal with the Oirats, here described as 'the four Ööld' tribes. Tsedenbal's leadership symbolizes the collective Oirat dominance over the Halh, and the revenge of the Oirat on the Halh who defeated them in the eighteenth century.

> Our state is like a woman
> who slept with another man the next day after her husband died.
> Instead of paying tribute to the ancient state and Chinggis' name,
> now being afraid, they are licking the feet of the Russians.
>
> They are respecting the Russians who hate our ancestor Chinggis,
> They are squeezing all of us who have originated from H'elun mother.
> [We] have driven away running dogs,
> But are now guarded by hungry wolves.
>
> Although the oxen [*üher*] Halh people have a stupid origin,
> No one else lived (even though stupidly) in the stone age,
> Knowing this (long ancestral origin), in opposition to the four Ööld,
> [We Halh] have struggled generation after generation shedding blood.
>
> For 500 years they [the Ööld] have been drooling over the Khan's throne,
> But their heads were shot to pieces by Queen Manduhai.
> Now the remnants of the selfish four Ööld,
> Have climbed to the lord's throne by way of revolution.
>
> Releasing their hatred and revenge
> of five hundred years,
> Now upon the steppe,
> They are planting insults.
>
> The stuff that they have planted,
> without it being realized,
> Is bringing up you and all of us altogether
> To be ignorant and primitive.

(Narangerel 1990: 14)

Scholars have different views of the meaning of the term 'Oirat'. Some say that it means *oin irged*, or forest people, as opposed to steppe people. Some insist that it means *oir*, or affinity: that is, affines of the Mongols. These are not just mere quibbles, but important for the identity of the

Mongols. The question is whether or not 'Mongol' should include the Oirats.

Tsedenbal, although he used the Oirats for his political purposes, showed no interest in promoting Oirat culture as an alternative to the Halh as the basis of the Mongolian identity. I have argued that, according to the official Mongolian rhetoric, the Halh group is representative of all Mongols; all other Mongol groups are to be assimilated to the Halh. In this way, not only is Oirat history denied, but the entire Oirat culture is denigrated.

In the post-Tsedenbal era, particularly since 1990, Oirat Mongols have started to rewrite their own history and culture. The redefinition of what it is to be Mongol is therefore an interesting ongoing debate, as the following statement illustrates:

The Oirat Mongols, the descendants of Alan Goa, who are the inseparable components of Mongol felt-tent dwellers (*tuurgatan*), are a strong-willed, sharp-wisdomed, persevering, and industrious people who have not cast off their ancient tradition and customs, and who have a characteristic culture and civilization. The so-called Oirat history is a component of the history of the Mongol nation (*ündesten*). There has never been a separate nation (*ündesten*) or ethnic group (*yastan*). Furthermore, this is not an ethnic minority (*ündestnii tsöönh*) nor a subgroup *(baga yastan)* of Mongol. Our Mongol *tuurgan* (felt yurt) is composed of two basic parts. In ancient times, it consisted of the steppe people, *irgen* (Nirun Mongol), and the forest people, *irgen* (Oirat); later these became the Central Mongols (*Töv Mongol*) and the Western Mongols (*Baruun Mongol*) (Oirat mainly). (Dalai 1991*b*: 19)

In a recent definitive statement of Oirat identity, Oirat ethnogenesis is linked to original Mongols (*yazguuriin Mongol*) (Ochir 1993). The author redefined the term Nirun, suggesting that it means 'back' of a body (*nuruun*). He related it to the legend in the *Secret History* that, after the death of her husband, Alan Goa, the legendary ancestress of the Mongols, gave birth to three sons from her back (*nuruun*), claiming that she had been touched by a heavenly light. Ochir used the term *butach* (illegitimate children) to refer to the three sons who became the ancestry of the Chinggisid golden lineage (*altan urag*). Most interestingly, he pointed out that the supposed 'heavenly light' that impregnated Alan Goa was in fact a servant called Malig Bayat, who was the ancestor of the Bayat subgroup of the Oirats. It is thus established that it was an Oirat who fathered the illegitimate children of Alan Goa, who in turn became the ancestors of the Mongol aristocrats! (Ochir 1993: 9–10)

We have examined some basic issues: namely, the Oirats and Halh each accuse the other of being treacherous and treasonous. Overall, they are a match, for it is difficult to deny that the Halh submitted to the Manchus and helped the Manchu state to conquer the Oirats; nor can it be denied that at least some of the Oirat Mongol élites acted counter to the interests of Mongolia. My concern, however, is rather with the question of the ethnogenesis of the Oirats and Halh in Mongolia. It is quite clear that a Halh consciousness has been aroused, defined not only as against the Chinese and the Russians, but also to a considerable extent against the Oirats. I argue that the quarrel with the Halh put the Oirats in the position of a people somewhat alien. And this gives rise to speculations about their ethnic origin, and to the question of why on earth the Oirats always make a mess of Mongolia, as a Halh Mongol might well put it. All this would lead to a self-perception of themselves as the 'central Mongols' on the part of the Halh, a theme that has significance for their rhetoric against all other undesirable elements represented by non-Halh Mongols.

Political liberalization in the late 1980s allowed the Halh to rebel against 'Tsedenbalism'; large numbers of Dürbets have been driven out of office. Some Halh still strongly believed that there were many Dürbets in the Foreign Office and Interior Ministry, though the validity of this belief is difficult to confirm. The Halh complained that in the past the Dürbets were arrogant and proud, especially because of their ethnic, and perhaps kinship, relation with Tsedenbal. Today, however, those very Dürbets resolutely deny that their high positions in the MPRP and government were in any way related to Tsedenbal. Anti-Tsedenbal and anti-Dürbet feeling provoked a reaction in Uvs, the Dürbet homeland. There was a rumour in Uvs that the Dürbets in Ulaanbaatar were being beaten up by the Halh. In defiance of the centre, the Dürbets in Uvs built a statue of Tsedenbal. In 1991, at the funeral of Tsedenbal, held in Ulaanbaatar, there was a large Dürbet turn-out, paying their last respects to their leader. One Halh friend commented sarcastically, 'All the Dürbets in Ulaanbaatar attended.'

This kind of political mobilization of one ethnic group in Mongolia is perhaps not just limited to the Dürbets, but is also duplicated with other groups elsewhere, especially at the high political level. After the brief Buryat prominence in Mongolian politics from 1990 to 1992, as a result of the election in June 1992, almost all important posts were filled by the Halh: the president, the Parliament leader, the prime minister, the Defence Minister, the chief of police, the chairman of the National

Security Administrative Office, the vice-minister in charge of government personnel, and the ambassadors to Russia and China. It is noted
that ministers and section directors of government organizations also
have all been changed to Halh. However, not all Halh have benefited:
most of those promoted come from Zavhan and Gobi-Altai. The coalition of these two provinces is not too difficult to explain; they were
originally one *aimag*, Zasagt Khan, which only divided in the 1930s
(Galdan 1992). Note too that the Gobi-Altai Halh were involved in
political controversy under Tsedenbal, as I mentioned earlier.

The indignation of the Halh against the Dürbets is based on a notion
that the Halh people and territory constitute the basis of the Mongol
nation-state. However, for most of this century the Buryats, Dürbets,
and Inner Mongols were active in Mongolian politics. Some Buryats and
Dürbets were chosen by the Soviets to act as their agents to bring about
the desired socialist revolution and closer integration with the Soviet
Union. In this process, the Buryats and Dürbets have been seen as
traitors or foreign agents, while the Halh are national defenders.
Although this is a power game played largely at the higher echelons, its
ethnic ramifications are significant.

The Flight of the Kazakhs from Mongolia

In Chapter 2 I have written on how Mongolia adopted the Soviet model
and systematically reformulated its former tribal heritage to fit into the
socialist transformation. It is worth repeating that the nation is defined as
a Mongolian nation, based on the Halh. I have described how that notion
clashed with other non-Halh Mongolian identities. The intra-Mongol
redefinition has also found its parallel in inter-national redefinitions. In
other words, the definition of a nation based on a single culture must
logically lead to the question of how to solve the non-Mongol identities
in the Mongolian nation-state. Here it is significant that the status of the
Kazakhs, an important non-Mongol minority, has been reduced to an
equivalent one of the *yastan*s, rather than as opposed to the majority
Mongols. Understandably, the Kazakhs begrudged this status. In the
1991–2 Congress, they finally managed to elevate their status to a full
ündesten, as opposed to Mongol.

In the thirteenth century, the ancestors of almost all the Kazakhs were
brought under the control of Chinggis Khan. They were subjects of
Chagadai, the second son of Chinggis Khan. The Kazakhs and the

Mongols share a common ancient history and common roots in their languages, and both are or have been nomads. However, they differ in religion; the Kazakhs are Sunni Muslims, while the Mongols are Tibetan Buddhists. The name and identity 'Kazakh' emerged in the sixteenth century, when a Kazakh Khanate was founded in today's Kazakhstan. The Kazakh aristocrats trace their origin directly to Chinggis Khan or his sons. In the sixteenth century, the Kazakh Khanate split into three Hordes, or Züz: the Greater Horde, Middle Horde, and Little Horde. Once under the rule of the Oirat Mongols in the seventeenth to eight-eenth centuries, some Kazakhs later moved into Jungaria, after the majority of the Oirats were liquidated by the Qing–Mongol army in 1757. In the nineteenth century most of them were conquered by the Russians.

The Kazakhs in Mongolia are mostly Abak-Kerei and Naiman Kazakhs who settled in the Altai and Hovd regions of Mongolia after the 1864 Tarbagatai Protocol between Russia and the Qing Dynasty. The independence of Outer Mongolia also dislocated numerous Kazakhs. Aurel Stein reported that 15,000 yurts of Kazakhs moved from the Altai mountains on the Mongolian border into Xinjiang (Stein 1928: 553). In 1923 the Mongolian Kazakh population numbered 1,870 house-holds and 11,220 people (Jamtsarano 1934). Subsequently, many more migrated to Mongolia from Xinjiang in China. In 1938, there were 4,300 households and 21,000 Kazakhs (Anonymous 1992). Between 1921 and 1940, the Kazakhs were administered first in Chandamani Uul *aimag*, then in Hovd *aimag*. The Kazakhs, like all citizens of Mongolia, suffered the Red Terror in the 1930s. Between 1937 and 1939, two thousand Kazakh men were liquidated for the purported crime of organizing an anti-revolutionary group with the aim of separating Kazakhs from Mon-golia and reviving the Kazakh Khanate. In 1940, however, in order to assist the Soviet operation in Xinjiang,[17] a new autonomous *aimag* was founded out of Hovd *aimag* for the Kazakhs and the Altai Urianghais—Bayan Ölgii (Minis and Sarai 1960: 65; Baabar 1996: 495). Until 1945,

---

[17] The switch of allegiance of Sheng Shicai, the Chinese governor of Xinjiang, from the Soviet Union to Guomingdang in the late 1930s, left the Soviets wrong-footed in Xinjiang, and much of the Soviet economic and political interest in Xinjiang was put into jeopardy. The discontent of the Kazakhs, led by Osman, was a useful tool for the Soviets. 'They could not approach a man like Osman directly, but they could still foster chaos through arming small guerrilla bands like his through their intermediary, the Mongol nationalists' (Benson 1988: 156). Bayan Ölgii became the operational base for the Mongolian military assistance to Osman, who led his first resistance warfare against the Chinese war-lord Sheng Shicai in February 1940.

Mongols provided military aid to the Kazakh resistance fighter Osman (Benson 1988). The Chinese recognition of Mongolian independence in 1946 saw an end to this operation, but numerous Kazakh refugees went into Mongolia subsequently. The autonomous *aimag* managed to survive as a normal province, despite the abortion of the operation in Xinjiang.

Subsequent industrialization in Mongolia exerted a strong influence on the Kazakhs. Attracted to opportunities in coal industries in central Mongolia, many Kazakhs moved away from Bayan Ölgii to Ulaanbaatar and nearby coal-mines like Nalaikh (see Sanders 1993). This population movement was as much an economic migration as a political design.

According to the 1989 population census, Bayan Ölgii *aimag* had the following 'ethnic groups': Kazakh: 82,750; Urianghai: 5,100; Dürbet: 1,382; Tuva: 737; Halh: 393; Zahchin: 66; Bayat: 63; Torgut: 16. The Kazakh population of Mongolia had increased dramatically, reaching 120,500, a large figure in a country of just about 2.1 million in 1989.

In the 1980s, with increasing liberalization of Mongolian politics, there arose a demand among the Kazakhs to Kazakhicize Bayan Ölgii. Following the example of Kazakhstan, where the Kazakhs were turning Russian place-names into Kazakh ones, in Bayan Ölgii the Kazakhs started to do the same to Mongolian names. A Kazakh National Unity Movement was inaugurated in October 1990 in Bayan Ölgii *aimag*, to 'promote Kazakh autonomy in Mongolia, adoption of Kazakh as the local official language, and the appointment of a Kazakh to the post of vice-president of Mongolia' (Sanders 1996: 113).

After the collapse of the Soviet Union and the gain of independence of Kazakhstan, the Kazakhs of Mongolia have been moving to Kazakhstan in large numbers. By October 1991 4,000 Kazakhs had already left Mongolia. In a shrewd move to increase the native Kazakh population in Kazakhstan, in September 1992, 'the Kazakh government convened a world-wide Qazaq qurultay, inviting representatives of the Kazakh diaspora from all over the world to Almaty. On President Nazarbayev's initiative, a Standing Committee was set up to accelerate the pace of Kazakhs' migration from abroad to Kazakhstan.... The highly publicized "Resolution of the Qurultay" appealed for all Kazakhs to unite under a single flag on the soil of Kazakhstan' (Janabel 1996: 6). This call and the preferential treatment promised to the returning Kazakh diaspora have stirred a zealous response from Kazakhs from China, Mongolia, Iran, and elsewhere. By June 1994, some 60,000 Kazakhs had left Mongolia. According to a Kazakh who remained in Mongolia,

All the Kazakh students from universities, colleges and vocational schools in Ulaanbaatar and other central regions left for Kazakhstan. Most of them were carried away by nationalistic feeling, while some others had no choice but to follow their parents. All those Kazakhs living in different parts of Mongolia and who had almost forgotten their customs and traditions, people who were morally and politically bankrupt, left the country. Scientists and true patriots did not leave Mongolia. (Quoted in Ganhuyag 1994)

It is important to note that most of those who left Mongolia were those who were scattered by the Mongolian government in various Mongolian provinces, including all young students who tended to be nationalistic. Kazakh intellectuals were certainly responsible for this exodus, as one Kazakh alleges:

They (some Kazakh intellectuals) spread rumours that the Mongolian economy was crisis-ridden and would not revive in years to come, and they said that now that nationalism is reviving the Kazakhs, who were 'slaves' in Mongolia must leave the country immediately. These people master-minded and led the migration of the Kazakhs. (Quoted in Ganhuyag 1994)

The flight of the Kazakhs was spurred on by Mongolian nationalism in the wake of Mongolia's own independence. The withdrawal of Russian troops from Mongolia in 1991–2 promoted speculation that the independent Mongolian government was adopting an extremely nationalist or pan-Mongolian policy which would not tolerate any non-Mongols in Mongolia. Rumours are certainly a powerful means of communication, and they played a significant part in putting the Mongolian Kazakhs to flight:

Kazakh envoys had a number of meetings with President Ochirbat who made a visit to Bayan Ölgii *aimag* during which he outlined his position. During a meeting with President Ochirbat last February (1994), an old Kazakh man asked him, 'Do you want the Mongolian Kazakhs to leave? Do you want to set up a Pan-Mongol state which former Premier Byambasüren wanted to do? If so, we must decide our next move.' In reply President Ochirbat said, 'I don't want the Kazakhs to leave. The plan to establish a pan-Mongol state will never materialize and if it does, it will push the country to its destruction.' (Ganhuyag 1994)

Since the issue of the status of the Kazakhs has become a major problem that might tarnish the image of Mongolia in its international relations, Mongolian and Kazakh scholars have begun to redefine their ethnic relations.

As mentioned, Bayan Ölgii was founded for two ethnic groups, the Kazakh and the Altai Urianghai, the latter allegedly being a Turkic people. However, this is disputed by the Urianghai, who always think of themselves as Mongols. The increasing Kazakh domination in Bayan Ölgii has brought about much inconvenience to the Urianghai, and I heard that many of them have moved away. Their emigration from Bayan Olgii started in the 1960s, when the state farms were set up in central Mongolian provinces.[18] In recent years, some Urianghai Mongolian scholars have protested about the fact that they were treated as Turkic people, both by the state and by anthropologists. They have begun to reclaim Mongolian identity. In fact, they say that they are the *original* Mongols, the ancestors of the Oirat Mongols, and they even claim that the majority of the Halh were originally Urianghai. Furthermore, they maintain that the *Secret History* was written by an Urianghai, for not only is the book full of information about the Urianghai, but the Urianghais appear in it as the most trusted people of Chinggis Khan, eventually being appointed by Chinggis to guard his tomb (Baatar and Gantulga 1992).

Changes in political practice have occurred along with the new democratic movement. Earlier, officials were more or less appointed by the central government in Ulaanbaatar, and the Mongols were politically dominant in Bayan Ölgii. Now, however, the Mongols are being removed from almost all posts, and replaced by Kazakhs. The Kazakhs are thus said to have staged a *coup* against the Mongols. This dramatic change in the ethnic landscape of Mongolia is a reaction to the established myth of the modern Mongolian socialist nation. According to this idea, all the groups would merge into the largest *ethnos*, the Halh, and become a socialist Mongolian nation. In order to legitimate this process, interestingly, the Kazakhs in Mongolia had been regarded as originally Mongols, a view said to be supported by the famous Russian scholar Gumilev. The Kazakh national consciousness must now fight the ethnogenesis battle, to prove whether they are Mongol or Turk.

Some Mongols claim that the Kazakhs are Mongol on the basis that they are descendants of Naiman and Kereit, these being recorded in the *Secret History* as two Mongolian tribes (*aimags*). This reference to the *Secret History* as the ultimate authority showing that the Kazakhs are Mongols is in fact meant to persuade the Kazakhs in Mongolia not to associate themselves with Kazakhstan. Kazakhs there are seen as

[18] Kazakhs have also exerted a strong influence on the remaining Mongol groups. One Mongol writer even said that these Mongols might soon find their way into the record books as an endangered species (Tuyabaatar 1990).

probably being of the Turkic 'race'. Ishjamts, a Mongolian authority on ancient Mongolian history, illuminates the present context:

In the folk language, the Halh are called Mongol, while others are called by the names Dürbet, Bayat, Buryat, Tsahar, Dariganga, etc., as if they were not Mongol. This is wrong. In our country live the Halh Mongol, Dürbet Mongol, Darhat Mongol, as well as the Altai (Mongolian) Urianghai and many other *yastan* of the Mongol *ugsaa*. The Mongolian nation-family (*ündestnii ulus ger*) also includes Turkic *yastan* like the Kazakhs. (Ishjamts 1991)

However, Ishjamts also tries to sort out the origin of the Kazakhs from a historical perspective. He writes that the majority of the Naiman, Kereit, Nangiad, and Jalair and other original Mongolian *aimag*s migrated to the Kipchak steppe, eastern Turkestan, and Central Asia after the disintegration of the Mongol Empire, and were gradually assimilated into the Turkic peoples, later becoming part of the Kazakhs and the Uzbeks. In the sixteenth century, when the Kazakhs came into being as a distinct entity, the Turkicized Naiman and Kereit were a majority part of them. This shows how newly descent-conscious Mongol scholars emphasize the Mongol *ethnie* of the Kazakhs, rather than social, political, and religious factors, in forming the Kazakh ethnic identity.

In almost all the history books written by contemporary Mongols, the Hunnu Empire (second century BC to first century AD) is regarded as having been a Mongol empire, thus showing that today's Mongolian territory was from time immemorial Mongolian ancestral land. In this historical scheme, the Kazakhs, or the Turkic people in general, are largely ignored, causing some bitterness among Kazakh intellectuals. According to Bazilkhan, a Kazakh linguist, the Hunnu Empire was not a Mongolian empire, but a Turkic one. Archaeological findings suggest that Turkic people lived in central Mongolia well before the Mongols. As far as the Kazakhs are concerned, they used to live in the central region of Mongolia, and this, he argued, is the ancestral land of the Kazakhs. Naiman and Kereits were Turkic people, not Mongol. Therefore, it was the Mongols who squeezed the Kazakhs out of their ancestral land.

The above remarks are a response to the statement by some Mongols that the Kazakhs are immigrants, that they should go to Kazakhstan, and that if they go, they should abandon claims to Bayan Ölgii. The Kazakhs' stance is that they are first of all not Mongols; secondly, that this land is their land (the basis of their claim for the autonomy of Bayan Ölgii), and thirdly that either independence or unification with Kazakhstan would be justified.

Whatever is happening over there, it seems that most Kazakhs are still willing to work within a Mongolian national framework. They are now fighting a successful battle to enjoy equal (if not superior) rights in Mongolia. The end of 1991 and beginning of 1992 saw some unrest in Bayan Ölgii; meetings and demonstrations were organized, in direct relation to the ongoing discussion of the new Constitution. In particular, Kazakhs claimed that their historical tradition, mother tongue, and ethnic rights had not been fully guaranteed and protected in the draft Constitution. Throughout the session of the National Congress discussing the Constitution, Kazakh deputies repeatedly urged the Congress to take the nationality question more seriously. They insisted that it be reflected in the Constitution as a guarantee of human rights. All this points to the existence of an uneasy Mongol–Kazakh relation in Mongolia. While the Kazakhs claim that they are discriminated against by the Mongols, the Mongols insist, rather, that they are the victims of the Kazakhs. The following remarks made to me by a Mongolian MP lay bare the ethnic picture in Mongolia: 'Before 1990, in the one-man dictatorship period, it was said that there was no nationality question in Mongolia. The Kazakhs constituted only 6.8 per cent of the total Mongolian population. This is not a substantial number, so it was thought that there was no nationality problem in Mongolia. This is a rather one-sided view. Within the last seventy years, the Kazakhs received more favourable treatment than the Mongols. For example, more houses were constructed for them; the Party and Government satisfied their wishes to a greater degree. In my opinion, there is a nationality problem. There must be a nationality problem when nationalities exist. There are two nationalities, the Mongols and Kazakhs, in Mongolia. During the period of discussing the Constitution, you must have heard the issues put forward by the Kazakhs. They tried very hard to have the Kazakhs recognized as an *ündesten* in the new Constitution. Now they are recognized as an *ündesten*.'

4

Problems of Biological Reproduction and the Mongolian Crisis of Confidence

Introduction

The discourse of nationalism and ethnicity in Mongolia, as we have seen, emerged on the basis of profound social, economic, and political reorganization along Soviet lines. The homogeneous image which Mongolia used to present and which is imagined by the world community is no longer valid. Social crises of various kinds have begun to grip the imagination of the Mongols, a phenomenon not at all isolated, but widely felt within the former socialist-bloc states. In this and the following chapter, I explore two issues: namely, what the Mongols regard as the 'national efficiency' crisis and the problem of the dilution of 'Mongolness'. These two issues, in my view, constitute the core of the post-socialist Mongolian nationalist discourse. When the socialist experiment of internationalism failed, people looked into their biological roots to see whether the biological body could sustain the perceived social crises. In this context, I discuss the attempt of current Mongolian élites to combat their imagined biological reproduction problems. Genealogy and clan names (*obogs*), long lost, are now being revived and taken as viable principles of social organization.

We may briefly reiterate the background to the problems. Socialist reorganization constituted a transition from the traditional to the modern. 'Bypassing capitalism' and socialist 'new men' were two concepts coined not only to accommodate the embarrassing theory of Marxism that socialist revolution was to be accomplished only in industrial countries, but also to signal the determination of the Mongols to bypass the historical period of capitalism in their evolutionary process.

Suffering severe under-population, especially after a substantial proportion of men were liquidated in the 1920s and 1930s,[1] the new

---

[1] There is no official figure available. In a population of about 700,000, between 30,000 and 100,000 monks, males of certain ethnic groups, intellectuals, and political leaders are believed to have perished in the first two decades of the revolution.

nation-building and socialism-building project demanded greater man-power. In the last three or four decades great efforts have been made to achieve higher birth rates.[2]

Sustained population growth (see Table 2.1), however, occurred in parallel with industrialization and urbanization which was, as we have seen, linked to the Soviet and other socialist economies. This fast development absorbed a substantial proportion of the rural population into towns and cities, eventually leading to an unbalanced demographic situation in Mongolia. Today 56 per cent of the population lives in cities, 26 per cent in *sum* centres, 3 per cent in brigade centres, and 15 per cent in the countryside; of the total, only 7.5 per cent engage in real pastoral production (Hün 1992: 3).

This rapid industrialization and urbanization not only effected profound changes in the social and economic structure of Mongolia, but also precipitated a myriad serious social problems. The consequences are now sharply felt. The previously all-encompassing state can no longer accommodate and mediate these problems, as the entire planned economic system has collapsed, as noted earlier. After early euphoria that the Mongolian nation was prospering, in recent years its survival as a distinctive nation or race in the world, as some Mongolian intellectuals would allege, is felt to be under threat.

One of the most serious problems which threatens to destroy the fabric of society is alcoholism. Here I am not so much concerned with the problems themselves, the severity of which is difficult to gauge, as with the social reaction to the perception of these problems. The Mongolian authorities have been combating alcoholism for decades, through ideological indoctrination and by limiting sales.[3] Now alcohol has been transformed into one of the most treasured items, tantamount to a means of economic transaction. Russians are the main scapegoat for transmitting this opium to the Mongols, who claim that prior to the arrival of the Russians they drank only in moderation.[4] Since the door to China was reopened in 1990, it has been widely reported that often the first thing

---

[2] The fast birth rate needed to bring the current Mongolian population to 2 million was the occasion for a national celebration in 1987. The government's Central Statistical Board determined that one of the 260 babies born on 11 July (Mongolia's national day) was the two millionth citizen. Twenty-five of the babies were selected as 'Two Million Babies' (Worden and Savada 1991: 70).

[3] Even the late Tsedenbal was reputed to be a severe alcoholic.

[4] A favourite proverb bandied about is: *Döchi garaad döngöj uu, Tavi garaad tavij uu, Jira garaad jiragaj uu* (Start drinking only after reaching forty; drink slowly after fifty; and drink happily after sixty).

Mongols do upon their arrival in China is to drink. The opened channel has unexpectedly sabotaged the long struggle against alcoholism. The government and social workers have started to wage a war against Chinese alcohol by extolling Mongol *arhi* (vodka). The government alcohol inspectors frequently raid newly opened Chinese restaurants. In 1991 an uproar ensued when it was reported that somebody had died from drinking Chinese alcohol. The Chinese were accused of deliberately putting poison in the alcohol, to realize their scheme of 'extinguishing the Mongols'. The social atmosphere reached a hilariously fevered state when it was rumoured that the cheap alcohol contained in a plastic bottle which looks like the figure of an old man (*övgön arhi*) now consumed in Mongolia was actually used for wiping and cleansing corpses in China.[5]

To the hysterical anti-Chinese discourse that the Chinese are now plotting to poison the Mongol nation without shedding blood is added another dreadful fear: a sudden, apparent rise in insanity and feeble-mindedness. This new perception chills Mongols to the bone, for it suggests that the Mongolian population (explored below) might be mentally and physically degenerating.

Amongst other problems afflicting Mongolia is a surge of prostitution and criminal activities, quite an unexpected thrust, catching the whole society and government in bewilderment, as many claim that this has happened only in the last three or four years with the start of political pluralism. This is a blow to the Mongols' image of themselves as a law-abiding, peace-loving people. The shattered image has prompted the whole nation to reflect on itself. What is the future of the Mongols, now that there is little to eat, everyone is a drunkard, the streets are filled with foreigners, and above all, there are so many feeble-minded and disabled people?

---

[5] Kaplonski relates this hysteria to concepts of race in contemporary Mongolia: 'It was a fairly common experience to hear of people taking ill through Chinese food or drink. Children ended up in the hospital, comatose, because of Chinese sugar; a man went blind from Chinese alcohol; Chinese grain was infested with insects. The stuff the Chinese were selling as salt wasn't really salt, either. The list seemed to go on and on. In contrast I heard only one story concerning bad food from Russia, a report circulating in mid-June that warned of possibly contaminated eggs that had come from Buryatia' (1996: 82). The Mongols' accusation is not entirely groundless. Their rush into China coincided with the Chinese economic boom accompanied with inadequate market regulation. A wave of 'fake' products (*jiamao chanping*) hit all of China, causing huge damage to both consumers and the economy. These fake products are usually cheap; those sold by pedlars are generally despised by most consumers in China. Mongols, crisis-ridden, and short of cash, were usually unable to buy better-quality products in China.

'Something Wrong with Reproduction?'

Along with these Mongol thoughts, I focus here on one important issue: biological reproduction. I present the 'evidence' which is giving rise to Mongol worries, but I remind readers that this reconstruction is meant to demonstrate the Mongols' notions, rather than my personal opinion.

In Mongolia a new phenomenon has emerged in the last twenty or thirty years. The number of people with mental retardation[6] began to increase. A large-scale investigation (Radnaabazar 1991) of inherited diseases was eventually carried out between 1987 and 1990. Four hundred and fifty thousand people were examined, covering eleven provinces and three cities. The results alarmed the whole nation: there were about 21,000 mentally handicapped, 9.7 persons per 1,000. What is more surprising is that 76 per cent of them were under 25. Note the juvenilization of the mentally handicapped population.

Statistics published in 1989 show that the number of mentally handicapped people under 18 years old was 21,904 (*Nigüülel*, 10 Nov. 1991). We do not know the total number of mentally handicapped people in Mongolia, but the distribution in terms of age-groups may give a clue (Table 4.1):

TABLE 4.1. *Breakdown of percentage of mental retardation by age cohort*

0–3	4–7	8–12	13–17	18–20
0.84%	5.99%	28.62%	19.80%	8.30%

21–9	30–9	40–9	50–9	60
23.13%	7.90%	3.20%	2.15%	0.71%

Source: Byambasüren *et al.* 1990.

The authors did not give the total number of respondents. We presume this table is meant to reflect the situation in the country, and comparing the table with statistics on the population numbers in each age-group, we can see that the total number of mentally retarded people may well exceed 30,000. Byambasüren *et al.* (1990) asserted that 29.2 per cent of all cases of mental handicap are of hereditary origin, 10.45 per cent

---

[6] Mentally retarded people are colloquially called *den dunchuud* (shaky, dim), or *teneg* (fool). In recent years, such people with mental retardation have been referred to as *oyun uhaani homsdoltoi hün* (persons lacking intelligence). Mental illness, such as depression, schizophrenia, paranoia, etc., is called *setgel medereliin övchin*. However, throughout the chapter, I refer mainly to the former.

caused by alcohol, 1.96 per cent by brain damage during delivery or at early age, 1.43 per cent by improper delivery, 2.87 per cent by encephalitis, 1.11 per cent by other external factors, and 14.05 per cent by both hereditary and external influences. In 38.96 per cent of the cases the causes had not been identified, and could well include both hereditary and external factors. The authors made a distinction between congenital mental retardation and psychosis. The number of mentally retarded people constituted 50.1 per cent of the mental cases. They were 39.1 per cent of the mental patients who received psychiatric treatment, although only 10.5 per cent of those were in mental homes. The authors further divided mental retardation into three categories: mild, median, and serious. The mild category constituted 79.17 per cent, the median 18.36 per cent, and the serious 2.48 per cent. School-age children between 8 and 17 years old accounted for 48.43 per cent of all mentally retarded people. This category proved difficult to identify, for they were easily confused with mentally ill people. Many of them commit crimes, and 44.2 per cent of all the criminals who could not bear responsibility for their crimes in Mongolia were mentally retarded people (Byambasüren *et al.* 1990).

There is also the question of the general health of the Mongolian population. If venereal diseases and smallpox, etc. prevailed in the past, today Mongolia is plagued by diseases of the kidney, uterus, heart, and liver, as well as fatigue and flu. It is said that few healthy children are born into Mongolian society these days. In 1991, 70–80 per cent of the children aged between 0 and 15 suffered from diseases of various kinds. This has created a public outcry. It is warned that if the situation goes on like this, there won't be any Mongols with healthy bodies to protect their independence (Ariunchimeg 1992).

Reproduction Processes as Seen by the Mongols

Social attention is focused on biological reproduction for an explanation and answer to this perceived threat. We describe how the Mongols are thinking of this problem. Adultery and promiscuity in Mongolia have a long tradition, and are socially tolerated provided certain norms are observed. The most important is to uphold, at least publicly, the marital bond, which invariably results in neither side acknowledging paternity. Mongol scholars suggest that this cultural pattern in a small isolated population makes it possible for cousins and half siblings to mate, and that this must be seen as indirectly contributing to genetic abnormality. Another contributing factor was the non-availability of contraceptives during the socialist period, as the state encouraged the fast growth of population. There is a widely publicized case (Enhbat 1991): a couple in the countryside gave birth to five children, two of them being born mentally and physically handicapped. Both the husband and the wife are healthy, and do not drink alcohol or smoke cigarettes. Their pedigrees were then studied, and it was found that the couple have the same biological father. This account is not unusual.

The Gobi, the desolate desert region of Mongolia, which once sparked off the wildest imaginings, is now of special social concern to both Mongol intellectuals and Western development advisers. In certain regions of the Gobi, herding is an economically highly risky activity. Thus men have left their homes in search of new economic opportunities, which can only be found in the towns. An unintended consequence of this migration is that women and children are left alone. This often results in numerous sexual encounters with the men who remain behind. Below I summarize an account written by a school teacher, Chuluun (1992).

The *sum* concerned is called Altanbulag in the Dornogobi province. It has a total population of 2,318. There are fifty-three unmarried women between 31 and 79 years of age who head their households and have 144 children. It is difficult to say who the fathers are, yet many of these children have already intermarried. There are also forty-six unmarried women between 18 and 44 who live with their parents. With three exceptions, each one of them has between one and eight children. The genealogies of forty people in one official organization in the *sum* centre have been studied, and it was discovered that thirty-seven of them are closely related. Twenty-four out of thirty-six families in Zamiin Shand brigade of the *sum* are in close-kin marriages (it is not indicated how close they are). In this *sum* there are thirty mentally handicapped people, of whom twenty-three were born after 1960. One quarter of the children born every year are labelled 'fathers unidentifiable' in the population census.[7]

The author points out that the few (two to three) local leaders of the *sum*, who periodically tour the region, have impregnated numerous

---

[7] Potkanski and Szynkiewicz (1993) confirm that a matrifocal family pattern has developed in the Gobi region: 'An unstable matrifocal family brought about the atrophy of the patriline and the disappearance of patrikin. Most people do not know the name of their father, and those who do know cannot identify [their] parents' (1993: 28).

women, whose children, unbeknownst to one another, often intermarry. These sexual encounters with local women coincide with the herding season. For example, in Hatanbulag *sum* of Dornogobi province 19 per cent of annual human births are concentrated in February and September (Zayabaatar 1990)—that is, many unmarried herdswomen get pregnant in May and December. It is noted that May is the animal birth delivery season, when people come from towns to help. December is the season for the final animal census in the year. Representatives from *sum* and province, roaming men in search of their lost animals, soldiers, and even teenage boys pour into the country to enjoy themselves. Conversely, the local men go to school and army never to return.

We can thus identify several 'problems': out-migration of the local male population and seasonal mating of local women with men from elsewhere; this results in illegitimate children, whose paternal identity is unknown, which may result in unintended inbreeding in succeeding generations.

Illegitimacy is apparently linked to the large number of single mothers in Mongolia.[8] Data on legitimacy and single parenthood are very unreliable. According to a sociological study conducted in 1989, there were 65,000 women-headed households out of 490,654 households in Mongolia (Enhtuya 1991). However, in 1991 it was estimated that there were 85,000 women-headed households in Mongolia (Ganbat 1991). In Ömnögobi province, 14 per cent of all households are headed by women,[9] and in some *sum*s, the percentage rises to 30 per cent (ibid.). Mongols say that illegitimate birth is not only an indication of the moral collapse of Mongolian society, but also contributes to mental retardation. There are also many single-father families; but the exact number is unavailable.[10]

Briefly, the two million-odd Mongolians are scattered over a vast territory as large as Western Europe. Mongolia has been divided into 328 *sum*s. So, a relatively small number of people live in a *sum*, and

[8] The emergence of single-parent families in Mongolia is not a recent phenomenon. We should make a distinction here, between widows and women having no husbands. The large-scale single-motherhood phenomenon might have arisen after Buddhism was reintroduced in the seventeenth century. The drain of men into monasteries left numerous women unmarried.

[9] A UNESCO study conducted in 1995 showed that female-headed households in rural areas of Mongolia accounted for approximately 12 per cent of the herding households (Skapa and Benwell 1996: 140).

[10] Men's problems in Mongolia have also attracted attention from politicians. One deputy of the Congress, J. Adiya (1991) proposed to establish an independent centre of Mongolian anthropology, dealing specifically with 'social questions of men'.

TABLE 4.2. *Distribution of mental retardation*

Aimag (province)	year created	1990 population	territory (thousand sq. km)	inhabitants (per sq. km)	no. of *sum*s	no. of mentally retarded	% of mentally retarded of total population
Arhangai	1923	89,200	55	1.62	17	724	0.8
Bayan Ölgii	1940	99,300	46	2.16	12	48	0.04
Bayanhongor	1941	78,700	116	0.68	19	1,429	1.8
Bulgan	1937	56,700	48.9	1.16	15	576	1.01
Gobi-Altai	1931	65,100	142	0.46	17	1,637	2.51
Dornogobi	1931	58,600	111	0.53	13	691	1.17
Dornod	1931	82,600	123.5	0.67	14	816	0.98
Dundgobi	1941	51,900	78	0.67	15	1,026	1.97
Zavhan	1923	93,600	82	1.14	23	1,724	1.84
Övörhangai	1931	100,400	63	1.59	18	1,033	1.02
Ömnögobi	1931	43,500	165	0.26	14	808	1.85
Sühbaatar	1941	53,500	82	0.65	12	689	1.28
Selenge	1931	92,000	42.8	2.15	16	1,384	1.50
Töv	1923	105,900	81	1.31	26	1,125	1.06
Uvs	1931	91,800	69	1.33	19	1,181	1.28
Hovd	1931	81,100	76	1.07	16	552	0.68
Hövsgöl	1931	106,900	101	1.06	21	3,547	3.31
Hentii	1923	76,700	82	0.94	19	908	1.18
Darhan	1962	88,600	0.2	434	7	729	0.82
Ulaanbaatar	1639	575,000	2	287.5	9	825	0.14
Erdenet	1978	58,200	0.06	970	4	451	0.77
Total		2,149,300	1,566.5	1.37	328	21,904	1.01

during the period of Soviet domination there was no inter-*sum* population flow due to strict administrative controls. With urbanization the population has been flowing one way from rural areas to urban centres. In recent years, it seems, people have often married or had sexual affairs within their immediate geographical areas. Radnaabazar (1991: 3) reports that each year about 80–120 marriages occur in each *sum*, and on average 69.9 per cent of the partners are found among relatives within a radius of 15 kilometres, and 10.9 per cent within a radius of 15–30 kilometres. If this new trend continues, argues Radnaabazar, it will result in a higher frequency of close genetic reproduction. Evidence can be found by examining the distribution of mental retardation and population density within given administrative districts. I made a special chart (Table 4.2), using Radnaabazar's data on mental retardation and other social data on geography, to analyse his evidence for this trend. A sophisticated analysis would certainly involve examining other variables. However, a crude analysis is sufficient here to show the kind of correlation which alarms the Mongols.

The table indicates that in isolated provinces with relatively small populations there are more cases of mental retardation. The larger the population and the more migration, the smaller the number of mentally handicapped people. For example, in Ulaanbaatar, in a population of over half a million, there are only 825 mentally handicapped people (0.14 per cent), while in Hövsgöl, there are 3,547 out of a population of only 106,900 (3.31 per cent). As we notice, not all small population provinces produce larger numbers of mentally handicapped people. In Ömnögobi, for example, although it is legendary for producing such people, in fact, the total is smaller than expected (1.85 per cent). The reason is perhaps, as mentioned above, that there is an influx of people from outside periodically. In Dornod, there may be different reasons for the small proportion of mentally retarded (0.98 per cent). Here there are several Buryat *sums* with few mentally handicapped people, perhaps because there is a high incidence of inter-ethnic marriages, or because Buryats still maintain some limited exogamy (see below). It appears that the more remote the province from the capital and railway lines, the smaller the number of ethnic groups in the region, and the more mountainous the terrain, the greater the incidence of mental retardation. Bayan Ölgii, the only exception to this pattern, is a predominantly Kazakh province; the Kazakhs retain their exogamous clan system much better than the Mongols.

The Mongolian argument that the abandonment of the traditional cultural concepts of incest and exogamy contributes to the high level of mental retardation is far from conclusive. There might always have been inbreeding by isolated herders, in spite of the traditional notion of exogamy. Exogamy, as a rule for avoiding marriage amongst same *obog* or clan name carriers, does not prohibit marriage between close kin in the category of mother's brother's daughters. In fact, such matrilateral cousin marriage was a preferred form of marriage. It is far from certain that mental disorder is more common now than before; one could argue that it is just noticed more due to modern medical diagnosis. Nevertheless, Mongolian intellectuals and the state believe this to be the case, and have been conceptualizing this 'crisis'. Consequently, the emerging nationalist discourse is grounded in biological metaphors that are designed to restore pride in the purity of the Mongolian nation. This is very important for our understanding of contemporary Mongolian nationalism.

Culture to the Rescue

Whether or not the Mongolian genetic quality is degenerating, the point
is that Mongols *think* it is. As one journalist warns in despair: 'The...
second serious genetic disease is called Down's syndrome. People suffering this disease are called Mongol, because they resemble the Mongols
physically. If our few Mongols continue to fill our gene pool with feeble
people, then, very soon, people in the world will name ordinary idiots as
Mongol' (Sharab 1991). This quote suggests that Mongols agonize over
the prospect of a direct link between mental retardation and racial Mongoloid features. The Mongols feed on this link, a stereotype prevalent in
Western popular media.[11] The impact of the Western stereotype has
clearly motivated Mongols to break the link between the two by establishing that 'Mongol' is a respectable term. In recent years, Mongolian
scientists have started to make an unprecedented attempt to define the
Mongolian population or race (*töröhten*). There are two notions: first, that
the Mongolian 'race' is subject to ecological determination (their anthropological constitution and physiology are ecology-determined). Secondly,
although it is implicit, we should not fail to discern the idea that Mongols
as a people are a biological unit, rather than a sociological unit. It is
significant that this idea may be linked to the work of the famous Russian
scholar Gumilev, who is very popular in Mongolia; according to many
Mongols, he defined the Mongols as a biologically distinct population, an
'ethnos'. On his theory, 'ethnoses' rise and fall on a time-scale of between
1,200 and 1,500 years, leaving only 500 years for the Mongols before they
disappear, a prospect chilling to many Mongols.[12]

From 1990, articles began to appear in newspapers about gene pool
protection. The Mongolian president issued a special warning about this.
The background is as follows. It is perceived that along with urbanization, the countryside has been deserted. One result, as noted in the
previous section, is that the sparse populations in the countryside have

[11] See Stuart (1996) for a detailed study of images of Mongols in Western consciousness.
This is the first in-depth study of the Western production and reproduction of a 'Mongol'
racial category for mankind, a 'Mongol body' (Mongol eyes, the Mongolian blue spot), and
a form of mental retardation known as trisomy 21 (Mongoloids, Mongolian idiots).

[12] It appears, however, that Gumilev was unpopular among Soviet anthropologists. 'All
Soviet ethnographers are anxious to disavow any biological element in the study of ethnos,
especially if it could denote some sort of racist overtone' (Dragadze 1980: 163). After
glasnost, however, Gumilev's theory of *ethnos* began to win him such honour that the
Russian Academy of Sciences had him elected one of its members (Becker 1992: 309–21).
In an obituary published in the *Mongol Messenger* (Erdenebileg 1992), the author suggested

had to marry within small local units, creating 'blood closeness' (*tsus oirtah*). There is a strong genealogical amnesia; not many people remember generations beyond their immediate relatives, and this creates the possibility of violation of the traditional marriage principle—that is, exogamy. Therefore, the Ministry of Health seeks to revive the traditional social organization and to co-operate with modern biological sciences (Batsuur 1988). What is of interest is that the formerly condemned pre-revolutionary social organization is now explicitly recognized as having important values.[13]

People have begun to develop an interest in the ancient system of clans and there is a campaign to revive the forgotten *obog* system. The State Small Hural (1990–2) was planning to pass a law on the *obog*, for each family and individual to know his origin, to keep a genealogy book.[14] The

that Gumilev had been persecuted in the former USSR for defending the Mongol invaders, saying that the wars unleashed by the Mongols were of a defensive nature. 'The name of Lev Gumilev will always be cherished by the Mongols, for his work is for them a gulp of the fresh breeze of free-thinking in the sultry and sad years of barrack socialism' (ibid.).

[13] The biological interest taken by Batsuur is important, for he later became head of the National Development Ministry. Under his initiative, and according to a presidential decree on demographic policy in 1991, the National Development Ministry and the Health Ministry elaborated *Hün* (Man), a long-term governmental programme aimed at dealing with the general population crisis in Mongolia (approved by the government in July 1992). An article in the *Mongol Messenger* newspaper reported: 'The authors of the programme tried their utmost to perceive all real possibilities for preserving the genetic fund of the Mongolian nation, offering first of all to reconsider the problems of women, children and family.... The programme envisages, in particular, measures on preventing births of mentally handicapped children. For the first time, the programme authors set national standards of health. They estimated that population health protection depends on medical care only by 20%, and largely depends on control of social problems. A laboratory for studying human physiology, morphology and genetics will be set up in Ulaanbaatar with the help of the UN Population Fund' (Solongo 1992).

[14] Elbegdorj, an MP, told me in late 1991 that immediately after the election law was passed, the State Small Hural would discuss the law on genealogy. I have no information on whether it has been passed. However, in 1994, the Mongolian Parliament approved the national security concept of Mongolia put forward by the National Security Council of Mongolia. 'The security of the population and its gene pool' is a main article in the 'Concept of National Security of Mongolia'. The internal factors which are believed to adversely affect the insurance of the security of the population and its gene pool include: '2. damage of the gene pool as a result of inbreeding; an increase in the number of mentally deficient and intellectually retarded persons exceeding the admissible ratio to that of normal people and thus exceeding the world average indicator'. The proposed ways and means of ensuring the security include, *inter alia*, '1. formulate and pursue a comprehensive Government policy aimed at ensuring the gene pool, health and sustained growth of the Mongolian population; revive, on public initiative, the tradition of keeping track and being aware of the family genealogy up to 7–9 generations of one's ancestors;...3. consider as a priority task the prevention of inbreeding, alcoholism and drug addiction which would negatively affect

genealogical campaign is advocated by both individuals and government. In 1991 several books and numerous articles appeared, describing specific ways to keep genealogical records. TV and radio have not been idle. This movement has had an immediate response from the whole nation. *Ugiin bichig* (written genealogy) is regarded as the most valuable inheritance a family can have. Those with old genealogy books are highly respected for knowing their origins. Schools and teachers are also taking an active part in this nation-wide project. In the new-style genealogy book, historians suggest that the following should be included:

1. Ethnic identity
2. *Obog* and *yas* (lineage) in paternal line
3. Parents, and individual's ranking among siblings
4. The ages of parents when the individual was born
5. Lunar calendar calculation:
   —century
   —year and the element of the year
   —the mark (*menge*) of the year
   —day and the element of the day
   —constellation
   —week
   —time
6. Names of birthplaces: *aimag*, *sum*
7. Basic administrative jurisdiction
8. If adopted, then the biological parents' *obog*s, and the time and age of adoption
9. Married whom, of which ethnic group, when, and children: age, gender, and names
10. Job, title, and medal received
11. Peculiar character and special talent
12. Mistakes made, crimes, and punishment services
13. The time and reason of death.

(Dashnyam and Ochir 1991)

Medical doctors, however, prefer to use medical means to prevent pregnancy of people who are in danger of giving birth to mentally ill children.[15] More importantly, it is suggested that the maternal side also

the Mongol gene pool, and comprehensive study of Mongols as human beings and of the Mongolian population; promote the policy of early diagnosis of and preventive measures against mental diseases and insurance of psychological security of the population' (National Security Council of Mongolia 1995).

[15] Some people oppose putting medical information in the written genealogy; they feel that such a practice might stigmatize one person and his entire circle of relatives.

be recorded. People are advised to write down all the generations they can remember. We can now see a clear change in kinship system in Mongolia. Indeed, many people would prefer to use the term *uragiin bichig* instead of *ugiin bichig*, the former meaning 'family book'.[16] What this implies is that people are no longer concerned only with their patrilineal origin, but more with the immediate bilateral relatives they can recognize, so as to serve their modern marriage strategy.

The essence of reviving the *obog* system is thus many-fold. Each person is advised to revive bearing the *obog* name, so that people of the same *obog* can avoid marriage. If the spouse is from the same *obog*, however, one is to find out the genealogical depth; only after nine generations is it safe to marry. According to some Mongols, this conforms to the modern genetic theory that 'genes disappear after nine generations'. Because sexual promiscuity is common, it is particularly urged that everybody remember who is the father.

Scholars' discussion of a return to the traditional *obog* system often takes the form of opposing nomadic nationalism to sedentarism. It essentially suggests that during the socialist period, the problem of nomadic social organization was not solved; instead, the very 'race' of the Mongols was weakened. The revival of the *obog* system poses questions like: what is the best way to develop a nomadic nation in modern times?

At present, however, the cultural practices of the ancient Mongols are the focus of contemporary Mongolian nationalist ideology. The Mongols say that the factor separating human from animal is that man knows his origin and abides by the rules necessitated by this knowledge. The knowledge of origin is thus essential, because it first imposes the incest prohibition, without which there would be degeneration of body and mind. Man's attainment of this knowledge marks the transition from nature to culture.[17] A well-cited proverb is, 'He who knows not his *udam* (descent) is no different from a strayed monkey in the forest'. The collapse of this system, which people have forgotten or have been made to forget, is taken by the Mongols as a deculturation process, a shift back from humans to animals, or worse than animals, because even Mongolian horses know how to keep their herd healthy (see below).

The current nationalist ideology in Mongolia rejects the idea that cultural institutions in pastoral-nomadic or tribal society represented

---

[16] *Urag* means matrilateral kin from the standpoint of the male or bilateral kin from the point of view of a third party. To a certain extent, it overlaps with *töröl* (kin).

[17] The Mongols are speaking just like Lévi-Strauss, who also had this theory about the separation of human culture from animals!

something far behind world civilization. This is a remarkable shift from the Mongols' previously critical treatment of the feudal period. 'The Mongolians occupy a high position in human civilization.' Such or similar statements appear in almost every article dealing with Mongolian culture today. The status of one nationality is allegedly judged by its survival strategy and its competition with other peoples, and by the cultural mechanisms which guarantee such good human qualities and competitiveness.[18] These provide, according to many Mongols, the elements of civilization and culture.[19]

The Mongol Concept of Incest Prohibition

It appears to be a widely held view that mental retardation in Mongolia is caused by inbreeding as a result of forgetting the now glorified *obog* system. Let us examine the grounds for such a belief, and the action taken by the government to revive the *obog* system. These problems involve, in my opinion, the questions of incest and exogamy.

Societies invent rules prohibiting sexual intercourse between variously defined 'relatives'. An anthropological yet most influential explanation is given by Lévi-Strauss (1969). In his opinion, the incest taboo facilitates the exchange of women during bargaining between social groups. Sisters and daughters are therefore used not for mating but to gain external social relationships or power. Socio-biology, on the other hand, has been active in providing an alternative explanation. Socio-biologists, applying an evolutionary theory, argue that close inbreeding results in defective

---

[18] Enhbat (1991) has written in a racist mode: 'The English and European royal families, in order to keep their power, married within their own families and hence developed "royal diseases". But such problems never happened to the Mongol Khans and lords. . . . The Jews living in Germany, under pressure, had to marry among close kin, and they gave birth to numerous mentally handicapped children. But this was never a problem for our Mongolian black-boned *arat*s and ordinary herdsmen.'

[19] These ideas are strikingly similar to the social significance of genealogy and name attributed to De Mattos, a Portuguese scholar. In his celebrated *Manual da Genealgia Portuguesa*, published in 1943, Mattos declared that genealogy had historical value that affects the nation. He believed that genealogy should serve as the family identification papers. Bouquet (1993: 151) gives a succinct summary of Mattos's argument of the moral significance of the name: 'There is nothing more nationalistic, he argued, than the constitution of a name, since it reveals tradition, which is the "very substance of a nation's greatness". If the procedures for composing a name were in "chaos", this did not augur well for the moral health of the nation more generally. De Mattos's remedy consisted in trying to achieve a balance between the ethical rights of expression involved in naming, and the obvious (to him) need for restraint and order to avoid decadence.'

offspring, and propose that natural selection processes have produced incest-avoidance mechanisms in the human genotype (see Leavitt 1989 and 1990 for a review of the relevant literature). We may briefly examine the Mongol case.

The Mongols say that their incest-avoiding mechanisms come from observation of animal 'family' dispersal, especially in horses, which prevents close inbreeding. Mongolian horses have an incest-avoidance instinct; that is, the stallion in the herd will drive away its own female yearlings once they are sexually mature. People say that if even animals do this, humans, as higher beings, must be more developed in this respect. Like horses, human beings drive away their daughters as soon as they reach reproductive age. The Mongols leave one seed male animal in a herd which consists of both female and sterilized or castrated male animals. But they do not let the same seed male mate in the same herd over several generations, and they attempt to bring in a different breeding male from somewhere else. In the Mongolian countryside during the mating season one can see herdsmen exchanging male breed animals. They understand that inbreeding would result in weak-bodied animals which normally could not survive the severe winter season and other calamities, such as drought.[20]

This suggestion that the Mongolian incest taboo is related to the observation of animals is not peculiar to Mongolia, but is also general knowledge in Inner Mongolia (see Borjigin 1990 for the Inner Mongolian case). The following saying is found in both regions: *Hün mori hoyor holiin udam tatna* (Both man and horse should maintain distant descent). This accords with the argument of socio-biologists that if natural selection has provided non-human species with genetic mechanisms for avoiding inbreeding, then humans are also likely to have such mechanisms (see van den Berghe 1980: 153). It is a widely held view that humans developed the incest prohibition largely through their observation of the disastrous results of consanguineous marriages; hence the incest taboo stems from a social reflection upon a natural phenomenon.

It seems that I am defending the Mongol point of view when I say that they have invented mechanisms to avoid inbreeding in order to keep themselves healthy. In fact, this indigenous Mongol 'kinship theory' is not unique. Löfgren in an interesting article shows how 'thinking with animals' has become part of historical processes of class formation and

---

[20] Owen Lattimore confirmed this practice in his travel book (1941: 194).

conflict, cultural hegemony, and resistance in Sweden (1985: 194–5). In this regard, it is interesting to mention Mary Bouquet's (1993) claim that English 'pedigree thinking' has directly contributed to the obsession with genealogy and kinship in British anthropology: 'Animals are transmuted into "persons" whose "breeding" closely resembles that held responsible for the "origins" of the English person. Primitive "pedigrees" are translated into genealogies, paving the way for kinship to become the centre-piece of British social anthropology during the first half of the twentieth century' (1993: 208). However, despite this evidence of pedigree thinking amongst Mongols, their incest notion is culturally embedded and prohibits breeding within the same patrilineage.

There is no Mongolian equivalent to the English word 'incest'; the closest concept may be found in the expressions such as *tsus oirtah* or *töröl oirtah*, literally, 'blood getting close' or 'kin getting close'. As is common in Central Asia, Mongols distinguish patrilineal kin from matrilineal kin, *yasan töröl* from *mahan töröl*, literally, kin in the bone from kin in the flesh (Krader 1963: 55). Another variation is that Mongols distinguish *yasan töröl* from *tsusan* (blood) *töröl*. These notions are similar to those of Tibetans. The Tibeto-Mongolian medical canon *Dürven Ündüs*, states that a person's father contributes bone, brain, and spinal marrow, while the mother contributes flesh and blood (Dürven Ündes 1959: 43). The Mongols, with their patrilineal descent system, regard all persons of the same *obog* as having the same *yas* (bone). The term *töröl*, however, is more puzzling. *Töröl* has two meanings: unilineal kin group or a bilateral kin group including close relatives on the mother's side. The incest prohibition applies to the former group (*yas*), who practice exogamy. The question then arises as to whether marriage or mating with *töröl* on the mother's side is equally forbidden. In fact, as I have said, the earlier notion, or the patrilineage principle, determined that flesh was not dangerous; only people bearing the same bone were prohibited from mating. Therefore, matrilateral kin were potential marriage partners. In other words, the classificatory mother's brother's daughter was eligible for marriage.[21] Today, however, Mongols also distinguish a new idea of *tsusan töröl* (blood kin), referring to people sharing the same bone and/or flesh.[22] Thus kin of the same patrilineal bone are now seen also as blood relatives, along with matrilateral kin. Marriage between either of them is regarded as *tsus oirtah*, hence dangerous and to be prohibited.[23]

However, the patrilateral prohibition remains ideologically dominant. Let me outline how Mongols count their generations through their body bone joints. 'Generation' in Mongolian is the same word as for bone joint: *üe*. The generations above an individual are counted through the joints of the arm, and the generations below through the joints of the leg. The individual is body or head; the neck joint represents father, the shoulder joint the grandfather, the elbow joint the great grandfather, etc., until you reach the finger tip. Similarly, when you count the generations below you, the neck represents the son, the thigh joint the grandson, the knee joint the great grandson, etc. The ninth generation is at the toe tip.[24] There are several ways to refer to the ninth generation. As the above list suggests, one way is *jiliihui*, meaning 'missing', 'lost'. One could also simply say *sunjirav*, which is a verb, meaning 'something becoming far or distant', implying that kinsmen beyond the ninth generation can marry each other, for there is no 'bone' involved there any more. The *üe* is also divided into two parts: *oir* and *aglag* (close and remote). The *oir* refers to the 'not yet distant' (*sunjiraagüi*) generations— that is, within five generations—and *aglag* to the 'distant' (*sunjirsan*) generations—that is, beyond the fifth generation. But marriage within nine generations is prohibited lest *tsus oirtah*. This system was not only a technique for counting, but also represented a sense of physical *identity* mapped on to the concept of patrilineal ancestry.

It is thought that the closer the generations, the closer the joints to the body, the more dangerous is marriage to life (*ami*). The furthest generation is least harmful to the 'life' or individual. After the ninth generation, a ritual was held to initiate a new lineage. This action is called *yas hagalah* (to break bone), which means that the new lineage and the

---

[23] See Firth *et al.* (1969) and Wolfram (1987) for discussions of the English notion of a relative by blood. Wolfram suggests that the English have a peculiar notion of heredity passing through blood. Blood in this case is both husband's and wife's; the confluence of blood from these two distinctive sources results in 'normal' offspring. Incest is thus popularly believed to results in 'idiot' or deformed children.

[24] A similar practice apparently existed in medieval Europe. Goody writes: 'in the thirteenth century, the Germanic calculus was represented by the human body, the head being the common ascendant, the shoulder the brother and sister, the elbow first cousins, and so on down to the nails, which stood for the seventh degree, at which point, as in Roman law, kinship stopped' (1983: 136).

parent lineage have no bone connection, and thus members of the two lineages may marry.

The above is a synthesized account of the idealized Mongol view of the efficacy of the Mongolian kinship system, by which they believe it is possible to avoid mental degeneration. Whether or not such a system indeed performs any genetic function must be left to genetic historians to determine. People today retain only a memory of previously strict social sanctions against consanguineous marriages: Mongols never entered the home of a family with children born of an incestuous marriage (within nine generations). If such a tent was accidentally entered, they would not accept food. If they met such a person outside, they would pass by on the windward side lest they be polluted by the air!

Social Transformation: A Historical Picture of Mongol Kinship

The meaning of *obog*, a concept or organization which has been much idealized, is not totally clear. The Mongols now say it is the 'surname', but this is difficult to accept. The modern idea of 'surname' appears to have come from the Russian patronymic, though people now also confer on it the Russian idea of *familiya* (surname). Recent archival research in Mongolia shows how, when, and why this particularly system was chosen. On 10 July 1925, in the Twenty-fifth Government Assembly, O. Dorj Meren suggested: 'From now on the whole people should be registered irrespective of man or woman, young or old. Also each individual should be given a surname (*obog*), so what about taking the names of the father or mother as *obog*?' His suggestion was accepted by the government, and the Interior Ministry organized a special committee manned by L. Dendev, Tseveen Jamtsarano, and O. Dorj Meren to draft a law on this issue. The committee soon released the following: 'All Mongolian people should be registered irrespective of men or women, young or old. Those who know their old *obog*s should retain them, and if they don't know their *obog*s, they should adopt the names of their fathers or mothers, grandfathers, great grandfathers, or any people of generations above that. Or they can adopt whatever surnames which suit them. Their names should not exceed two words' (Samand 1991).This clearly shows that the patronymic-cum-surname-cum-*obog* was a modern invention to facilitate the state census of the population in the newly established Mongolian People's Republic. It also suggests that at the time of its adoption, *obog* was not used as a surname, or Mongols did not don *obog* as their surname. This is still the case in Inner Mongolia, where a Mongol usually has one single given name, quite unlike the Chinese practice of having a surname, *xing* or *shi*. However, there do exist *obog*s, which can at best be called patrilineage. The point is that, until recently, although many knew their *obog*, it never served as a surname.

Obog was perhaps a clan institution in the pre-Chinggis period, but the concept in the later period is something different. Indeed, the original Mongol *obog*s became so mixed up due to constant military organizational reshuffling, that the *obog* in post-empire Mongolia was no longer a residential group. Vladimirtsov ([1934] 1980) treats *obog* as an ethno-nym-carrying clan, and perhaps wrongly ascribes to it such features as exogamy, clan worship, blood vengeance as a sign of solidarity, territorial unity, etc.[25] Bacon (1958), by contrast, distinguishes *obog* from clan. Although she does not really make a differentiation between the *obog* of the thirteenth century and that of the later period, her general point is useful. The basic difference, in her opinion, lies in time and group membership. 'Clan' normally operates by group membership, while *obog* is a generational principle used mainly for purposes of exogamy. Both organizations are called *obog*, and it is perhaps futile to delineate the nuances of the difference. However, we may nevertheless suggest that the present-day Mongolian notion of *obog* confuses the principle of generational exogamy and clan solidarity. David Sneath (1996), in a recent study, suggests that we should make a distinction between what he calls 'élite-centrist' and 'rural-localist' models of social organization in Mongolia. In this light, I suggest, the new concept of *obog* is 'élite-centrist'. Although there is such a huge discrepancy, Mongol intellectuals are trying to build a new genealogical culture for the Mongol nation based on the 'image' of the Chinggisid 'written' model and the common folk's generational exogamy.

The new concept of *obog* in present-day Mongolia is not of a social group but is ideally based on a nine-generation limit to exogamy, as we have seen. In my view, it was the commoners without written genealogies who resorted to generations as the bar of exogamy. It should be noted that the Mongol Chinggisid had extended written genealogies. For example, the genealogy of Sechen Khan Sholoi of the Halh (b. 1577) recorded 11,966 males' names, covering 328 years, from 1577 to 1905

---

[25] See Naran Bilik (1989) for a comparative study of Mongolian *obog* with Chinese and English surnames.

(Dashnyam and Ochir 1991: 6). The Borjigid were, until recently, exogamous as a totality.

How do we account for the decline of the *obog* system in Mongolia? Mergen Gegeen, an eighteenth-century Inner Mongolian (Urad) lama, tells us that early in the Manchu period, the Manchus reintroduced the *obog* organization based upon the Manchu model among several Inner Mongolian tribes. However, they refrained from introducing it in Outer Mongolia, where, according to him, the *obog* was not recoverable (Szynkiewicz 1977). The decline of the *obog*, either as a corporate group or as an exogamous principle, is related in a complex way to other social changes in Mongolia. This qualitative change in Mongolian kinship organization was, in my opinion, profoundly influenced by Buddhist ideology, as opposed to shamanic ancestor-worship ideology.

Buddhist karmic ideology is in fact a complete antithesis to the genealogy principle. In Buddhism, people are concerned with their karmic fate, and see happiness in their ultimate rebirth, while the clan or genealogical system assures a perpetuation of the clan or lineage. Buddhism in Mongolia and Tibet denigrated the procreative function. Ekvall (1972) writes about how family values weakened among the pastoral Tibetans:

Family and living ancestors and descendants too are thereby lessened in importance. The living ancestors, soon to lose their identity in the lottery of Karmic rebirths, are not a part of a long line that extends changeless into the far past and claims worship and remembrance in tombs and monuments. The living descendants too, though useful for facilitating the withdrawal of their parents from mundane concerns, do not have that crucial importance which belongs to those who will honour and worship their ancestors, for those parents will soon become generalized *being* instead of retaining identity as specific *beings*. They themselves feel no compulsion to have descendants to honour and worship them, for they too will soon lose identity in the changing cycles of rebirth.... In such a universe of values there is no overriding imperative to have progeny. (1972: 280–1)

In Mongolia before the revolution, apart from monks, lay men and women over 50 or 60 also usually shaved their heads and took religious vows. Men were called *ubashi*, and women *chivganch*.[26] They devoted the rest of their lives to the sacred. The lack of interest in their descendants on the part of older people in Mongolia may provide a clue to the decline

---

[26] In Ordos, well into the 1970s, older men and women shaved their heads and took little interest in the 'mundane' life.

of the institution of the family, and ultimately to patrilineage as an organization.

It is legitimate to question the importance and significance of the *obog* in such a social value system. Men were encouraged to have religious but not social responsibility. Women then had the sole responsibility for bearing and educating children. Children were prized, not by elders of the family or lineage, but by women, who needed them for economic and psychological reasons, but not for extending the line generation after generation.[27]

Let us then briefly review social reproduction in the Buddhist period in Mongolia. The Manchu annexation of Mongolia in the seventeenth century resulted in a reorganization of Mongolian society. The Halh were organized into eighty-six banners (Shirendyv and Natsagdorj 1968: 189–90). Banner boundaries were fixed; these fiefdoms belonged to different feudal lords, and the residents were not allowed to go beyond the pasture of the banner. In principle, this would result in endogamy within the banner's small population (remember that in the early twentieth century the total population of Halh Mongolia was only just over half a million, and that over one-third of all males were lamas). This must have led to the destruction of exogamy. Kinship schemes cannot be considered without reference to their political, demographic, or economic implications. The Manchus were only too aware of what kinship alliances between major Mongol groups would mean. During the reign of the Kangxi emperor, the Manchu state categorically forbade any marriage between Halh, Oirats, Tangut, Barga, and Inner Mongols (Xie 1985: 237).

However, while the mobility of lay men and women was restricted, monks were free to travel. Larson, who had an intimate knowledge of 'old' Mongolia, was quick to spot frequent illicit relations between monks and women: 'Very few priests stay in their temples in the entire year. They return to their homes or travel wherever they are needed, to read prayers for the sick, dispose of the dead, decide on a marriage day, select a new pitch for an encampment, or execute any of the various errands to collect funds for the lamasery which they frequently undertake. They travel on horseback, as everyone does in Mongolia, and usually sleep in a different tent each night' (1930: 99). 'The Mongolian

[27] This is a contrast to the pre-Buddhist Mongols. They respected elders, boasted about good origin, and were concerned with perpetuating their 'seed of seed' (*üriin ür*, or *uragiin urag*) and preserving the hearth (*golomt*).

woman is not the property of her husband, but a free and independent personality who can and does do exactly as she pleases. She takes the passing lama or friendly traveller as lover without shame or censure' (1930: 71). Forbath also observed similar conduct more explicitly: 'The Mongolians are so hospitable that once they have admitted a stranger to their house—or tent—they endeavour to study his pleasure in all things. Sometimes their hospitality goes so far that the host's wife or daughter is offered to the guest for the night' (1936: 51–2).[28] What seemed 'exotic' customs to these travellers nevertheless help us to infer that roaming lamas provided an alternative to endogamy. Another category of people who could travel freely in Mongolia were the Chinese merchants. They fathered numerous children, who are now called *erliiz* (see Chapter 5).

The Mongol *obog* system was already disintegrating by the beginning of twentieth century. Nevertheless, the idea (ideal) of lineal exogamy was still alive. Actual kinship was a matter of expediency and practicality, but the ideal lingered as a 'memory'. Many of the features now identified by Mongols as 'problems' were already present before the revolution. We need to explain their intensification during the socialist period and the reasons why they have been caught up in nationalist discourse recently. Before we go into a case-study, we need to look at the social and economic practicality of kinship.

Socialist 'Loss-of-Kinship' and the 'Revival of Kinship' in a Market Economy

Decline of kinship in the socialist system happened especially in the *negdel* (collective) period. At the start of collectivization (achieved in the late 1950s and early 1960s), relatives were prevented from close economic co-operation.

Therefore *negdel* organizers took care to create unrelated production teams (*suurs*) out of a conviction that kin interests would otherwise take precedence over collective ones. This was an ideological choice in the struggle to create a new society built in the national interest, instead of one based on kinship groups, which were considered as units of a closed system, outdated and associated with

---

[28] This was not a long-established Mongolian institution. During the Yuan Dynasty, the Mongols in fact forbade such a practice as carried out by some non-Mongol peoples. Marco Polo (1931: 72) described a similar practice in the province of Camul. However, such behaviour of men offering their wives to strangers was heard of and consequently banned by Mönh Khan, the Mongol emperor.

feudalism. There was also a practical wish to avoid nepotism and corrupt practices to the detriment of the collective, and of state property. (Potkanski and Szynkiewicz 1993: 26–7)

The *negdel* was instrumental in a major reshuffle of population, so that the majority of the herders were not herding in their *törsön nutag* (natal land), but elsewhere. The specialization of production also reduced kin interdependence. The *negdel*, by developing all essential facilities, in fact worked more effectively than the kinship ties. Rosenberg (1982) made a detailed study of how the *negdel* strove to offer far better services than the rich individual patron herders, and how the state exerted all its power to supply Soviet machinery to the *negdel*s. The system proved advantageous, and even the rich were persuaded rather than coerced into the collectives (see also Humphrey 1978). The *negdel* was thus in some ways a continuity of the earlier system. I propose to call it a quasi-'kinship' society at the local level. Just as ethnic group ties were decried (yet also underpinned) in order to achieve a unified socialist Mongolian nationhood (see Chapter 2), a sub-*ethnos* at the local *sum* level was created, through the erosion of kinship ties and alienation from private properties.

The removal of this *negdel* structure in 1991–3 has forced the herders to resort to kinship ties. There have re-emerged communities like the *neg usniihan* or *neg nutagiinhan* (communities of one water source or natal land). People have begun to cluster together, developing real or fictitious kinship, this time often legitimating their claim to pasture on the basis of birth. A message is clearly transmitted: a link between kinship and one's birth place is now crucially established at the lowest individual level. The proposed privatization scheme of the new Mongolian government in 1991–2 to make individual units of herders independent of each other has propelled herders to seek their own devices, and the most serious problem happens in the territorial organization or pasture redistribution. A Sussex University project, 'Policy Alternatives for Livestock Development in Mongolia', discovered that territorial conflicts have already started (Bazargur *et al.* 1993, Potkanski and Szynkiewicz 1993). They cautioned that further reshuffling may cause severe conflicts, and urged that a new land tenure system must be legally established.

Kinship during the socialist period was not totally lost, however. An active kinship was maintained vertically, that is, with urban kin. Potkanski and Szynkiewicz (1993) call this the *idesh* exchange system, providing meat in winter to urban kinsmen:

The initial ban on networks in production was relaxed with time, following a change in kinship interests, reoriented now towards closer ties with kin based outside the pastoral economy and thus having access to different types of goods and services. The reorientation was of an earlier date, but its importance increased with the economic deterioration paralleling the process of collectivization. It served to create a network accompanying goods exchange between unequally supplied areas, the countryside and the town. Thus evolved the idea of *idesh* (or *yidesh*), that is of redistribution of goods between individuals living in two economically distinct areas. Two aspects of the exchange were equally important: first, assistance extended to kin, and second, making up for the shortcomings of the state-owned trading companies. The latter were unresponsive to demand from the countryside, and besides, had few resources. Their efforts had to be supplemented by private initiative. Since the latter was more or less forbidden, informal goods exchange took the innocent form of assistance to kin. (1993: 27)

The system operated on one principle: a gigantic rural and urban disparity. The urban centres were provided with modern services and 'luxuries', which were acutely insufficient in rural areas. On the other hand, rural products like meat and dairy products, essential for the Mongol life-style, were desperately needed and prized by the urban Mongol dwellers. The system was generated by the fact that population mobility was 'illegal'; herdsmen were not given internal passports until the late 1970s, and they were thus not allowed to use urban public services, unless specially authorized by the officials. In Inner Mongolia, although a 'citizenship' card was not issued until the late 1980s, a different but similar system operated, as a person was tied to a work unit in the city, while the country people were tied to the land.

In Mongolia, the *idesh* flow from rural to urban centres gained currency only in the late 1980s, but it has now fully blossomed. In the socialist period, urban residents were in fact assured of a meat supply, while the rural population had little access to meat. The country people provided more milk products than meat to city kinsmen, like *airag* (koumiss), cheese, or butter. Imagine the situation (in 1991–2): an urban resident is entitled to only 90 grams of meat a day, while in the countryside, animals have been privatized. If in earlier times, the urban residents had a better economic standing, this is reversed now. It is expedient for urban dwellers to return to become herders. It was reported that the former Mongolian prime minister Byambasüren's son was the first to become a herder. In Zavhan *aimag*, for instance, the official number of herders in 1991 was more than double that in 1990 (Humphrey *et al.* 1993: 32).

The collapse of the socialist redistributive system at both the urban and rural levels gave rise to individualized kinship safety-nets. And it is here that urban and rural interaction becomes directly linked, based on the principle of exclusion and inclusion. In the past the rural people had to rely on urban markets and other services which were not available through official channels; the network has strengthened now that urban kin have to rely on rural kin for meat and other supplies. Outsiders (ethnicized) are excluded, and insiders are welcome. This kind of 'practical kinship' networking is now serving the Mongolian attempt to revive or reconstruct the long forgotten *obog* system (see Humphrey 1983: 283–98 for the Buryat 'practical kinship' during the Soviet period).

Reviving the 'Tradition': A Buryat Case

Dashbalbar, a predominantly Buryat *sum*, illustrates the process of reviving genealogies and the importance attached to them by the local people. Genealogy in Buryat Mongolian is called *ugiin bichig* (or *ugai besheg*, in colloquial Buryat), in contrast to Halh genealogy, which used to be called by various terms—for example, *uragiin bichig*, *udam sudur*. Today, the phrase *ugiin bichig* has gained currency in Mongolia, borrowed from the Buryats. The famous Buryat Mongolian scholar B. Rinchen declared that *udam sudur* was primarily concerned to show who were the descendants of a given ancestor. The aim of Buryat genealogy was to find out from whom a living person was descended, who were the ancestors (Humphrey 1979). The Buryats keep their genealogical records better than the Halh. One may attribute this to their more shamanic tradition, which pays more respect to ancestors. Each Buryat clan is named after a certain 'father' (*echige*). However, the development of Buryat genealogy was shaped through their relationship with the Russian state, and the use of genealogy became institutionalized. Humphrey (1979) writes that the Buryat use of genealogy was largely in response to land and tax issues in Russia. Therefore, it was a politically determined group solidarity.

The Buryats in Mongolia today, however, have almost completely abandoned their genealogy. *Echige* names have been forgotten by the younger generations, although the older generation still remember which *echige* they belong to. The abandonment of genealogy and *echige* was a recent phenomenon, only after the Buryats moved into Mongolia early this century. As elsewhere in Mongolia, the patronymic became the surname. The destruction of Buryat community ties was achieved by two means: Stalinist ethnocide (see Chapter 3) and the complete reorganization of society. The most important factor, maybe, was the collectivization of property. As we have seen, collectivization had a devastating effect on kinship ties. Production was no longer kin-based, and there was no private property which would tie individuals together. The Buryats told me that because of this their young people became alienated from herds (*malaasaa höndüirsen*), left home, and pursued studies or careers. Few of them ever returned home to settle.

In 1966, none the less, six huge Buryat genealogies were collected and published in Mongolia (Sumyabaatar 1966). They were not for any practical purpose, but to be used for 'scientific research' to study ethnogenesis, literature, and ethnic relationships. No further effort was made until 1990, when a newspaper was issued by the Buryat Cultural Heritage Society, which was named 'Ugai Besheg' (Genealogy). The first issue published a Buryat national genealogy, tracing their ancestors well beyond Chinggis period, and linking them to the Borjigin genealogy as known in the *Secret History*.

In Dashbalbar, *ugiin bichig* or *ugai besheg* began to be taught in school from 1990. The only way to avoid the tragedy happening among the Halh, the locals said, was to revive the *ugiin bichig*. One Buryat said to me: 'In the past, we were made to be ashamed of knowing our genealogy. The Halh would laugh at this; they said that we were still in the primitive clan stage, while they have already entered the socialist stage. Some even accused us of showing nationalism by remembering genealogy. In the 1930s, the Buryats were accused of being Japanese spies. From 1934, a policy was carried out to exterminate the Buryats. In Dashbalbar, 242 men were purged, ten of them were sentenced to ten-year imprisonment, all the rest were executed. They were good lamas, intelligent people, multi-linguists who knew history. I have only one thing to complain about: the destruction of the Buryat *ugai besheg*. This is the most terrifying thing. If the Interior Ministry found it, they would kill all the people mentioned in it. So, frightened people burned it, they buried it in the well, and some memorized it by heart. The Buryats never used parents' names as *obog*, but now all these have been lost. We must revive it before it is too late.'

The task of reviving the *ugiin bichig* and 'tradition' lies on the shoulders of the school, especially the Mongolian language and history teachers. Pupils are asked to bring their genealogical books (if they have any) to class. Contests are held for students to compete in remembering how many generations they know. This is more or less a revival of a tradition of the Buryats: Buryat children used to recite their genealogy before their parents and grandparents. Now when children meet, they often recite their genealogies to each other to outshame their opponents, just as in the past when Buryat men met, they wrestled. In October 1990, Oyun, the headmaster of the Dashbalbar school, developed a concrete scheme: 'The General Direction of Conducting Education in Dashbalbar *Sum* 10 Year School'. The scheme is divided into eight sections. The second section is about education in folk tradition and customs:

1. To know one's genealogical roots (junior and intermediate classes);
2. The customs of greeting (shaking hands is not a Mongolian custom) (junior and intermediate classes);
3. The traditional concept of taboos and sins (junior and intermediate classes);
4. The morals to be respected: merit;
5. The first six items for the aid of all beings;
6. The mentality of respecting and loving Nature and Mother Earth;
7. The origin and history of the Buryats;
8. The reason for respecting and worshipping the mountain and *obo* (ritual cairn);
9. The three manly games (wrestling, archery, and horse-racing).

The children are taught to remember the clans (*echige*) of the Hori Buryats, as well as the Aga Buryats. The other Buryat groups are ignored, for they are not thought to be proper Buryats. The majority of Buryat pupils know their clans after consulting their parents, while none of the Halh children knows theirs. They all say they are Borjigin Halh upon consulting their parents.[29] Both the Buryat and the Halh pupils are then classified into their clan groups, and their names and clan names are listed on a large wall chart. The teachers designed this in order to mark exam scores under each pupil, in an attempt to compare which clan's children are brighter. It was found, to the pride of the Buryats, that the Buryat children do better in class than their 'Borjigin' Halh 'elder brothers'. The reason is, I was told, that the Buryats have been more exogamous than the Halh, and that has helped keep the Buryat children clever.

One afternoon, Thursday, is left free specially for children to have various 'national' games, folk-tales, and technologies, etc., which is essential, according to the headmaster, to be a proper human being. However, he also told me that he found it difficult to carry his project

---

[29] The Borjigin clan is the imperial clan of the Mongols, and every Halh aspires to be Borjigin. In fact, this is the most widely known clan name to all the Mongols. Therefore, those who do not know their clan names usually say they are Borjigin.

further, because talking about Buryat history would be embarrassing to Halh children.

The genealogical principle has also been applied well beyond the school. In 1990, along with political and economic reforms, there was a reshuffling of personnel in the *sum* organizations. As a result, many were dismissed from work. Those dismissed were, according to informants, of bad *udam* (descent), who had bad or polluted (*búzar*) blood. As one local leader explained to me, 'A bad-blooded person is stupid and wouldn't do his work well. On the other hand, those who work well, keeping the collective and private animals well, keeping the pens clean and strong, are of good descent. We look at the parents: like father like son. Today, the weeding-out of *sum* and *negdel* personnel is based on this, only those with good family background are retained.'

People are no longer tolerant of a local case of incest[30] and link it to the wider national problem: that is, the high frequency of mental retardation among the Halh and in some neighbouring *sum*s. The Buryats are confident that as long as they rapidly revive the genealogical principles they will avoid similar tragedies.

Although there has been some kind of relationship between relatives in Dashbalbar and Ulaanbaatar or Choibalsang, the capital of the province, the current interest in kinship is more 'practically' oriented, as elsewhere in Mongolia. The urban–rural relationship in Dashbalbar started quite early, and it has taken a semi-official form. A link has been established between the local administration and about two hundred intellectuals in Ulaanbaatar and Choibalsang. They are called *nutagiin nöhöd* (homeland friends), and their aim is to help develop their homeland by providing technology and information. Their main achievement is the establishment of a local museum. In return, they go to visit their homeland almost every summer for holidays. In addition, there are now perhaps two major modes of interaction between the Buryats in the capital and those in the home villages. One is political, the other economic. This *nutag* kin relationship is being carefully cultivated by both sides. (I will discuss the concept of *nutag* in the wider context in Chapter 6.)

In 1990, newly emerged Buryat democratic politicians went back to their hometown, and chose it as their constituency. This link provided

[30] There is one woman, married to her brother, who has given birth to seven children. The brother is physically handicapped; the sister has been looking after him all the time, and she declined to marry anyone else lest her brother be deserted. She got emotionally involved with her brother, and they live like a married couple. The public used to take a sympathetic attitude to the sibling couple, but not any longer.

them with strong political support. Dashbalbar cast most votes for the democratic parties. Not only did *sum* leaders become Democratic Party members, but their delegate was able to become a member of the State Small Hural. This political support, however, demands reciprocity from the indebted politicians, to render financial support to the home village. But the economic crisis paralysed the politicians. In spring 1991 the newly elected *sum* leader went to the capital and held a meeting with the 'homeland friends'. He managed to make an agreement that teachers come to teach, doctors to heal, and economists to help draft the economic development programme of the *sum* in the following summer. It was expected that more than two dozen of those who promised would come, and the *sum* prepared to provide all facilities. Eventually three turned up. One of them was a senior doctor practising Tibeto-Mongolian medicine. During his one-month working holiday, he provided extensive counselling to the local clinic and patients. He particularly emphasized that the Buryats in Dashbalbar must do all they could to avoid *tsus oirtah*.

The chairman of the Senior Citizens Union in Ulaanbaatar, once a diplomat, tried to make his home village, Dashbalbar, a supplier of meat to his business in Choibalsang, utilizing the two railway lines, one running from the secret uranium town Mardai, the other from Choibalsang to Siberia. He promised to provide employment to the local youth. He further suggested that his relatives solicit support from the strategically located Buryats in Inner Mongolia and the Chita region. The genealogy-reviving movement in Dashbalbar has thus another important motive: to establish wider kinship relations with the Buryats across the international frontier. As I mentioned in the previous chapter, visits between them have become possible. The younger people are eager to know what relatives they have across the borders. To do so, they often nag their elders to count their relatives. These practical concerns may have been the primary reason for the renewed interest in genealogy in Dashbalbar.

In Dashbalbar people are perceiving an increasing danger of hereditary diseases due to their isolation and relatively homogeneous population. Genealogy is a symbolic concern as well as a practical strategy for wider economic and political interaction. This can be contrasted with the situation in Dadal. In Dadal the revival of genealogy is a matter of pride and knowledge, not so much a medicalized nationalist concern, for the population has consciously been engaging in mixed marriage between three ethnic groups, Buryats, Halh, and Hamnigan, in relatively recent decades. This is seen locally to have served as a 'healthy' blending of genes.

Conclusion

Let me briefly bring up the wider implications of the kinship revival in Mongolia which has become such an important element in Mongolian social consciousness.

The 'Soviet' twentieth-century organization confined the Mongols to small, scattered territorial units, which I call 'socialist feudal enclaves'. Aspects of pre-revolutionary culture and social organization were suppressed to achieve a socialist way of life and a socialist Mongolian nation. The artificiality of this system was exposed to the fullest extent when the system itself, which had been brought in by an external power, was removed by that same external power.

Once the previous state system was removed, there immediately emerged severe pasture problems, constrained urban–rural relations, and increased contacts with the outside world. In the resulting chaos the Mongols have to find a cosmos, a belief system, to replace the socialist system. Opposition to Soviet policies, combined with idealization of the past (especially the aristocratic version of history), have led intellectuals to raise an outcry about alleged subnormality and its link with abandoning traditions. In reaction to this real or perceived threat, the Mongols are now trying to revive their genealogies and the *obog* system. This reinvention of tradition and revival of 'national pride' (*ündesnii baharhal*)—the *obog* system—is a manifestation of the Mongols' nationalistic belief that perhaps this could regenerate the Mongols in a new era of renaissance. The Mongolian nationalist discourse suggests one interesting point: a nation is analogous to a human body. If a nation is to survive, the body must be kept healthy and strong.

When the state loses its importance or effectiveness, the *obog* system is urged to take up the responsibility of guaranteeing the survival of the Mongol 'race'. Over the last seven decades the state tried to eliminate kinship/ethnic links in order to achieve a socialist nationhood. Now, with the virtual collapse of the state, the (imaginary) *obog* has become the foundation for building a new nationalist nationhood.[31]

The implication of this return to *obog* is the deconstruction of the socialist Mongolian *ethnos*, and indeed, the defiance of this artificially developed idea of 'nation'. At the same time, by developing the kinship

---

[31] The contrast that I am drawing here, society versus kinship as the basis for a nation-state, is also noted by Spivak (1992) in a study of women 'bondage-slaves' in decolonized India.

system, people are able to make links with kinsmen outside Mongolia, who officially belong to another *ethnos*. This, as I shall point out, challenges the entire system of the nation-state, and more so the legitimacy of dividing Mongol groups into three mutually hostile states. This challenge is perhaps not yet strident, but it is certainly one dimension of what I call Greater Mongolia sentiment.

In fact, every 'ethnic group' wants to revive the ethnic/kinship principle denied by socialism in order to invigorate its own *yastan*. The revival of exogamy, *obog*ism, and the 'archaic' principles, criticized and suppressed so much under Marxist evolutionary principles, now serve a national revival, and an economic survival based on a selectionist competitive mechanism of inclusion and exclusion.

My study should bring out one theoretical question concerning kinship as a symbolic system, as Lévi-Strauss (1969) suggests. A dualistic division of the social world into wife-givers and wife-takers can be projected on to the whole cosmos. Although I have not systematically described Mongolian kinship, the reader will not fail to discern that the Mongol kinship organization has undergone a complete transformation. This is reflected in the difference between the ideal form of kinship (remaining in memory) and the actual practice. Kinship ideology does not mean that people necessarily practise it, but the underlying pattern is such that this ideology may, under special circumstances, be appreciated and lived up to. As this chapter shows, the difference may even be of biological significance. More importantly, this ideology can be used on the political level in relation to states and nations, as we shall explore in the following chapter.

5

The Discourse of Race in Mongolia

Introduction

The crisis now perceived by the Mongols is the danger that they might be too feeble to defend themselves in this hostile world, and that the Mongols as a nation will not be able to reproduce and perpetuate themselves as a result of prevalent inbreeding. Inbreeding is largely seen as a result of forgetting the age-old rules which have been subjected to obliteration in the striving towards the different social relations required by socialist construction. Various strategies to combat this problem have been formulated, and, as described earlier, one of the most important is a call for a return to exogamy. However, while they feel their nation is weakened by inbreeding, the Mongols also see a problem with out-breeding. It is felt that Mongolian culture and 'blood' are subject to too much foreign 'pollution', and the loss of Mongol nationhood is apocalyptically heralded unless this process is halted. What we see here is a classic contradiction. However, the now proposed out-marriage is no longer aimed at breeding with people too distant; the ideal partners are still people within the state—that is, Mongolian citizens who are not classified as foreigners. Out-breeding must be controlled, otherwise pure Mongolness may be diluted.

Thus a national endogamy is now being undertaken to preserve the 'purity' of the gene pool (*udamiin sang*). It is in this context that the concept of blood (*tsus*) becomes crucial. As we have seen, this is a curious combination of the traditional metaphors of bone and flesh with modern biological concepts. There are a number of issues entailed in this concern: preservation of pure Mongol blood, and hence the preservation of the Mongolian nation and its independence; the question of the Russians, Chinese, and 'Mongols' in Russia and China, as well as the relationships of women with both Mongol and foreign men. The idea of a national crisis is therefore closely related to the Mongols' unenviable geo-political location, and is also a conscious effort to strengthen national identity. However, what is thought most dangerous are those marginal peoples who consider themselves as Mongols.

To put this new idea in context, let me return to two key concepts: pan-Mongolism (*narmai Mongoliin üzel*) and Halh-centrism (*Halh töviin üzel*). Pan-Mongolism has its roots in the idea that all Mongol-speaking people were once united under a paramount leader who established the largest land empire the world had ever seen. Pan-Mongolism, as the first modern Mongolian national consciousness, developed around the turn of this century. It became a powerful call for all Mongols to unite and create a Mongol nation-state, a direct response to the great surge of nationalism throughout the world. But pan-Mongolism did not succeed, due to strong Russian and Chinese objections. As I noted in Chapter 2, contemporary Mongols have long ceased to harbour this political ideal. The current aspiration may well be more accurately expressed as Greater Mongolia sentiment, whereby Mongols of the world could communicate with each other culturally and economically across the political boundaries that separate them. However, any culturally expressed Greater Mongolia sentiment is still met with strong suspicions from three states: Russia, Mongolia, and China.

Halh-centrism is a concept which I define as the pride of the Halh as the 'guardian nation' in independent Mongolia *vis-à-vis* other Mongol groups. This concept was nurtured during the socialist period, when the identity of Mongolia was closely founded on one group, the Halh; other Mongol groups within the Mongolian territory were supposed to be assimilated to the Halh. Nationalism-cum-Halh-centrism, until recently, was an effort to guarantee Mongolia's hard-won sovereignty and independence from China with the help of the fraternal Soviet Union. Pan-Mongolism, or even the moderate Greater Mongolia sentiment expressed by Mongols who have fallen outside this political Mongolian domain, is seen as undermining the sovereignty and independence of Mongolia, largely because of the pronounced hostility shown by the Russians and the Chinese.

With the decline of Russian power in the late 1980s, Mongolia lost a protector, albeit an exploitative one. The Mongols are now more exposed to an ultimate enemy, physically similar to them, yet of completely different civilization, rich, populous, and indeed the historical supplier of wealth to the Mongols. Should Mongolia be occupied by China, they fear, Sinicization would be thorough and rapid. The overdependence on Soviet Russia has, however, led to an internal

Russification, which many Mongols also resist. The anti-Communist revolution in 1989–90 was also an anti-Soviet revolution. The new nationalism in Mongolia is thus a movement to revive Mongol identity, a 'renaissance' (*sergen mandal*) which includes several cultural features such as the cult of Chinggis Khan, reviving the Mongol script. Although this is basically a reaction to Soviet socialism, this revival of Mongol tradition on the part of the Mongol nation dominated by the Halh ironically bridges the gap between them and other Mongols, especially the Inner Mongols who have never given up their traditional Mongol identity. The democratic revolution thus unleashed a tremendous social force which formerly had been suppressed. The resurgence of 'ethnic' identities that do not correspond to the Halh Mongolian national image, and the influx of Inner Mongols when borders were partially opened in 1989, were felt by many to undermine greatly the ideological foundation of the Mongolian state. The perceived threat is thus a loss of independence not only from within, but also from without.

We are thus dealing with an attitude from the centre: Halh-centrism to the periphery. I therefore reverse other approaches, which take the Mongols as the periphery of either China or Russia, and suggest that there are now two peripheral peoples, Buryats and Inner Mongols, peripheral to both Mongolia and Russia or Mongolia and China respectively. Interestingly, both these groups have members inside Mongolia, either immigrants or refugees. There are also what are usually called *erliiz*: progeny of mixed parents, Mongols with Chinese or Russians, etc. The reason that I put the *erliiz* people living in Mongolia and the Inner and Buryat Mongols in the same category is that the latter two are indeed perceived by the Halh to be culturally, and even biologically, assimilated by the Chinese or Russians. Some Mongols explicitly call Inner Mongols *Hyatadiin erliiz* (Chinese half-breeds) and Buryat Mongols *Orosiin erliiz* (Russian half-breeds) (see Chapter 6). Despite the difference that the latter two live outside Mongolia, while the former (*erliiz*) share the same language, territory, and political culture with the 'pure Mongols', they all fall outside the Halh concept of 'purity'.

In this chapter I discuss the concept of *erliiz* and how it has become politically stigmatized. I suggest that twentieth-century geo-politics in Inner Asia has nurtured a political culture in Mongolia such that it has become 'politically correct' to denigrate *erliiz* so as to demonstrate one's genuine 'Mongol' identity. *Erliiz* is thus the 'other' of Mongol (see Chapter 6).

Erliiz, *the Threshold People*

Let us try to find a theoretical frame for the categories of people in Mongolia. The multitude of relationships in Mongolia must be set against Halh-centrism. Mongolia is no longer a periphery of Russia or China, but itself a centre, albeit not a very powerful one. However, certain categories of people are what Victor Turner (1979) calls 'inter-structural' human beings, or threshold people; they are betwixt and between two fixed points or 'states'. Turner's theory, although originally applied to *rites de passage*, a ritual situation, could be equally applied to our case. Let us examine Turner's theory of this marginal man, without going into its other implications.

'State', here, means a stable one, that is either 'pure' Mongolian or pure Chinese or pure Russian. 'State' refers to any type of stable or recurrent condition that is culturally recognized. To be in transit from one state to another is to be in 'a state of transition'. The 'transition' is 'a process, a becoming, and in the case of *rites de passage* even a transformation' (Turner 1979: 234). According to Turner, in this liminal period, the subject of passage is structurally 'invisible'. A society's secular definitions do not allow for the existence of a not-boy-not-man. They are 'structurally indefinable "transitional-beings, or liminal persona"'. Turner also points out that the liminal person is defined by a name and by a set of symbols. In our case, we may say, these are *erliiz*. They are given a special term, and put into a special classificatory category, neither Mongol nor Chinese nor Russian. Conversely, they could be labelled either 'Mongol' or 'Chinese' or 'Russian', depending on the situation and circumstances. This is to say that their identity is ambig-uous. Moreover, what is unclear and contradictory tends to be regarded as 'ritually' unclean. Therefore, biological or cultural non-conformists may be regarded as *erliiz*, against whom society usually makes a rather 'legitimate' discrimination (Douglas 1966).

Our case of *erliiz* is surprisingly similar to the situation in Japan. Ohnuki-Tierney (1987), in a study of classification of people in Japan, reveals how the concepts of purity and danger shape the Japanese way of thinking. Total strangers/foreigners are thought to possess some power; they are to be kept out, but admired and emulated. They are stranger-deities, as it were, worthy of 'emulation' but at the same time 'threaten-ing' (1987: 146). In addition to these stranger-deities, there are also various groups of people who do not fall into this scheme of classifica-tion. They are 'marginals—neither insiders nor outsiders'. The intensity of Japanese discrimination against marginals is evident in the following passage:

The Japanese attitude towards marginals is at best ambivalent and usually down-right negative. Included among the marginals are the Japanese who were born or raised in foreign countries, such as Japanese Americans. They are supposedly Japanese, and yet they are regarded as falling short of a full-fledged Japanese identity because their upbringing and behaviour show departures from those of the 'fully Japanese'. A recent addition to the category of marginals are the children of Japanese parents whose work required them to raise their children overseas. They are derogatively labelled *han-japa* (half-Japanese,...), and they are clearly marked as such. All people who lie 'betwixt and between' in the conceptual scheme of the Japanese meet with prejudice and discrimination. (Ohnuki-Tierney 1987: 147–8)

The Mongols living in China and Russia share an analogous common experience: their loyalty is not always trusted. The Chinese would never fully trust the Inner Mongols, even though Mongolian history has been incorporated into the Chinese historical and symbolic framework (Mongols are regarded as offshoots of the Han, and Chinggis Khan is a Chinese national hero). Nor do the Russians trust the Buryats, as mentioned. These two Mongol peoples are not accepted by the Halh either. Inner Mongols (especially the Tsahar) are associated with the Manchu army banner system, which constituted the Manchu imperial force.[1] The Buryat Mongols were also organized into Cossack regiments serving the Russian state. Both groups of Mongols are typical interstructural beings. However, these interstructural images *vis-à-vis* Chinese and Russians have been added to by a new interstructural position *vis-à-vis* the Halh. I will discuss the Inner Mongolian case in the next chapter.

[1] The hatred of the Halh for the Inner Mongols is perpetuated by interpretations of history, especially the involvement of the Tsahar Mongols in both Baron Ungern von Sternberg's army (Alioshin 1941: 219) and the Chinese occupation army in Mongolia. Many units of the Chinese occupation army in Outer Mongolia in 1919–20 were composed of Tsahar Mongols. The Mongolian anti-Chinese revolution was more an anti-Tsahar revolution: 'The Chakhars started looting. They broke down trunks, stabbed with knives and awls, cut off [their] ears, drove wooden spikes under [people's] nails, and cut off [their] fingers. The Mongols hid their girls. Then they (i.e. the Mongols) locked their girls in those trunks. The Chakhars abducted their (i.e. the Mongols') women and girls ....The Khal-kha–Mongolian chancellery moved their subject army and beat (the Chakhars)' (Poppe 1978: 40). During the debates over the name of the Constitution at the second Congress in late 1991 (see Ch. 7), many Mongols objected to the term *tsaaz*, a name proposed by the parliament. A poster pasted near the State Department Store showed a man enslaving a Mongol hero, Chinggunjav, the rebel against the Manchu in the mid-eighteenth century. The oppressor was named Manchu and Tsahar!

The term *erliiz* is an intriguing one. We cannot find it in the older dictionaries, but modern dictionaries published after the 1950s usually contain the word, without giving an etymology. So we do not know if it is Mongolian or Chinese in origin. Related to *erliiz* is *hurliiz*. A *hurliiz* refers to one born of an *erliiz*. I presume that it could be a Mongolian term, or at least coined according to a Mongolian word-forming principle (we know that great grandfather is called *elents*, and the generation above him is called *hulants*; note the similarity in the word formation, both using the *e* and *hu*). Another explanation is that the word may have derived from the term *ers* (or *eresu* in classical Mongolian spelling) which means neuter in Mongolian phonetics. We know of two different occasions when this term would be used in 'traditional' Mongolia. One is to refer to a hermaphrodite, the other to refer to an offspring born of a cross between a domestic dog/cat and a wild one. Most interestingly, the northern Chinese for hermaphrodite is *er yi zi*, which resembles closely the Mongolian *erliiz*.

Erliiz-ness, as a quality in animals, is something that the Mongols have long desired; herdsmen normally exchange breed animals to improve the animal stock. It could not only give them animals of greater economic value, but the *erliiz* was also regarded as more powerful than the indigenous animals. However, the practice of cross-breeding very different breeds has been only a recent phenomenon, possibly influenced either by the Russians or the Japanese. Modern Mongols might find it natural to employ the term *erliiz* to refer to this scientific practice. Today, indigenous animals are regarded as more capable of standing the severe Mongol climate.

However, on no occasion did the Mongols use the term *erliiz* to refer to any human beings except hermaphrodites. It is therefore interesting to note that Tsevel's authoritative dictionary (1963) gives two meanings to the item *erliiz*: 1. offspring of parents of two different national or ethnic (*ündesten yastan*) backgrounds, 2. a cross-bred animal. Tsevel's definitions are certainly a new departure from the earlier Mongol usage. Tsevel's definition implies that even a marriage between a Halh and a Dürbet would result in an *erliiz*, for Halh and Dürbet are officially *yastan* in Mongolia. Inter-ethnic marriage certainly existed before, but only recently have people become anxious about it. Such an *erliiz* is not only despised, but has recently been excluded from the Mongol community.

The Mongols' traditional marital practice, as noted, is based on the practice of exogamy; and exogamy in reality is aimed to produce hybrids.

But there is a crucial difference between the present and the past: *erliiz* today refers to anybody only one of whose biological parents is 'Mongol'. In the past, however, an *erliiz*-like concept would have been applied only to those people whose paternal 'bone' was foreign.

In medieval Mongolia, in order to preserve bone purity, people of suspicious births were kept away from the clan and allowed to form a different lineage. According to the *Secret History*, Bodonchar caught a pregnant woman from the Jarchiud clan and married her. Because the first son was a son of *jad* (foreign), he was given the name *Jadiradai*, and became the ancestor of the Jadaran clan, while the legitimate sons of Bodonchar formed the Borjigin clan (*Secret History*, section 40). With this concept, the Mongols intermarried with different stocks of people, yet without breaking up the tribehood or nationhood. What is implied here is that the group which should be excluded is the foreign 'bone', rather than foreign 'flesh'.

Like a *jad* who must not be accommodated in a clan, in the modern Mongolian nation-state, people of foreign descent (either maternal or paternal),[2] especially on account of their political background, are thought to be dangerous to the sovereignty of the nation. *Erliiz* thus becomes a problem to the modern Mongolian nation-state—an ideologically patrilineal society—which, however, has no mechanism to sideline a suspiciously born child as the earlier Mongols did, because the Mongol community has been expanded to its maximum limit—the nation-state.

Today, *erliiz* connotes not merely something biological, but also a mentality, specifically related to the cultural transformation of the socialist Mongolian period. The evaluation of the current transitional stage is determined by the mood of the society and its current ideology. It is useful to note how the Mongols now regard those names which were once a proud symbol of the transition from feudalism to socialism, from Mongol to Soviet. We can identify very easily several name-labels: *Biyeiin tamir sportin horoo* (Sports Association), *yasli tsetserlegiin kombinat* (kindergarten), *ofitseruudin ordon* (officers' palace), etc. All these words are now criticized as typical examples of *erliiz* concepts, for they are combinations of Mongolian and Russian words. Thus there is the concept of *erliiz*

---

[2] Although Mongols do not yet dare to apply this principle to denounce Chinggis Khan, we have a prominent Western scholar, who, unconsciously thinking in terms of the European notion of consanguinity, observed meticulously the racial impurity of Chinggis Khan: 'It is interesting to note that even Chinggis Khan was not a pure Mongol, but had Turkic blood (his mother was from a Turkic tribe) and seems to have spoken the Turkic language better than Mongol' (Eberhard 1982: 40).

setgelgee (bastard mentality), as opposed to *Mongol setgelgee* (Mongol mentality) or *Mongol Uhaan* (Mongol Idea). *Mongol Uhaan* is probably a new concept in opposition to *Sinjleh Uhaan* (science), and the adherents of the notion of *Mongol Uhaan* often tend to be ultra-conservative. The 'bastard mentality' is seen as one learned from the Russians in particular. For example, the Mongols say that they did not originally drink alcohol, and that the Russians taught them to get drunk. Mongols no longer regard alcohol as *ideenii deej* (gem of food), something usually cherished and used more often on ritual occasions than for mere daily consumption. They now insist that they did not shake hands, but exchanged ritual scarves (*hadag*) or snuff bottles. Nor did they clap hands to cheer or show appreciation of a speech or performance, but called out *Hurui, Hurui.* The Mongols claim never to have quarrelled among themselves; the Russians taught them to do so. As a result, the Mongols have become the most hot- and bad-tempered people in the world, it is said. Like the Russians, they now kill people as they would animals. Menacing phrases now come out of Mongolian mouths constantly, like *Alnaa shu* (I will kill you), in contrast to the 'traditional' Mongolian character, which is characterized as *uuzuu taivan* (relaxed and peaceful).

Even conflicts between political parties have been explicitly described by ordinary observers as the product of the '*erliiz* mentality', for this is not a Mongolian habit but a copy of the Russians. The Mongols would never talk of *il tod* (*glasnost*) or *ilen dalangui* (openly), but would say: *honi alabch hoton dotroo; hodood hagarabch togoon dotroo* (in the pen if a sheep must be slaughtered; in the pot if intestines must be broken). The moral is: keep your skeleton in the cupboard. *Glasnost*, an ideology of political transparency, is not altogether appreciated in Mongolia. Mongols emphasize social harmony. Openness, or *il tod* for that matter, suggests disagreements and quarrels. As a result of this *erliiz* manner, the most common expressions today are said to be: *Bitgii hudlaa yaraad bai* (Don't you always tell lies!) or *Bitgii hutsa chi* (Don't you bark!).

Erliiz, then, has become a concept in contrast to something 'pure', a social memory of an idealized past. It seems to denote the negative side of Mongolian society; anything 'bad' is *erliiz*.

Marriage Strategies: Mongol Men and Foreign Women

Erliiz, as shown above, is both a biological and a social concept; it denotes the result of biological and social cross-breeding. It is therefore appropriate to examine Mongolian marriage strategies. Here let me reiterate some of the basic principles of Mongolian kinship.³

The traditional Mongolian concept of kinship during the Buddhist period (seventeenth to early twentieth centuries) was a patrilineal system based on genealogical reckoning. The *obog*s, the earlier clans, ceased to exist as political organizations, and were scattered all over Mongolia. The *obog* was no longer a corporate group. It became a classification of relatives, largely for the purposes of exogamy (Szynkiewicz 1975, 1977). As an ideal, the *obog* was nine generations deep, within which people were regarded as kin and were prohibited from marriage. Non-kin were called *hari*, and they were eligible for marriage. As is common in Asia, the Mongols distinguished between paternal links (using the metaphor 'bone') and maternal links (flesh). The 'bone' (*yas*) broke, as it were, after nine generations. However, the 'bone' of the Golden Family, or Chinggisids, was not subject to this principle, but went on multiplying over time unbroken.

One may say that this principle of 'bone' and 'flesh' has existed at all times in Mongol history, varying only in the degree to which it is taken into account in practical kinship relations. It creates a most salient feature of the Mongolian kinship system: generalized exchange. Marriage with women of the Father's Sister's Daughter category was forbidden, while marriage with the Mother's Brother's Daughter category was possible and encouraged. There is an implicit status difference between wife-giving and wife-taking lineages; the *nagats* category (Mother's Father or Brother) is senior in relation to the individual, while the *zee* category (Father's Sister's Son or Sister's Son) is seen as junior to the individual. This 'generalized exchange' was extensively used by the Mongols and neighbouring peoples to form alliances, and continued to be used in the Soviet period.

Under such a system, women passed between patrilineal groups. The transference of a woman from one to another involved property—that is, bride-wealth and dowry. In principle, the amount of the dowry was proportional to that of the bride-wealth (Sugita 1980: 59). A woman had a considerable degree of independence, as she controlled her own property. This put women and men on a more or less equal economic level, and women had considerable power in deciding the domestic

³ There are a number of works available in English concerning Mongolian kinship. See Aberle (1953), Vreeland (1957), Bacon (1958), Krader (1963), Pao (1964), Jagchid and Hyer (1979), Szynkiewicz (1975, 1977, 1987*b*), Humphrey (1983), etc.

budget. Through manipulating such property relations, the woman's patrilineal group maintained symbolic and real superiority in the marriage alliance (see Humphrey 1992*b*).

This process has been predictable in general terms; but now let us think, on the political and kinship level, about the identification of one particular symbolic mechanism of ethnic relationships in this region. Traditionally there was a pattern which related the *Taiji* and the *Tabnang*. *Taiji* means prince and *Tabnang* is a family or lineage married to the *Taiji* as 'son-in-law' or wife-taker. This terminology is confirmed from at least the thirteenth century (Jagchid and Hyer 1979). The Mongol–Manchu marriage relationship and Mongol–Russian marriage relationship have both, at various times, constituted fragments of what Lévi-Strauss calls 'generalized exchange'. The Mongol élites married either Manchu women or Russian women, and this, through repetition of alliances, created Leach's pattern of 'matrilateral cross-cousin marriage' (1961).

I argue that such a politicized marriage alliance model has been used symbolically and strategically in the region in such a way as to maintain internal colonialism. In his postulation of a model for national development, Hechter (1975) rejects the diffusionist theory which holds the periphery to be isolated from the core and suggests that the industrialization process will eventually swallow the periphery, thus creating homogeneity. Hechter sees the periphery as a deliberate creation by the core. Peripheral status is institutionalized, a stratification system which he calls a 'cultural division of labour'. This structure corresponds to the Mongolian situation.

We could divide the pre-revolutionary Mongolian male population into three major classes. About one-third of the male adults were monks, who took vows of celibacy. Then there were the ordinary citizens. Thirdly, there were nobles, the hereditary rulers, albeit nominal, many of whom preferred not to marry Mongolian women, but tended to marry women of the Manchu royal family. 'Marriage exchange' in this case was conducted between Mongolian hereditary princes and Manchu royal families; the women exchanged were primarily women of these families. We may say that this was not a generalized exchange, but a 'restricted exchange'—that is, direct exchange of a woman for a woman—for Mongol noble women also married into the lower echelons of Manchu royal families. In reality, the Mongols were in debt to the Manchu, not for women's value, but for the royal grace. The Manchu and the Mongols formed marriage alliances, such that, as far as the Manchu were con-

cerned, their women tied the Mongolian princes to the Manchu royal
family, and the Manchu became the 'mother's brothers' of the Mongols.
As the colonial power, they could control the wife-taking Mongols. The
Mongol princes, on the other hand, needed royal support to enhance
their own prestige. Interestingly, it seems that although the practice was
restricted exchange, in reality, because of this status difference, the
reverse flow of Mongol women was invisible.

This situation can be explained by Lévi-Strauss's (1969) theory of
hypogamy (marrying up) and hypergamy (marrying down) (see also
Leach 1954 and 1961). In his theory of harmonic/disharmonic regimes,
Lévi-Strauss asserts that hypogamy—the Mongols marrying high-status
Manchu women—is a sign of instability within a patrilineal system; it
is a structural phenomenon which represents the tension between
paternal and maternal lines. The Mongols, in effect, by marrying Manchu and Russian women have become *Tabnang*, or sons-in-law, of the
Manchu or Russians. In such a hypogamous system Manchu women
played a pivotal role in relations with their own higher-status group.
This pattern of marriage finds a version in modern Mongolia: the
Communist male élites married Russian women (see Humphrey 1983:
34–8 for analogous marriages among Buryats in Russia). Such a marriage, although sometimes a deliberate controlling mechanism initiated
by the wife-givers, was also favoured by the Mongol élites because it
satisfied their snobbery and also gave them more power. We have a
typical case in the late Mongolian prime minister Tsedenbal, who married a Russian wife.

Tsedenbal was widely known as a henpecked husband (*tolgoi deeree
avgaigaa zalsan*—'He courteously invited his wife to [sit on] his head',
people say) (see Fig. 5.1). The use of the term *avgai* for 'wife' is
interesting, for it is a respectful term, which replaced the traditional
'contemptuous' terms *ehner*, *gergii*, or even *hüühen*, girl or prostitute.[4] In
fact, the earlier terms were not so much disparaging as affectionately
modest and self-deprecating. The use of *avgai* perhaps reflects a new
understanding of an independent existence for the wife.

Be this as it may, Tsedenbal's Russian wife, Anastasya Tsedenbal-
Filatova, was the *de facto* behind-the-scenes boss of the Mongolian
Secret Service (she was awarded the title 'Honoured Chekist'[5] by the

[4] 'See Rinchen (1968) for the transformation of *hüühen* from meaning girl or daughter to
prostitute during the Buddhist period.
[5] The term 'Chekist' comes from Cheka, the initials of the security organization that
preceded the KGB.

С. Цогтбаяр «Тоглоом»

FIGURE 5.1. 'Toy', Tsedenbal 'covered' by his Russian wife. Drawing
by S. Tsogtbayar, *Ardchilal*, 1–10 May 1990.

Interior Ministry on her sixtieth birthday). It is said that Tsedenbal was
afraid of his wife, and he certainly tried every means to soften her with
the highest state medals. Filatova emerged as an 'iron lady' who did not
like being called 'the wife of Tsedenbal'. She was awarded her own
fiefdom, becoming chairwoman of the Children's Fund in 1973. From
this base she gradually became more powerful, and in the end her power
exceeded even that of her alcoholic husband. She is widely held to have
controlled the entire party and government, as well as the cultural life of
the Mongols.

Filatova's dominance and abuse of power became one of the main
reasons for anti-Dürbet and anti-Russian sentiment in Mongolia in the
1970s and early 1980s. Gorbachev was said to be concerned about the
role Filatova was playing; he called her 'queen' (of Mongolia), and he was
instrumental, it is thought, in removing Tsedenbal from the Mongolian

leadership in 1984. Filatova's continued abuse of power jeopardized Soviet–Mongol friendship.[6]

Thus, one might even say that Soviet control of the Mongols was through women as well as by the army. The situation in the 1930s was vividly described in a book originally written in 1939 by a Mongolian officer called Byamba, who defected to the Japanese army (Byamba 1991). Scholars in Mongolia are dubious about the value of Byamba's book, suggesting that it might represent a Japanese intelligence stratagem to sow discord amongst Mongol soldiers or induce them to rebel against Soviet Communist domination. Nevertheless, the picture of Mongolian political life in the 1930s is strikingly accurate, and more interestingly, Byamba even then argued like a nationalist anxious about the racial purity of the Mongols.[7] According to Byamba, almost everyone who visited Russia or studied there came back with a Russian wife. 'There were more and more people with Russian wives. There appeared people who urged their Mongolian wives to serve them like Russian women. Some sent their Mongol wives to visit Russian cities, and they came back to offer sugared black tea to Mongols as a sign of having visited the Soviet Union' (1991: 17). Later, Choibalsang was said to have been responsible for trying to Russify Mongol women. He encouraged them to dance and to apply cosmetic oil to their faces day and night, so as to look civilized.

I was told that during the socialist era marrying Russian women became more than a fashion, as the practice was supported by the Mongolian state. Those with Russian wives were given priority in housing allocation. A Mongolian who married a Russian wife did not have to work in the countryside. He could stay in the city and be given a flat.

What role did the children of such marriages play in Mongolian society during the period of Soviet domination? I do not have statistical data to show. But it seems that they were more Russian than Mongol.

---

[6] Mongols' criticism of Tsedenbal and Filatova has ebbed away in recent years. A special fund has been set up to protect and study Tsedenbal's heritage. It has been discovered that after 1984, when Tsedenbal was dismissed, the Mongolian state did not pay any pension to the Tsedenbal family until 1995. The government newspaper *Ardiin Erh* (27 Apr. 1995) blamed the extremism of the early 1990s for the impropriety accorded the former Mongolian leader and first lady. It reported that Filatova, in her capacity as director of the Children's Fund of Mongolia, had built over 300 kindergartens throughout the country, as well as the international children's 'Friendship' summer camp, the children's palace, and the wedding hall.

[7] This documentation of Byamba is discussed in detail by Coox (1985: 160–73) in his monumental study of the Soviet–Mongolian–Japanese military conflict at Nomonhan in 1939.

Normally they received a Russian education, and today few of them can speak Mongolian. Tsedenbal's children have Russian citizenship, rather than Mongolian. The mothers' families usually facilitated their stay in the Soviet Union, and as their fathers were usually politically powerful, they were able to reside permanently in the Soviet Union. Because they were so thoroughly Russified, despite the patrilineal principle of the Mongols, many voluntarily gave up their Mongolness. Undoubtedly, there are also many who have remained in Mongolia. Under such circumstances, they did not suffer any discrimination; instead, they represented a new model, indeed the new generation of Mongols the nation was striving to achieve.[8]

To sum up, with the end of Manchu period (during which Mongol nobles married Manchu princesses), the Mongol élite turned its eyes towards the new source of power; Russian women were welcomed in the Soviet period. However, although Mongol males were forming unions with foreign women, Mongol women's relations with foreign men were strongly disliked by men; and even more so today.

Women, Erliiz, *and Mongolian Nationalism*

Now, 36 per cent of the entire Mongolian population is reported to be *erliiz*, of which 31 per cent is Chinese *erliiz* (Batnairamdal 1991). It is calculated that in the capital Ulaanbaatar alone there are 85,000 Chinese *erliiz*. The rest are concentrated in such places as Hovd, Zavhan, and Selenge *aimag*s and Darhan and Zuunharaa cities. These numbers must not be dismissed as pure fabrication; although it is impossible to calculate the exact numbers of people with non-Mongol ancestry, they are an important social reality.

The grounds on which the Mongols are apprehensive of the *erliiz* must be explained first in the context of male–female relationships, and second in the context of the 'international order' between the three peoples: Russians, Mongols, and Chinese. These two contexts are not as far apart as they might seem; as mentioned, marriage strategies have long been part of Inner Asian politics.

The era of nationalism at the beginning of this century saw marriage become a controversial issue for the first time. One of the complaints in

---

[8] See Isaacs (1989: 65–6) for a discussion of the legacy of colonial racial mixing and the fate of children of mixed unions.

the petition sent by Mongolian representatives to the Russian emperor for support of Mongolian independence in 1911 was that the Manchu government had decided to allow the Chinese to marry Mongol women: 'Originally, marriage between Mongols and Chinese was forbidden; but as a result of the "New Policy", it was declared last year that such marriages have been approved. This is not only breaking the old laws but it is an example of the wicked intentions of (the Chinese). How can we Mongols submit to this ignorant kind of government?' (Onon and Pritchatt 1989: 12). The Mongolian prime minister Tserendorj, in the 1920s, warned again: 'Our girls are greedy for sex and money, and they are increasingly having sex with foreigners. But women are the mothers of our nation. In the future I am afraid our descent will degenerate' (Batnairamdal 1991).

Why did Mongolian women bear the brunt of the blame for marrying foreigners? They continue to be scolded by men today, as will be discussed shortly. This phenomenon can only be explained by women's role in the nation-state. Athias and Yuval-Davis suggest that there are five major ways in which women are involved in ethnic and national processes:

(a) as biological reproducers of members of ethnic collectives;
(b) as reproducers of members of ethnic collectives;
(c) as participating centrally in the ideological reproduction of the collectivity and as transmitters of its culture;
(d) as signifiers of ethnic/national differences—as a focus and symbol in ideological discourses used in the construction, reproduction and transformation of ethnic/national categories;
(e) as participants in national, economic, political and military struggles.

(quoted in Walby 1992: 82)

I have already shown in the previous chapter that Mongolia has been encouraging women to produce as many children as possible for the good of the nation. Women, as the 'mothers' of the Mongol nation, then, shoulder a responsibility to perpetuate the Mongol nation, its culture, etc. Women would be blamed for their failure to fulfil these roles, especially should they be used to reproduce members of other nations or ethnicity, as the concern of the Mongol élites clearly demonstrates.

Although 'traditionally' women passed between groups of men in Mongolia, at least for the last two hundred years this system has ceased to function among ordinary people. In fact, women, should we exaggerate a little bit, were not marriage partners at all in Mongolia itself. I will argue this by discussing the social implications of a topic mentioned in the previous chapter. The culmination of Buddhism in the nineteenth century coincided with the arrival of Chinese merchants in large numbers (Sanjdorj 1980). The fact that one-third of Mongolian males were lamas left many women unmarried. It is true that lamas had sexual liaisons, and that many lived a more or less normal family life. Nevertheless, the large numbers of lamas fundamentally altered Mongolian social life. A substantial proportion of Mongol men renounced their sexual and reproductive rights to their own women, who in turn had to find other partners. The single Chinese males who came to Mongolia on trade missions provided excellent alternatives. The Manchu did not allow the Chinese merchants to take their wives to Mongolia, to ensure that they eventually returned home. On the other hand, they were strictly forbidden to take Mongolian women for wives, lest they settle down. However, such restrictions did not stop husbandless Mongol women and wifeless Chinese men from establishing informal sexual liaisons. So we see a large number of lamas and Chinese merchants having sexual relationships with Mongolian women, yet the children thus born having no patrilineal identification. The children of the merchants did not go back to China, but were raised by single mothers. As a result, in regions near monasteries and Chinese trading centres, kinship norms were widely disturbed by early this century.

At the beginning of the twentieth century when there were about 600,000 Mongols, there were also some 75,000 traders, 15,000 Chinese workers and craftsmen, and 5,000 Chinese agricultural labourers. The Chinese community was predominantly male and of long standing (Sanders 1987: 47). Many of the Chinese subsequently left Mongolia after the revolution, leaving behind their progeny who had been reared by Mongol mothers.

Ideology could sometimes blur nationalist principles. Ideological enemies, even if they were Mongols, were often equated with national enemies. Thus, in the 1930s, the Chinese community served another purpose; it established relationships with the womenfolk of the large number of political prisoners during the Stalinist purges. The women had no alternative, for their properties were confiscated, and no other Mongols were allowed to approach them or to help them. According to Byamba, the Interior Ministry issued the following order: 'Cut off all relations with the family members of MPR's soldiers, clerks, and other official personnel now punished as anti-revolutionary! It is forbidden to support those family members whose properties are confiscated'

(Byamba 1991: 30). Byamba reported that several hundred families were thrown on to the streets. Information about those people who were deprived of property, their whereabouts, and how they were living was made unavailable to Mongols. '(The dispossessed) under pressure of life, approached our most hated Chinese traders and vegetable farm-ers....These people who lost their citizen's rights found it difficult to live further. I will tell you one sorrowful thing: the wife of the leader of the Army Headquarters, colonel general Maljin, after losing her hus-band's life, has recently married a Chinese trader. I can tell many more such stories' (ibid.).

The statistics on *erliiz* mentioned at the beginning of this section indicate the alarm of Mongols at the level of hybridity. The very attempt to keep track of the number of such Chinese *erliiz*, whether as a reality or a fabrication, is none the less a reflection of the current concern. Today, concerns are aired by men, rather than women. Mongol women are blamed for this 'problem'. They are warned off starting relations with wealthy foreign men. Men in 1990–3 would resentfully say that Mon-golia is now so rich that those foreign 'experts' are most eager to stay to enjoy not only Mongolian meat, but also Mongolian women, two pro-ducts Mongolia is supposedly famous for. It seems that Mongol men are convinced that Mongol women are now known to foreigners as *zeer* (antelopes), which suggests that foreigners come to Mongolia not only on safari, but also to hunt for women game.

Earlier I referred to Lévi-Strauss and the 'exchange' of high-ranking women, who come into the nation from outside to serve as reproducers of the body politic. In this context, it is strangely apt to find that the Mongol imagination today sees Mongolia in the form of a woman lying with her legs open, waiting to be raped (see Fig. 5.2), and envisages the classical Mongol script (which was scrapped under Soviet influence in the 1940s) in the guise of a pregnant woman (see Fig. 5.3). The clever cartoon shown here uses the traditional terminology for the elements of the script, named after parts of the body, in order to make a stunning verbal-visual pun. By invoking this gendered image of Mongolia and the Mongol language, Mongols not only lament the previous Russian con-quest and exploitation, but show a desire to keep Mongolia under 'male' control. Yet they still anxiously envisage a danger of further heterosexual conquest. And here men engage in an uphill battle to protect this femininity by using 'tradition'.

Spivak analyses a novel by Mahasmeta Devi which depicts a map of the newly independent India being covered with the body of a female

МОНГОЛ УХААН ДУТЛАА ГЭЖ ҮҮ?

Монголоо юу... арьсаа юу...

Энэ шуудайн амы нь пээ гээд хоосолчихжээ.

Тэрэнтэй унтсан гэхгүй, монголтой унтсан гэвэл яана.
Зургуудыг Ч. ХИШИГДАВАА

FIGURE 5.2. 'Short of Mongol Idea?': *Top*, 'Selling Mongolia ... or skin?' *Middle*, 'This bag is opened and emptied.' *Bottom*, 'What if they say that they did not sleep with her but with Mongolia?' Drawing by Ch. Hishigdavaa, *Gal Golomt*, no. 1, 26 June 1991.

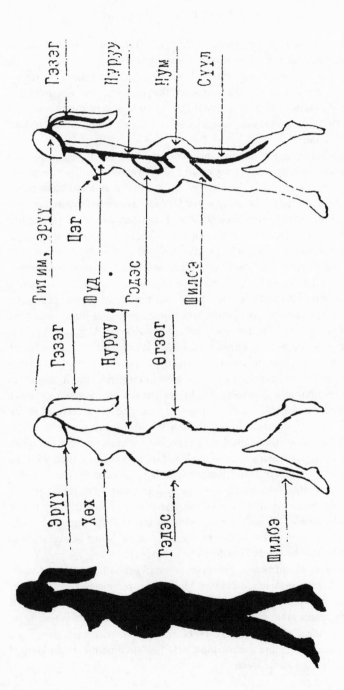

FIGURE 5.3. The classical Mongol script resembling a pregnant woman, using the traditional terminology for the elements of the script, named after parts of the body. Drawing by O. Buuvei, *Urlah Erdem*, no. 5, May 1991.

tribal bonded-labour prostitute (1992: 112). The image implies that in the international political economy a seemingly decolonized India resorts to its own 'internal colonization' (1992: 99). Although the contexts are different, we should not fail to discern that in India and Mongolia, the image of a colony, internal or external, is often imagined and represented (by both the colonizers and colonized) by a female body subject to rape and exploitation.

The ideal male–female relationship of the Mongols has been expressed by the symbolism of *yin–yang* or *arga–bilig*, represented by two joined fish symbols expressing the ideas of inseparability and complementariness. Traditionally, the female gender was associated with domestic space, while males were associated with the outside. However, unlike sedentary societies, in which women were often subordinated, in nomadic Mongolian society women in practice enjoyed a fairly equal status with men, and in terms of labour value they were and are more important. Men were known to be lazy and to be talkers, and women to be doers. This division into 'outside' and 'inside' was transformed into yet another relationship: men became lamas, and women stayed at home providing economic support for the male monk population. Although socialist policies eliminated this formal division of labour, men continue to be associated with 'outside' and social visiting, which often involves drinking alcohol. Women attribute this to Russian influence (the Russians are known as notorious drinkers). Might one suggest that women are more and more disenchanted with Mongolian men and are searching for an alternative, a new image? In popular talk the Mongolian image of men is of parasites who do not produce wealth but squander money on drink. Women compare their image of wealthy foreign 'civilized' men with the 'hopeless' Mongolian men. The attitude is reinforced by the fact that domestic violence seems to have been increasing in recent years in Mongolia. Some Mongol women told me that they would never marry Mongolian men. 'What's wrong with giving my life and body to a foreigner who is at least kind to me, instead of being beaten up and cursed by this bad beastly evil-hearted (Mongol)?'

Jankowiak found similar processes among Huhhotians of Inner Mongolia, where men married Han or Mongolian women, but insisted that Mongolian women should only marry Mongols (1993: 30–59). But recently, more and more city-born Mongolian girls are preferring to marry Chinese men. In the eyes of these women, Chinese men are more 'civilized', more industrious, and less dominating than Mongol men fresh from rural areas.

In Mongolia, such attitudes give rise to sayings about how hopelessly disloyal the Mongol women are (Nergui 1991):

1. *Dagaj yavhad darga saihan; Darlaj baihad danjaad saihan!*
   It is nice to be with a *darga* (leader) if you want to follow anyone; it is nice to go out with a *danjaad* (Chinese merchant) if you want to bully (exploit) anyone.
2. *Oron orni harchuud bayan um; Oldoj baival Oros ch yaah ve?*
   Ordinary people from foreign countries are rich, who cares if he is a Russian as long as one (man) is available?
3. *Balarya gevel Halhtai bai; Bayajya gevel Hyatadtai suu.*
   If you want to suffer bankruptcy, marry a Halh; if you want to get rich, marry a Chinese.

Although I never actually heard women talk in these crude terms, I think that statements like these might well emerge during a quarrel between women and men. As I have explained, in this ideologically patrilineal society, where women are seen as passing between groups of men, there is a particular mentality among women. They do not see themselves as particularly tied to either group, the father's or the husband's. Women's reaction to men's worries is often indifference. While this was a 'merit' in the past, in a nationalist era men now seek to control women's thinking and reorient them, to turn them away from the 'going out' perspective and ensure they remain behind to marry Mongol men.

As we have seen, men have not been very successful in this endeavour. In actuality, marriage choices by women seem to be very much affected by cultural stereotypes; parents too use these stereotypes when searching for a good family for a daughter. On a wider scale, there are stereotypes delineating the men and women of different ethnic groups. To my initial surprise, the Buryat women I knew said that they would in principle prefer to marry Halh men (I was surprised because the Halh in general are held to be lazy and stupid). However, the Buryat women, who themselves are said by the Halh to be 'industrious', are attracted to Halh men's 'gentle nature', which contrasts with the 'dominance' and 'bull-like brutality' of Buryat men. Meanwhile, some Halh women express an interest in marrying Buryat men, for they accept the idea that their own men are lazy, whereas Buryat men are 'active' and 'go-ahead'.

The evaluation of stereotypes may change along with dominant social concerns at particular historical periods. In the present highly urbanized Mongolian society, where parental and male dominance in marriage arrangements no longer obtains, people see that women are 'non-nationalist' and are concerned above all with their individual liveli-hood and interests. It is here that Mongol men feel uncomfortable and incompetent. They thus invoke, or invent, 'disloyal' remarks by women, in the hope of re-subjugating them.

This leads to an interesting contemporary drama of gender relations in Mongolia. From the Mongol male point of view, a struggle is going on between Mongolian and foreign men over Mongolian women. From 1989 a Miss Mongolia contest has been held annually. Many prize-winning beauties have been going out, however, with rich Japanese or Koreans. The 1990 Miss Mongolia, Amarsaihan, married a South Kor-ean businessman. This fact deeply hurt the pride of many Mongolian men. A society for protecting *Saihan Büsgüi* (beautiful women[9]) was subsequently set up. The purpose of the society is, according to some members, to protect the beauties from being encroached on by rich foreigners. In early 1992 a 'Gentleman' contest was held to improve men's image. It is said that there are several clubs which teach men how to dress and how to treat women gently. This is an unprecedented attempt by Mongol men to enhance their standing in 'competition' with foreign males. But many are doubtful about how far this campaign can go, for Mongol men are fatally handicapped in financial resources. It is even suggested by some that there should be a law to prevent Mongol women from marrying foreign men, especially Chinese.

Probably the most dramatic episode was the following: Gantömör, a Congress deputy, suggested during a debate in 1992 in the National Congress that the Constitution should allow a Mongolian man to have two wives, insisting that this was a Mongolian tradition. His suggestion was broadcast on the evening TV and radio programme, and he became the laughing stock of the whole country. However, 21 per cent of the deputies voted for his proposal. So perhaps this was not merely Gantö-mör's idiosyncratic excuse for having two wives. Has it some deeper background? Polygyny is regarded as a better option than prostitution. The Mongols are painfully aware, with the coming of capitalist foreign-ers, that because of the economic crisis, more women will sell their bodies. They are afraid that should the Immigration Law be passed, foreign men would pour into the country and sleep with these women,

---

[9] The phrase should be translated as 'beautiful married women'. *Büs* is a symbol of right and power in Mongolia. A man is called *büstei* (wearing a belt), while a woman loses her belt upon marriage, and becomes *büsgüi* (beltless). The current use of *büsgüi* as equivalent to 'Miss' suggests how mixed up the whole terminology denoting women's marital status has become in Mongolia. See earlier discussion of *ehner*, *hüühen*, etc.

and in a decade, a whole generation would be *erliiz*. The Mongolian 'gene' would be lost for ever, and so, they think, would Mongolian independence (see Fig. 5.4). Polygyny, then, is thought to be the best mechanism to guarantee a pure Mongolia. The suggestion was in the end laughed off, and was considered an insult to Mongolian women. This is, however, a typical case of men using 'tradition' against women, and it is not unique. Laurentin writes on African men's appeal to 'tradition' in order to control women: '[R]emembrance of the good old days is accompanied by nostalgic regret on the part of older men . . . Among young and old alike there is a profoundly anti-feminist spirit which springs from a feeling of impotence upon realizing that women will refuse to return to the state of dependence they knew a century ago' (quoted in Ranger 1983: 257).

These 'traditions' are perhaps not just idiosyncratic ideas held by men that we can easily laugh off. They underlie a basic problem of gender

ГОНШУУЛ №14. 1991.

Тайлбаргүй Ц. БАЯНЗУЛ

FIGURE 5.4. 'Hasn't your immigration law been passed?' A cartoon joke representing Mongol fear of foreign immigrants. Ts. Bayanzul, *Tonshuul*, no. 14, 1991.

relations in the post-socialist 'democratic' countries. We noted earlier that in the socialist period women obtained a number of rights, most notably equal pay and the maternity allowances for many children. Today, the bankrupt state is no longer able to pay them. Single mothers are particularly hard hit by the crisis, as they are the first to lose their jobs; at home what awaits them are numerous children with gaping mouths to be fed. It is these vulnerable women and their children who become beggars or prostitutes in Mongolia. Indeed, it is against this general background that women resort to foreigners' 'mercy', and it is largely for this very reason that they have been blamed. This is a recurring phenomenon, yet the state and men are blind to the root of the problem. Watson (1993) sagaciously observes the rise of masculinism in post-socialist Eastern Europe: 'Indeed, the very uniformity of the Eastern European experience indicates that the re-creation of the gender order in the transition to capitalism is in fact predicated on the rescinding of a range of rights accorded to women under state socialism' (1993: 71). She finds that women are being marginalized in political representation and economic participation. Most dramatic of all is women's subjection under the anti-abortion campaign waged by men; in the words of a member of the Polish Senate: 'We will nationalize those bellies!' (1993: 75)

The Halh 'belly-nationalization' campaign, as it were, is now targeting even Inner Mongols. Inner Mongols, being in China and living amongst Chinese, are naturally, as the Halh would say, becoming more Chinese than Mongol; their 'dubious' claim to be Mongol must be closely guarded, not only to protect Mongolia from possible Chinese sabotage, but also to avoid genetic evolution. In a recent newspaper report on Inner Mongols claiming asylum or doing business in Mongolia, discussants were alarmed and annoyed at the phenomenon that more Halh women have been marrying Inner Mongols. They called for an urgent stop to this (Nagaanbuu 1995). Apparently, Inner Mongols go to Mongolia, their motherland (*eh oron*), to preserve their Mongol 'blood' by marrying 'authentic' Mongol girls, but Halh Mongols regard this as a dilution of their Mongol 'blood'.

Erliiz: *Revealing Traits of the Father*

The Mongolian government officially recognizes the Mongolian citizenship of the *erliiz*, as the MPR law on citizenship of 1974 stipulates, for

Mongolia is acutely short of people: 'If the parents or one of them is an MPR citizen, then the registration of their natural children as MPR citizens irrespective of their place of birth shall be their duty as an MPR citizen. For evading the registration of their children, the guilty persons shall be brought to responsibility in accordance with MPR legislation (Butler 1982: 585). But society may not accept them psychologically, and many have had to adopt as their surnames names of their Mongolian maternal uncles or mothers. The social attitude to them always involves the traditional kinship value: the distinction of bone and flesh. By this principle, children born of Mongol mothers but foreign fathers are not Mongolian but, fundamentally, either Chinese or Russian. Their patrilineal identity is to be exploited as permanent evidence against them.

The flow of foreign men into Mongolia violates a crucial principle: patrilocality. The children stay on with mothers, and thus residence is matrilocal. This highlights the difficulty of matrilocal residence in a patrilineal society. The Mongols see the children as agents, and they think that the second generation, despite their citizenship, will inevitably comply with the patrilineal principle; that is, their 'bone' loyalty will be to this specific foreign person whose national identity is firmly established in a different country.

In the most fundamentalist views, *erliiz* are said always to reveal traits that are alien to Mongols. Any ambiguity becomes clear when the children become adult; by then they are thought to be terribly dangerous. The *erliiz* are imagined to be hidden moles, gradually transforming themselves to expose more of their patrilineal bone, so that they may stage a quiet *coup d'état* in Mongolia. Many Mongols are terrified by the thought that these hidden *erliiz* might buy up Mongolian land, should it be privatized, and then transfer it to the Russians or the Chinese, especially the latter.

Mongols apparently think that certain ethnic traits are innate, not learnt. For example, language! The pure Halh dialect is something so subtle that no one can learn to imitate it very well. The Buryats who have long lost their own dialect would also tell me that when one is old one can no longer control one's tongue, but finds oneself intuitively slipping back to the Buryat pronunciation. A Chinese *erliiz*, when old, would often pronounce Mongolian badly with a subtle Chinese flavour, so it was claimed.

Another example is that the Mongols say that the Chinese walk differently: they take small steps, typical of the *danjaad* (burden-carrying merchants, or pedlars), or, as indeed their own proverb would say, 'A man bearing a burden walks faster'. A Mongol, on the other hand, walks clumsily, with a bow-legged gait.[10] Significantly, it is said that *erliiz* who have grown up with their Mongol mothers are supposed, when they grow old, to walk like a *danjaad* or *hujaa* (nicknames for a Chinese).

It is undoubtedly true that the Mongols' physical features are different from the Russians, and even the Chinese, although the latter are also Mongoloid. Mongols are thought of as having small narrow eyes and high cheek-bones. This physical feature has now acquired some nationalist elements. The typical Mongolian physical structure is said to be drastically changing, especially with contacts with the Russians and Chinese. People frequently pointed out to me that there are fewer and fewer pure Mongols, fewer and fewer Mongols with high cheek-bones, especially in cities and in the economically and agriculturally more advanced region north of Ulaanbaatar and along the railway. This region is said to be famous for its non-typical Mongolian faces, so much so that people doubt if there are any real Mongols there. Hövsgöl is also a province where the Russian *erliiz* allegedly concentrate.

Erliiz, 'Surnames', and Politics

In Mongolia, the problem of the *erliiz* seems to be most emotionally related to the Chinese, and thus it is part of a wider politics. The concern over the Chinese *erliiz* intensified after the beginning of the Sino-Soviet ideological split in the early 1960s. It was predicted that a war between Soviet Union and China was inevitable; Mongolia, lying between the two, would certainly be the first to suffer. Rather than staying neutral, Mongolia sided with the Soviet Union, thus incurring strong Chinese aggression. Border skirmishes between China and Mongolia were frequent. During China's Cultural Revolution, some local Chinese in Mongolia seemed to have been incited by the call of Mao Zedong, and they fought street battles against the 'revisionist' Soviets and Mongols. People recall that the tension between Chinese and Mongols was extremely high. The Chinese and Inner Mongols living in Mongolia were under constant surveillance. In the early 1980s, ostensibly as a sign of support for Vietnam in the Sino–Vietnamese War which started in 1979, the

---

[10] Bow-legs may be due to riding horses as well as to rickets, or may even be genetic. Some Mongols see this as innate, not learnt.

Mongols repatriated several thousand Chinese back to China. While Chinese nationals were discriminated against, let us see how Chinese *erliiz* were treated. As I mentioned earlier, such *erliiz* are numerous, and many of them have received a better education than 'pure' Mongols, for they live mostly in cities.

An incident in the life of Mongolian politics reveals how *erliiz* were categorized in Mongolian politics. In one of Tsedenbal's diaries, there is a list of names of top leaders, divided into three categories, each category written in a circle (Dojoodorj 1991):

Inner circle: Jagvaral, Haayagiin Sodnomdorj, Luvsangombo, Dügersüren, Zagasbaldan, Lamjav.

Middle circle: Jalan-Aajav, Chimid, colonel Jamsranjav in Moscow, his brother Tömör-Ochir.

External circle: *erliiz nar* 'the half-breeds'.

This list was written between 5 and 8 July 1981, apparently in reaction to a rumour spread among the public that 'ethnic' Dürbets from Uvs province were dominating the country (see Chapter 3). Tsedenbal was himself a Dürbet, and was alarmed at the hostility of the rumour. Meanwhile he was briefed by a trusted official that some Dornogobi Halhs were forming a strong faction in the higher government organs. The 'circles' are the people he hoped to discredit. So the inner circle comprises Halh from the Dornogobi *aimag*. The people in the middle circle are connected to each other by marriage: for example, Jalan-Aajav and Chimid are spouses of two sisters; Jamsranjav and Tömör-Ochir are brothers of Jalan-Aajav. As we notice, the external circle is constituted by *erliiz nar*. It is interesting to note what Jalan-Aajav revealed:

The external circle's *'Erliiz nar'* are related to me. Tsedenbal is a man who would flare up when he heard the word 'Chinese *erliiz'*. As for the real Chinese, he disliked them to their bones. In the past, there were many Chinese living in Zavhan province (Uliastai city) where they ran shops and planted crops, etc. Tsedenbal would call all people from Zavhan *'erliiz'* and he might have sincerely believed so. (Dojoodorj 1991)

Much of the political intrigue is not known to me, but it is clear from this that Tsedenbal was deliberately engaging in a stratagem. In order to counteract the rumour that the Dürbet Mongols were dominating Mongolia, he labelled even certain Halh as *erliiz*, thus relating them to the Chinese, which was of course a most serious accusation in view of the hysterically hostile relations with China. Thus, even the staunchest Communist could use the most primordial instinct! It seems that a new political culture in Mongolia was born and set in motion. This was perhaps the first time that the notion of *erliiz* was used at the highest political level with the aim of discrediting political rivals. This political culture acquired a more popular base when *glasnost* gradually made Mongolian politics more transparent.

Since 1989, when the border between Mongolia and China was opened, the Chinese economic success has displayed a striking contrast to the collapsing Mongolian economy, and it is understandably a great boost and pride-inspiring factor to the long-oppressed Chinese nationals and those who have been accused of being Chinese *erliiz* in Mongolia. Many Chinese and Chinese *erliiz* have begun to use this opportunity to transfer cheap commodities from Mongolia to sell in the Chinese market. Of course, they are not the only people to take advantage of this new economic opportunity; indeed, the majority of Mongols have been involved. However, some individual cases have been publicized by people who are frightened by this unexpected and seemingly uncontrollable 'Going to China' phenomenon. Clamorous rumours circulate saying that some people have deserted their Mongolian passports or their Mongol identities, and openly declared their Chinese affiliation. Some *erliiz* have already begun to use the surnames of their Chinese fathers, etc. This social discourse ultimately pushed the concept of *erliiz* to the centre of the Mongolian nationalist concern. In consequence, genealogy acquired a further political function to check individuals' ancestral origin. This gives added vitality to the current usage of the *obog* as patronymic-cum-surname, as it serves to identify whether one was born of a foreign father or a Mongol father.

For this reason, 'to guarantee independence', there has recently been another dramatic witch-hunt of those of Chinese blood among the upper circles. This was accompanied by the rise of speculation as to patrilineal descent, as the largest problem in Mongolia is perceived to be precisely people of illegitimate birth. People in important positions are constantly subjected to popular scrutiny and rumour. Punsalmaagin Ochirbat, the president of Mongolia, has been a target of such gossip. His surname, or *obog*, is his mother's name, and it is widely believed that his father was Chinese. He had to stand up and scotch the rumour. He insisted that his natural father was a lama over twenty years older than his mother. His stepfather was an Inner Mongolian called Böhöön. So there are three grounds on which such gossip is based: Ochirbat is from Zavhan *aimag*, which is famous for Chinese *erliiz* proliferation, as I noted above; he bears his mother's name as his surname, thus hiding his patrilineal identity;[11] his 'Inner Mongolian' stepfather grew vegetables and cleaned toilets for a living, a job no genuine Mongol would do (see Chapter 6).

Many also suspect that the deceased former leader of Mongolia, Tsedenbal, was illegitimate. Suspicion is aroused by his surname. Tsedenbal's family background is not known to the public; his father is said to have died while he was young. This is a good ground for suspicion, and indeed, this is a good way to show disapproval of anyone who is not particularly liked by the public. His surname is *Yumjai*, suspected to be his mother's name. He was thus accused of being a *butach* (bastard). His own explanation for his surname was posthumously published in *Ardiin Erhe* (27 December 1991), in which he stated that *Yum* means 'mother', and *Jai*, 'save' (*avrah*). This further fanned speculation that he was genuinely illegitimate. Interestingly, top Mongolian leaders are all suspected of being *butach*: Choibalsang, Tsedenbal, and Ochirbat all have their mothers' names as surnames. President Jambyn Batmönh's surname is said to be his mother's brother's name.

As we have seen, the Mongols apparently think that a person without a genealogy can pose a great threat to society. The main kind of such potentially dangerous people are *butach*, a child whose father is unidentified. The etymology of this term comes from *buta* (bush)—the child is procreated in the bush. But it has further connotations. A *butach* person is said to be harsh and cruel and proud in character; as the Mongolian saying goes, 'The head of a fatherless boy swells, so does the bottom of a motherless girl'.

Butach and *erliiz* became touchy and hotly debated issues during the public debate of the proposed new Constitution in 1991. In an article (Surmaajav 1991) entitled 'Don't Let a *Butach* Take the Helm of the State', the author suggests: 'Our president should have learnt to work under the guidance of his father; have received golden teaching from his father; be one whose temper softened at the taste of his father's palm;

---

[11] In his autobiography *The Heavenly Hour* (1996), Ochirbat devoted a large space to explaining why he adopted his mother's name as his *obog*. His father, Gonsiin Gendenjav, was a lama, who was forced by Communists to return to secular life in the 1930s and married Ochirbat's mother, Tsogtiin Punsalmaa. He died in 1947, when Ochirbat was 5 years old. Ochirbat then became head of the family and was registered as Gendenjaviin Ochirbat. In 1951, when he entered school in Ulaanbaatar, he gave his mother's name as his *obog*, for he could not remember his father's name. 'It was a taboo to mention one's father's name, and since he was already dead, how could I know whether or not I should mention his name' (1996: 44). Ochirbat also painstakingly traced his mother's ancestral origin to the Hunnu period, and claimed: 'I belong to the Boma tribe or the Alag Aduu *obog* which existed in the ancient Hunnu period' (1996: 34).

have the self-control ability not to catch alcohol addiction; have the pure spotless Mongol Idea; and be a man of capacity.' According to this view, fatherless Choibalsang and Tsedenbal did much harm to Mongolia. They were cruel, not only because they had not been educated by Mongol fathers, but, some say, because there could be some foreign blood or gene which was guiding them in their schemes. Ochirbat was criticized for maintaining a good relationship with China, even after the 1989 Tiananmen Square massacre. It was suspected that he might allow Mongolia to fall under Chinese control.[12] Much public attention was given when he sent one of his daughters to Beijing to study. Until then, Mongolian leaders generally sent their children to the Soviet Union or Eastern Bloc countries.

A politician even suggested that the president, prime minister, deputy prime ministers, leader of the parliament, and its deputy leaders, MPs, and ministers should be subjected to genealogical screening before they are elected (Lhagvadorj 1991). The issue became so serious that the State Small Hural dominated by the Halh made an unprecedented attempt to introduce an article into the Constitution on the eligibility of persons for the presidency. The first draft Constitution stipulates that an eligible candidate should be an indigenous Mongol born in Mongolia, who can trace his or her ancestry three generations back. This is a tough condition, especially when genealogy has almost completely broken down. The following remark demonstrates that only a Halh, preferably a central Halh, is felt to be suitable to be president. It is interesting to note what merits this group of people are said to possess, and it is more interesting that Halh here is reduced to central regions:

Our president should be a democratic (*aradach*) Halh coming from the depths of the masses like Hicheengui Said Tserendorji, A. Amar and D. Damba. Furthermore he should be a son of central Halh (*töv Halh*) from Arhangai, Övörhangai, Bulgan, or Dundgobi. I, who am saying this, am from Hovd province. Other leaders of the state and government could be from any ethnic group from any place. (Surmaajav 1991)

As in the case of Tsedenbal, who attempted a political killing by calling his Halh co-leaders *erliiz*, the current hunt for 'bad blood' is

---

[12] Kaplonski also notes a strong suspicion against Ochirbat: 'During the 1993 campaigns, Ochirbat was felt by some to be unsuitable as a candidate for president because he was rumoured to have a Chinese father. Narantuya, who did not like Ochirbat, said that this was in part because of everything that had happened while he was in office: various scandals, embezzlement, etc. She also admitted that it was partly because he was Chinese. "We don't like Chinese," she announced in her typically straightforward fashion' (1996: 79).

not just a matter of 'ethnic purification'. Since 1990, the bad blood hunt has been waged by the 'pure' Halh and Communists in order to discredit anybody who undermines Communist control. Enemies are called *erliiz*, and denigrated as the bad blood of society.

An example of the hysteria involved can be seen in Baabar's account (1992) of his encounter with a member of the *Mongol Uhaan* (Mongol Idea) society, a secret society in Mongolia, comprising only Halh. This quasi-Fascist group is supported by Communist hard-liners. They have a network of informants keeping a close eye on the 'ethnic' composition of the leadership. They have been bidding for Halh control of the government and state, which is now (1990–2) under the control of more diversified ethnic groups. They approach important personnel of Halh ethnic origin and attempt to recruit them into the organization. The purpose of the organization was laid bare by a secret agent who approached Baabar, who is also a central Halh: 'We should save our motherland. The entire leadership is falling into the hands of the Chinese and Buryat immigrants. In order to save our motherland from this dirt, some of us have organized a secret organization. Since we know you are a pure-blooded man of central Halh, we came trusting that you will support us.' The 'secret agent' then pointed out that President Ochirbat is a Chinese, because his stepfather is Chinese. Despite his being Mongol by birth, 'he (Ochirbat) ate Chinese food from a young age, and became a Chinese through food' (see Chapter 6). The prime minister D. Byamba-süren was called a Buryat immigrant. The chairman of the Mongolian Democratic Party, Bat-üül, was said to be 'urine of Buryat immigrants'. The first deputy prime minister, Ganbold, was named a Chinese *erliiz*. The vice-president and leader of Parliament, Gonchigdorj, was also related to the Chinese, because 'his wife has Chinese blood. So his children are not normal. The father of such children must be loyal to China.' He went on further to claim that the MP Ulanhu is also a Chinese *erliiz*. 'Look at his name: isn't it the same as the late Inner Mongolian leader Ulanhu?' After he was corrected by being informed that Ulanhu is a Dürbet from Uvs, the secret agent said: 'Well, don't you see? Dürbet means bad blood! The deputy prime minister, Dorligjav, is also a Dürbet. But where are our Halh?' Baabar was to find out only later that he was also labelled 'Chinese *erliiz*', simply because he did not endorse the view put forward by the 'Mongol Idea' society.

The MPRP (Communist-dominated) organ *Bodliin Solbitsol* (7 January 1992) published a threat from a police officer, Choisürengiin Vasha, a typical Russified Mongol, judging from his name: 'People say we should not shed blood. One can only become healthy when one is constantly bled and combed. Similarly, the bad blood of the society should be let out so as to make it healthy. A certain elderly person told me this. It is right!'

The discourse of blood is not uniquely Mongolian, despite the supposed 'tradition' invoked by the police officer. The idea of blood as a political symbol is, as Herzfeld (1992) has convincingly argued, a Western tradition. He points out that the Western humoral classification of human races 'persisted, not only in scientific theory, but also, and especially, in the sphere of ethnic politics and prejudice' (1992: 22). Eugenicists of the nineteenth century such as Francis Galton saw the racial organization of humankind as essentially unchanging. Galton's view was a major influence on the immigration policies of Anglo-Saxon countries (ibid.). The spread of this ideology of 'unchanging nation or race' lies behind the 'ethnic cleansing', or what the Mongolian police officer called 'blood-combing', type of mentality. Herzfeld writes: 'The association of blood, war, and intellect constitutes the conceptual foundation of the ideas of identity that we find ensconced in much European classification of persons. Distilled and intensified through the selective filter of a national educational system, . . . it rationalizes feral actions' (1992: 28).

The Role of Rumours in Mongolian Politics

In this section I discuss the social transmission of opinion. In earlier sections I have made use of printed and oral rumours, in the milieu of contemporary Mongolian politics (in addition to my own observations), because they are important sources and have tremendous social impact. In Mongolia, it is not easy to distinguish between news and rumour. Newspapers themselves cultivate rumours. For example, the Social Democratic Party newspaper *Üg* (Word) has a special column called *Jig Jug* (strange things) for (true) rumours.

Almost every family has a radio hung up on the wall, and it is turned on all day. Not only in the house, but even in offices people listen while they work. They are then able to keep in touch with everything that happens. Mongolian TV[13] and radio programmes have become much

---

[13] In 1990, 6.5 per cent of the population owned TVs (137,400 sets) and 30.5 per cent owned radios (443,200 wired-radio outlets and 205,000 transistor radio sets) in Mongolia (State Statistical Office 1991).

politicized, and they broadcast the quarrels and debates of different parties and factions. However, radio and TV have a limited range of programmes. It is newspapers which are the main bearers of rumours and news. Newspapers have thrived recently. I counted more than forty newspapers and a dozen magazines in Ulaanbaatar alone, in a country without a paper-making factory.

In Ulaanbaatar, what happens in one night is quickly spread to the whole city by the next day; as the Mongols say: *muu yum morin ulaatai* (bad news travels by horse relay). This is due not only to the importance of mass media, but also to the character of the Mongols. The Mongolians have a strong curiosity for news, reflected in their much ritualized greeting language, *sain baina uu?* (How are you?), followed by *sonin saihan yu baina?* (What's the good news?). From *sonin* (meaning 'news', 'interesting', or 'strange') there develops a famous Mongol characteristic, curiosity (*soniuch zan*). This curiosity may have its roots in the nomadic pastoral way of life, as people live dispersed over a large territory. When a visitor arrives, the whole neighbourhood comes to find out *sonin*. It is still very much so in rural Mongolia.

Rumour or news is also gender-oriented. The stereotype of the eloquent Mongolian man can be contrasted with the quiet Chinese man, and the less articulate Mongolian woman with the sharp-tongued Chinese woman. In Chinese society it is the women who transmit news, often sitting together and gossiping, while the men stay away and do not participate in the 'women and children's talk'. In Mongolia, on the other hand, women stay at home, and men go out into the pastures, often galloping to somebody's *ger* to exchange *sonin*. Mendicant lamas (*badarchin*) are also news-carriers.

Note also the structure of the transmission of news. Like the entire political and economic system, the whole country is (or was until recently) pyramidal in shape (see Chapter 2). The centre, or capital, is the source of information, and the countryside has no or less information. So the city transmits information to the countryside. The transmission used to be through the Party, administrative channels, and official newspapers. Mongolian radio and TV did not play an important role here until July 1991, when for the first time the Mongolian TV programme covered all of the county centres. In 1992, newspaper delivery to *sum* centres was usually two weeks behind, and in some places, a month. It was this control of information, and its relative inaccessibility, that made the news especially important. In Dadal people closely follow political controversy in the capital, and they are often excited about what's happening there. They ask the city-goers not only to buy goods, but also to bring back news, and to verify verbal reports.

I should, however, explain another important aspect, which I believe lies behind the very problem of why Mongols are engaged in so much political controversy and gossip, as described above. Mongols are relatively prone to believe something easily (_itgemtgii_), and they emphasize kind-heartedness, which they express as 'the white (milky) heart' (_tsailgan setgeltei_) (see Lubsangjab 1980). Evil is seen as black. People are thus _soniuch_ (curious), watchful for the black, in order to prevent it from polluting the white. By this means a public sanction is achieved. The Mongols' contrast of black and white often leads them to extremes (_tuilshrah_): when they think somebody is good, he is supposed to be as good as Buddha; if bad, he is compared to a devil. This cultural characteristic is consciously or unconsciously manipulated from above by the Party, which constantly sets out to distinguish who is black and who is white: who is the enemy, who is the comrade.[14]

An accusation against somebody in a newspaper will soon spread all over the country. People are interested in the accused, not to defend him or her, but to find traces of the wrongdoing. The Party was the Truth (the newspaper of the Party is _Ünen_ (Truth), a translation of the Russian _Pravda_). What could be more legitimate and more enforcing than the 'truth'?[15] The _soniuch_ character then leads to _tsuurhal_ (rumour). He who has access to the newspaper becomes the truth-teller, and the listeners spread it among their friends. This _soniuch_ character of the people and the _sonin_ provided by the newspaper then form a consensus, and the accused person can be effectively neutralized, or politically killed.

This information exchange channel presents a continuity with the traditional society, now reinforced by the authority of the newspaper, the written 'word'. I should explain another important element here. The word _medee_ (information) derives from the notion of _medeh_, to know. In Mongolian, to know something entails not just knowledge or cognition of it, but control or command of it. If I _medeh_ somebody, this means he is under my control, or under the control of my information. People as objects or targets of information can thus be successfully

[14] The Mongol character of distinguishing black and white is exemplified by Jankowiak (1993: 45) in an Inner Mongolian case: 'He (a Mongol father) attempted to transmit this ethnic identification to his son by periodically sitting in the hallway of his apartment complex and pointing out the "bad Hans" and the "good Mongols".'
[15] Recently, of course, there has been a challenge to the authority of the Party and government papers; people explicitly ridicule _Ünen_ for not telling the truth.

turned into puppets under the 'mouth' of the knower. The Mongols often say: *biye biyeen medenee* (they know one another, so they control each other).

This has a deeper background in recent history. Formerly the Mongolian Secret Police effectively utilized information provided by the people (so-called workers' information: *hödölmörchidiin medeelel*), and then turned people against each other. This use of fear, I was told, destroyed interpersonal relationships, making it difficult for the Mongols to work together. '[V]irtually everyone (Mongol) had a double life, that anyone could be an informer, that the weapons of the "weak"— rumour, gossip and innuendo—were those of the "strong" too' (Humphrey 1994: 25). A Mongol could be a liar and the victim of a liar. With rare exceptions, most of the purged people had purged others. The blending of heroes and anti-heroes has prevented the emergence of a 'clean' party or leader able to form an effective opposition. People know who was an informer and what he did. Whenever I asked somebody to talk about someone, I hardly ever heard people praise each other or point out how such a person could be a leader. Such jealousy can be characterized by the widespread Mongolian saying: *Mongol Mongoldoo Muu, Mod Yarandaa Muu* (Mongols are bad to each other as wood hates its knots).

It is against this social and psychological background that newspapers not only publish journalistic reports, but also become platforms for personal insults and rumours. The authority of such a paper is curiously greater than that of papers which transmit more formal news, about the development of the country, etc. Information about human factors is now recognized as part of citizens' rights, and these rights are such that people rise up and attack whoever they like. Humphrey writes of the pre-democratic Mongolian situation: 'it is not possible to make a simple correlation between the official ideology and the public, and resistance with the private, since almost all social life is necessarily played out in conversations, which are somewhat public and somewhat private' (1992: 25). Today the previous resistance has been transformed into public/private attacks on individuals and groups, and this is the medium by which ideas about 'ethnicity' and 'race' are disseminated.

Conclusion

This chapter has suggested that there are several important factors in the emergence of the category of *erliiz* and the Mongol attitudes that give rise to it. *Erliiz*, being a category 'betwixt and between' some culturally and politically defined fixed cores, is not merely a biological concept. However, its biological aspect has been constantly exploited in such a way that *erliiz* has become a commonly recognized stigma. It is, then, a weapon to be used. We have examined how vulnerable *erliiz* have been in Mongolia, in contrast to the imagined vulnerability of the Halh Mongols. This will remain a problem until the society is confident of its cultural and national stability.

But perhaps the most important factor, as I argued in Chapter 2, is the role of the state in creating nationalism. Chachig Tölölyan (1991) provides an illuminating statement which is relevant to the socialist period:

In [the nation-state], differences are assimilated, destroyed, or assigned to ghettos, to enclaves demarcated by boundaries so sharp that they enable the nation to acknowledge the apparently singular and clearly fenced-off differences *within* itself, while simultaneously reaffirming the privileged homogeneity of the rest, as well as the difference *between* itself and what lies over its frontiers. (1991: 6)

Nationalism, in the context of Mongolia, is an ideal concerned with being 'pure' and 'original'. While the cores, Mongolia or China or Russia, are in political controversy, the peripheral or inter-structural beings or ideas or concepts are subject to tremendous pressure, as scapegoats for many national problems. Nationalism is not just one 'core' against another, but more a core guarding against its own peripheral being, for indeed the real bloodless danger comes from there. A constant theme in Mongolia is really the battle between pan-Mongolism and Halh-centrism. It appears that pan-Mongolism is now equated with *erliiz*ism. In Chapter 6, I look at how the Halh Mongols are constructing their own community *vis-à-vis* the Inner Mongols, and how the Inner Mongolian ambiguous status is being magnified and thus 'fenced off' symbolically from the 'pure' Mongols.

6

Inner Mongols as 'Other' to Mongols

Introduction

I start this chapter by discussing the methodological issue that I raised in Chapter 1: namely, the situation of an *erliiz* anthropologist studying a community from which he is excluded. I set out my initial intention to explain why I, a Mongol, have now become an *erliiz* in Mongolia; my aim here is to understand this personal predicament, but not to attempt to vilify the Mongols' actions and norms. I have tried to explain their intangible 'actions' by analysing the new norms or notions that have emerged over the socialist period. As Holy and Stuchlik point out, 'The meaning of human acts lies in actors' intentions, purposes, motives, or reasons for performing them' (1983: 37). 'Communities are to be distinguished', suggests Anderson, 'not by their falsity/genuineness, but by the style in which they are imagined' (1983: 15). I now intend to treat Mongolia as a Halh Mongolian community, largely because the Halh Mongols have become acknowledged as the baseline nationality of Mongolia, just like the Han in China. I have already indicated how they developed over recent centuries in political and historical terms. In this chapter, I turn to the present symbolic construction of the Halh Mongol community in relation to the Inner Mongols, and first of all to myself.

In talking of a community, I run the risk of myself 'imagining' Mongolia as a closely knit collectivity, and this runs counter to my previous analysis of the social, national, and ideological diversities in Mongolia. Holy and Stuchlik rightly object to 'relating disembodied systems of notions to collectivities', but insist on 'relating notions, or knowledge, to social processes, to observable actions' (1983: 47). I think that a context-sensitive approach makes it possible to relate *some* commonly held ideas to a certain notion of 'community'. I shall discuss disagreed-on notions—for example, how the Mongol élite split over national symbols—in the next chapter. This chapter will discuss symbolic concepts of the Halh, whom I take, following A. P. Cohen (1985),

to be a community. Cohen develops the thesis that community is symbolic. Community is a place in which one learns how to be social and
continues to practice being social, a 'culture'-acquiring process. There
are symbols, rather like grammatical rules, and only by acquiring these
symbols or rules can one communicate meaningfully. Anyone who does
not possess this symbolic equipment is likely to be excluded socially.
Thus I am not talking about the truth or falsity of knowledge or notions,
but about the attitudes that arise from them. This, then, is a collective
cultural, ideological experience and model that every Mongol has been
subjected to through life in a family and in a myriad of social encounters.
I am probably talking about a mentality, which is apt to be 'felt', if not
observed.

The symbolic construction of the Halh community is in my opinion
best understood in a confrontational situation. To take an example, most
Inner Mongols can no longer appreciate the traditional Mongolian food
customs, their palate being more adjusted to the new culture they have
developed in their interaction with the Chinese. The same is true of food
in Mongolia, which is now perhaps more geared to Russian cuisine. Food
is part of a cycle which includes production and excretion. These are
great, visible points of disagreement (even though they are not readily
observable to outsiders). A Halh symbolic community becomes readily
'observable' when these food and excreta categories are constantly
employed in verbal combats between Halh Mongols and Inner Mongols.

As Geertz points out, concerning problems of etic or emic points of
view, both sides try to 'figure out what the devil they think they are up
to' (1983: 58). But in my case, this is less of a problem, since I am a
participant engaged in this quarrel, either to prove or to dislodge some
of what I feel to be mistaken notions. There are many commonly held
notions, although there are many that are alien to either side. The
problem of making a sociological study of this 'web' is that it is impossible to ask people directly about deep symbols adhered to more or less
unconsciously. Only through rounds of pleasant and unpleasant
exchanges did the web the Mongols had built become visible to me. I
somehow engaged in a perhaps 'deep play', however shallow it might
seem to be in any particular case. Geertz writes, 'Understanding the
form and pressure of...natives' inner lives is more like grasping a
proverb, catching an illusion, seeing a joke—or...reading a poem—
than it is like achieving communion' (1983: 70). And in this process of
flirting with the Halh Mongols in an effort to achieve understanding, I, at
least a half-native, whose 'Mongol' integrity was constantly felt to be at

stake, tried to figure out how *they* were weaving a symbolic web, from which I have been largely excluded.

The Conflicting Concepts of Homeland

I now want to return to a theme mentioned in Chapter 1, where I wrote that I went to Mongolia as a pilgrim. I argue that this sense of diasporism is widespread among contemporary Inner Mongols. In other words, their current ethnic identity is not confined to Inner Mongolia or China; their Mecca is now to the north, in Mongolia. A de-localized Inner Mongol is thus little concerned with his or her immediate homeland (*nutag*), as it is thought to have already been lost, or that it no longer provides a sanctuary. The state frontier, earlier demarcated by the Manchus and later maintained by the Chinese, is seen as illegitimate. This new notion of homeland devoid of tribal or national boundaries sets itself against the still new concept of a homeland based on a modern nation-state ideology.

It is commonly known that Inner Asian pastoral nomads have no concept of land as property (Jagchid 1988); but the lack of a sense of property does not mean that they have no sense of a homeland. Confrontation with the agriculturalist Chinese has clearly demarcated their sense of boundary: the natural domain of the nomads is behind the Great Wall, an area not attractive to the sedentary, unless for strategic reasons. The division into Inner and Outer Mongolia, and the strict prohibition of Chinese agricultural migration north of the Great Wall, reinforced the naturally held view that this was Mongol territory. This view was held not only by the Mongols, but also by the Han until recently. Mao Zedong, in his declaration to the Inner Mongols in 1935, recognized that the Chinese provinces set up in 1928 by the KMT government—that is, Suiyuan, Chakhar, and Jehol—would be abolished and returned to the 'Inner Mongolian Nation' (*Neimenggu Minzu*) once revolution was achieved (Mao Zedong 1991). The idea of this territorial domain and boundary was so deeply embedded in modern inner Mongolian leaders such as Ulanhu, that his Inner Mongolian autonomous region, albeit of limited rights, managed in fact to cover much of the territory north of the Great Wall, thus restoring the traditional *nutag* (pastureland, homeland) of the Mongols.

The concept of homeland in Inner Mongolia has increasingly transcended the smaller pastureland (*nutag*) assigned to individual herders or belonging to individual Mongol banners, as introduced by the Manchus. The loss of the entire Inner Mongolia to the Chinese administration in 1928 created a collective sense of crisis; the fight for one individual pastureland was thus enlarged to the entire Inner Mongolian land. This can be seen clearly in a famous nationalist song in Inner Mongolia, 'Gada Meiren'. As the story goes, in the late 1920s, the prince of a Horchin banner sold pasture to a Chinese war-lord, Zhang Zuoling, allowing the latter to open the pastureland for cultivation. Having lost pastureland, and failing to persuade the prince to change his mind, a banner military leader, Gada, rebelled to bring back the banner's pastureland with armed forces. This localized incident was soon spread and commemorated with vigour through epic story-telling by travelling bards; it was also composed into a popular song which is still sung by almost every Mongol in Inner Mongolia:

> A gosling of geese
> is flying nigh from south.
> Why do you fly away,
> but not stay on the long and great Sira Mörön river?
> If you ask the reason for
> the rebellion of Gada Meiren,
> He was fighting for
> the land of the whole Mongols.

(my translation)

The appeal of this song lies not only in its solemn and stirring melody, but most importantly in its content. De-localizing the event, Gada Meiren's heroic struggle is interpreted not just for his own banner land, but for the land of the entire Mongols.

Another important and popular song in Inner Mongolia is 'I am a Mongol' (*Bi Mongol Hün*), based on a poem written by a Halh Mongolian poet, Chimed:

> I was born in a herding family,
> saturated with thick cattle-dung smoke,
> I regard as my cradle
> the grassland, my homeland (*atar heer nutag*).
>
> I love like my own body
> the homeland (*nutag*) upon which I dropped.
> I regard as my mother's milk
> the crystal clear river.

This is a Mongol,
A person who loves the motherland (*eh oron*).
(my translation)

This song clearly states that Mongol identity is closely linked to grassland and water, which are both a *nutag* (homeland) and an *eh oron*
(motherland). Although the motherland in the original poem refers to
the MPR, for Inner Mongols it is the abstract notion of motherland or
their homeland upon grassland and river that appeals to them. Their
sense of homeland is clearly not a localized one, contained in the present
boundary of Inner Mongolia, as it would be in Mongolia.

Clearly, the Mongols have a definite sense of homeland, which, however, begs some explanations. The *nutag* concept rests on the traditional—perhaps shamanistic—view that a specific land is possessed by
ancestral spirits, and is thus confined to a particular people. The *nutag*
boundary is marked by *oboo*s (ritual cairns), which are not only land-
marks, but embody the local spirit. The central *oboo* is the location of
communal worship.[1]

When someone moves away from his native land, he should take
stones from the homeland, and add them to the new *oboo* honouring the
local deities. Mongol tradition held that one should be buried in one's
natal land or homeland (*törsön nutag*) after death.[2] Upon one's return
home, the first thing one should do is to drink the water (*ugaasan us*).
This water element is interesting, because, within a week or two, a new-
born baby is washed or 'baptized' in a tea or meat soup using the local
water, and in the course of this ritual a name is also given to the baby.
The Buryat Mongols usually bury the placenta under the yurt, a sacred
spot to which men would travel miles to pay homage (Humphrey
1991*b*). The homeland is thus said to be connected to one's umbilical
cord (*hüisen holbootai*). An emotional metaphor for a natal land is
törsön nutag ugaasan us (land that gave me birth, and water that baptized
me).

Nutag, in the everyday practical conception, consists of the four
seasonal pasture-residences; this could stretch several hundred miles,
and it could be reinforced by an administrative border. Under normal

---

[1] *Oboo*s are both centres and found on boundaries. See Bawden (1958), Tatar (1976),
Pozdneyev (1978), Sneath (1991), and Humphrey and Onon (1996) for *oboo* worship among
the Mongols.
[2] A classical example is the burial of Chinggis Khan. He died somewhere in today's
Gansu province in China, but he was buried near where he was born, Burhan Haldun in
Mongolia. It is important to note that his birthplace was decreed to be sacred.

circumstances, people will not move out of their *nutag*, unless because of calamity, war, etc. To move away is regarded as bad luck. Interestingly, contrary to the usual image of roving nomads, the rural Mongol space concept is rather limited. A house is a castle to an Englishman, where he is the king; similarly, the Mongol's castle is *bor ger* (brown or ordinary yurt) or *har* (black) *ger*, and he is Bogd or Khan, the holy emperor of this yurt. Thus we have the phrase, *bor gerteen bogd*, or *har gerteen khan*, an image that one is confined to one particular place, and has never seen anything beyond the immediate knoll.

In Mongolia, there was formerly no concept of what we call emigration or immigration, as the flow of population between banners was strictly prohibited. The administrative confinement to a certain *nutag* gave rise to a notion of pastureland-cum-homeland-cum-motherland, in which members of other than the titular group were prohibited from settling. We then see the emergence of the term *tsagaachin* (a beggar of *tsagaa*, sour milk), denoting immigrant. Paul Hyer (1978) noted three *tsagaachin* groups in early twentieth-century Inner Mongolia: the Harachin Mongols who migrated to Jirem League from Josot League, due to heavy Chinese pressure; the Halh refugees who fled the revolutionary changes in the MPR in the 1930s; and the Buryat migrants from Siberia to the Hülünbuir region and Silinggol region of Inner Mongolia. All these groups were stereotyped as *tsagaachin* and subject to a certain amount of discrimination by their recipient host communities, although the latter were generous enough to offer pastureland to accommodate them. However, the very notion of *tsagaachin* (foreigner, sojourner) indicates that these people were expected to leave the territory eventually (Hyer 1978). *Tsagaachin* is a stranger or outsider, whence derives a typical phrase: *tsagaachiig tsagaagaar hatgah* (to prick a sour milk beggar with bitterly sour milk).

The above description refers to the Manchu period, but not to the earlier period of the Mongol Empire. Today, despite holding this localized idea of *nutag*, which was reinforced by the Manchu for better political control, Mongols nevertheless retain the myth of their original ancestral land. The Malinowskian charter of myth still holds great significance for the different Mongolian groups. The myth states that the Mongols established their first state, *Mongol Uls*, in today's Mongolia, set up the first capital in Kharakorum, and dispersed or expanded through Chinggis's and his descendants' war effort; and it fundamentally inculcated in the consciousness of various Mongol groups the notion of their geographical origin. This reverence of the ancestral land is not, however, an admiration of the people there, but of the mythical ancestral hole, as Isaacs writes:

The physical characteristics that bear on group identity extend in critical ways to the place, the land, the soil to which the group is attached, literally, historically, mythically.... Octavio Paz identifies each human being's solitude not only with the 'nostalgic longing for the body from which we were cast out, but also for the place from which the body came or to which in death it will return,' seen by many ancients as 'the centre of the world, the navel of the universe,' as 'paradise where the spirits of the dead dwell,' and as 'the group's real or mythical place of origin.'... Almost all the rites connected with the founding of cities or houses 'allude to a search for the holy centre from which we were driven out.' Thus 'the great sanctuaries—Rome, Jerusalem, Mecca—are at the centre of the world or symbolise and prefigure it.' (1989: 51–2)

Mongolia, as the place of origin of all the Mongols, has always been seen as sacred, and allegiance to it is often expressed symbolically. An Inner Mongol would ride a horse by letting it face north. After returning home, the saddle would be put with its front also facing north. Indeed, the horse statue on the roof-top of the Inner Mongolian Museum originally faced north. During the Cultural Revolution it was destroyed, and a new horse statue was built with the head facing south. The Chinese were said to have objected to this symbol of the Mongols riding northwards to Mongolia. Such a symbol commands a powerful political message. According to a generally held belief, a Barga (in eastern Inner Mongolia) would put his horse and saddle westward, an Oirat eastward, and a Buryat southward. This symbolic construction of the Mongol groups points to their ancestral land, which is in today's Mongolia.

The success of the nationalist revolution in Mongolia from 1911 onward, and the failure of that in Inner Mongolia, powerfully reinforced the notion of the ancestral land lying in today's Mongolia. The recent de-localization of Inner Mongolian identity enables Inner Mongols to symbolically attach themselves to Mongolia without much constraint. To put it simply, 'Mongolia is a country of Mongols, and I am a Mongol, so I have rights to live there.'

This 'de-localization-in-the-imagination' of the Mongol identity is certainly at odds with the nation-state system upon which modern Mongolia is founded. As argued earlier, Mongolia is a country built on the basis of the Halh. Homeland for Mongols in Mongolia refers strictly to the territory of the Mongolian nation-state, not other areas inhabited by Mongols; an expatriate must be someone who could establish common identity with the dominant nationality in Mongolia, that is, Halh. In this Mongol world, to claim one is a *Mongol* would not automatically entitle him or her to apply for Mongolian citizenship. The homeland for Mongols in Mongolia is a pure Halh-land, with a clearly demarcated boundary, consisting of the famous landscapes of mountains, rivers, and deserts of Halh-land, as envisaged in one of their most famous patriotic songs written in 1933 by Mongolia's foremost poet, D. Natsagdorj (1906–37):

MY NATIVE LAND

High stately mountains of Khentei, Khangai and Soyon,
Forests and thick-wooded ridges—the beauty of the North,
The Great Gobi desert—the spaces of Menen, Sharga and Nomin,
And the oceans of sand deserts that dominate the South,
This, this is my native land,
The Lovely country—my Mongolia.

The crystal rivers of sacred Kherlen, Onon and Tuul,
Brooks, streams and springs that bring health to all my people,
The blue lakes of Khövsgöl, Uvs and Buir—deep and wide,
Rivers and lakes where people and cattle quench their thirst,
This, this is my native land,
The Lovely country—my Mongolia.

The vast land of Khalkha [Halh] among the deserts and highlands,
Land where we rode along and across from the green days of our health,
Towering mountain chains where deer and wolf are hunted,
And the finest valleys where splendid horses run,
This, this is my native land,
The Lovely country—my Mongolia.

(quoted in Tsedev 1989: 13)

In recent years, both Buryatia and Mongolia have issued calls to Mongols in the rest of the world to come home to help develop their homeland. The Buryats, I heard, only called on the Buryats, not on other Mongols.[3] During my field-work in north Mongolia among the Buryats, I was often asked if there were Buryats in Ordos, my 'homeland', and

---

[3] Indeed, there seems to be a movement in Buryatia even amongst Buryats to claim that Buryats are not Mongols. The minister, M. F. Zavgorodayaya, and the secretary of Obkom (regional committee), Ts. O. Ochirov, noted recently that on the territory of Buryatia there is not a single Mongol, ignoring the fact that the Tsongol, Sartuul, Hongodor, Ekinar, and Ashabagad are Mongols migrated from Mongolia (Chimidorjiyev 1991: 48).

people expressed strong interest in establishing economic links with them. Recently I talked to a young Buryat scholar, and asked him if he would welcome Inner Mongols and Halh Mongols in Buryatia. He replied no, because Buryatia is in economic difficulty and cannot afford them settling there. After all, he said, both Inner and Halh Mongols have their own homelands. But he admitted he would welcome back every Buryat from Inner Mongolia and Mongolia, and that the Buryat state would do its best to allocate residence and provisions. Likewise, Mongolia takes a keen interest in the few Mongols who have emigrated abroad. They use every opportunity to seek out Mongol people or students, but only the Mongols from Halh-land. While I was in Mongolia, when people asked me when I was returning home to Inner Mongolia, they would use the term *eh oron* (motherland). Everybody should have a motherland. An Inner Mongol's motherland is China, as some say, nowhere else.

Naming and Categorizing

As we have seen, homeland is an important concept, invoking political loyalty. Borneman (1992) writes of two Berliners questioning each other's loyalty, a situation that may reflect that of two Mongols. At the check-point one was asked: 'Where are you going?' The answer revealed not only the intended destination, but also the political standpoint and an understanding of post-war history. The question would elicit simultaneously a name, a categorization, and a periodization. 'Naming and categorizing are always contested acts because they are essential sources of power in the construction of local, national, and international loyalties' (1992: 12).

The naming of the two Mongolias has been controversial. The MPR is a twentieth-century political national identity, and its old name, *Ar Mongol* (Outer Mongolia), is now almost outlawed by the Halh, for it refers to an identity previously attached to the Manchu state and China. *Övör Mongol* (Inner Mongolia) implies an even deeper loyalty, symbolized in the name: *övör*, 'bosom' or 'inner'. The implications of the terms depend on who is speaking. *Ar* in *Ar Mongol*, means 'back' or 'outer'; thus, it can also have a positive connotation, not loyal to the Manchu. This is a much politicized explanation. A modern primordial and sentimentalist explanation from Inner Mongols is: *ar* and *övör* are two sides of a body, back and front. The two Mongols are organically one, as are the southern and northern sides of a mountain or any physical landmark. We now see a frequent use of 'Southern Mongolia' (*Nan Menggu*) and 'Northern Mongolia' (*Bei Menggu*) by some politically conscious Inner Mongols, delineating geographical separation, but not political division.[4] Of course, the original meaning was entirely different: Inner Mongolia was subjected to internal administration—that is, direct rule—while Outer Mongolia had a separate administration, hence indirect rule from the Manchu court. The official names under the Manchu were *Gadaad Mongol* (Outer Mongolia) and *Dotood Mongol* (Inner Mongolia).

Contemporary Chinese continue to exploit these names; they stick to the use of *Övör Mongol* and *Ar Mongol* or their Chinese equivalents of Inner Mongolia and Outer Mongolia—*Nei Menggu* and *Wai Menggu*—although Outer Mongolia is officially recognized by the People's Republic of China as an independent country. Unofficially for the Chinese, *Nei* and *Wai* no longer connote separate administrations; the term *Menggu* or *Mongol* suggests their inclusion in China by default.

National identity is formed not just on the level of symbols, but also on that of citizenship. The socialist Mongolian nation (based on Halh) is a political identity which sets itself apart from China, a Chinese nation. Just as the Mongols in Mongolia are *Mongoliin Irgen* or *Mongolchuud* (Mongolian citizens or Mongols), the Mongols in China, for the former, are *Hyatadiin Irgen* or *Hyataduud* (Han Chinese citizens or Han Chinese).[5] Or, as a minority in China, they are *Övör Mongol*, rather than simply *Mongol*. But ironically, they have started to abandon even the term *Övör Mongol*, instead calling the Inner Mongols *Övörlögch*,[6] a term not used in any old Mongolian dictionary, but interestingly glossed in Ya. Tsevel's *Mongolian Explanatory Dictionary* published in 1963.

---

[4] This geographical delineation comes from the earlier expressions *Monan Menggu* (Mongolia south of the Gobi) and *Mobei Menggu* (Mongolia north of the Gobi). It is curious indeed that Mongols have come to envision themselves as being separated by the Gobi, because it is not a borderline, but rather a zone. Gobi is in both Mongolia and Inner Mongolia.

[5] In earlier documents, the Republic of China was referred to as *Dundad Irgen Uls* (Central Citizen's State), which is a literal translation of *Zhonghua Minguo*. However, the People's Republic of China is named *Bügd Nairamdah Hyatad Ard Uls*—literally, the People's Republic of Han.

[6] I believe *Övörlögch* is derived from the verb *övörlöh* (to harbour); *gch* is a suffix denoting a person—hence 'one who harbours something, e.g. a thought'. This is similar to the term *tergüülegch* (chairman), which comes from the verb *tergüüleh* (to lead, to chair). It is interesting to note that the same rule cannot be applied to *Ar* (Mongol); there is no such a term as *Arlagch*.

H. Nyambuu wrote as late as 1992 in his comprehensive handbook of Mongol peoples, identifying *Övörlögch* as equivalent to *Övör Mongol-chuud*. He wrote, for example, that the Uzemchin, now a *yastan* in Mongolia, 'has many *obog* (clans) pertaining to Halh, *Övörlögch* and Barga'. He further suggested that *Övörlögch* is also a distinct dialect, as opposed Halh, Oirat, and Buryat-Barga (1992: 161). Citizenship is a controversial matter; international convention demands the absolute loyalty of citizens to the nation-state, superseding ethnic origin. Therefore, Inner Mongolian loyalty is supposed to be to China.

By naming China a Han Chinese nation-state (*Hyatad Uls*), the MPR unwittingly labels the Inner Mongols as Han Chinese. Such a naming is perhaps done not out of ignorance, but as a deliberate manipulation, as a demonstration of a contrast—that is, to make difference clearer, rather than less clear. An unclear name is always dangerous, for it could well imply a claim for legitimacy. The MPR, by differentiating its neighbour explicitly, has made itself a 'pure' Mongol nation-state.

I mentioned that Mongols in Inner Mongolia are at best described as *Övör Mongol*. There seems nothing wrong with this labelling; yet a further analysis would reveal some problems. The crucial question is whether an *Övör Mongol* identity is an ethnic identity or a regional one. For Mongols in Inner Mongolia, *Övör Mongol* is not an ethnic identity, but refers to Mongols in Inner Mongolia, the latter being an administrative concept which does not denote any 'ethnicity'.

Borchigud (1996) has made an interesting study of how the term evolved in Inner Mongolia. In the 1950s, Mongols in Inner Mongolia refused to say they were *Övör Mongol*, but rather used the term *Mongol*. To the Chinese, however, *Mongol* referred to Mongols in the MPR. Mongols in Inner Mongolia must be qualified as *Neimeng ren*, or *Övör Mongol hün*, as opposed to *Hebei ren*, or *Beijing ren*, for example. This was an identity based on region, with its particular cultural traits, but not essentially different from other peoples in China. This place-based identity allowed for the Han Chinese and other ethnic groups also to claim the identity of *Neimeng ren*, to the great resentment of Mongols in Inner Mongolia. Borchigud argued that from the 1980s, the ethnically based identity of Mongols began to gain prominence, thanks to a new preferential policy towards ethnic minorities implemented from the early 1980s. This 'ethnic' definition of identity cut across the regional boundary, creating a trans-regional ethnic identity. Thus, Mongols (or other minorities), regardless of their residence, are now officially able to identify with each other as belonging to one overall Mongol nationality.

The renewed interest in 'ethnic' roots is excellently described by Dru
Gladney, who reports that many Han Chinese now apply to merge with
other existing ethnic groups or to form separate non-Han ethnic minorities (1995). This special circumstance fosters a strangely ethnically
based identity that is certainly trans-regional in operation. The Hui
Muslims in China, despite their being dispersed all over China and
varying in dialects and cultures, are unified through one of the locally
defined Islamic principles, namely, *Qing Zhen*: purity and authenticity
(Gladney 1991). Gladney argues that the force behind imagining the
ethnic community is the state's classificatory system *minzu* (nationality).
For the Mongols, however, this state policy facilitates their long-held
desire or effort that Mongols should transcend their own internal 'feudal'
or 'tribal' boundaries. Inner Mongolia now operates an eight-province-
region Mongolian language co-ordination programme to serve Mongols
scattered in all these areas.[7] The de-localization of modern Mongolian
identity in China thus enables Mongols to cut across administrative
boundaries, and even national boundaries. Therefore it comes naturally
to them that Mongols in Mongolia or in other countries are to be
considered as 'one of us', or 'our Mongol', or 'Mongolian brothers and
sisters', all in basic kinship terms, rather than seeing them in terms of
their political and administrative affiliations.[8]

To recapitulate, for Mongols in China, their 'tribal' background has to
a large extent given way to their overall Mongol identity. It is important
to note that there is no political language denoting ethnicity beyond
ündesten (nation or nationality), which embraces every Mongol who
considers him or herself as a Mongol. Sub-identities like Ordos or
Tsahar have been left only as 'Mongols' (*Mongolchuud*). Therefore,
since Mongols in Inner Mongolia tend to see Mongols in Mongolia as
Mongolchuud, ignoring their sub-identities like Halh, a 'close' or indeed
a 'united' relationship is denoted. In contrast, I suggested earlier that
ethnographers in Mongolia have taken on board the term *ugsaatan* to
denote 'ethnographic peoples'. The differentiation of ethnic groups

[7] *Ba shengqu menggu yuwen gongzuo xiezuo xiaozu* (co-ordinating work team for Mongolian language of eight provinces and regions) started its operation in 1978. The eight
provinces and regions are Inner Mongolian AR, Heilongjiang, Jiling, Liaoning, Gansu,
Ningxia Hui AR, Xinjiang Uygur AR, and Qinghai.
[8] It is interesting to note that the motor vehicle registration plate numbers in Inner
Mongolia are now preceded by the Chinese character *Meng*, Mongol, denoting regional
identification. In the 1980s and before, the character was *Nei*, Inner (Mongol). It is difficult
to ascertain why and who made this change; none the less, this phenomenon supports my
argument that Mongols in Inner Mongolia are de-localizing their ethnic identity.

(*yastan*) of Mongol origin (*ugsaa*) is essentially an indication that the ties between these groups have been removed, leaving only their link through their remote ancient 'origin'. Furthermore, the concept of *Mongol ündesten* as used in Mongolia covers only the Mongol *yastan*s of Mongol *ugsaa* within the geographic and political boundary of Mongolia, but not those beyond.

The geographic-political identity principle is then extended to Mongols in these regions as *separate* from the Mongols in Mongolia. This approach is buttressed by Soviet policies. I have explained in the previous chapter how the Mongols in Russia were already stripped of the epithet 'Mongol'. They are no longer hyphenated as Kalmyk-Mongols or Buryat-Mongols, but are called Kalmyk or Buryat nations. The Mongols in Mongolia likewise 'invent' an *Övör Mongol* nationality as one of the ethnic minorities (*ündesnii tsöönh*) of China (Altantsetseg 1978). For them, to identify Mongols in Inner Mongolia as 'Mongol' would be to put them in the same category as Mongol in Mongolia. In fact, to distance themselves from 'Inner Mongols', and hence from China, was a consistent political policy directly charged by the Politburo of the Mongolian People's Revolutionary Party.[9]

An Ethnography of the Rejection of the Inner Mongols

The existence of an independent Mongolia has been a huge boost to the morale of Inner Mongols, who often say that the Mongols will not perish; even if they themselves perish, the Mongol culture, the Mongol blood, will be preserved by the Halh Mongols. For the Halh Mongols, however, Inner Mongolia is a lost land, not much different from any other distant territory of the old Mongolian Empire. Some non-academic, yet educated, young people told me that in their imagination

---

[9] One celebrated episode in a modern Mongolian ideological battle about how to write Mongolian history illustrates this point. In 1970, Ts. Damdinsüren, a prominent Mongolian scholar, published a Russian–Mongolian Dictionary, with a supplement of about one hundred pages providing a chronological outline of Mongolian history. The Mongolian Politburo held a special session to condemn the supplement. The minutes of the meeting show that Tsedenbal criticized Damdinsüren for putting Mongols with Buryats and Mongols in China together as part of the complete Mongolian history. This was denounced by the Politburo as pan-Mongolism. Such a 'pan-Mongolism' would, it was alleged, fall prey to the expansionism of Mao Zedong, who always regarded Mongolia as a part of China. Following the Politburo resolution, most of the distributed dictionaries were withdrawn, and in the new edition, the supplement was scrapped (Jadambaa 1990).

Inner Mongolia is just a small province with about two to three thousand Mongols! This ignorance is not surprising, because no history and geography of Inner Mongolia are taught at school, although children learn Chinese history and geography. In none of the Russian-made world maps (the only sort available in Mongolia) is the location of Inner Mongolia marked. When I told a group of university students that Inner Mongolia is almost as large as Mongolia, and that there are two Mongolian Autonomous Prefectures in Xinjiang and several banners in Höhnuur (Qinghai), etc., they could not believe their ears. When I told them that there were about four million Mongols in China, they called me a liar.[10]

Some Mongols told me that in the 1960s, at the height of the Soviet Mongolia–China rift, they were made to believe that the Inner Mongols (and the Chinese) constantly violated the border agreement, posing a threat to Mongolian independence and sovereignty. Indeed, one Buryat told me that his father was deemed a hero for shooting Buryats and Barga coming to Mongolia from the Hülünbuir region of Inner Mongolia to unite with them. He said that the Buryats were convinced that they were indeed fighting spies and enemies from imperialist China. In many Mongolian anti-Japanese films, Inner Mongols are depicted as spies and in other unpleasant roles; audiences would imitate the funny, Chinese-flavoured *Övörlögch* accent. Today, this artificially standardized Inner Mongolian accent, as I call it, is often parodied when people make fun of Inner Mongols, without distinguishing the enormous dialectal variations there. Lattimore comments on the Mongolian language: 'It is a beautiful language. The Mongols love it as the French love their language, and like the French they are jealous of it and like to hear it well spoken' (1962: 205). This jealousy has deprived almost all Mongols outside Mongolia of their 'Mongolness'. The slightest accent, or a harmless particle *ba*, would betray and let down an Inner Mongolian, as the latter is believed to be a Chinese word. Speaking with such an accent or using a particle *ba* would entitle one to being called *hujaa*, a derogative term referring to the Chinese.

As an Inner Mongol, I have had numerous experiences of being called *hujaa*. Once in the free market, I bargained with a local, and eventually declined to buy his stuff; he snapped: 'I will sell it to our Mongols, not to

---

[10] One may expect that with increasing contact with China, Mongolia's knowledge of China and Inner Mongolia will increase. One of the laments expressed to me by a Mongol scholar is that Mongolia has few Sinologists. China is emphatically the least known country to Mongolia, although it is their most important neighbour.

bad *hujaa* like you.' My accent had betrayed me. Another experience has left a lasting memory. Again in the market, I commented unwittingly to my friends that traditionally Mongols did not wear someone else's second-hand garments. Someone from the crowd threw a sentence to me: 'Just what Mongol do you think you are, you stinking *hujaa*!'

The Inner Mongols are not only suspected of political disloyalty, but are also queried in regard to their genetic purity. There is a widespread belief among the Halh Mongols that the Inner Mongols have been physically assimilated to the Chinese. According to propaganda in the 1960s, in every Inner Mongolian family a Chinese soldier was installed to facilitate the production of half-breeds. Mongol men were conscripted and served elsewhere. I have often been asked if it was true that during the Cultural Revolution there were one or two Chinese living in every Mongolian family. Even some scholars (including diplomats), notably Halh, tried to convince me that most Inner Mongols have 'lost their gene pool' through the above process, and that voluntary ethnic intermarriages had increased. They would say that this was not only their view, but also that of some distinguished Japanese scholars who were familiar with the Inner Mongolian situation. This deeply held conviction leads the Halh to believe that Inner Mongols, once they become Chinese, must be thrifty, exploitative, and, above all, disloyal to Mongolia. Undoubtedly, the Halh claim of an assimilation process is not entirely unjustified; one may debate the extent to which the Inner Mongols have been assimilated. But the point of the Inner Mongols fleeing to Mongolia is to avoid that assimilation.

In Mongolia I met three Inner Mongols who fled to Mongolia in 1963. I was told that they were subjected to constant surveillance, and had to report to the Mongolian Interior Ministry once every week to declare that they had not been doing anything harmful to the nation. They were the lucky few who managed to stay on in Mongolia, but they did not get passports until 1989. Despite their newly gained freedom, few of them wanted to stay on in Mongolia. One of them said to me before his departure to Warsaw to seek his fortune: 'I came to Mongolia a convinced nationalist and believed in Mongolian brotherhood, but I am afraid I was wrong. They have never treated me as a Mongol but always as a Chinese. I would rather be a slave to a foreigner than despised by my own people!'

It seems that Halh discrimination against Inner Mongols had a more popular support. Baabar (1990), in his famous dissident booklet, *Don't Forget! Or Perish*, written in 1988, wrote: 'Since the time when the Russians developed a rift with Mao, the Chinese immigrants living in

Mongolia, Mongols mixed with different degrees of Chinese blood, and the Inner Mongols obtained by Choibalsang, have been discriminated and oppressed with the "internationalist principle".[11] It is true that the Mongols, who are originally inharmonious with the Chinese, once injected with Tsedenbal's medicine against "the deeds of the Chinese threat, poison and destruction", have greatly supported this internationalism' (Baabar 1990: 44).

The following remarks by an Inner Mongol bear out the current difficult relations between Inner Mongols and Halh Mongols:

The train was so crowded that many people did not have seats. Five minutes before the train took off, three men got on and talked with each other in Mongolian. They had to stand, for there were no seats available. I was sitting with two other Inner Mongolian Mongols who spoke only Chinese. I managed to question the three newcomers in broken Mongolian and found out they were Outer Mongolian merchants. I passed the message to my two companions, and together we decided to give our seats to them to show our hospitality to our Mongol brothers from the other side of the border. They accepted our offer right away. I introduced the three of us as Inner Mongol Mongols, but we did not talk further because of the language barrier. After four hours' journey standing on the crowded train, the three of us were nearly exhausted, but the three of them not only did not show any sympathy to us, but also pretended not to see our suffering. As we had another ten hours' journey to go, I asked them to take a turn standing and let us sit for a while, but they did not respond to my request at all. Finally, my two companions had to pull them out of the seats. After that, they went to another carriage. Later when I went to the rest room, I saw one of the Outer Mongolian merchants talking in broken Chinese to a Han. At that moment I felt cheated and very angry toward him and asked him in Chinese: 'Why did you pretend to us that you couldn't speak Chinese?' He did not respond. Later I

---

[11] Mongolian discrimination against the Inner Mongols is not a unique phenomenon, but part of the Communist style 'internationalism' also practised in Eastern Europe. Hungary, for example, took a harsh attitude to the Hungarian minority which was subjected to brutal discrimination by the Romanian Communist regime: 'The question of Hungarians living in neighbouring countries was declared taboo by Hungary's political leaders during the Ràkosi era. This stance was also encouraged by the prevailing viewpoint regarding international law and politics which, after World War II, submerged minority rights into the category of universal human rights. This relegated the matter of minorities, with few exceptions, to the exclusive domestic jurisdiction of individual states. From the end of the 1940s, the Marxian interpretation of internationalism in Hungary reckoned less and less with the nationalities, and regarded even the existence of Hungarians beyond the borders as nationalistic pleadings. Consequently, the issue of Hungarians living in neighbouring countries became a topic about which it was inadvisable to speak in public. In their criticism of earlier Hungarian nationalism and irredentism, Hungary's Stalinist ideologues and propagandists frequently adopted the anti-Hungarian arguments of the nationalists in the neighbouring countries' (Joò 1994: 97).

also heard other stories similar to mine from some local Mongols who speak Mongolian. Those Outer Mongolian Mongols treat us Inner Mongolian Mongols as running dogs of the Han. They think of us as simply assimilated by the Han and not equal to them or to our masters—the Han. (Borchigud 1996: 177)

The Inner Mongol in this story is one who cannot speak Mongolian, but it would make no difference if he could. 'Mongolness' remains the Mongols' primary standard for judging Inner Mongols, so is it the Inner Mongols' towards the Halh. Some Inner Mongols point out that they are more Mongol than the Halh Mongolians, because they still preserve the old script and Mongolian customs—for example, paying respect to elders. They still worship Chinggis Khan, while the Halh Mongols abused his name for seventy years. They argue that the Halh cannot deny their Mongolness on these grounds. Vanchigdorj, a famous Inner Mongolian film director, wrote his impression in a poem:

> Although the linguistically united Mongolian felt-tent dwellers
> have the same mentality,
> there is a difference between
> cyrillic and classical scripts.
> Although my speech is poor
> mixed with Chinese
> I cannot understand despite my effort
> a language muddled with Russian.
>
> (Vanchigdorj 1991)

The verbal battle goes into one very sensitive area. The Inner Mongol tends to argue emotionally when he is being rejected: why should I give up my good job and salary to come to Mongolia and suffer? The Halh Mongolian would snub: 'Why don't you go back then, if you cannot stand this difficulty, and if you prefer Chinese life? After all, we have not invited you to come.'

Despite the effort of the Inner Mongols to prove that they are also Mongols, their accidental and fateful association with the Chinese has brought them great misfortune. The Inner Mongols are indeed the direct victims of the political struggle between the two countries. The naming and categorizing, as shown above, have put the Inner Mongols in a limbo situation like that which Owen Lattimore commented on *vis-à-vis* the Hui people in China:

In times of political crisis, Moslem Chinese in Sinkiang are invariably caught on one or the other horn of a dilemma. If they stand with their fellow Moslems, sooner or later an attempt is made to reduce them to a secondary position and treat them as 'untrustworthy' because, in spite of their Moslem religion, they are after all, Chinese. If they stand with their fellow Chinese, there is a similar tendency to suspect them of subversion and disloyalty, because, it is feared, their religion may prove politically more compelling than their patriotism. (1950: 119)

The Inner Mongols, similarly, are caught between the two. The tragedy is not that they have not gained freedom, but that they are subject to a stereotype of assimilation. They are regarded as traitors, a fate beyond their own will and control. Internal enemies are always more dangerous than foreign enemies, just as a traitor is more condemned than a real enemy and cannot be forgiven.

Inner Mongol identity can also be a useful thing for the xenophobic Mongols, who avoid being accused by the Chinese of being racist by denigrating Inner Mongols. In 1995, about one hundred 'Chinese' illegal immigrants were expelled from Mongolia. What is interesting is that most of these so-called Chinese were actually Inner Mongols, as Bruun and Odgaard correctly note: 'The population issue has been complicated by the fact that many illegal immigrants may now be Inner Mongolians of Mongol descent, putting the Mongolian government at risk of allegations of racist discrimination if treated differently than ethnic Chinese' (1996: 40).

In the following sections, I outline some scenarios of interaction between Mongols from China and Mongols in Mongolia. For the sake of contrast, I have portrayed a rather simplified picture of the two cultures: Chinese and Mongolian. This is not a systematic elaboration of cultural norms of Mongolians and Chinese, but rather a description of how they see each other, often highlighting some differences, stereotyping each other. The term 'Mongols' refer to Mongols in both Mongolia and China. In terms of tradition, they form a fairly common culture *vis-à-vis* the Chinese. When referring to Mongols in Inner Mongolia, I use 'Inner Mongol'. I am not suggesting that Inner Mongols have become Chinese, but they are suspected of having acquired some of those cultural norms which are so fundamentally opposed to Mongolian culture, and this often forces Inner Mongols into defensive positions.

Man and Animal versus Culture and Nature

Historians are familiar with the pejorative view of the Chinese about the nomads. The latter are seen as barbarians, often presented in the image of 'beastly animals'. However, there are few published materials to indicate how the Mongols and the Chinese engage in this symbolic game in modern life (see Jankowiak 1993, Hyer 1978).

In Mongolia, there is the following joke: a Mongol who could not speak Chinese went into a shop run by a Chinese who couldn't speak Mongolian. Having failed to communicate verbally, the frustrated Mongol made a gesture by pointing his second and third fingers at certain goods. The smart Chinese shopkeeper immediately responded by showing his thumb and little finger.

This silent, body language communication reveals the basic attitude and opinion of the two peoples to each other. The Mongolian gesture refers to the Chinese as a sly donkey, whereas the Chinese is suggesting that the Mongol is a stupid cow. Symbolic expression in animal categories is important as a means of stereotyping. Leach (1972) writes that people classify animals as 'closer' and 'more distant' from themselves, and as 'good' and 'dirty', etc. They use the same classification for people around them. However, the same animal in different cultures may have different meanings. The Chinese have a different animal classification system from the Mongols. For the Mongols 'cattle' is a positive category, but for the Chinese it is negative: a cow is clumsy, and easily controlled by man. As we know, cattle play an important part in Chinese agriculture; they are obedient, subject to human domination, and used not for meat but for labour.[12] A donkey for the Mongols, on the other hand is an evil animal; moreover, it is not a typical Mongolian animal. They would point out that it is imported from China. Indeed, the donkey is not one of the five types of animals (*tavan hoshuu mal*) that are classified as 'Mongolian': namely, horse, camel, cow, sheep, and goat. In the imagination or as evidence from real life proves, the Mongols' image of a Chinese merchant is of a person riding a small donkey, carrying bags and going from family to family.[13] The donkey is contrasted with the horse, which is believed to be associated exclusively with Mongols. The image of

[12] 'Cattle' in the Chinese symbolic system connotes a certain temperament: *niu pichi*, 'oxen temper', which means stubbornness. Strength is also expressed by the idea of the ox: *niujin*, 'oxen strength'. The view that the ox is to be controlled dextrously is expressed in the following proverb: *chian niu yao chian niu bi zi* (an ox must be led by the halter).

[13] The mistrust of Mongols towards Chinese merchants is well-founded. As mentioned in the previous chapter, the Manchu Qing Dynasty separated their Mongolian and Chinese subjects, forbidding them to interact; yet, in order to supply the Mongols with commodities otherwise unavailable in Mongolia, Chinese merchants were allowed to trade in Mongolia. Over time, the Chinese merchants accumulated enormous wealth through various means, impoverishing the Mongols. In this process, the Mongolian language acquired an interesting bit of vocabulary: to buy or sell is *hudaldah*, the root of which stems from *hudal*, 'cheating'.

Mongols as a nation on horseback is not only a self-identification, but also a stereotype of the Chinese, as they call Mongols *mabei minzu* (nation on horseback). While a horse may sound neutral or simply reflect the nomadic way of life or martial spirit of the Mongols to the Chinese, to Mongols it is often personified, as a companion loyal to its masters or a friend to be loved; but a donkey is something for which Mongols feel unable to cultivate such a feeling. They see a donkey as stubborn and tiring; it will not only try to throw off the rider, but, if possible, trample on him and kick him when he falls. As Mongols say, he who falls off a donkey will have bad luck. The donkey may be domesticated, but it is not herded. What is more, donkeys are servants (*zarch*) of man, and should be treated harshly. It is thus not surprising to find that the image of the Inner Mongols among the Halh Mongols is one of people riding donkeys and mules. The Halh often amuse themselves with a story. In the 1950s, Ulanhu,[14] the then Inner Mongolian leader, called on every Inner Mongolian family to have at least one horse. Mao Zedong heard this news; suspecting that the Inner Mongols would ride horses and escape to Outer Mongolia, he banned horses in Inner Mongolia, instead introducing donkeys and mules (remember, the mule is a hybrid). This transfer of image shows that some innate qualities are seen as associated with both humans and animals.

We can distinguish two words to refer to animals in Mongolian: *mal* and *adugus. Mal*, a term usually reserved for the five domestic animals: horse, camel, cow, sheep, and goat, denotes stupidity and obedience. Sometimes a drunken person becomes a *mal*, as in the phrase *mal shig teneg* (as stupid as *mal*). *Adugus*, on the other hand, is a much more general term referring to creatures other than human beings. The term connotes cruelty and uncontrollability; it is thus derogatory. These two terms may be interchangeable; animals objectively in the category of *mal* are called *adugus*, particularly when they annoy the master. Donkeys and mules are, however, always called *adugus.*

Different Mongol groups also use animal terms to refer to each other, but those animals are invariably the five 'Mongolian' domestic animals mentioned above. For example, the Halh are commonly known by other

---

[14] Ulanhu (1906–88) was the founder of the Inner Mongolian Autonomous Region in 1947. From 1947 to 1966, he was the paramount leader of Inner Mongolia, concurrently holding numerous posts in the Chinese government. Purged in 1966, he re-emerged in 1973, and in his later career in Beijing he served as the minister for the United Front, vice-president of the People's Republic of China, etc. (see Bulag, forthcoming; Hyer 1969).

Mongols as *üher* (cow) Halh,[15] by which it is implied they are as stupid and docile as cattle. This stereotype has been largely accepted by Halh,[16] as in the poem by Choinom quoted in Chapter 3. In that poem, the Halh, also slightly resentful of this stereotype, nevertheless manage to assign a better quality to the cow, namely: the Halh, stupid as they may be, nevertheless survived as a nation. Halh Mongols call the Inner Mongols *yamaan* (goat) Tsahar,[17] because they are reputedly as restless or turbulent as goats, reminiscent of the role of the Tsahar in either rebellions or militancy. The image of the Tsahar is interestingly reflected in the stereotyping proverb: *Tsahar ügei dain boldag ügei; Ahar ügei isgii boldag ügei* (There would not be a war without the Tsahar; there would not be felt without sheep hair). Today, Inner Mongols have a self-designated animal stereotype—sheep; it is imagined that they are as helpless as sheep, waiting to be slaughtered by the Chinese. To the Halh, Buryats are known as *buha* (bull, not castrated); they are not only stubborn, but have misplaced their loyalty by giving it to the Russians, as the following stereotyping phrases show:

1. *Buriadiin buha yülden; Buruu ishilsen süh yülden.*
   The Buryat bull is stubborn; the axe with a wrong handle is obstinate.
2. *Dür ügei buha; Döröö ügei Buriad.*
   Bulls without nose-rings are like Buryats without stirrups.[18]

There is a difference, from the Mongolian point of view, between the terms *üher* (used by the Inner Mongols for the Halh) and *buha* (used by

[15] The Chinese see the Mongols collectively as cattle, but the Inner Mongols, perhaps a little bit 'cooked', regard the less 'cooked' Halh as 'cattle'.

[16] The stereotype of Halh being cattle seems to have folkloric support. A Mongol prince well versed in the ancient lores told Haslund the following legend: 'The Khalkha Mongols derived their origin from union between one of the nature spirits and a cow. The cow that gave suck to the first Khalkha Mongol infused into him the love of cattle-rearing and nomadic life and, that the coming race should not forget their origin, the Khalkha women are charged to wear a coiffeur reminiscent of a cow's horn, and their dresses were furnished with projections on the shoulders which called into mind the prominent shoulder-blades of the cow' (Haslund 1934: 69).

[17] The homogeneous Tsahar image of Inner Mongolia, as seen by the Halh, has left its mark among some Western scholars. John S. Major wrote as late as 1990: 'In the Chinese Inner Mongolian Autonomous Region, most of the Mongols are Chakhars [Tsahars]; the rest are Oirats, a people traditionally divided into the Eastern Oirat and Western Oirat confederations' (1990: 15).

[18] The counter-rebukes from Buryats are reflective of their dismay at the indeterminacy of the Halh: *Halh hün not ügei, hyalgasan dees bat ügei* (The Halh are unstable, just as ropes made of horse tails are not strong). *Dür ügei sarlag, döröö ügei Halh* (Yaks without nose-rings are like Halh without stirrups).

the Halh for the Buryats), and it is as follows. The term *üher* connotes docility but also perseverance. The Inner Mongols see the Halh as meek, but as having gained their independence because of their persevering spirit. *Buha,* not being castrated, is seen as unruly and difficult. Indeed, the Buryats have often been blamed for not being loyal to the Mongols. The difficult relationship rests on the fact that many Buryats voluntarily became Russian subjects rather than performing military service and paying taxes to the Halh Mongol princes in the seventeenth and eighteenth centuries.

Let us see if we can explore cultural categories a bit further. Different perceptions pertaining to animals, as demonstrated, engender enormous misunderstanding. The Chinese, as is well known, have never had any charitable notion of non-Chinese, especially Mongols. In the past, they described the wild lands of the north as lands of carnivores, and even referred to the human inhabitants by various wild animals' names. Collectively, they are *shou,* wild beasts.[19] The realm of humans lies in the Middle Kingdom of the Chinese; only those who accept the Chinese way of life would be regarded as 'civilized'. Although this extreme discrimination has long been discredited officially, its imprint is nevertheless long-lasting, and consciously or unconsciously emerges in day-to-day interactions between Hans and Mongols. This is no place for a systematic discussion of the topic. Below, I provide simply a random comparison of differences of perception of certain notions. To start with, the two people's views are deeply embedded in their modes of production

---

[19] Thierry presents the Chinese perception of non-Han in terms of animals: 'The nature of Barbarians is to wander like animals in zones unsuited to sedentary culture such as steppes and mountains; animals are different from men precisely in that they have to wander in search of their subsistence, having only temporary lairs in which to rest their heads. Likewise with the Barbarians. This animal nature of the non-Hans was shown in their very name. The importance given in China to the harmony between the thing and its name is well known: every name must agree perfectly with the profound nature of what is named. Thus the graphic classification of the name of each type of Barbarian under a radical marking his animal nature is an ontological necessity. So one finds in the ideograms designating some Barbarians the root "reptile" (the Mo, the Wei, the Lao, etc.), the root "worm" (the Ruan, the Bie, the Dan, the Man, etc.) and above all the root "dog" (the Di, the Yan, the Qiang, the Tong, etc.); some may be written equally with the root "dog" or the root "reptile" (the Wei, the Lao). This animal classification is sometimes replaced by classification under a radical "grass" (the Mongols, the Liao, the Miao, the Lolo, etc.) which then stresses that they are linked to wild vegetation and not to agriculture, sedentarization. The term that is still used to describe the Barbarians, *yeman,* is composed of the character *man,* which we have seen above classified under the radical "worm", and the character *ye,* which signifies "rustic", "wild", "rude", "non-urban", and by extension, "who is not in power"' (1989: 78).

as their dominant social identity: nomadic pastoralists versus sedentary farmers.

From the farmers' point of view, to be human is to do with pens and poems and cultivating land, and anything different is deemed barbarous. This can be seen in their traditional view of the body. A strong or robust person is not liked in Chinese culture, and is associated with several metaphors of abuse: A tall person is usually regarded as either clumsy or stupid: *zhangrou bu zhangxin* (grow flesh but not brain), *sizhi fada, tounao jiandan* (he who has well-developed four limbs is simple-minded), or *laoxin zhe zhi ren, laoli zhe zhi yu ren* (those who work with their brains rule and those who work with their brawn are ruled). In China, a tall child (*sha da ger*, the stupid tall) has a lot of trouble among class-mates; he or she is regarded as not having a good brain, and is often laughed at. Often a low academic record is attributed to the big body which is thought to have taken away too much nutrition from the brain. A small, short person is called *duan xiao jing han* (not of imposing stature but strong and capable). Susan Brownell, in a study of Chinese perceptions towards body and sports, finds that they have diverged somewhat from the traditional ones (1995: 35). In traditional Confucian genteel culture, physical labour was despised. This attitude often caused clashes with the rulers of northern nomadic pastoralist origin. During the Tang, polo was criticized by the scholar-officials and Taoist priests, who regarded it as dangerous to the 'vitality' of the horses and players. This contempt for physical exertion is long-lasting. 'An ancient proverb is said to characterize Chinese culture even today: "esteem literacy and despise martiality" (*zhong wen qing wu*). Many Chinese people say that sports are identified with the second half of this formula, which explains the historically low social status of sports and sportspeople' (ibid. 35).

Mongol and Chinese cultures are often polarized in terms of literacy and martiality. Although the majority of urban Mongols are predominantly university teachers, cultural workers, and party and government officials, their image amongst Chinese is martial (*shang wu*) (see Atwood 1994, Jankowiak 1993). Therefore, these stereotypical images are not occupation-related; rather, they hark back to a time when their distinctions were crystal clear. But these seemingly outmoded or anachronistic values do in fact indicate a hidden desirability that affects people's attitudes to one another.

There is always a danger in taking the contrast too far. Obviously, both Mongols and Chinese appreciate wisdom and physical strength. Although Chinese love their robust heroes, few of them are deemed 'wise'. Mongols appreciate wise men, but they do not judge a man's wisdom on a physical basis. Paul Hyer made an interesting observation of the traditional Mongolian notion of wisdom: 'A traditional, ideal-type image which the Mongols admire and try to project is one of reserved wisdom, not open, flashy brilliance. A corollary to this is a common feeling that one should not attempt to persuade others to his views. The feeling is that wisdom makes itself known and does not have to be openly propagandized' (1978: 69).

Dialectics of Food and Faeces

Animals, grass, food, and faeces are important categories for human thinking (Lévi-Strauss 1966, 1978; Harris 1986). They acquire added potency when people of different cultures interact. Louden observes:

Perhaps because of a tendency to concentrate attention on faeces as the most conspicuous example, body products and their smells are liable to be dismissed as a topic only worth a scatological bagatelle. This is understandable but mistaken. A strong case can be made for them as playing a much more important part than is generally granted in human social interaction . . . it is to be expected that certain body products, however variously interpreted and emphasized, are raw material for thought and action in all human societies. (1977: 162–3)

An interesting event which took place in Mongolia illustrates the delicate relationship between Inner Mongols and Halh Mongols. Many Inner Mongols now come to Mongolia to do business, either independently or as representatives of Chinese firms. Usually they take the role of interpreters communicating between the two. Once, at a banquet, some Inner Mongols and Halh drank too much, and started to sort out their differences by mouth and fist. At one stage, a Halh businessman shouted down his Inner Mongolian counterpart: 'Don't keep on pretending to be a Mongol, you are after all fed on shit!' I was not present at the banquet, but the insulted Inner Mongol is a friend of mine, and he told me the story. He said he felt that his whole personal integrity was at issue. It happened that they had been discussing, while they were sober, the different foods preferred in Inner Mongolia and Mongolia, only to discover how the traditional food ways have diverged. It is not that the Inner Mongols do not eat meat, or less meat, but that they cook it in a different way. He told the Halh that pork is much more easily available than mutton, and being an urbanite, he admitted that he had to consume a lot of pork and vegetables. This candid discussion left a bad impression on the Halh. When the power of vodka conquered their self-control, further fuelled by the difficulty in the business negotiation, suspecting that the Inner Mongolian brother was not helping them in this matter, the Halh brother came out with the above insult.

This is easy to understand once we are aware of differences in the lifestyle of the nomads and the Chinese. Let us not stop here, but go into their different attitudes toward foodstuffs and their differing ideas of hygiene. Before turning to meat and grass, I will first discuss notions of body odour, hygiene, human faeces, and animal dung.

The sense of smell plays a prominent role in the greeting ritual of the Mongols. Today, Mongols still sniff (*ünseh*—sniff, now also means 'kiss') each other's faces in greeting them (see Largey and Watson 1972 for similar customs among the Eskimos, Filipinos, etc.). Odour plays an important part in human relationships, in recognizing or rejecting the other and contributing to social divisions. Guérer (1993) described how the 'Jewish smell' nauseated the Germans, and German people's body stench equally tortured the French. Odour may even lead to punishment and ostracism. Mongols in Ulaanbaatar are repelled by the smell of Russians, and are reluctant to move into the flats newly evacuated by Russians, for they face a formidable task of clearing out the cockroaches. Cockroaches, Mongols say, are found only in flats lived in by the Russians, because they like the Russian odour. In Inner Mongolia, Mongols tend to hold their noses when they pass Chinese public baths. On the other hand, the Chinese have long noted the 'unbearable' smell emitted by Mongols and their *ger* (yurt). On account of this, they applied the epithet *Chou Dazi*, 'stinking Tartar', to the Mongols.

I should make a distinction between two kinds of body odour. Body odour as it is understood in the West is called in Mongolian *hulungsu*, in Chinese *huchou* (fox odour). Among the Chinese, anyone who has such a body odour is problematic, and even a whole clan may be stigmatized. Newspapers and magazines in China abound in articles on this topic. In the mid-1980s, statistics appeared suggesting that one-tenth of the Chinese population and all Europeans suffer from body odour, but it was particularly mentioned that Mongols are the people among whom this smell is *least* prevalent. This gave rise to claims among ethnically conscious young Mongols that the Chinese in fact 'stink' more than the Mongols, and that with the improvement of health and sanitation, the Mongols are actually the cleanest people in the world.

The second type of body odour is a matter not so much of particular physical secretions as of general cleanliness. The sanitation of the Mongol has a poor reputation historically.[20] However, this seems to have been a phenomenon of urbanization, where facilities are not complete. It cannot tell us much about the belief system or tell us why, in modern Mongolia, sanitation is probably better than in Chinese Inner Mongolia. I have observed that in Mongolian villages in northern and eastern Mongolia each family has its own latrine. One seldom sees people urinating or defecating in the street, as is common in China.[21] *Buxu suidi daxiao bian* and *Buxu suidi tutan* (Don't urinate and defecate everywhere and Don't spit everywhere) are two signs posted all over Chinese street corners. The government has been making face-saving campaigns to get rid of this habit, but the progress is very slow.

Non-Mongols can easily misunderstand the apparent disorder (difference) created by the nomads' transient lifestyle. Cohen rightly notes: 'While the white community may see the gypsy as "dirty", the gypsy has a more highly developed ideology of bodily purity and pollution than is generally current in British society. Indeed, the gypsies exploit their ideology to symbolize their ethnic boundary' (A. P. Cohen 1985: 41). For Mongols, there are definite rules regarding where to urinate and defecate.[22] In Mongolian, the formal word for a lavatory or latrine is *zorlon*. But to relieve nature is to *mori harah* (to go to look for the horse) or *garaad ireye* (to go out and come back), according to regions. This means that Mongols' toilets are never inside the dwelling; this would pollute the pure (*ariun*) fire hearth (*gal golomt*), the symbol of the genealogy of the family, which is located in the middle of the *ger* (yurt) (see Cammann

---

[20] 'The Mongol attitude toward disposal of waste was, from our point of view, rather casual. Men and women simply relieved themselves anywhere at all, completely unashamed by the presence of strangers' (Cheney 1968: 65). However, despite this picture of late nineteenth-century Urga, Pozdneyev described Urga as 'relatively clean, and there is by no means the filth and stench which fills the streets of the Chinese cities.' Cheney attributed this fact to 'climatic conditions—low humidity, abundant sunshine, and cold winters—and to the scavenging of the hungry dogs' (1968: 66).

[21] A friend of mine told me recently that he watched an interesting short satirical piece shown on Mongolian TV in 1995. A Mongol man criticized another for urinating at the corner of a building: 'Why do you urinate everywhere? Who taught you to do that?' The accused replied, 'My teacher is in Ereen.' Ereen is a border town in Inner Mongolia where thousands of Mongols go to do petty business every year. The satire implies that the Mongols are now picking up some bad Chinese habits.

[22] In Ordos, the women's 'toilet' is to the east of the *ger*, behind the litter pile, the men's 'toilet' to the west. This division of 'labour' is related to their work; women get up early, clean the *ger*, throw away the litter and find their convenience nearby, while men's first job is to look for horses to be saddled for the day.

1963, Humphrey 1974*b*, Wasilewski 1975, for descriptions and analyses of Mongol dwellings). The Mongolian *ger* has no space designed for a toilet; relieving nature is structurally and symbolically an outdoor activity.

Apart from designating relieving nature as an outdoor activity, there are several expressions to render neutral what is otherwise a dirty business. *Biye zasah* or *zorlond oroh* are more formal than *baah* (shit) and *sheeh* (urinate), the latter expressions usually being reserved for children. *Biye zasah*, for defecate, is literally 'correct the body'. The significance of this is that to defecate is to straighten and bring back to normal the function of the body. *Zorlon* is perhaps the equivalent of the Chinese latrine, a place where one has to *go in.*[23]

The Mongols' attitude towards human excreta can be better understood by referring to their medical theory. In Mongol–Tibetan medicine, the primary excretions or impurities are three in number: urine, faeces, and perspiration. There are seven principal constituents which help to sustain life: food, blood, bone, marrow, flesh, fat, and sperm. Everything starts from food. In this theory, all constituents are divided into two categories, refined and unrefined. Thus, food is separated into nutrition and excreta, and the latter is useless (Rechung Rinpoche 1973).

In Mongolian, excrement is called *baas*, applicable to both human and animal faeces, indicating dirtiness. However, as we know, there is a whole range of honorific terms by which to refer to animal dung, distinguishing between animal species. For example, *horgol* for sheep and goat dung, *argal* for cattle dung, *homool* for horse, etc.[24] These words have a different meaning, as they refer to types of fuel, and they do not

---

[23] A story illustrates how these variations cause misunderstanding among Mongols. An Inner Mongolian friend of mine recalled how he was ridiculed by Halh Mongols: 'Once we were having beer with two Halh. I said I needed to go to *zorlon*. They laughed and told me that it is rude to say that. They pointed out that in Mongolia they only say *mor'oo haraad ireye*. I know this expression since I heard it many times from people on the grassland. But you know Mongols in Huhhot often say *zorlond ochih* in order to avoid saying *sheegeed ireye* (go to urinate). In my place, people usually say *biye zasah* for *baah* and *sheegeed ireye* or *mor'oo haraad ireye* for *sheeh*. And I know people from Gorlos say *shees sheelgeed ireye* (go to urinate urine).' My friend, while being a bit resentful when Halh Mongols mocked his urban expression, alludes to other Mongols who would use expressions which are as much laughable as incorrect. *Shees sheelgeed ireye* is now a famous expression mocking a Han linguist of the Mongolian language in Huhhot. Once while visiting a Mongol family in Silingol, in the midst of dinner, the Han professor stood up and said in his beautiful Mongolian accent, *shees sheelgeed ireye*. He has since then become a laughing stock amongst Mongols, not only because he used the phrase on a wrong occasion, but because the phrase is unidiomatic, although it is grammatically correct.

[24] See Tangad (1989) for the various cooking usages of different animal dungs in the four seasons among the Halh.

indicate dirtiness. Dry dung is regarded as clean. Dung can also be dirty, but only when it is not yet dry and is not yet fuel. Muddy dung in the animal pen is called *baas*. Now, interestingly, for Mongols, human faeces have no practical or ritual use, so remain *baas*, something to be hidden and buried. At least in the case of the Ordos Mongols, there are two rubbish piles: one is for ash, while the other is for the kind of rubbish called *lag* (in different regions, *hog, bog*), which means anything swept away from the *ger*. Mongols categorize human faeces as untouchable and harmful. They should be kept far away from the *ger*, behind the pile of *lag* or *bog*, away from either the ash or the animal dung piles. People never imagine that it could perform a fertilizing function.

Let me elaborate further on the question of animal dung. As is clear, despite the fact that Mongols have developed such a negative attitude toward human excreta, they do not object to animal dung; they have developed a cultural system which is in favour of animals. In their belief, animal dung is clean, and it is the source of fire. One is not allowed to sit on a pile of dry cattle dung, for it would 'pollute' the dung. Cattle dung has a special use for strengthening the animal enclosure in winter, in order to make the pen warmer. Mongols also distinguish between sheep dung and goat dung, which are believed to have different 'warm' and 'cold' natures. For example, goat dung cools off the sheep in summer, while sheep dung constitutes a warm cover on the frozen field to protect goats.[25] Medically, cattle dung is used to heal arthritis. In summer, the Buryats burn *argal*, to fumigate the home, to smoke out mosquitoes.

Faeces of animals are 'food' to fire.[26] Fire worship is the most import-ant ritual in Mongol society, as it represents genealogy. It also cleanses foreigners and dirty things.[27] Until recently, a bride was taken in only

---

[25] The idea is that in hot summer, goat dung (mixed with sheep dung) would be helping sheep in driving away some heat. The same is true for goats in winter obtaining warmth from mixed dung. If herded separately, sheep in summer easily get what Mongols call *haluun övchin*, or hot disease, and goats in winter become 'frost-bitten', as it were. An experienced herder is careful about the herd composition, ensuring that appropriate ratio of sheep and goats is maintained. In modern Mongolia, however, for reasons of accelerating development towards socialism and modernization, some 'scientific' methods of specializing herd species are used. Such methods are workable only in a climate that is favourable to sheep or goats in most seasons, or where they have good infrastructure to maintain such a herding practice. In the harsh climate of Mongolia, they often prove to be disastrous.

[26] The Mongols are against placing any unclean thing or sharp objects in the fire. Fire is regarded as sacred and basic to the well-being and prosperity of the family. Extinguishing the family fire signifies a curse or an end to a family.

[27] In the thirteenth century, John di Piano Carpini wrote: 'Whence it recently came about that when Michael, one of the chief dukes of Russia, came on a visit to Bati [Batu],

after she had passed between two fires. This is to say that anything foreign, or *hari*, which is not of the clan or family, is regarded as unclean, hence polluting, and has to be cleansed by the most powerful substance, fire. Thus, the hearth is a pure place, *ariun gal golomt*. A fascinating illustration of the ritual importance of fire in the life of the Mongols is as follows:

If a traveller meets another person collecting dung in the steppe, he may ask '*argalyn zorig xairlana yy*' (will you grant me the strength of this fuel?). He will take one or two lumps of dry dung and put it inside the front of his *deel* (gown) until he reaches home, or goes into a tent along his way. There he will follow the fine custom of putting the dung on the fire, saying '*argalyn zorig*' (the fuel's strength). (An alternative interpretation of the words would be: 'grant the dung its destination'—'the destination of the dung'. In other words, the traveller has arrived safely.) (Tangad 1989: 93)

To sum up, for the Mongols animals and fire are linked not directly, but through dung. The fire and animals together serve human beings, the fire transforming the animal meat into food. The food in the body becomes nutrition and excrement; one supports life, the other is dangerous and waste.

As we have seen, human waste, despite its universal nature, connotes something rather different for different peoples. The Chinese perception of the matter differs from that of the Mongols. For the Chinese, human waste is rather useful, because it constitutes the major source of the fertilizers which are indispensable for growing crops and vegetables. Chinese farmers, in north China for example, collect human excreta near houses, and stock them up in winter and fertilize the field in spring, or throw the liquid in the vegetable field constantly in the summer.

In the agricultural world, the categories of food and excreta seem always to be linked, but largely through the field, rather than fire.[28] In time, faeces and food could transform themselves, and become each other. Panoff (1970) has presented a fascinating analysis of the Melanesian attitude to food and faeces:

If food becomes faeces, then it must have been faeces in the beginning, thus avoiding the fact the faeces comes indeed from its contrary, food. This kind of reasoning may have facilitated the recognition of the part played by decayed

they made him first pass two fires. After that they told him to bow towards the south to Chingis Chan [Chinggis Khan]' (Dawson 1955: 10).

[28] Fire in Chinese society has little to do with genealogy. Fire worship, at the *zao* fire, is for the kitchen god, concerned chiefly with food.

leaves and rotten matter in the swidden cycle, and may also have encouraged the use of human latrines as a source of manure. Indeed, the fact that the nutritive substance of the taro is called 'snake excrement' seems a necessary corollary to the statement that rotten leaves are 'givers of food'. Rotting matter is thus the substance of food—as well as its source, and its end. One of the themes of this sequence, then, is that the same is born from the same to give the same; rather than that the other is born from the same to give the same. (1970: 250)

The same analysis could be applied to the Chinese case. In Chinese, there are two words to refer to faeces: *shi* and *fen*, and one word for urine, *niao*. Looking at the ideograms, we know that *shi* is a combination of corpse and crop. It is dead food, as it were. *Niao* is a combination of corpse and water. When they are both used as manure, they are called *fen*, and then the ideogram is related to field and crop. The manure's status can be further enhanced by calling it *fei*, which also means fat. Manure is thus a fattening agent. *Fen,* referring to both human and animal excrement, has little of the meaning of dirt, but connotes something beneficial, normally to be associated with *fei*, fertilizer. In fact, human faeces lying around in traditional Chinese villages are also cleaned up by roving pigs, which also become food.

This recycling process is not accepted by the Mongols. For Mongols, food and faeces are separate, and they should never return to each other. Because the Mongols regard human waste as the dirtiest and most untouchable thing, they frown upon vegetables grown by the Chinese, because the fields are fertilized by human night-soil. Mongols believe that proper human beings eat the meat of animals, which are fed on wild vegetation. In fact, they thereby label the Chinese as in the category of 'animals'. But animals that are to be consumed should not be linked to human waste; nor should they consume what is humanly regarded as dirt. Chickens and pigs are despised and are inedible for this reason. Mongols think that the food of animals should come from *baigaal,* nature. *Bai* means existing. It is there. It is pure and clean. The Mongols' secular philosophy implies protection of nature, which gives food to the animals, which in turn provide both fuel for fire and meat and milk for people.

The concern for purity is so strong that most traditional Mongols refrain from eating Chinese vegetables. In Mongolia, there is a chronic shortage of vegetables; the little that is available is mostly grown by Chinese residents in Mongolia. This concern has now been extended to the Chinese flour donated to Mongolia in recent years. I heard many Mongols complain that Chinese flour has a funny taste, and they would enquire whether the wheat was fertilized with chemicals or human waste. Chinese flour, they say, is not only less nutritious, but is poisonous in terms of the long-term health of the Mongols. They extol the goodness of the pure, nutritious Mongolian *buudai* (wheat) and, the gem of all, the *ohi*, pure Mongolian *arhi* or vodka, brewed from Mongolian red *buudai*. When Mongol wheat and flour are insufficient, they import flour from China, America, and Japan, the Chinese flour being accepted grudgingly only as a last resort.

Dialogue of Mutton, Milk, Pork, and Vegetables

The high value assigned to nature and also to the traditional Mongolian pastoral way of life means that anybody who is not raised in such milieux is seen as non-Mongol, and even as biologically something different. Such an attitude may have become a part of the recent revival of tradition in Mongolia.

Deviation from food norms, Mongols say, brings physical deterioration. Chewing sinew, for example, is thought to be better for teeth than chewing gum; it strengthens the teeth, cleanses them, and functions as toothpaste. Older people would often scold children for not following the tradition. They are proud to show how good their teeth are. In Mongolia, I frequently heard people say that because of the shortage of meat due to the ration system, their teeth became loose, and they expressed the need to have a good gnaw at meat.

A meal without meat is hardly a meal for Mongols. To be deprived of meat can indeed be equated with starvation. The value of meat lies in its symbolic importance as a tangible representation of human control of, and superiority over, nature. (Interestingly, for the Chinese, by contrast, meat signifies both barbarity and power.) Vegetables to the Mongols mean degeneration of physical strength, which is incompatible with the pastoral life. Such an attitude may have contributed to the underdevelopment of vegetables as an alternative to compensate for the meat shortage in Mongolia.

Leach (1972) writes that food is always related to the cultural worldview subconsciously. In the English system, edible 'meat' comprises fish, birds, and beasts, but not reptiles or insects. The former are warm-blooded, hence subjected to cruelty. Edibility is also related to ritual and kinship relations between creatures and human beings. 'Pets' are never eaten. The English are also ashamed of killing animals of substantial size.

Hence meat of cattle becomes beef, pig becomes pork, sheep becomes mutton, etc.

Fiddes writes of the English meat-eating system: 'That we so readily presumed non-human primates to be vegetarian is itself significant, for meat eating is one key trait by which, traditionally, we have characterized ourselves as human' (1991: 55). Fiddes tries to classify the various stages of human evolution; and following the archaeologists and evolutionists, he sees hunting as the turning-point of man's evolutionary elevation from animal to human. Although I do not accept this as universally true, the Mongols may have developed, because of their hunting tradition, a notion of being superior, and in light of this swollen idea they equate any helpless, not-so-mobile sedentary people with vegetarian animals, as easily able to be controlled and dominated.

In both Mongolian and Chinese, there are no special terms for the flesh of various animals as is the case in English. Animal names are followed by the term 'flesh' (*mah* in Mongolian or *rou* in Chinese) to give the name of the foodstuff. The Mongols eat the flesh of all five domestic animals, though horse flesh is consumed less. There are two theories relating to this relative avoidance. During Chinggis's time, horse was eaten. After his death, Khubilai Khan decreed the offering of horse flesh as a sacrifice, and ever since then, horse has no longer been eaten by the Mongols. Another theory is that the avoidance began after the introduction of Buddhism into Mongolia. In Buddhist doctrine, the horse is seen as celestial, and consuming horse flesh therefore incurs punishment (Lovely Ordos 1985: 195). One may perhaps also add a more Leachian idea: that Mongols refrain from eating horse because their identity is closely related to it, or they have personal relations with their horses.

'Flesh' (*mah*) refers indeed to the flesh of anything that is living, including ourselves; fish, poultry, and insects are flesh, but not all are 'eaten'. Therefore, 'flesh' does not mean 'edible' to the Mongols. Flesh of pigs and donkeys is frowned upon. They are both alien to Mongolian culture. The pig, moreover, is represented in Buddhist ideology as the lowest creature; its meat is so degraded that it is equated with faeces.

Perhaps we should explain the Buddhist influence further. Although we do not have much data that would shed light on pre-Buddhist Mongol dietary rules, according to the material that does exist, such as the *Secret History*, what were later regarded as dirty things such as birds and fish, etc., were consumed by the Mongols at that time (thirteenth century). However, in Mongolian Buddhism, all human beings are destined for three bad spheres of existence: that of ghosts suffering from hunger and thirst, that of animals, and that of inhabitants of various hells. Since we are dealing with the issue of eating animals (mutton and pork), we will concentrate on the middle sphere. Animals are divided into two categories, those feeding on other living creatures, and those not. In Buddhist theory, the former, by killing, acquire bad karma, and stand little chance of reincarnation; but the latter have a better chance, for they do not take life and hence do not produce bad karma.

In secular Mongolian culture, a distinction is made between animals which eat clean grass and those which eat 'dirty things'. The Mongols call sheep *buyant mal* (virtuous animals) for this reason and for their contribution to feeding human beings. But similar status is not given to pigs, because they eat human excreta and other rubbish. Pigs in Buddhist theory have a further significance. Two edifying tales in the Buddhist canon *Kanjur*, popular in Tibet and Mongolia, tell of the fear of being reborn as a pig (Eimer 1989). Furthermore, pigs and chicken are thought to be incompatible with pastoral nomadism. Clearly, the most important reason is that both would hold up migration, but the Mongols have developed some secondary theories. They would say that sheep are often irritated by chicken feathers, which stick in sheep's throats. As for pigs, they, like the Chinese, can do nothing but destroy the pasture, as demonstrated in this saying: *Gahai Hyatad hoyor olshirvol, gazriin hörs üldehgüi* (If pigs and Chinese multiply, the turf will perish).

Once in the free market, I saw an old man hunting for mutton. He rushed up to a counter, but when he realized it was pork, he spat and cursed: 'I would rather eat shit than eat this dirty thing.' People complained about rising prices, and seeing that pork was more expensive than mutton, they often expressed their disbelief: how could the price of the meat of the dirty pig grown on mud and shit be higher than that of the meat of sheep, raised on pure grassland?

Mongolian and Chinese cultural concepts are further divided by different philosophies of cooking. According to the Chinese, the substance of a thing is hidden in the food, and it has to be boiled hard, which means the longer it is cooked, the more nurturing substance would be extracted, and the more effective it is in treating any imbalance of the *yin–yang* system. The usual practice in north China is that pork is thoroughly cooked so that the flesh and bone are separated. This idea is not only related to their cookery, but also to medicine. For example, Chinese herbal medicine is usually cooked in a *shaguo* (earthenware pot) for hours, and the soup is then drunk.

Mongols, however, have a quite different practice: meat is usually cooked rare. Mongolian herbal medicine is usually in the form of powder, drunk with boiled water, or at most boiled for a few minutes.[29] Mongols think that meat should not be cooked too long because the nutrition would then be destroyed; the fresher it is, the more energy it gives to the body, which often lasts for the whole day. The aim of eating to a Mongolian is to generate the spirit (*süld*) which sustains life. Mongols consume a lot of soup, but this has a rather different meaning. Mongol soup is not full of random ingredients, but is usually made from bone. The *mös*, the marrow of the bone, is extracted into the soup, and this gives 'spirit' to the Mongols. Although this is now generally forgotten, in the thirteenth century, the most prized food was soup. In fact, the Mongols at that time divided all foods into *shülen* [*shöl*], 'soups', and *undan* [*undaa*], 'drinks' (Buell 1990). Today too, the soup of meat is utilized, with added noodles or millet, and it is followed by the serving of boiled meat. Sometimes, soup is regarded as more spirit-giving, and therefore more important symbolically, than the meat itself. This means that acceptance of the Chinese way causes the spirit (*süld*) of the Mongols to drop or decline, for the Chinese meal does not provide, in the opinion of the Mongols, those spirit-giving substances.

Of course, not all Mongolian foods were just soups and drinks. Rather, it appears that these liquids contain the spirit of the red food (*ulaan ideen*) and the white food (*tsagaan ideen*) respectively. The term 'red food' refers to meat, and the term 'white food' to dairy products. This leads to the most fundamental classification of the Mongol diet. John di Piano Carpini, a thirteenth-century European envoy to the Mongol imperial court, remarked on this distinction, which is still made today:

They drink mare's milk in very great quantities if they have it; they also drink the milk of ewes, cows, goats, and even camels. They do not have wine, ale or mead unless it is sent or given to them by other nations. In the winter, moreover, unless they are wealthy, they do not have mare's milk. They boil millet in water and make it so thin that they cannot eat it but have to drink it. Each one of them drinks one or two cups in the morning and they eat nothing during the day; in the evening, however, they are all given a little meat, and they drink the meat broth. But in summer, seeing they have plenty of mare's milk,[30] they seldom eat meat,

---

[29] In Inner Mongolia, the Mongols are suspicious of Chinese medicine, thinking that it could be poisonous after being boiled for hours. Conversely, the Chinese are afraid of Mongolian medicine, saying that their bodies are not strong enough to stand its rawness.

[30] See Serruys (1974) and Humphrey (1981) for various texts and rituals for the libation of mare's milk.

unless it happens to be given to them or they catch some animal or bird when hunting. (Dawson 1955: 17)

It is also believed that meat, especially sheep mutton, has a 'hot' (*haluun*) nature; therefore consumption of it in summer dry weather in Mongolian conditions would be conducive to various diseases. Fermented mare's milk (koumiss), on the other hand, by its cooling (*serüün*) nature, is suited to summer consumption, and this is also believed to clean up 'poison' stored and developed in the bowel during the long winter. This is called *hor tailax* (to detoxify). Even now in summer rural people in Mongolia eat less meat, but live largely on dairy food and noodles; only elderly and weak people drink mutton soup (*shöl uuh*). It seems that human bodies react differently to meat and dairy products, as one Mongolian scholar expounds: 'In summer, various kinds of white food will drive away humidity from the stomach, so that one feels light in body, sharp in mind, clever in reading books, alert in sleeping. Excessive meat in hot summer will, however, makes one feel heavy in the body, lazy, sleepy; the blood boils (*höörh*), the face colour darkens and the whole body will feel uncomfortable' (Dandii 1990: 4). This binary division is interesting, for the Mongols consume these two not only according to seasonal availability and possibilities of storage but also according to their interpretation of the principle of *yin–yang* (*arga–bilig*).[31]

However, this custom has less force today. It demands an extreme self-discipline—which is normally lacking—and nowadays, many Mongols think that meat is the sole kind of food. I have realized that excessive meat consumption *in all seasons* is a phenomenon that has developed only in recent years. Many Mongols now complain of various symptoms if they do not eat meat. Many say, for example, that they feel dizzy; some say that their teeth ache, because they have not touched something hard, as I mentioned.

Mongols also say that human beings should choose the quality of their food, defined by the purifying quality of the Mongol appetite. They do not like things mixed, but to see them crystal clear, in their original form. Anything mixed looks suspicious, impure, and dangerous to health. They distinguish *idesh saitai* (refined consumption) from *idesh muutai*

---

[31] It is not clear whether the principles of *yin–yang* and *arga–bilig* (means and wisdom) are the same. The Mongols today claim that the Chinese borrowed the Mongolian *arga–bilig*, from which they developed their own *yin–yang*. For interpretations of *arga–bilig* in politics, see Erdene (1991) and Gaunt (1993).

(unrefined consumption). It seems that they emphasize nutrition, rather than variety or colourfulness, as in the Chinese case. A person who consumes food unselectively is looked down upon, regarded as a lower being. This explains why the Mongolian diet is so monotonous, consisting mainly of meat and milk plus occasional wild garlic, berries, etc., and why they hardly use any spices. This binary classification into pure and impure food gives the Mongols a suspicion of the consumption of a variety of foods in the Chinese style (*idesh muutai*). Chinese eating habits are interpreted by Mongols as stemming largely from their poverty.[32] Being poor, they would allege, the Chinese cannot afford to be selective; inaccessibility of quality food to them is said to have contributed to their 'inferior' physical stature.

The Chinese are known to the Mongols to have no specific food taboos, and yet, contradictorily, they are also known to abhor mutton and dairy food. Mongols have partly explained this in terms of poverty or unavailability. That this is not a plausible explanation may be verified by the huge consumption of mutton all over China, despite the fact that people allege that it has a nauseating smell, *shanqi*, a phrase specifically referring to the rank odour of mutton. It is difficult to say when exactly the Chinese overcame this psychological barrier. The ethnic food division is nevertheless also acknowledged by Chinese anthropologists like Fei Xiaotong. In his newly formulated concept of *Zhonghua Minzu* (Chinese Nation), Fei suggested that the Han, traditionally indulging only in agriculture, should be adventurous and adopt the minority lifestyle by tending animals and eating more animal meat. In this way, he argued, not only would the population of the Han region be reduced by out-migration, but also, in their new environment they would not cause environmental damage by desertifying grassland. Most importantly, changing their life-style would alleviate the pressure on dwindling arable land (Fei 1989). This is not just the wishful thinking of an eccentric anthropologist, but seems to be a major shift in government-fostered policy (see Brown 1995).

But even without government prodding, the Chinese have started to develop an appetite for mutton—for example, *menggu kaorou*, or Mongolian barbecue, which is, however, unknown to Mongols. In mainland China, and indeed amongst Chinese communities all over the world, one

---

[32] Jacques Gernet (1962: 135) explains the inventiveness of Chinese cooking in terms of 'undernourishment, drought and famines' which compelled the Chinese people to 'make judicious use of every possible kind of edible vegetable and insect, as well as of offal'. For views on Chinese 'famine plants' and 'poverty food', see Chang (1977).

of the famous dishes is called *shuan yang rou*, or hotpot.[33] While regional variations like Beijing hotpot, Sichuan hotpot, etc., have developed this dish is purportedly of Mongol origin, although it may be a Hui Muslim one. Ironically, this dish has been introduced only in the last few decades, and in Mongolia it is almost non-existent. This attribution of a mutton dish to Mongols is important, for it reflects a deep cultural attitude rather than practice. As one legend in Inner Mongolia goes: once Khubilai Khan was on a campaign. He stopped to ask his cook to prepare a meal. Soon sentries rushed in to report that enemies were approaching. Khubilai ordered his cook to serve the food immediately. The panicked cook sliced mutton into the boiling water, and served the mutton slices with some sauces. Within minutes, the dinner was over, and Khubilai met the enemy charge. After the victory, Khubilai remembered that the food he had had earlier was rather different, but tasty, and asked his cook to serve the same food again. Since then, this has become a famous 'Mongolian dish'. The Manchu adopted it, and made it a court dish. The recipe was kept secret for hundreds of years, until, in the last century, a retired eunuch stole it, and the famous dish spread to the public. This addition to the Chinese diet perhaps tells us that taboos against certain meats are not only culturally imposed, but also have a political dimension: Khubilai Khan is well known as the Mongol emperor who moved his capital to China, and thus he represents a 'northern barbarian' influence in the heart of Chinese culture.

The Chinese traditionally had little appetite for dairy products over the centuries, although in recent years they have demonstrated considerable interest, a point to which I will return. A 'cultural materialist' explained this phenomenon as follows:

One explanation for the Chinese aversion to milk is that they are physiologically 'allergic' to it. Adult Chinese who drink quantities of milk generally get severe cramps and diarrhoea. The cause is not really an allergy but a hereditary deficiency in the ability of the intestines to manufacture the enzyme lactase. This enzyme must be present if the body is to digest lactose, the predominant sugar found in milk. Between 70 and 100 per cent of Chinese adults have a lactase deficiency. (Harris 1978: 149)

This is tantamount to saying that it is biologically determined that the Chinese reject milk products. This ecological-determinist theory cannot explain, of course, the present-day large consumption of *certain* dairy

---

[33] Thinly sliced mutton is dipped in boiling water. As soon as the meat changes colour, it is eaten with sauces.

products in China.[34] In recent years, under Western influence, yoghurt has become as popular as ice-cream. The point is not that the Chinese do not eat mutton or dairy food, but that they have not accepted them culturally as part of their diet. Late acceptance of this purportedly 'Mongol' diet could perhaps be explained in terms of cultural hierarchy. The Chinese accept new foods, such as the royal 'Mongol dish' hotpot and 'Western' ice-cream and yoghurt, only if it comes from *above*, from a culture seen historically as politically dominant; otherwise, these ethnic foodstuffs or other things could be excuses for Chinese discrimination against ethnic minorities in China.[35]

We may now tentatively conclude that milk products and meat products in Mongol culture are in a harmonious relationship, rather than in opposition to each other. Abstention from either milk or meat would mean renunciation of Mongol identity, for these two are strong cultural labels which distinguish identity. Today in Mongolia, there is strong advocacy for reviving this food pattern. It serves two purposes at least: safeguarding the health of the Mongols as they see it and, by relying on these traditional food patterns, getting through this difficult period of economic crisis.

The Mongols, as explained above, often decline to eat vegetables grown by the Chinese. Nor did they eat many vegetables in the past. Vegetables are called by Chinese names, like *baitsai* (cabbage), *loovan* (carrot), *lajuu* (pepper), etc., and only a few Mongol words exist in popular use: *mangir, taana, songino, sarmisag*, etc., almost all for garlic

[34] The Mongols are as 'lactase allergic' as the Chinese, but, it seems, only to unboiled milk. The Mongols never drink milk as in the West, but always make it into yoghurt, cheese, butter, koumiss, etc. For a comparative study of lactose absorption in Mongolia, see Takahasi and Suvd (1993). It has been found that the phenotypic frequency of adult lactose absorber in Mongolians is relatively low compared to that of other milk-using populations in Europe, Arabia, and Africa. A comparison of the frequency with those of two Chinese populations, Han and Inner Mongolians, shows no statistically significant difference!

[35] The famous Chinese dissident Wei Jingsheng made an important observation in his open letter to Deng Xiaoping in 1992: 'When I was imprisoned in Tibet (Qinghai), I overheard a lot of conversations which helped me to learn the discrimination and despise of the Han cadres against Tibetans. Everything that has something to do with Tibet would be looked down upon. For instance, Tibetan dogs are famous dogs. But Han cadres would rather raise dogs they bought from inland. They would laugh at me when I told them how good Tibetan dogs were. They were only convinced of what I said when it was shown on TV that foreigners would pay a lot of money for a Tibetan dog. For another instance, they would not believe that Tibetan butter was the same thing as butter in a western restaurant. How could it be possible that old Tibetans eat the same thing as foreigners? Yet another example. Yak meat is the most delicious of meats. But the Han cadres in Tibet would say something like "As there is nothing else to eat, we have to buy some yak meat"' (Wei 1992).

or onion types of vegetables which grow wild. They are never served as a separate course, but are rather served diced, in very small quantities, as spices would be elsewhere. As Mongols would say, they should not be grown on night-soil, but gathered wild or grown on 'pure' soil.

Mongol resistance to vegetables is still observable in the cities.[36] Many Mongols at the Chinese vegetable markets hesitate before buying them, asking what they are for and how to cook them. Some Chinese vegetable-sellers told me that the Mongols are hopeless. Each time, they only bring a little to market, so of course their profit margin in selling vegetables is small.[37] This dietary difference might also have contributed to the formation of a caste type of community in Mongolia: the Chinese residents are mostly engaged in vegetable growing and working in the vegetable markets.

The Mongols believe that they are born not to be associated with vegetables and raising pigs. The experience of pig raising in Inner Mongolia, and also Mongolia, is interesting. I remember that my family started to raise pigs towards the end of the Cultural Revolution, and the results were often disappointing. After a year the pigs we raised tended to be spoiled and very selective in their food, and by the end of the year they were often only half the size of those raised by our Chinese neighbours. After several tries, we had to quit this uneconomic endeavour to add more nutrition to our diet in the ever-worsening economic conditions during that period. In Ulaanbaatar, I met some families raising pigs who shared the same problem. And they tended to be looked down upon by neighbours for mis-activity. Nor are the Mongols capable of growing vegetables. In Ulaanbaatar, in 1991, for example, I found that the size of local garlic was pitiably small, and that cucumber tasted rather bitter. I found that these deficiencies were of rather recent origin. When the Russians were there, I was told, the cucumber tasted normal and good and the garlic was big; but after they had gone, the garlic grown by the Mongols would either not grow at all, or was small, and cucumber turned bitter. In fact, some Mongols say that the biggest garlic is grown by the Chinese, the medium size by the Russians, and the smallest by the Mongols. The garlic grown by Chinese is not enough in quantity, however. The ultimate explanation, then, is that the Mongols are

---

[36] Vegetable growing in Mongolia, especially in Ulaanbaatar, was developed first by the Chinese, and later by the Russians.

[37] The recent influx of the Inner Mongols, Chinese, Japanese, and Westerners is beginning to boost the Chinese market, to the delight of the Chinese, but the dismay of some Mongols.

'destined' not to be vegetable-growers. They say their fate is different, not only as individuals, but as a nation.

The notion of inherent ability is interesting. This is perhaps a psychological factor embedded in the cultural system, and here we see the application of the idea to the entire people: Mongols are ordained to be associated with the five domestic animals, nothing more, nothing less!

It should be clear by now why the local Mongols say the Inner Mongols are raised on shit. By saying so, the Inner Mongols are put into the category of lower beings. But, as shown above, this insult has a deeper background. Vegetables and pork have become, in the life of the Mongols, not something totally inedible, but a value, and certainly a weapon for dealing with the *erliiz* Inner Mongols.

The anecdotal stories and arguments I have put together above show how diversified the two Mongol communities have become. As mentioned in previous chapters, Mongols feel hybridized through various factors, especially the Sovietization process, and are now desperate to claim some authentic Mongol origins. The point is that hybridization is an internal process, something that has to be defended against. Curiously, then, what is internalized is usually taken as something authentic, endogenous to the group concerned. Therefore, one may say that Inner Mongols will not, in practice, try to stop eating stuff supplied by their supposed enemy; nor will Halh stop importing products from outside. In fact, this argument of who is eating what of the enemy is no more than a boast of one's alleged purity or adherence to the tradition. The point of the argument is not its authenticity, but rather its belief quality—however distorted that may be. This may be illustrated by another interesting case of Halh mocking Inner Mongols. Inner Mongols wash their hands and faces in basins, while Halh Mongols wash with running water. The Inner Mongolian practice is cited by the Halh with disgust, reminiscent of the food–faeces recycling principle, for the dirt that is supposed to be cleansed remains in the water. The more you wash, the more dirty the water becomes. It is thus suggested that Inner Mongols, acquiring Chinese customs, cannot even wash their faces. A more civilized Halh would use running water. An interesting device can be found in every Mongol family, both in cities and in rural areas. A small water tank is placed above, from which water flows out. Inner Mongols I encountered would often cite this difference, and they are indeed puzzled, wondering if the Halh indeed have a point. This sometimes pushes Inner Mongols to find an answer to reverse their cornered embarrassment by pointing out that washing in a basin may in fact be a Mongol tradition, or that in the past, Mongols would blow water into their hands and wash their faces when no basin was available. The running water device, although it may sound authentically Mongolian in principle, is in fact Russian in origin.

Argument of this kind usually puts Inner Mongols on a lower level. In the minds of Inner Mongols are notions that they are indeed victims of assimilation, and it is to escape this assimilation that they want to go to Mongolia. Although they argue that they are the more authentic Mongols keeping the classical Mongolian script, which Halh Mongols aspire to revive but are unable to do for practical reasons, Inner Mongols do actually prefer the Cyrillic script. For them, Cyrillic does not represent a bad memory of the eradication of their culture under the Russians; rather, it is a means for progress, something they can use to compete with the Chinese. The overwhelming concern over Sinicization creates a mentality that anything that is not Chinese is acceptable and desirable.

This structural dilemma thereby prevents Inner Mongols from providing a convincing argument to elevate their own image. And what is curious is that, for all the Inner Mongols trying hard to assert their Mongol identity by showing some pathos, hoping to arouse empathy from their *ah duu* (brothers) from Mongolia, the latter, rather than showing much sympathy, choose to pour scorn on them.

Conclusion: Inner Mongols as a Mirror

Inner Mongols are important ingredients in the formulation of Halh's self-identity or self-congratulatory remarks about their luck. Inner Mongols are an ultimate image of what, if they lose independence to Russia or China, they would be like. For Halh Mongols, to be like an Inner Mongol is said to be like being in hell. Halh Mongols pour scorn upon Inner Mongols as if their state or situation was their own doing, or a conspiracy with their home societies, thus a sin; once in that state, they are believed to have become a bridge or tool in the hand of the powers intending to take over Mongolia. In the case of the Inner Mongols, their quality or loyalty is regarded as much worse than those of their political masters, as formulated in the phrase: *Hyatadaas door doloon dahin* (seven times worse than the Han Chinese).

This is a curious situation, whereby the identity of Inner Mongols is determined by two opposing powers: China, to assimilate them, and Mongolia, to reject them. The above proverb needs some analysis.

Chinese were the ultimate enemy against whom Mongols made their nationalist revolution. For centuries the two constituted opposing civilizations. The dichotomy of agricultural versus nomadic is so deep that a number of norms have developed. The distrust towards the Chinese is such that the argument between Halh and Oirat is whether surrendering to Manchu Chinese or moving the capital closer to China constitutes a sin against Mongolness. The opposing sides, Mongols and Chinese, despite howling abusive language at one another, waging frequent warfare, etc., none the less show each other respect, or reckon with the forces of the other. However, any Mongol losing something 'Mongol', in terms not of retaining the cultural tradition, but of keeping the ability to be a self-sustaining entity, is to be despised by both sides.

I argue that while the definition of 'Mongol' may be universal, cutting across internal differences, a separate Halh-based Mongol identity and a Mongol nation-state apart from Buryatia and Inner Mongolia have been moulded and shaped. Mongolia can now afford not to recognize or to downplay the Mongolness of the Buryats and Inner Mongols. Inner Mongols and Buryats can imagine no legitimate link to the geo-body of Mongolia. I suggest that Mongol 'brothers' have grown up and, with their own inheritance from the fatherly stock of culture and history, set up their own separate households. It seems that the Buryats have undergone this process, and are relatively successful in being Buryat in their own Buryat Republic within the Russian Federation (Hamayon, forthcoming). Inner Mongols, however, are undergoing a more painful process, not only because of the Chinese cultural and political pressure despite the Mongols' 'legitimate' titular status in Inner Mongolia, but because of a profound sense of loss of identity, especially after this recent encounter with Mongolia.

The Mongols still retain much of a pastoral ideology. Pastoral nomadic societies do not exist in isolation, and nomads usually live in relatively 'symbiotic' relations with sedentary agriculturalists, or what Khazanov calls the 'outside world' (1984). Both the nomads and the agriculturalists benefit from the exchange, although they can survive without the goods provided by the other. The Mongols traditionally, as well as today, still use Chinese silk, Chinese grain and tea, Chinese-made snuff bottles, and indeed a whole range of goods from the sacred to the mundane. The cultural and biological systems of these two regions are not fixed rigidly. Over centuries, due to the climate and to economic necessity, some agriculturalists have become herders, while some nomads have settled. Despite this interaction and the age-old economic relationship, pastoral ideology glorifies nomadic values and disparages agricultural culture. If we believe Dikötter's (1992) thesis that Chinese racism was deep-rooted in the self-image constructed from the discourse between humans and carnivorous barbarians, we have reason to believe that the Mongolian racist idea equally arises from this 'symbiotic' inter-action. To the Mongols, Chinese agriculturalists fall into the category of animals, or animal-humans, to be herded by the Mongols from horse-back. Such values, in modern times, will surely present severe obstacles to efforts to develop a Mongolian civil society. But a profound contra-diction permeates contemporary Mongolia, where the expression of Mongol values is not always sustained or consistent. Nomadic values and culture must necessarily be conditioned by interaction with agricul-turalists. A joke may illustrate this relationship. Some years ago, a Mongol showed the achievement of Mongolia to a foreign guest. He pointed at one building and said that it was built by East Germans, another by Russians, yet another by Chinese, etc. The guest was bewild-ered, and asked what the Mongols were doing. The Mongol said proudly: 'Don't you see? We were building socialism.'

This joke is not just a dig at the laziness of the Mongols, but suggests how the nomads have depended on the sedentary people to provide the material base on which to build their own culture. Perhaps I am too harsh. Yet, under today's nationalistic ideology, the Mongolian renais-sance is not being brought about by Mongols, but again by relying on foreigners. In 1991, to celebrate the seventieth anniversary of the Mon-golian People's Revolution started in 1921, Chinese builders from Bei-jing were invited to embellish the State Department Store (which was originally built by the Chinese), the Peace and Friendship Bridge, and the gate of the Ulaanbaatar city council. But this anniversary was one celebrating the Mongolian revolution against Chinese rule! Indeed, a profound contradiction lies also in another, more interesting case. A residential complex in the Zaisan district, beyond the Peace and Friend-ship Bridge, to the south of the government building, was built by the Chinese in the 1950s. The Mongols pointed out to me the malice of the Chinese even in constructing the building. The shape of the complex was said to be in the form of a pistol, with its muzzle pointing to the government building, the heart of the Mongol nation-state.

Douglas suggests, while discussing the relationship between sex, food, and animals in Israel, that sexual concern is primarily with the integrity of territorial boundaries. The taboo imposed on certain animals also extends to marriage with outsiders: 'In this case, the concern is to insist on not exchanging women' (1971: 78). She does not say that people are conscious of their boundary-building activity—indeed, symbolic boundaries are more powerful if they are unconscious. Her theory suggests that symbolic boundaries occur 'naturally' within a culture. However, symbolic boundaries may be caused by historically developing political relations of domination (or fear of domination). In the case of the Mongols and the Chinese, we could say, maybe, that each side fears the domination of the other—and this is reflected in the kind of symbols they use. The Chinese historically feared the physical strength and prowess of the Mongols. The Mongols today fear the encroaching population, culture, and life-style of the Chinese; that is, they may see the threat as not so much one of being directly ruled by the Chinese, as of the insidious subversion by their culture.

These ideas have been exposed and exploited as a reflection of nationalism. At this stage the Mongols would be well advised to know their rules of cultural grammar. He who forgets the grammar is regarded as marginal in the context of symbolic boundaries, and polluted. Marginal beings are always dangerous. They are dangerous to the centre, and vice versa. They are themselves in danger. Cleansing of things like dirt has always been intrinsic to human thought. 'The use of the word "dirt" does rather more than signify the particles which lie under the finger nail: it also expresses an attitude, "ugh!", and prescribes a remedy, "scrub!"' (A. P. Cohen 1985: 14).

The ethnicized identity of the Mongols in China is essentially an identity based on genealogical origin and blood. In Mongolia, as we have seen, people have also developed a renewed interest in genealogy and blood. However, for Mongols in Mongolia, blood is not something unchangeable; it is ecologically, environmentally, culturally determined. There is bad and good blood, there is dirty and pure blood, but all is Mongolian blood. It would not be too far-fetched to suggest that no mutual accommodation will be reached as long as this blood discourse continues. Blood may not always be thicker than water! But to a Mongol, what could be more precious than Mongolian blood?

7

The Choice of National Symbols:
Reinitiating a Nation-State

We now move on to discuss the collective construction of the Mongol nation-state in terms of the symbols of nationhood intended to be recognized and distinguished by others. This is a culmination in two senses: it is the most formal construction as far as the Mongols are concerned, and, for me, I was lucky enough to observe the choice of nation-state symbols, the names of the state and the Constitution, and the designs of the state emblem and flag under the new regime towards the end of my field-work. These became the most important issues in Mongolia for almost half a year from mid-1991 to January 1992.

The first post-Communist rewriting of the Constitution had been anticipated ever since the democratic revolution started in early 1990. The new Constitution was regarded not only as a reflection of demo-cracy, to be embodied in the highest state law, but also as a chance to redefine the image of Mongolia. This was a change in national identity emerging from the debris of socialism. These symbols were chosen entirely by the Mongols, thus providing a gauge to measure Mongolian nationalist sentiment. This nationalism, as expressed through choosing national insignia and enshrining them in a Constitution, is what Hayden (1992) defines as 'Constitutional Nationalism'. According to his defini-tion, 'constitutional nationalism' is

a constitutional and legal structure that privileges the members of one ethnically defined nation over other residents in a particular state. This type of structure reflects an old tension in central European politics and thought...It is a departure, however, from currently accepted democratic constitutional norms which view the individual citizen as the basic subject of constitutions. Instead constitutional nationalism envisions a state in which sovereignty resides with a particular nation (*narod*), the members of which are the only ones who can decide fundamental questions of state form and identity. (1992: 655–6)

The essence of constitutional nationalism is definition of the state in ethnic terms. In its overwhelming concern to use this highest law to define the nation using insignia from a specific 'ethnic group', or what is perceived as 'the' Mongol nationality, and by insisting that the president of Mongolia must be an 'indigenous citizen', Mongolian nationalism has become 'constitutional'. As I have already noted in Chapter 4, the National Security Concept of Mongolia explicitly stipulates that the Mongol state will protect the 'gene pool' of the Mongols. Katherine Verdery, in her examination of constitutional nationalism in post-socialist Romania, suggests that the reason for the 'ethnic' characteristics of the 'citizenly' rights is 'both the preformed ethnic identities of earlier nation building and the constitutional reification of nationality in the socialist period, under circumstances that obstructed the formation of "civic" or other countervailing identifications' (1996: 89). In similar vein, I have examined the socialist 'construction' of ethnic identities in Mongolia and their manifestations explicitly in ethnic or indeed 'blood' terms. It is no surprise, then, in parallel with their emphasis on democracy, that Mongols jostled to define their national identity and enshrine it in their constitution.

Dominant Symbols

A symbol, in the Durkheimian sense, expresses social solidarity, and it has psychological effects on people who identify with it. Totemic symbols are related to ritual and myth, belong to the realm of the sacred, and are tied to the entire social organization (Durkheim 1965). Similarly, Smith writes that a 'collective name "evokes" an atmosphere and drama that has power and meaning for those whom it includes, and none at all (or a quite different resonance) for outsiders... the name summons up images of the distinctive traits and characteristics of a community in the minds and imaginations of its participants and outsiders—as well as posterity—though these images may differ widely' (1986: 24).

This discussion should modestly touch upon the debate in anthropology about symbols, whether they are socially 'natural', reflecting the social totality and solidarity as Durkheim contends, or whether they are 'man-made', and thus subject to different interpretation by members of the society. Raymond Firth has argued that although national symbols have some primordial quality, 'a change in type of government may be symbolized by abandonment of the old flag and creation of a different one' (1973: 341–2). In earlier chapters, I have already demonstrated that within the Mongol nation-state there is no single ideology, and no single norm or notion. I take advice from Holy and Stuchlik: 'Even within the same culture, the same symbols can have different meanings for different people. If this is so, talking about the meaning of a cultural symbol as such, without paying attention to who bestows and perceives the meaning of it, as structuralists and others whose methodology is informed by formal semantics usually do, becomes a rather misguided enterprise' (1983: 30). As we shall see, the Mongols not only disagree passionately about the meanings of the symbols, but also engage in a controversy as to whether they are 'dirty' (*buzar*) or 'clean' (*ariun*) in terms of ideology. In the past, these symbols were not so problematic, for they had their place in a religious and decorative cosmos characterized by an upward, vertical outlook. In today's nationalist, horizontal world, existence, or the meaning of life, is defined in relation to somebody else.

Barnett's study (1977) of the changing caste ideology in present-day South India shows how different members of a caste hold widely differing ideas on what it means to belong to that caste, and how they differ in interpretations of various symbols. Internal debate over 'dominant symbols', to use Turner's phrase (1967), is guided by actors' understanding of what society should be. And it is here that ideologies, in the context of the actors' own actual social relations and social positions (ideologies that are inseparably linked to the 'outside world'), make the debate over symbols meaningful.

As our case will show, the Mongols have been manipulating and constructing symbols, trying to make them efficacious enough to 'command instantaneous respect and loyalty' (Firth 1973: 342). Studies of symbolism often neglect the fact that this is no easy task. 'Invented tradition', to apply Hobsbawm's and Ranger's (1983) useful concept to these symbols, does not always command automatic support, and much can be learned from looking at the conflictual process whereby particular symbols come to achieve prominence.

Let us begin to think about this in the Mongolian context by examining ideas of what a symbol of the state is (its ontology, as it were) for the Mongolians.

The *Secret History* records that Chinggis Khan erected a four-pennant black standard (*tug* or *süld*[1]) and a nine-pennant white standard when he declared the founding of Mongolia in 1206. Tradition tells us that the white standard symbolizes peace, and the black standard is for military purposes. Rinchen (1977), a prominent Buryat Mongolian scholar,

---

[1] *Süld* means soul, spirit, intellect, as well as symbol and emblem. Today it seems that the meanings of soul or spirit have all but disappeared.

attempted to explain the connection between these standards and the Mongolian shamanistic tradition. He wrote that a person has three souls. One receives 'spirits of the bone' from the father and 'spirits of the flesh' from the mother. These spirits are called *ejen sünesün*, or host souls. One also acquires another, immortal soul—the everlasting soul. The body is only the temporary dwelling of these spirits. After one dies, the everlasting spirit wanders for three years. After the flesh disappears from the bone, and the host soul of the bone subsequently dies, the everlasting spirit is introduced into the communion of the ancestral spirits. Depending on the status of the person in his clan, his spirit may become the protector spirit of the whole clan. After this introduction, his everlasting body (*mönhe biye*) is kept as an icon, or representation, by the members of the clan in their dwellings; to this people offer sacrifices, forming the ancestor worship of the shamanistic Mongols. According to Rinchen, there are five forms of spirits (*onggon*), amongst which are *süld* or *tug*—the standards made from the white or black fringes of stallions' manes and tails. These standards 'were the everlasting Bodies of the Lord-Spirits of the clans, and after the elevation of Chinggis Khan's clan over all the Mongol clans, the Lord-Spirits of the imperial clan of Borjigin became the Lord-Spirits of the Nation, and their Everlasting Bodies—the shamanic standards—also became the dwellings of the Lord-Spirits of all the Mongols' (1977: 180).

Rinchen is a modern scholar with modern perceptions; his ideas are not necessarily an exact reflection of what the ancient Mongols thought. However, we note that the state emblem in Mongolia is called *süld*, and the state anthem is called *süld duu*. This is not just an arbitrary metaphor, but may be said to represent the idea of a spirit residing in an object. This is obviously related to the shamanistic tradition.[2] This Mongol idea *does* seem like Durkheim's. However, my analysis is different, since it interprets Mongols' conflicts and disagreements over not only the property of Mongolia's dominant symbols, but also over what should be adopted for Mongolia's national symbols.

Traditional Symbols and the Invention of Tradition

Since national symbols are inventions, the Bogd Khan Mongolian (1911–21) symbols are a starting-point for our analysis. The new Mongolia

---

[2] See Humphrey 1971 for analysis of the Buryat iconic images which are endowed with spiritual or magical efficacy.

was influenced by the Russians in many ways. The Asian policy of the Russian government of Nicholas II was carried out largely by the Russian Ministry of Finance, in which some Russian Orientalists participated. Kotvich (1872–1944), a Polish Mongolist, was a patron of the famous Buryat Mongol scholar-politician, Ts. Jamtsarano. Based in Mongolia, Kotvich represented the Ministry of Finance on the Russian Committee for the Study of Central and Eastern Asia, and he gave advice to the Mongols. Other Russian scholars such as A. Pozdneyev (1851–1920) and A. Rudnev (1878–1958) also offered advice to the Mongols as to how to run state affairs. The interest shown by the Russians in supporting the Buddhist, theocratic Mongolia was in fact one aspect of the Russian policy toward Tibet and Mongolia, and indeed the 'Great Game' played between Britain and Russia over Tibet (see Hopkirk 1990). Agvan Dorjeev, a prominent Buryat Mongolian monk played a crucial role in liaising between Tibet, Mongolia, and Russia; he had master-minded the exile of the thirteenth Dalai Lama in Urga (now Ulaanbaatar) in 1904 (see Snelling 1993). Meanwhile, the Inner Mongols were pressing hard for unification with Outer Mongolia. In fact, the most powerful civil leader in the first few years of the Bogd Khan Mongolia was Khaisan Gun from Inner Mongolia.

We can see that all these elements were at work in the shaping of the Mongolian state symbols. Hobsbawm very briefly mentions Mongolia's copying of the English and French tradition during this period: 'In the period 1870–1914 there were, as it happens, unusually few "new states". Most European states, as well as the American republics, had by then acquired the basic official institutions, symbols and practices which Mongolia, establishing a sort of independence from China in 1912, quite rightly regarded as novel and necessary' (1983: 266). The Bogd Khan state thus introduced a whole range of state symbols in accordance with Western tradition, and one should not be too surprised at the fact that the state anthem was actually composed by a Russian. Indeed, the anthem was similar to an Inner Mongolian melody collected by Rudnev. In his article entitled 'Renascent Mongolia', Rudnev wrote:

> Liberated from the centuries-old servitude to China with the powerful aid of Russia, the Mongol state acquires, bit by bit, all the external criteria of a sovereign country. Introducing a monetary unit and founding orders (of merit) were followed by the Khutukhtu's decree on the performance of the Mongolian national anthem by military orchestras.
>
> The anthem was written according to a special order of the Mongolian government by the Russian composer, Mr. Kadlets (Kadlec), using Mongolian

220 *The Choice of National Symbols*

FIGURE 7.1. Mongolian state emblem adopted in 1911.

tunes presented him by the Oriental School (*vostochnyi fakul'tet*) of the University of St. Petersbourg. (Quoted in Kara 1991: 149)

The Bogd Khan state soon began to realize the importance of a flag, as it was stated in an official document: 'All the countries have their own flags; our Mongolia enjoys self-ruling rights, so it is proper to specially make a flag to express independence' (Nyambuu 1979: 18). For the first time, a *soyombo* symbol was inscribed on a state flag. The *soyombo* was supported by a lotus flower, and accompanied with two Tibetan words, *e* and *bam*, meaning *yin–yang* (*arga–bilig* in Mongolian) (see Fig. 7.1). The three pennants of the flag were inscribed with the Tibetan seed syllables, *om, a, hum*. What is interesting is that the new independent Mongolia was not called Mongolia, or *Mongol Uls*, but *Olona Ergügdegsen*, 'Elevated by All',[3] implying a religious, but not a geographical-ethnic concept of the country.

[3] There seems to be a considerable controversy as to the name of the independent Mongolia. Sanjmyatav (1991) records that there was a heated debate in the Khiagt tripartite conference in 1914 as to whether Mongolia should keep its original name Outer Mongolia (*Gadaad Mongol*), preferred by the Chinese, or *Mongol Uls* or simply *Mongol*, an option insisted on by Mongols. To the dismay of Mongols, who pointed out that Mongols used the

The selection of the *soyombo* and the name of the state were both a reflection of the dominant ideology of the then religiously minded Mongols. But they seemed to have brought dissatisfaction among the Buryat Mongols. The Buryat Mongolian scholar-politician Jamtsarano wrote in his letter to Kotvich:

Now all papers are marked: '*Olona ergügdegsenii terigün on*' ['First Year of Elevated by All'] with the month and date. This [refers to] the Indian Makhasamdi Khan;[4] Naran Gereltu [Radiant as the Sun], the name of the Khaan, is also from Indian mythology. One circumstance has struck me, namely the absence of a Chinggis tradition; so that when I spoke to Khand [Khanddorj] Van about the *Khar Sülde* [Black Flag] of Chinggis and the grave in the Ordos,[5] and advised him to try and use these holy relics to unite the Mongols, he was taken aback. 'Really? Oh—Oh! We will certainly do as you advise.' (Onon and Pritchatt 1989: 99)

The Halh Mongols left out Chinggis Khan and his black flag in their state symbolism, perhaps due to the triumph of Buddhism in Mongolia and the decline of the Mongolian Chinggisid aristocracy. Jamtsarano might not be so criticial of the Buddhist symbols acquired by the Mongols, but as a pan-Mongolist politician-scholar who had visited the Chinggis Khan shrine in Ordos in 1910 (Jamtsarano 1961), he nevertheless advised Khand Van, the Mongolian Foreign Minister, to use the symbolism of Chinggis Khan. Khand Van, a direct descendant of Chinggis Khan, might have been receptive to Jamtsarano's advice, for in January 1913 one of the five columns of armies sent by the Bogd Khan Mongolian government to liberate Inner Mongolia marched in the direction of the Yellow River, which is in the territory of Ordos (Onon and

term '*Mongol Uls*' in the Mongolian version of Russian–Mongolian protocols in 1912, Russian delegates denied its existence in the Russian version (1991: 18). Onon and Pritchatt (1989: 16) note that 'some Mongolian historians later named their newly-established nation, based on the Great Chinggis Khaan's tradition, "*Ikh Mongol Uls*" (great Mongolian nation) or "*Ikh Mongol Tör*" (great Mongol dynasty). It was also called "*Bogd Khaant Mongol Uls*" (holy khaganate Mongol nation).' Recently, a Mongolian historian suggested that the name of independent Mongolia in 1911–15 was '*Olnoo Örgögdsön Mongol Uls*' (Elevated-by-All Mongol Nation). Moreover, the term 'Elevated by All' should be understood in the Mongol context: that is, all Mongol Nation elevated by all Mongols, rather than in the Indian tradition (Jamsran 1992: 68).

[4] Makhasamdi is the legendary founder of India. In Buddhist-influenced Mongolian historiography, Makhasamdi is regarded as the ancestor of the Mongols. See Sagaan Sechen's classical *Erdeni–Tovch* (The Bejewelled Summary), written in 1662, in which he established a genealogical link between the Mongol kingship and the Tibetan and Indian kings (Krueger 1967: 41).

[5] For a detailed description and historical record of the *Süld* shrine and the cult of Chinggis Khan in Ordos, see Sainjirgal and Sharaldai (1983).

222   *The Choice of National Symbols*

Pritchatt 1989: 20). Ordos Mongols to this day would say that the Halh
Mongols at that time wanted to take control of the shrine of Chinggis
Khan. According to a recent Chinese book denouncing pan-Mongolism,
the governor of Ushan banner in Ordos responded to the call for unification with the independent Mongolia by co-operating with the invad-
ing Mongolian troops to transfer the Chinggis Khan shrine to Mongolia
(Shi 1993: 146). This military expedition ended in failure, but triggered
numerous attempts by Japanese, Chinese, and Inner Mongols to take
control of Chinggiss's shrine to rally Mongols behind their respective
causes: anti-Chinese, pan-Mongolist, or anti-Japanese.

What we have seen here is an interesting blend of Tibetan Buddhist
together with Russian ideas, introduced by Russian Orientalists. This
was possible because the Mongols were desperately looking wholly
towards the Russians for help. Note the tendency of the Mongols to
respect outside influence.

State Symbols in the Socialist Period

The Russian influence continued in the socialist period.[6] The Mongolian
army of partisans adopted the *soyombo* symbol as their coat of arms,
stripped of its religious decorations. However, the *soyombo* was not called
süld, but either *erhem üsüg* (distinguished word) or *temdeg* (mark). Revolutionary Mongolia did not have a state flag until 1924, when Bogd Khan
died and Mongolia was declared the Mongolian People's Republic. The
first Constitution (adopted in 1924) of the MPR introduced a *süld*
emblem for the first time: this was the *soyombo* on a base of a lotus
flower (see Fig. 7.2). The designation *süld* (emblem) to the *soyombo* has to
be attributed to a Buryat Mongol, Elbegdorj Rinchino, who suggested at
the first National Congress that the original term *temdeg* (mark) should
be replaced with *süld* (Otgonbaatar 1986: 62). It appeared, however, that
the deputies did not understand why *soyombo* should be chosen as a
national seal and mounted on the national flag. The prime minister,
Tserendorj, gave his authoritative opinion: 'Although I have not seen
any explanation written in any document, according to the old people,
Öndör Gegeen (the first Jebtsundamba) used it to mark the "Sovereign
Mongolian Nation" (*Büren Erht Mongol Uls*)' (H. Nyambuu 1979: 45–6).
The *soyombo* symbol, then, started to enjoy both religious and nationalist

[6] See Stites (1984) for the primary symbols of Bolshevism adopted in 1917–18.

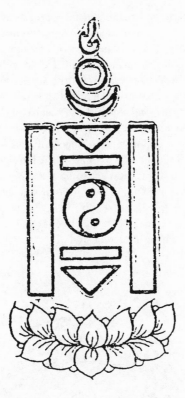

FIGURE 7.2. Mongolian state emblem adopted in 1924.

appeal. At the fifth MPRP Congress in 1926, when an anti-Buddhist policy was adopted, the Buryat Mongolian scholar-politician Jamtsarano argued: 'The phrase *e-bam* designating the heart and brain of the Joyous Buddha, which symbolizes the people's freedom, is beautifully inscribed in our country's *süld*; it has the meaning of developing religion and state in parallel' (Dashtseveg 1976: 27). But this persisting religious overtone warranted suppression when the victory over religion was declared in the 1930s.

After fifteen years of political and ideological struggle, the 1940 Mongolian Constitution specified the nature of the MPR: 'The Mongolian People's Republic is an independent state of workers (herders, workers, and intelligentsia), who have annihilated the imperialistic and feudal yoke, ensuring a non-capitalistic approach to the development of the country to pave the way to socialism in the future.' A new emblem was designed to reflect this new party ideology. The state emblem consisted of a circle in which was depicted an *ard* with a lariat in his hands, galloping on horseback toward the sun. Around the edge of the circle, on two sides there were depicted in small circles the heads of a sheep, a cow, a camel, and a goat. In the centre of the upper part of the circle was a five-pointed star, a Communist symbol. At the bottom was a scroll inscribing the full name of Mongolia in classical script: the Mongolian People's Republic. The emblem had no *soyombo* (see Fig. 7.3). However, the state flag continued to have a *soyombo* in the middle. In 1945, the *soyombo* was removed from its lotus seat, and was capped with a Communist five-pointed star (see Fig. 7.4).

This emblem was in fact a product of the new Communist international division of labour, as demonstrated by the following episode from

FIGURE 7.3. Mongolian state emblem adopted in 1940.

FIGURE 7.4. A Communist star-capped *soyombo* symbol.

Choibalsang's diary kept during his visit to Soviet Union at the end of 1939 and early 1940. On 3 January 1940, at 8 p.m. in Molotov's office in the Kremlin, Choibalsang introduced a draft of the Mongolian emblem to Stalin, Molotov, Voroshilov, Beriya, and Dekanazov:

Seeing the draft emblem, (Stalin) said that there should not be crops in your emblem; there should be a man on horseback, surrounded by various domestic animals. 'In general, do you grow crops on a large scale?' he asked. I said, 'Not so much.' He then said, 'If there are no such crops why did you make such an emblem? No crops.... Mongolia is not an agricultural land, you have no crops. Mongolia is a pastoral land. It is extremely wrong to think that Mongolia has too many cattle. Your Mongolia should increase your cattle number to 200 million. Have you understood?' (*Ünen*, 3 January 1992)

Clearly the introduction of the horse and other animals in the Mongolian emblem was made at the insistence of Stalin.

This emblem gives a hint in fact of 'internal colonialism'. The 1940s was a crucial period in defining the status of Mongolia, whether or not it should be part of the Soviet Union. The deletion of the *soyombo* from the state emblem became a cause of concern among some Mongols. Two camps appeared in the deeply disturbing background of ideological assault from the USSR. Ts. Damdinsüren published an article on the *soyombo* script in 1944 (*Shinjleh Uhaan*, no. 7), writing that the seventeenth-century Western Mongolian Zayabandid Namhaijamts reformed the classical Mongolian script and called the new version *tod*, meaning clear. But Öndör Gegeen Zanabazar of the Eastern Mongols, rather than accepting the *tod* script, invented another script system, which he regarded as even clearer, and gave it a foreign (Indian) name, *soyombo*.[7] Damdinsüren pointed out that while the Western Mongols (Oirat) were fighting for national independence, the Eastern Mongols (Halh) headed by Zanabazar knelt down before the invaders (the Manchu). Damdinsüren's implied argument echoed his involvement in abolishing the classical Mongolian script and adopting the Cyrillic script in 1941, thinking it even 'clearer' than the *tod* script and closer to the spoken Mongolian.[8] At the same time, this article was an attempt to justify the deletion of the *soyombo* symbol from the Mongolian emblem in 1940.

His academic rival, B. Rinchen, opposed abolishing the classical script and the *soyombo*. A popular story goes that Rinchen shook his head when he talked about the Cyrillic script, but nodded to the classical script, because the Cyrillic script is written horizontally, while the latter is

---

[7] At least six different scripts have been used by the Mongols at various stages of their history: the classical script, the hP'ags-pa script, the *tod* (clear) script, the *soyombo* script, the Vaghintara script, and the Cyrillic script (for more information see Academy of Sciences MPR 1990). Bousiang (1984: 92–103) mentioned another script called *Ali Gali*, invented by a Harchin lama, Ayushi Gushi, in 1587.

[8] Damdinsüren later confessed to having committed three sins: he had eulogized Stalin and Choibalsang, destroyed the Mongolian classical script, and married a foreign wife and eliminated his Mongol descent (*Zasgiin Gazariin Medee*, no. 1, 1992).

vertical.[9] Another story tells how Rinchen shrugged off the 1940 Mongol emblem in a conversation with Molotov, the Soviet ambassador to Mongolia. When Molotov asked Rinchen about the meaning of the five-animal cattle emblem, Rinchen replied: 'It means Mongols are as stupid as the cow, as easily taken in as the sheep, as naughty as the goat, and as apathetic as the camel.' But Rinchen liked the horse. In 1945 he wrote an article entitled 'The *Soyombo* is a Sacred Symbol of Mongolian People's Struggle for Independence' (*Shinjleh Uhaan*, no. 9). This was an act of defiance. Encouraged by Choibalsang, who by then might have regretted his negative role in the 1930s, Rinchen also made a hugely successful film about a rebel Halh prince, Tsogt Taiji. Rinchen depicted him as a national hero fighting against the Manchu. In the film, Tsogt Taiji is wearing a *soyombo* crest on his helmet. This was a deliberate anachronism, because Tsogt Taiji was killed by Hoshuut Mongols in a religious dispute in 1637 in Tibet,[10] and the *soyombo* was not invented until 1686. Whatever the case, Rinchen saved the *soyombo* from complete

---

[9] Today supporters of the classical script call it *Hümüün Bichig* (Human Script) (see Fig. 5.3), while those who support the Cyrillic script call it *Mongoljin Bichig* ((female) Mongol Script) (the suffix-*jin* denotes female gender). There is also a newspaper called *Hümüün Bichig*. The vertical way of writing was not an indigenous invention, just as the script itself was borrowed from non-Mongols. However, just as nationalist Mongols during the independence movement could assign new meaning to the *soyombo*, so post-socialist Mongols have used their imagination to invest new meaning in the conspicuous Mongolian script, as Ts. Erdenebileg (1994) has: 'The Mongol script, written top downwards, symbolizes their (Mongols') desire to link the Heaven and the Earth, sing praises to the earthly life and to immortalize space and time. This is indeed a marvellous symbolism. The Mongol script reminds us to love and protect nature, which has created man. Mankind is the offspring of the Father Heaven and Mother Earth. According to an ancient Mongolian belief, a human being is made of three elements. They are the "supreme element", or intellect, the "middle element", or the mind, and the "low element", or flesh and blood. These three elements are closely connected with each other and the "highest element" controls the "middle and low" elements. The Mongol script links human intelligence with the mind and body, and considers them as a sacred treasure. In this sense, the Mongol script is an expression of humanness.... The Mongols act in a most sincere and frank manner. And they link this sincerity with their heart. The Mongol script, written top downwards and left to right is a sign that the written words come from the heart. The Mongol script could very well be called a confession of heart and soul.'

[10] Tsogt Taiji was one of the Halh princes involved in a Halh internecine war in the early 1630s. The civil war was closely related to the Manchu expansion in Mongolia south of the Gobi. Some Mongol tribes defeated by the Manchu fled to the Halh region; Halh princes started to fight each other for control of these Mongols. In this struggle, Tsogt Taiji was defeated and expelled from Halh-land. The contemporary depiction of Tsogt Taiji as an anti-Manchu Mongol hero was largely based on his later association with Ligdan Khan, the last Mongol Khan, who was vehemently against the Manchu expansion into his territory. However, it should be clear that Tsogt Taiji joined the Halh civil war in order to expand his own rule over the refugees of Ligdan Khan (see Oyunbilig 1987).

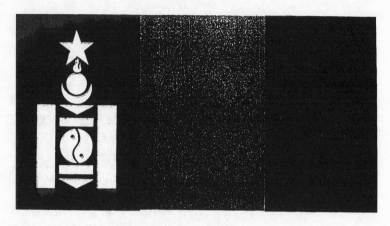

FIGURE 7.5. Mongolian state flag adopted in 1961.

abolition by pro-Soviet influences, and popularized it as a symbol of independence.

In 1961, the third Constitution introduced a new set of symbols. The emblem it prescribed deprived the horseman of his lariat, thus making him unidentifiable as to occupation. The animal heads disappeared, and were replaced by sheaves of wheat, joined at the bottom by a cog-wheel, and interlaced with a ribbon-scroll of red and blue, bearing in Cyrillic the acronym BNMAU[11] (MPR). The flag has three equal vertical stripes, red–blue–red. The red stripe at the hoist bears the *soyombo* in golden yellow, with a yellow star above it (see Fig. 7.5). In the centre of the emblem is the symbolic figure of a working man on horseback galloping upward toward the sun—communism—against a background of a relief typical of the MPR mountains (see Fig. 7.6). According to the Constitution, 'The state emblem of the Mongolian People's Republic reflects the essence of the state and the idea of friendship of peoples, and shall show the national and economic peculiarities of the country.'

One cannot fail to observe that these symbols are linked primarily with the Communist vision of industrialization and urbanization. In the emblem, a complete ideological vision of the Mongols is represented: 'Mongolia, represented by a herdsman, has jumped across a black field (capitalism) from a yellow one (feudalism) on to a red one (socialism)'

---

[11] The full name is *Bügd Nairamdah* (Friendly to All) *Mongol Ard Uls* (Mongolian People's Republic).

FIGURE 7.6. Mongolian state emblem adopted in 1961.

(Sokolewicz 1982: 129). One may interpret the emblem as a graphic embodiment of the socialist Mongol nation based on Stalin's four criteria for defining a nationality: 'a common language, a common territory, a common economic life, and a common psychological make-up manifested in common specific features of material culture' (Stalin 1953: 349). It also reflects the ideological formula 'socialist in content, national in form.'

The *soyombo*, capped by a star in the flag or put within a star in the emblem, was a limited expression of nationalism, allowed perhaps because the Soviet Union needed the MPR's support in its row with China. It was a controlled and directed nationalism, and the symbol was therefore manipulated to express the following idea: anti-Chinese patriotism (or nationalism) and the alliance with the Soviet Union (internationalism).

We have seen that the *soyombo* is an important symbol throughout the socialist period, tracing its origin to the deep past. But what does it mean? The contemporary official exegesis is as follows:

Since ancient times, the *Soyombo* ideogram has been the national emblem of the freedom and independence of the Mongols. At the top of the ideogram is a flame, which symbolizes blossoming, revival, upgrading and continuation of the family. The three prongs of the flame signify the prosperity of the people in the past, the present and the future.

Below the sign of the flame are the sun and the crescent, traditionally symbolizing the origin of the Mongolian people. The combination of the flame, the sun and the crescent expresses the wish: May the Mongolian people live and prosper.

The triangles at the top and bottom of the *Soyombo* are a general expression of the people's willingness to defend the freedom and independence of the country, while the rectangles are the symbols of honesty, justice and nobility. There are two at the top and bottom, personifying honest and selfless service to the homeland.

The fish, in Mongolian folklore, is a creature that never closes its eyes, i.e. remains vigilant. The two fish in the emblem symbolize the unity of the people: men and women. The cumulative meaning is: May the whole people be united, wise and vigilant. The two vertical rectangles on the sides of the emblem signify fortress walls and are a graphic representation of the ancient Mongolian saying: 'two men in friendship are stronger than walls of stone.' In the *Soyombo* they have the meaning: May the whole people be united in friendship, and then it will be stronger than the stone walls of a fortress. (Academy of Sciences MPR 1990: 4–5)

This official interpretation is almost a complete copy of Rinchen's detailed analysis of every component of the ideogram, but omitting his explanation of the lotus, a Buddhist symbol explained as symbolizing purity of heart and thought (Rinchen 1958). It is interesting to find that a design like this has such deep and complex meanings. It could well be a mantra. 'The shortest form of a Mantra is the germinal syllable (Skr.: Bîja) or the mystic seed. This term, in Mantrayâna, means the primal syllable, the primal note or creative word from which the Buddhas develop. Prior to any creation in substantial form, according to Indian philosophy, there was the primal, original word, the first sound in the vastness of space, the sound from whose vibrations all other things developed' (Lauf 1976: 109). Indeed, *soyombo* is derived from the Sanskrit word *swayambha*, whose literal meaning is 'self-sprung', 'existing by itself', or 'independent', and is attributed to the first Jebtsundamba Hutagt. It is the initial grapheme of the script invented by the first Jebtsundamba Hutagt. The grapheme does not have any specific role in the script apart from its religious function. Mantras have an esoteric, hidden meaning which can only be discovered from special instruction by a guru. Therefore, different people put forward different views regarding their interpretation. According to Zhukovskaya, the original *soyombo* was depicted in early Buddhism in the form of a crescent, the sun, and a

FIGURE 7.7. Mystic mantra monogram, 'The All-Powerful Ten'.

tongue of flame, and it was interpreted as the symbolic fusion of an individual with Adibuddha in the Buddhist practice of meditation (1991: 251). In the past, hard pressed by ordinary Mongols who wanted to know the meaning of the *soyombo*, lamas would say that the *soyombo* was used in the 84,000 secret Buddhist teachings (Rinchen 1958). I would suggest that the *soyombo* symbol is simply a Mongolian version of the mystic mantric monogram 'The All-Powerful Ten', or *Nam-bc'u-dban-ldan* (see Fig. 7.7). All these are of course unacceptable to the nationalist-minded Mongols. However, only recently have the deep mystical and hidden meanings of the *soyombo* been deciphered and explained by

Mongolia's modern guru B. Rinchen, as mentioned above. And the hidden meanings lie not in its esoteric tantric function to improve one's meditation, but in nationalism, to throw a charm or spell to defend Mongolia's sovereignty.

Democracy, Nationalism, and Change of Symbols

As we see, the Mongolian Communists, under the direction of the Soviet Russians, frequently changed the emblem and flag to reflect the policy of the state, transforming Mongol society from religious to secular, from pastoral to industrial and socialist. A 'national' symbol in a socialist state is not designed to evoke primordial national sentiments, but is a symbol of the leading role and power of the party and state (Arvidsson and Blomqvist 1987). But perhaps we may say that a socialist symbol may over time be turned into a national symbol, commanding the same quality as that expounded by Firth. In some socialist countries, indeed, historical circumstances demanded that national symbols be retained. In Poland, for example, because of the historical fate that the Poles suffered under the Nazis, Polish Communists wanted to cling to their national symbols and thus legitimate themselves as being a native force, rather than an alien one. The same national symbol was used later by opposition groups in order to out-manœuvre the Communists (Mach 1985, Jakubowska 1990).

Mongolia is one of the few countries that, like Poland, retained the national symbol in its Communist-national flag (in this case, the *soyombo*). However, unlike the Polish case, where the national symbol was used to de-legitimate the power of the Communists, the anti-Communist Mongols have used their flag little, still less their emblem. Instead, the portrait of Chinggis Khan was used in nationalist anti-Communist movements in 1989–90. Chinggis Khan's portrait had much more emotional power, because he represents the ancestor of all the Mongols, the founder of the Mongol state, and was the identity-giver of the Mongol people. For over seven decades, it was not permitted even to mention his name. Carrying his portrait was a form of protest, a demonstration of the return of an independent identity. It opposes not only communism but also Soviet colonialism, and to those Mongolian subgroups and Mongolian democrats, it also embeds a notion of Greater Mongolia. It is obvious that the existing public symbols did not fulfil the nationalist criteria, and the protests of 1989–90 underlined the need to change the public symbols.

Disillusionment with Mongolian state symbols at the end of the socialist period can be seen from popular jokes. These were so widespread that the official titles came virtually to have a double meaning. For example, in Soviet bloc countries, there appeared a joke in the 1970s about the name Mongolian People's Republic (in Russian abbreviated as MNR): *mojno ne rabotat* (You are allowed not to work), characterizing the laziness of the Mongols. I heard that these were being retold by some Mongols to laugh at the impossible situation in Mongolia. The Mongols also coined some jokes, perhaps sharper ones. At the same period, alcoholism became increasingly a social problem in Mongolia, as reflected in the following language-game involving the letters BNMAU (acronym of the Mongolian People's Republic): *Bügdeeree Nülj Manaid Arhi Uugaad, Uusan Arhi n' Manaid Novsh Bolood, Bolson Novshüg Manai Avgai Ugaav* (All together drank alcohol at my home, the consumed alcohol became filth, and my wife cleaned the filth). A simpler version runs as follows: *Bügdeeree Nüleeg Manaid Arhi Uuya, Uusan Arhia Manaid Nülj Bööljne* (Let's all gather at my home and drink alcohol, Let's vomit what we drink altogether at my home). The idiocy in the acronym alludes not only to a serious problem in the country but to the stigmatization of the nation.[12]

I now want to discuss how post-socialist Mongolia changed its national symbols. Ever since its establishment (in 1990), the State Small Hural (SSH), or the Mongolian version of parliament, had been drafting new laws, including a new Constitution. The highest political organ, as prescribed by the old constitution, was the Great People's Hural (Congress). After 1990 some power was taken away from the Congress and shifted to the newly elected parliament. The SSH was a functional standing committee of the Congress. However, it was regarded as a rival power, because the majority of the MPRP members in the SSH were democratically minded; the SSH had to defend its draft Constitution before the Congress in which the overwhelming majority of deputies were conservative MPRP members from the countryside.

Before moving on, I should briefly mention the social background of the politicians. The SSH members were mostly young journalists, writers, scholars, lawyers, and economists who had been educated in the Soviet Union or Eastern European countries. Many of them were

---

[12] In Czechoslovakia, similarly, people twisted slogans to ridicule the state. For example, the two most important slogans, 'The Soviet Union—our example' and 'With the Soviet Union for ever', have been made into a joke, 'With the Soviet Union for ever but not a day longer' (Holy 1993: 213).

non-Halh, such as Buryats, etc. They gained their reputation as anti-Soviet nationalists and democrats in the early 1990 demonstrations, and they thus became national heroes. The deputies of the Congress were mostly *negdel* (collective) leaders, élite herders,[13] and MPRP bosses, who were initially overwhelmed by the democratic process. It was the dual values of democracy and education, and the fresh euphoria and enthusiasm in the immediate aftermath of the revolution, that carried those 'democrats' into the newly established SSH in July 1990. However, as time went on and the economic crisis deepened, people began to question the existence of the SSH. The new laws were ridiculed as *Mongolin huul' gurvan honog* (Mongolian laws last only three days). The democrats' failure to save the economy and further social crises provoked some to regret the old days and search for a new Khan to iron-rule Mongolia. An often heard proverb was *Deedes n' suudalaa olohgüi bol doodos n' güidlee olohgüi* (If those above cannot find their proper seats, those below will not be able to run errands).

The Congress was convened against a more serious background of privatization and the abolition of the *negdel*s. The *negdel* leaders' political future thus seemed rather uncertain, and they were particularly hostile to the SSH and the government. Meanwhile, the MPRP also had to defend itself and keep itself in power. After the August 1991 Soviet *coup* the call to outlaw the MPRP had become clamorous. The Mongolian situation was rather similar to the post-Communist Eastern European situation as accurately described by Hroch (1993), which I quote at length:

For the current situation in the region is in many respects a unique one in European history. The old order, based on a planned economy and rule by a nomenclature, has suddenly disappeared, leaving a political and social vacuum. In these conditions new elites, educated under the old regime, but now at the head of the national movement, have rapidly occupied leading positions in society. The educated strata of the non-dominant ethnic groups strove towards similar goals in the nineteenth century, but they had to contend with the established elites of the ruling nation for every position, and a condition of their success was acceptance of the traditional forms of life, moral codes and rules of the game of the class above them. Today, by contrast, vertical social mobility into the highest levels of wealth or power is subject to no traditional usages, but often appears to be simply the resultant of individual or national egoisms. The vacuum at the top of society has created the possibility of very swift careers, as a new ruling class starts to take shape, recruited from a confluence of

[13] These people were the 'model herders' who came first in the socialist competitions, etc., and were then rewarded by the regime and used as role models.

three principal streams—apprentice politicians (some of them former dissidents), veteran bureaucrats (the more skilled managers from the old command economy), and emergent entrepreneurs (sometimes with dubious capital resources). The fight within, and among, these groups for positions of privilege has so far yielded the most intense conflicts of interest in post-Communist society; and wherever members of different ethnic groups live on the same territory, it generates the leader tensions of a nationally relevant character today. (1993: 17–18)

Broad public debate on the new Constitution began in Mongolia with the publication of a draft in June 1991. An earlier draft in English was circulated abroad in May, to enlist the assistance of the International Commission of Jurists (Sanders 1992: 511–12). In keeping with the rebirth of strong national sentiment in Mongolia, the title for the Constitution was given as *Ih Tsaaz*; the English translation pens it *Yassa*,[14] evocative of the name of Chinggis Khan's legendary code of laws. The country's name was *Mongol Uls*, simply Mongolia, which is also the name of Chinggis Khan's Mongolia. While the May draft did not specify the emblem and the flag, the June draft did: 'The Mongol national (state) emblem is a golden *soyombo* on a pure white flower base.' It is interesting to note that the emblem was the same as that of 1924. The flag remained a *soyombo* flag, the star being removed.

During the public discussion, it was critically noted that the white flower is ambiguous: the Mongols think that the flourishing of white flowers in summer suggests diseases in summer, and other calamities in winter. The Mongols are sensitive to the term *tsetseg*, 'flower', because it is the popular name of smallpox. Many suggested that if there were to be a flower at all, it should be named 'lotus'. Many objected to the continuance of the red colour in the flag, seeing it as alien, introduced into the country from 1919. One interesting view would equate the two red colours with Russia and China, with the blue Mongols squeezed between two giants, hence an inauspicious arrangement. As a result of public reaction, the SSH decided to suggest a different emblem and flag. On 5 October, two artists' designs of emblem and flag were published in the *Ardiin Erh* newspaper.

[14] This translation is incorrect. *Ih Tsaaz* (Great Law (Prohibition)) refers to an Oirat edict in the seventeenth-century, while *Yassa* is the thirteenth-century pronunciation (still preserved among the Oirat Mongols) of Chinggis Khan's *Ih Zasag* (Great Code of Laws). *Zasag* derives from the verb *zasah* (to correct, to balance). The government is now called *Zasagiin Gazar* (governing, or correcting place). It was earlier called Council of Ministers.

Tsültem, designer of the 1961 emblem, proposed a combination of the emblem of the Huns[15] (entailing fire, sun, and crescent), the emblem of thirteenth-century Mongolia (the white standard), and the more recent Mongolian emblem (the *soyombo*). At the bottom is a man on horseback holding a bundle of arrows, a motif taken from the legend of Alan Goa, the female ancestor of the Mongols. According to the legend, Alan Goa gave each of her five sons an arrow to break, which they did; but, as she predicted, they were unable to break five arrows taken together. His second version was a reform of the 1961 emblem. The wheat, the star, and the landscape were deleted, leaving only the horse and the *soyombo*.

The state emblem designed by Tengisbold is round in shape, symbolizing heaven. The background colour is blue. On the top are nine stars, meaning 'may the universe and life continue for ever', as Mongolians have high respect for the number nine. A falcon is depicted holding in its claws five arrows, symbolizing unity and strength. On the breast of the falcon is the ideogram *soyombo* on a lotus flower, which means, according to the artist, that even if Mongolia becomes weak, it will have the strength to revive again. His second version depicts a white horse with a white standard flying on the breast of a falcon.

The new state flag designed by Tengisbold is blue with six white and red stripes running on two sides of the flag, in the centre of which is the *soyombo*, again depicted on a lotus flower. The white stripes symbolize the pure-hearted Mongolians, and the two red stripes stand for male and female elements, and have their source, according to Tengisbold, in the theory of relativity of the ancient Indian philosopher Nagarjuna. The *soyombo* and the lotus flower are painted in gold.

The SSH chose Tengisbold's falcon emblem for discussion in the Congress. The name of the country in the second draft Constitution remained 'Mongolia', and the name of the Constitution, *Ih Tsaaz*. Due to limits of space, I eclipse the broad public discussion, and go directly to the debates in the Congress, of which indeed many would say that they reflected the state of mind of the whole nation. I have arranged the debates in sequence. My sources are mainly the government newspaper *Ardiin Erh*, Mongolian TV and radio, which covered the Congress debates extensively, and my own observations and discussions with people.

---

[15] An early nomadic empire in Central Asia. The name is also spelt Hsiung-nu or Hunnu.

Names of Constitution and State

The Congress started on 10 November 1991. For ten days the deputies argued about the names of the Constitution and the state. It was not until 21 November, the eleventh day, that the deputies agreed to the temporary name of the state as the Republic of Mongolia (*Bügd Nairamdah Mongol Uls*) and the Constitution's name as *BNMU-in Ih Zasag Huul* (Republic of Mongolia's Great Code). The Congress had originally been expected to last only three weeks. It was then estimated that should the pace continue like this, the whole process of discussing the Constitution might take 1,650 days, or more than four years. They had something more important to discuss: the entire content of the new Constitution and also the evaluation of the new government record. It seems that the SSH was over-confident of its proposal and expected easy approval by the Congress. They might have thought that their version reflected both the national renaissance and democracy, two of the most dominant thoughts of the period. It turned out, however, that these had become the most questionable issues and a focus of political struggle. Below, I give a summary of the eleven days of debates.

The new parties immediately formed a coalition accusing the MPRP of being solely responsible for the delay,[16] and they struggled in every possible way against the MPRP. The MPRP in turn accused them of not listening to the opinions of the people. The MPRP was totally against the proposal of the SSH, and tried every means to sabotage it by taking advantage of their overwhelming majority. At the beginning of the Congress, the MPRP distributed a *Lavlagaa* (guide) ordering every MPRP member to abide by the order set out: namely, the MPRP member should hold on to the old names, the MPR, and the Fundamental Law (*Ündsen Huul*), which was the old name of the Constitution since 1924, etc.[17]

An interesting tactic used by the MPRP leadership was to tell the deputies from the countryside not to be frightened by the SSH members.

[16] The seats occupied by parties in the Congress were as follows (*Ardiin Erh*, 12 Nov. 1991): MPRP: 360; MDP: 17; MNPP: 5; MSDP: 5; MFLP: 1; non-party: 39. The factions established during the People's Congress were: MPRP: 350; MDP: 30; MSDP: 7; MNPP: 11; agricultural co-operatives: 124; Democratic United Front: 93; Youth for Democracy: 10; deputies' independent faction: 64; army deputies: 14; non-party: 7; medical doctors: 20; women deputies: 9. Members of the above parties were also subdivided into groups by profession or even opinions. On certain issues, less formal groupings emerged across party and factional boundaries.

[17] *Ardchilal*, no. 17, 1991.

They had the same rights. *Ta nar öörsdiin har uhaanaar shiid*, 'Make up your mind by your own plain instinct'—that is, don't be fooled by the new thinkers. In spite of appearances, this was not in fact a de-ideologizing effort. The majority of the deputies began to express their views in the old, accustomed ways. Those so-called nationalists were actually strenuously defending the Communist system, opposing any democratic change, the parliamentary system, and land reform. In order to combat the urban democrats, the MPRP appealed to the rural deputies by endorsing and promoting Buddhist values. In so doing, they became nation-defenders. Their logic was this, put simply: return to the original 'Mongol Idea' (*Mongol Uhaan*) and religion, thus become Buddhist and 'Mongol'; fight against anything foreign, from people to ideas, thus against democracy and economic change.

Conservative MPRP pigheadedness was opposed by those (headed by Zardikhan and D. Tangad) inside the MPRP who supported the democratic process. They split away from the party and formed a new party, the Renaissance Party, and they also joined a coalition consisting of other small parties. The MPRP, however, was joined by the '821' group, widely criticized as a Fascist group, later to become the Independence Party.

Democrats, who opposed the term *Ündsen Huul* (Fundamental Law) for the new Constitution, argued that it was not only a foreign production, but had also played a negative role. It was because of this *Huul* that many people were killed and so much tragedy occurred in Mongolia. The *Ündsen Huul* was closely linked to the content of the previous Constitutions, and not only was the content wrong, but the term associated with it was not desirable. The democrats, or the majority of the SSH members, insisted on the name *Ih Tsaaz*. Chimid, the secretary of the SSH, explained that, according to Mongolian state tradition, the core law is called *Ih Tsaaz*; *tsaaz* is a Mongolian word meaning *huul* (law). This explanation did not receive support. It was agreed by some MPRP members that it means law, but it connotes *yal*, or crime, and 'cutting heads' (see Fig. 7.8). It is thus characteristic of criminal law, which does not correspond to the content of a Constitution, nor to the democratic spirit. The debate between the two resulted in the third option, *Ih Zasag*. The importance of the term lies in *Zasag*, which means governing. Moreover, it was recalled that Chinggis Khan's *Yassa* was also called *Ih Zasag*. Many then cajoled the deputies, saying that if you worship Chinggis Khan, then you must vote for the term *Ih Zasag*!

However, opponents were convinced that *Zasag* could not have the meaning of law. They pointed out that *Zasag* is a tainted word, specific-

С. ЦОГТБАЯР, Н, ЧУЛУУН нар
зурав.

FIGURE 7.8. '*Ih Tsaaz* means . . .'. Drawing by S. Tsogtbayar
and N. Chuluun, *Üg*, no. 32, Dec. 1991.

ally related to the concepts of *zasaglah* or *zahiraadah*, too much administrative bureaucracy, which was characteristic of socialism, and is therefore the antithesis of freedom and democracy. Both these terms were also
characteristic of the feudal period, and thus did not fit today's parliamentary democracy. Dashbalbar, the leader of the '821' group, argued
that *Ih Zasag* would be a cruel name, and should it be adopted, then half
of the two million Mongols' heads would be cut off!

Numerous rounds of voting were carried out, but still the issue could
not be settled. The president had to persuade the political groups to meet
and exchange ideas. As a compromise, the leaders of the parties agreed to
a solution: *Mongol Ulsiin Ündsen Huul* (Mongolia's Fundamental Law).
Despite this agreement, because of the stubborn insistence of some
deputies who were resolutely opposed to *Mongol Uls*, the Congress failed
to ratify it. After further debates, another compromise was reached. The
name of the Constitution was called *Ih Zasag Huul* (Great Code),[18] on 19
November.

[18] I was surprised that nobody talked about the native word *Juram* (Code of Laws), as
appeared in the *Halh Juram*, the famous eighteenth-century Halh Code of Laws. Some

Discussion then started on the state name. Three names were proposed: *Mongol Uls* (Mongolia), *Bügd Nairamdah Mongol Ard Uls* (the Mongolian People's Republic), and *Bügd Nairamdah Mongol Uls* (the Republic of Mongolia). But none of them got a majority.

The SSH's choice of *Mongol Uls* was explained by Zardikhan (incidentally, he is a Kazakh, now Mongolia's ambassador to Kazakhstan), the deputy leader of the SSH: all the countries in the world call our country the land of blue sky. With 2,200 years of state tradition,[19] historically it has been known as *Mongol Uls* since 1206. Dispelling the worry of some deputies who argued that a change of name would jeopardize the status of Mongolia in the UN, Zardikhan assured them that no such problem would occur. He explained that the main reason for changing the name was because of the word *ard* (people). In the first Constitution, *ard* had a clear class connotation, cutting off 24.8 per cent of the entire population as non-*ard* (feudal lords, rich men, etc.) and laying the foundation to persecute them. Thus *ard* is typically associated with socialism, and is incompatible with today's attempt to build a civil society. Today, economic reform has made possible the birth of private property ownership, pluralism has swept across the nation, and the traditional religion has been revived.

However, the staunchest ex-Communists insisted that a change of name would endanger the independence of Mongolia. They were particularly worried that both China and Russia would not like the term 'Mongolia'. They also argued that the change would cost too much for a poor economy. Some argued that the term *ard* no longer denotes class, but refers to all strata of people. The '821' group insisted that they would fight for the old name BNMAU. Pessimism began to develop in the hall as to whether the Congress could indeed ratify the Constitution. Dramatically, General Mönhdorj, a vice-minister of the Defence Ministry,

---

people told me that they did not like it, because it is now related to the term for socialism, *niigem juram*. Alas!

[19] Mongols claim that the first Mongol state should be dated from the Hun Empire, not Chinggis Khan's Mongolia. There seem to be several reasons for this. First, the Mongols assert they have a much longer history than 800 years. Second, the Hun Empire is ideologically more acceptable to the Russians than Chinggis Khan's Mongolia. Hun is also acceptable to the Kazakhs, many of whom would argue that they did not come from the thirteenth-century *Mongol* tribes Naiman and Kereit as popularly believed. In Inner Mongolia, Chinese scholars are eager to cultivate the Hun link with the Mongols. Wang Zhaojun, a Han Dynasty court girl married to the Hun Chanyu (chief) is a celebrated motif extensively exploited to promote Mongol–Chinese friendship (see Lin 1979). The Inner Mongols themselves, however, would stress Chinggis Khan's Mongolia.

collapsed and died during this verbal cross-fire, supporting the name *Mongol Uls*. The political factions had to adjourn to discuss their strategies. The following day, the representatives of different factions read their resolutions. The MPRP still insisted on BNMAU; so did the Independence neo-Fascist group. The Democratic Party and Republican Party preferred to postpone the ratification. But a compromise was finally reached when the leadership managed to control the situation and let the deputies vote for 'the Republic of Mongolia' (*Bügd Nairamdah Mongol Uls*).[20] As a result, 67 per cent approved the motion, thus temporarily cracking this hard nut.

Emblem, Flag, and Seal

On 22 November 1991, a working group of deputies was commissioned to choose the state symbols. On 25 November, article 12 of the Constitution, which describes the meaning of the symbols, began to be discussed. Then the emblem and flag designer Tengisbold explained his designs. He rejected the criticism that his bird emblem was a copy of the American eagle. He said that a lot of countries use birds as their emblems, therefore similarity is inevitable. Explaining the white falcon in the emblem, he said that the Mongols were in fact the first in the world to have a bird emblem, but lost this tradition later. He was referring to the falcon dream omen as recorded in the *Secret History*. Yesügei and his son Temüjin (later Chinggis Khan), en route to find a wife for Temüjin, met Dei-sechen of the Onggirat tribe, the future father-in-law of Temüjin. Dei-sechen said that he had had a dream the previous night: 'A white falcon grasping both the sun and the moon, came flying and perched upon my hand... Yisügei-quda, this, my dream, showed you coming, leading your own son. I dreamt a good dream' (*Secret History*, section 63). However, the design was rejected by the majority.

---

[20] Baabar made an interesting point about the origin of the name *Bügd Nairamdah Mongol Ard Uls*. In his view, *Bügd Nairamdah* is not a literary translation of the Latin term *res publica*; rather, it is a rendering of the Chinese characters *Gonghe*, in *Wuzu Gonghe*, (Harmony of Five Nations) as propagated by Sun Yat-sen. Therefore, the phrase denotes the harmony of the Mongols with the other four nations in the Republic of China: namely, Chinese, Manchu, Muhammadans, and Tibetans. Baabar also notes that the MPR was the only 'People's' Republic until 1948, providing a model for some Eastern European countries after their 'socialist revolution'. The model was also copied by the Chinese Communists, who named their country 'People's Republic of China' (Baabar 1996: 344–6).

Scholars were called in. Professor Ch. Dalai, a historian, said that he would prefer a horse in the emblem: 'Honourable deputies, when you change the emblem, try to keep the horse. This petrol oil stuff will eventually be exhausted, and in 200–300 years' time, who knows what will be more useful than horses?' Anthropologist H. Nyambuu recounted the history of Mongolian state symbols: namely, the *soyombo*, the white standard, and the falcon. But no immediate solution was in sight; the article had to be shelved to be discussed in the second reading of the Constitution.

The first reading of the Constitution was completed at noon on 23 December 1992, having lasted more than a month, without being able to resolve many issues. The second reading started that afternoon, and the Congress immediately took up the question of state symbols.

Interestingly, the Deputies' Association made a new proposition: in addition to the state flag (*dalbaa*) and state emblem (*süld*), there should also be a state standard (*tug*). This was to be a ritual honour standard, representing the white standard of Chinggis Khan's Mongolia, and it should be made of the tails of one thousand white stallions. The Association suggested that it should be specially protected in the state palace. Chinggis Khan's black standard should be kept by the Defence Ministry.[21] This suggestion was accepted by the deputies.

Horse and *soyombo* were left as options for the emblem. The falcon failed to enter into the competition, although stubbornly supported by the SSH.[22] The herdsmen deputies objected to the deletion of the horse from the emblem. By supporting the falcon, the SSH made itself vir-

---

[21] Zuunai, a deputy, wrote on 24 Dec. 1991 in *Ardiin Erh*: 'The state flag (*töriin dalbaa*) should keep the *soyombo*, and being printed on cloth, it should become a symbol of state administration (*töriin zahirgaanai beleg demberel*). The state white standard (*töriin tsagaan süld*) is meant to show that *Mongol Uls* is the hearth of the Mongol *tuurgatan* (tent-dwellers, hence all the Mongols in the world).' The contemporary Mongols' understanding of the white standard as opposed to the black standard is largely derived from a propagation of Academician B. Rinchen in the 1950s. In an article rebuking the mistaken notion that the pendant of the standard was made of yak tails, Rinchen wrote that it was made of the tails of stallions, and that white standard symbolized peace and the black standard war (see O. Pürev 1990).

[22] According to a survey conducted among 270 deputies and published in *Ardiin Erh*, on 30 Nov., 63.3 per cent of them preferred to change the emblem, 27 per cent supported the falcon emblem proposed by the SSH, and 8.9 per cent were in favour of the old one. The following elements obtained overwhelming support to be incorporated in the emblem: *soyombo* (80 per cent), horse (75.8 per cent), sun (70 per cent), fire (51.8 per cent). But bird symbols got only 1.4 per cent support.

FIGURE 7.9. 'Dad! The State Emblem Bird!' Drawing by Ts. Bayanzul,
Tonshuul, no. 15, 1991.

tually an opposition to the Communist-turned-Buddhist herdsmen
deputies (see Fig. 7.9). Two factions appeared, one supporting the
horse, the other the *soyombo*. Deputy Norovragchaa advocated a *set* of
state symbols, arguing that a combination of state standard, *soyombo*
emblem, and flag would make a complete history of Mongolia. The
white standard was a product of Chinggis Khan's time, the *soyombo*
was after his time, and the flag would represent the future. Horse
supporters criticized those who said that the horse is in fact not so
much respected in Mongolia (it is slaughtered to be eaten or sold to
the Russians!). If that is so, they argued, then the fish in the *soyombo* is
equally eaten by people, so how could such a thing be worshipped? They
insisted that Mongols should never be separated from the horse, and said
this was the people's opinion (see Figs. 7.10, 7.11, 7.12).

Scholars were again called in to elaborate on the *soyombo*. Two
fundamentally different views emerged, which echoed the great debate
between Damdinsären and Rinchen in the 1940s. The issue was whether
soyombo is Mongolian or foreign, whether or not it symbolizes independence. Since Buddhism is legitimate now, one scholar (ironically the
curator of the Damdinsären Museum) argued: 'Our famous scholars

FIGURE 7.10. Where are we going? A Mongol on horseback looking behind at the sunset. Drawing by N. Chuluun, *XXI Zuun*, no. 2, Oct. 1990.

and lamas say it (the *soyombo*) is a marvellous product, having the triple function of looking with eyes, hearing with ears, and meditating with mind. Amongst all the nations in the world, only the flags of Japan, India and Mongolia look spectacular. Mongolia is known to the world by this *soyombo*.' However, Sühbaatar, an anti-religious and anti-Chinese historian, observed scornfully: 'The *Soyombo* was only ever a religious symbol. It was never a state symbol. It is also an artificial speculation to say that it is a symbol of independence. Whatever it says, it is meaningful only in Sanskrit, not in Mongolian. Even "*tug*" is of Chinese origin.'[23] These

---

[23] He did not give an explanation. I suspect the etymology is *dao*, an ideogram resembling a standard.

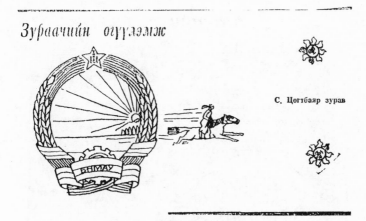

FIGURE 7.11. A Mongol on horseback galloping out of the emblem. Drawing by S. Tsogtbayar, *Üg*, no. 15, Sept. 1990.

FIGURE 7.12. A disappointed herdsman talks to his horse: 'So all we've got for 70 years is that they say horses should be transported in lorries and eaten! Let's go home before it's too late.' Drawing by S. Tsogtbayar and N. Chuluun, *Üg*, no. 32, Dec. 1991.

debates ignited the atmosphere of the Congress to such an extent that many deputies simply walked out of the hall. Inside and outside the Congress, people were bewildered by the overwhelming choices of

FIGURE 7.13. A bewildered ordinary Mongol praying to numerous emblem designs proposed in the Congress: 'Mercy! My state emblems!' Drawing by S. Tsogtbayar and N. Chuluun, *Üg*, no. 32, Dec. 1991.

symbols, and they passionately debated which were genuine Mongolian national symbols (see Fig. 7.13). Mongolian artists tried their best to transform the mood of the Congress into something acceptable to the nation (see Fig. 7.14).

The discussion was postponed till 2 January 1992. This time, the competition was between Tsültem's improved version and a new design by Ts. Oidov. Tsültem changed his design from a horse to a *soyombo*, explaining that it was not a Mongolian tradition to depict animal figures on an emblem. However, his design did not arouse much interest among the deputies. Their attention was drawn to Oidov's design, which had a horse with a *soyombo* in its centre. The horse's tail and mane were drawn like streaming flames, suggesting that it was flying, reminiscent of a wind horse (*hii mori*). It had triple gems (*chandamni*) at the top, and five arrows

—Сүлдээ дагаан шонхроор бат-
луулбал
Сүүлдээ барнгдахгүй хэцүүдэх
болов уу?

Сүлдэндээ морно үлдээчнхвэл
Сүүлээ шарваад хашнгнах болов
уу?

Ж. БАТСАИХАН зураа

FIGURE 7.14. Artists racking their brains to design the Mongolian state emblem: *Left*, 'If a white falcon is drawn into the emblem, will it be uncontrollable later?' *Right*, 'If the horse remains in the emblem, will it be lazy and wag its tail later?' Drawing by J. Batsaihan, *Ardiin Erh*, no. 202, 16 Nov. 1991.

on the base of a lotus flower. The emblem was round in shape, rimmed by a swastika motif (see Fig. 7.15).[24]

Some began to pick faults. It was pointed out that this horse did not look like a Mongolian horse, but more like a Greek mythological horse. One deputy even joked that it was like a beer-bottle opener.[25] A deputy,

[24] The swastika can be found in rock paintings in Mongolia, and also in the earmarks of animals. The swastika is called in Mongolian *has*. It symbolizes *sain üil* (auspices). This ideogram became part of the Buddhist decorative art of the Mongols, embodying the meaning *Jargalang* 'happiness' (symbolizing passing over four seas in Buddhist cosmology—birth, pain, ageing, and death) and attaining a second meaning, *Um sain amgalang boltugai*, the starting phrase in almost all praise odes. The Mongols also call the swastika motif either *tümen ölzii* or *tümen nasan* (longevity) when drawn in such a way that it has no beginning or end (Chimid 1992).

[25] This metaphorical resemblance has gained popularity after the ratification of the national emblem. In a recent collection of political jokes in Mongolia from 1921 to 1994 (Tsenddoo 1994), only two items refer to the new emblem, and both link it explicitly with the alcoholism rampant in Mongolia: 'Why have Mongols started to drink heavily? It is

FIGURE 7.15. The new Mongolian emblem adopted in 1992.

Badarch, commented sarcastically, 'We have rid the national name of *ard*, now we rid the horse of a human being.' He pointed out that the swastika became the symbol of Hitler's Germany, and therefore must not be used in the Mongolian emblem. Others reminded the Congress that this swastika is depicted on chest surfaces, on felt, socks, and other things, and therefore should not be drawn on such a sacred thing as the state emblem. Tengisbold, the falcon emblem designer, taking

because a bottle top is worshipped in the national emblem' (1994: 83). 'The new Mongolian national emblem is used as a brand (for a product), but its circulation is poor. It is because bottled beer has become scarce, and has been replaced by tinned beer' (1994: 55).

advantage of the chaos, again pressed for his own design. A deputy, Sh. Sürenjav, got so furious that a fight ensued. The Congress adjourned at the demand of several political factions to find a way out.

On the sixtieth day of the Congress, 10 January 1992, after intense debates and votes, the Congress finally adopted Oidov's design, on condition that some modifications be made. The decision on the flag was relatively simple; the Congress decided that the old flag, with the five-pointed star on top of the *soyombo* removed, would do (see Fig. 7.16). However, the People's Great Hural decided at the last moment to call the Constitution not 'The Republic of Mongolia's Great Code', as had been agreed two months before, but 'Mongolia's Fundamental Law' (*Mongol Ulsiin Ündsen Huul*). 'At long last', comments the *Mongol Messenger*, 'a compromise was reached: those MPs who voted for the new emblem made concessions to their "opponents" by agreeing to the name of [the] country [as] Mongolia' (14 January 1992).

The Congress also decided unanimously to adopt a state seal (*tamga*). The seal was not as controversial as the other symbols. The seal handle is in a lion shape. Its face has a *soyombo* on a lotus flower, with the words *Mongol Uls* on both sides.

What needs to be explained, however, is the function of the *tamga*. To put it simply, the legitimacy of the dynastic state in East Asia was represented by the *tamga*, a symbol of power bequeathed from Heaven. In other words, the legitimacy of a family to rule a state over generations is marked by possession of the seal. The control of the legitimizing power

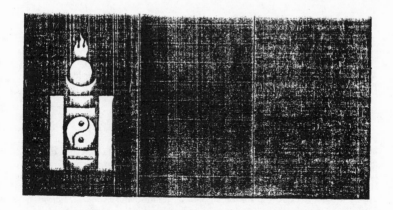

FIGURE 7.16. The new Mongolian flag adopted in 1992.

of the seal was the source of endless wars and struggles, and even changes of dynasty.[26] The Mongols also adhered to this mode of thought. Togoon Tömör Khan, the last Mongol Khan of the Yuan Dynasty, when he fled the capital, according to Sagaan Sechen, 'placed the jade jewel seal in his sleeve and took his queen and children' (Krueger 1967: 184). Because of this seal, the Mongols were able to continue their dynastic tradition (though their power drastically weakened). This was also the cause of the endless war between the Ming Dynasty and the Mongols, for without this legitimating device, the Ming Dynasty feared not being regarded as orthodox by its subjects (Cao 1990). The legitimating power of the seal can be further seen in the following account: 'With the surrender of Ligdan's son, the imperial seal is also said to have come into the possession of Abahai: this is a Manchu tradition legitimizing, as it were, his succession to the inheritance of Genghis Khan. Mongol popular tradition denies that the seal ever came into the possession of the Manchus at all' (Bawden 1968: 47). What made Bogd Khan Mongolia special is that it deliberately created a new seal to legitimate its independence, and also named the state according to Indian mythology, as we saw earlier. This was perhaps the first psychological change of the Mongols from their traditional outlook of the need for continuity in legitimation by an ancient seal. But the legitimacy of the revolutionary government was marked by the nobles' handing over the existing seal to the revolutionaries, thus returning to the old pattern. The re-establishment of the idea of the seal today is a reflection of strong nationalistic historicism.

Epilogue

We are now clear that these state symbols are not just simple Durkheimian symbols, but are conscious intellectual constructions, reflecting ideo-

[26] According to Endicott-West (1989), the *tamga* or *yin* (seal) used to be a purely Chinese institution, giving legitimacy to an office-holder. During the Mongol Yuan Dynasty, however, the Mongols' preference for hereditary transfer of office to the Chinese examination system further developed this institution, making it more Mongolian in character than Chinese. 'The *yin* privilege in the hands of the Mongolian rulers became an instrument for attempting to maintain the sharply defined social, political, and ethnic differences that existed to varying degrees in thirteenth- and fourteenth-century China' (Endicott-West 1989: 66). This institution was later adopted by the Manchus for controlling the Mongolian hereditary nobles in their respective banners, so much so that the banner government was called *tamgiin gazar* (seal office).

logical struggles. The invention of tradition is not an easy process. The Mongolian legislators declared the criteria for the selection of symbols to be 'the historical tradition, aspiration, unity, justice and spirit of the people of Mongolia'. Since I am chiefly concerned with symbols and identity, in the remainder of this chapter, I analyse the time and space dimension that came into this complicated (albeit simplified in my description) symbol-choosing process. The tremendous effort and emotion devoted to these symbols and names left the deputies little time to discuss other important articles of the Constitution. In fact, despite prolonged gestation, the final document was little changed from the draft submitted by the SSH. What mattered to the deputies was external metaphors rather than the content. Indeed, as Walzer puts it: 'The state is invisible; it must be personified before it can be seen, symbolized before it can be loved, imagined before it can be conceived' (quoted in Kertzer 1988: 6).

First, I wish to draw attention to emblem choice in Israel. The young nation-state has absorbed millions of Jews who have different origins in time and place in the Diaspora. While in exile, they called themselves Jews. 'All turned towards Jerusalem to pray, and in synagogues across the globe and across the centuries the salutation would ring out: "Next year in Jerusalem". Then, with the Ingathering of the Exiles into the new State of Israel, cultural differences of time and place became salient' (Paine 1989: 121). The content of Jewish peoplehood or nationhood is thus the source of competition over 'tradition', because 'after 2000 years of life in the Diaspora, the differences among Jews and Jewish communities around the world may be far greater than their similarities' (Dominguez 1990: 132). However, Handelman's and Shamgar-Handelman's (1990) analysis of the choice of the emblem of the new Israeli nation-state—the seven-branched lampstand, the menorah—shows how historicity is represented and encoded in symbols. The legislators avoided themes like the Diaspora or the Holocaust, the most important features of Jewish culture and history, which are the points most disagreed upon. Instead, they concentrated on the Jewish notion of redemption, a Zionist return to the sacred space and the ancient time of God. Thus, disputes over 'tradition' or heritage were effectively avoided, so that all Jews could define their Jewishness in Israel.

However, in Mongolia, there is simply no single time or space common to, or accepted by, all the Mongols, even in Mongolia. The debates and the disagreement (ideologically oriented) over the choice of the symbols should thus be explained in the context of interaction and exchange. Mauss ([1925] 1954) has developed a theory of the morality of reciprocity in gift exchange. The obligation to repay is linked to the belief that the gift retains a spiritual relationship to the giver in systems where things are 'parts of persons', and social identity, status, and prestige are thus at stake in gift exchange. Following the insight of seeing the gift in its quality of generating social solidarity, and the spiritual identification of the gift with the owner, Lévi-Strauss (1969) developed the theory of exchange of women and marriage alliance, which I have applied in this book. This insight could be extended to the symbols and ideas that form the core of group identity. The Mongol choice of symbols is only meaningful today if we see them as part of a whole field of interaction and, most importantly, in the light of nationalism. I have explained that Mongol nationalism has an overriding concern with purity. Thus the choice of national symbols is in fact a choice of purity. Yet 'purity' must be an arbitrary invention, and crucially it is defined in relation to an outside or non-pure other.

We have seen that Mongolian symbols are signs and objects selected and chosen from various historical contexts in the larger interaction with the outside world. There are several kinds of interactions: the ruling nomadic élite might whole-heartedly embrace the sedentary culture and bureaucracy, adopt an assimilationist policy, and in time, disappear; or they might maintain a nomadic superiority until its collapse, or the nomads might constantly seek legitimacy from outside. Whatever the case, Mongol identity formation has always been, in one or another context, related to the 'outside world' (see Khazanov 1984). This relation with the outside world includes raiding and trade, the principal purposes of nomadic warfare (Jagchid and Symons 1989). We have seen a flow of women, economic items, and ideas between the sedentary and nomadic peoples. Cultural influence between the sedentary Chinese and the nomadic Mongols is perhaps greater than might be imagined, as nomads introduced numerous cultural codes to the Chinese, which became an essential part of Chinese culture, and vice versa.[27] The same is even true of Russian–Mongolian cultural influences, though it is beyond the scope of this book to describe them.

---

[27] According to Chen (1989), Chinese concepts and philosophy spread to the Huns, the most representative of them being the *yin–yang* principle and the idea of five primary elements (metal, wood, water, fire, and earth). Mongols believe that they exported to the Chinese the twelve-animal representation of the lunar calendar (Bira 1988: 28). Whatever the case, it is clear that the two strikingly different peoples in fact share most of their elementary philosophical principles.

Just as the strategic situation of the Mongols between Russia and China provided a series of historical contexts in which the Mongol nation emerged as a complex entity directed towards, and influenced by, one or other of its neighbours, we can see parallel processes at work in their symbolism. In fact, the 'outside world' lent many, if not all, of their symbols, like 'gifts', to the Mongols. These were used by herdsmen as clan marks or livestock property marks (for example, the swastika, double-fish sign, the 'endless knot', the lotus, etc.)[28] (Perlee 1975, Humphrey 1974*a*). Clan and livestock property marks (brands) are called *tamga*, the term for the seal, including the Mongolian state seal. The *tamga* designs are now being examined by Mongolian scholars in order to trace clan (*obog*) genesis and ultimately the genesis of the Mongols. Thus, we have the curiously paradoxical situation in which what were originally 'outside' symbols were transformed by use into signs of self-identity, and are now being seen as traces of the essence of 'Mongolness'.

Nationalism is about purity, but the nation is not pure. The modern Mongolian nation is indeed a product of socialist construction, linked to the Soviet Union. The linkage itself is pollution, yet it is in symbols that Mongolia and the Soviet Union overlap most publicly and visibly.[29] This 'purity and danger' inevitably give rise to a structural dilemma, as the Mongols are situated between the Russians and Chinese. The purity or independence from the Russians must be solid, for China is also waiting to claim sovereignty over Mongolia. For the nationalist Mongols, however they are defined, merely stressing Mongol history, Chinggis Khan or whatever, against Russia is to court the danger of connecting themselves with China, which would be a denial of their own independence. We can see this from the case of Chinggis Khan, symbol of anti-Russian sentiment. In 1991, there was a rumour that Chinggis Khan in his best-known portrait is not Chinggis Khan himself, as the picture was painted by a Chinese painter. Scholars were invited to explain. Professor Ishjamts commented that whoever drew it, this was Chinggis Khan; on the basis of anthropological examination, he looks like a Mongol. Others did not think so, saying he looks like a typical Chinese emperor; Chinggis Khan should be much more powerful- and magnificent-looking. For a

---

[28] Many of these *tamga* signs are engraved or painted on rocks, and appear to be very old, certainly pre-dating the most recent, seventeenth-century, spread of Buddhism into Mongolia.

[29] The 1961 Mongolian anthem sings: 'Linking (our) fate with the Soviet land | (We are) in agreement with the progressive lot; | Holding firm the advancing direction, | (we) drive vigorously toward the ascending communism' (my translation).

time, this picture was not popular. By the end of 1991, a new picture depicting him as a warrior carrying a bow and arrows was issued in a calendar. But immediately historians commented that this was not Chinggis Khan either, but a Chinese general campaigning against the Mongols in the Ming Dynasty!

This situation creates despondency (*buhimdal*) in Mongolia. It is said by some Mongols that even the term *Mongol Uls* denotes dangerous pan-Mongolism, echoing perhaps the MPRP Politburo's concern in the 1970s. I have even heard the opinion that *Mongol Uls* is an inauspicious term, for its acronym *MU* sounds similar to the word *muu*, or 'bad'. This kind of psychology could only be imagined in a country in the structural position the Mongols are in, as well as with the identity that has been developed over this century.

Independence and Greater Mongolia are actually the core of the entire debate. There are two kinds of sentiments involved here. The first is nationalism, concerned with the independence of Mongolia, though this represents the greatest worry of the people (that Russia and China would be angry). Within this, Halh-centrism is an attempt to maintain the *status quo*. On the other hand, Greater Mongolian sentiment demands rewriting the entire history, from changing the name and symbols to reviving the cult of Chinggis Khan and the classical script. It is not conservative, but seeks help from other democratic Western powers. However, the Greater Mongolian vision was not to prevail. The 1992 election returned a government even more dominated by the MPRP than the earlier one. This was a government pervaded by the anxieties of Halh-centrism identified in the earlier chapters of this book. As Heng and Devan write: 'Postcolonial governments are inclined . . . to generate narratives of national crisis. . . . Typically, however, such narratives of crisis serve more than one category of reassurance: by repeatedly focusing anxiety on the fragility of the new nation, its ostensible vulnerability to every kind of exigency, the state's originating agency is periodically reinvoked and ratified, its access to wide-ranging instruments of power in the service of national protection continually consolidated' (1992: 343).

The compromise between the 'national' and 'socialist' symbols gradually shaped a 'Mongolian nation', one that was closely bound to the Soviet Union. Changing these symbols thus meant a challenge to seventy years' production and reproduction of the Mongol identity and entire social order, an identity and order which in terms of economy, ideology, and social life had not been entirely disastrous for the Mongols. Rather, this socialist system, however one may judge it from the ideological point of view, had indeed guaranteed an independent Mongolia. There is therefore a strong, legitimate basis for opposition to any change in the symbols. This is one reason why the MPRP supported retention of the *soyombo*. The Congress, instead of being a trial of the heritage of the MPRP, actually cross-examined the new government and democratic movement, forcing the coalition government to offer its resignation. The debates in the Congress were really a show-down which tested the political power of the new parties.

Although ethnicity was not the main topic of the drama, we may draw a broad outline. Given the diverse ethnic backgrounds of the deputies and the democrats' support of the falcon, one may sense an ethnic sentiment. Many Buryats I talked to did not feel particularly attached to the *soyombo*, and it is alien to all non-Halh Mongols. The falcon represents, in cosmic terms, shamanic spirits (see Humphrey and Onon 1996). It has a greater time-depth for the Mongols, with which, in fact, no other symbols (including the Buddhist ones) can compete. If we believe, as Tengisbold would argue, that the falcon was the emblem of the Borjigin-Kiat clan of Chinggis Khan and was associated with the cosmic symbols of fire, sun, and moon, then it was under this symbol that all the Mongols united. What is interesting about the Halh Mongols is that although they claim to be 'Borjigin Halh', they have now dis-avowed their very ancestor's emblem. What is certain, though, is that the 'democrats' were supporting what today may be regarded as a most undemocratic symbol of Chinggis Khan, yet its intended use was to promote democracy and Greater Mongolian identity; with this symbol all the Mongols can identify themselves. Unfortunately, the falcon for the Mongols is not equivalent to the Jewish menorah.

The entire Constitution has become an arena for political struggle. The democrats' ostentatious historical nationalism linked to Chinggis Khan was eventually crushed by the Communist Mongolian version of the Russian Constitution (Fundamental Law). The argument centred around the notion of humanity. The accusation that the term 'Funda-mental Law' connotes class struggle and political purges forced the Communists to apply the same tactic: making the accusation that the terms *Ih Tsaaz* and *Ih Zasag* imply killing more people (see Fig. 7.8). Buddhist humanity was exploited to condemn the 'cruel American sheep-eating hawk' (see Fig. 7.9)! By unscrupulously exploiting popular sentiments, the Communists re-emerged as a leading power, as the guardian of the Mongol nation, wearing, however, a Buddhist symbolic mask (see Fig. 7.17).

FIGURE 7.17. A former Communist fingering Buddhist prayer beads. From Tsenddoo 1994: 44.

It seems that a socialist state was essentially an anti-nation in its ultimate goal of international proletarianism. It was the antithesis of freedom cherished so much by the nation. A nation is, writes Holy, 'free not just when it has its own state but when that state is an instrument for the management and channelling of the nation's interests. The ultimate interest of the nation is, of course, its continued independent existence' (1993: 213). The socialist state has not satisfied this basic principle, and thus nationalism in a socialist country becomes 'anti-state'. Although this is valid for Mongolia to some extent, such a nation-against-the-state syndrome has to be qualified. In Mongolia, as I have mentioned, there are two forms of nationalism.

There is the democratic strand of nationalism, arising against the background of demanding freedom from the Soviet Union. It advocates a Western-style free market economy, and it harbours a dream of wider contacts so as to be no longer isolated in the heart of Asia. This nationalism is curiously spiced with ancient Mongolian freedom-loving ethics. It challenges the socialist state. But such enthusiasm faces a real or perceived perennial threat from China. This anxiety over a stalking China is in fact the very cohesive glue of the 'Mongol' nation. The guarantor of the 'independence' of Mongolia has been externally the USSR (Russians) and internally the MPRP, the ex-Communists. The USSR helped to create a 'Mongol' nation, and the socialist state provided the nation with virtually all its structures. Thus there is another strand of nationalism. The MPRP, by repeatedly narrating the national crisis, successfully legitimates its role as guardian of the 'Mongol' nation. Democracy and freedom do not provide enough legitimacy for defining a new Mongol nation, certainly not enough to overthrow the 'old' nation-state.

Like the miss-the-good-old-days syndrome permeating several ex-socialist countries, many Mongols, in the aftermath of ever more severe social and economic crises, have begun to regret the old days. People ask if overnight democratization accompanied by universal enfranchisement is really suitable for a nation without the prior historical experience of liberalization. The 'desire' for democracy, freedom, and economic prosperity, and the 'need' for stability, safety, and independence are two major ingredients of all Mongolian politics, and are likely to remain so for some time to come. They produce a unique balance of power in Mongolia, a blending of ideologies: half Communist and half democratic; but both claim to be nationalist.

Geertz (1973) differentiates nationalism in the 'new states' into two strands: 'The Indigenous Way of Life' and 'The Spirit of the Age', or 'essentialism' and 'epochalism'. 'To stress the first of these is to look to local mores, established institutions, and the unities of common experience—to "tradition", "culture", "national character", or even "race"—for the roots of a new identity. To stress the second is to look to the general outlines of the history of our time, and in particular to what one takes to be the overall direction and significance of that history' (1973: 240–1). These two themes are often so entangled with one another that 'nationalism is not a mere by-product but the very stuff of social change in so many new states; not its reflection, its cause, its expression, or its engine, but the thing itself' (1973: 251–2). In Mongolia, these two nationalisms, like the themes of pan-Mongolism and Halh-centrism that I have discussed in earlier chapters, are likewise entangled, and are indeed the very essence of Mongolian nationalism, as fully reflected in the new nation-state symbols.

Let me summarize several dominant current concerns of the Mongols and their reflection in the state symbols. The most favoured ones, and the most ready-made symbols, are the horse and the *soyombo*. These two lie in the depths of the Mongol heart, because they represent something of the present mentality and immediate concerns: the horse is essentially a symbol of Mongol identity, a nation on horseback, and as the proverb goes, *mori–ügüi hün moho* (a horseless person perishes). The flying winged horse resembles the wind horse (*hii mori*), which is also a sign of energy and spirit. In fact, the new emblem is a mirror of the phrase and idea that the Mongols are now most concerned with: *sergen mandah*, renaissance. However, the Mongolian term has the meaning not only of reviving, but also of prospering. Thus *hii mori*, although a symbol derived from Buddhism (see Bawden 1990), has been reinterpreted as symbol of the ever-living prospering spirit.[30]

The *soyombo* has become so mythical and powerful that nobody can have a dominant opinion about it. It expresses an abstract notion of the independence and longevity of the Mongols, nourished by the lotus, and supported by other motifs in the emblem. For example, the Mongolian 'genealogical' identity is symbolized by the three *chandamni* (triple gems) suggesting past, present, and future. The wheel, entwined with the silk scarf (*hadag*), is an expression of reverence and respect, and symbolizes continued prosperity. Finally, the swastika motif was chosen not for its happiness content, but for its connotation of longevity. In the newly adopted emblem (Oidov's design) the *soyombo* is placed against the background of the 'hill' pattern conveying the notion of 'mother earth', according to the official exegesis (see Fig. 7.15).

We have seen that the Mongolian Congress has created its symbols for the nation. Will they be acceptable? As a Mongol might put it, will the *süld* (everlasting spirit of the Mongols) contradict or correspond to the politically and ideologically chosen *süld*? None the less, as Kertzer puts it, 'a flag is not simply a decorated cloth, but the embodiment of a nation; indeed the nation is defined as much by the flag as the flag is defined by the nation' (1988: 7).

[30] Emphasis on the horse can also be interpreted as Mongols' 'nomadic nostalgia'. Similarly, Dru Gladney writes: 'The continued salience of "nomadic nostalgia" to contemporary Kazakh identity in Kazakhstan is clearly demonstrated by their recent selected national stigmata: the flag of Kazakhstan, which has the famous flying horses beneath the interior dome of the yurt on a field of the sky' (1996: 463).

8

Conclusion: Nationalism and Hybridity

In the final, yet temporary, valediction to both this book and Mongolia, I am not going to predict the future of Mongolia, as history will determine its course. I shall recapitulate and distil the previous points, and offer an alternative way of understanding Mongolian nationalism, juxtaposing it with a question about identity that is crucial in the post-modern world, 'What does it mean to be an *erliiz* or hybrid?'

This book started with the personal predicament that I encountered in Mongolia. I attempted to address the issue of the disparity between the 'imagined' image of Mongolia and the reality. By examining socialist modernization in Mongolia, I came to the conclusion that a strong Halh nation conterminous with present-day Mongolia has been shaped. The crucial problem lay in the very socialism which purported to eliminate inequalities and differences, but in fact created inequalities of different kinds that fostered politicized ethnicity. I treat the socialist system less as a purely political system than as a special method of organizing production and redistribution. The Soviet Union, Mongolia, and lower-level administrative regions within Mongolia, were organized in a hierarchy. The collapse of the socialist apex was due to failure to maintain this, and once the redistributive system was removed, we see revealed an exclusive type of ethnicity, based on territory, economic specialization, and local power, which it in effect created. These stratified 'localisms' are ubiquitous in the socialist countries. The 'independence' of the MPR from the Soviet Union is in this respect structurally no different from the localism occurring within Mongolia.

A new idea has begun to develop: that man is an ecological being definable only by a biological association with a particular locality. The Mongols now have an obsession with ecological and diet determinism. They suggest that people's genes change according to their diet and ecology; being away from the Mongolian steppe, not eating Mongolian mutton, and not breathing the wonderful Mongolian steppe air are sufficient fundamentally to change the genetic quality of the Mongols. This sort of nationalism conceptualizes the Halh, the 'indigenous'

Mongols, as 'pure' Mongols, and the other Mongol groups as 'impure', for they have their 'homeland' in today's China and Russia. A crisis of confidence in the very survival of Mongolia has led to public hysteria over kinship: that is, the biological reproduction of the nation understood in basic terms. The government now advocates on the one hand the revival of the long-defunct exogamous clan system and on the other hand a national, purity-conscious endogamy.

The new emphasis on 'blood' or 'genes' coincides with the emergence of the category of *erliiz*, a concept of 'half-breed' now applied to people as well as animals, and conceived of not only as a biological category but also as a cultural one. Earlier the *erliiz* had been a positive ideal, denoting health and strength, but now it is despised. Interestingly, the ex-Communists of the ruling MPRP, who earlier advocated 'internationalism' and integration, thus producing *erliiz*, have now begun to stress purity in an effort to curb the influence of outside ideas, goods, and people. I have argued that Mongols are now facing a choice between a purist, racialized nationalism, inherited from certain Soviet discourses of nationalism (Halh-centrism), and a more open, adaptive nationalism accepting diversity, hybridity, and multi-culturalism. All this is reflected in the fierce debate over national emblems and symbols which pitted democrats and ex-Communists against one another.

Sexuality, Nationalism, and Hybridity

Let me try to formulate a theoretical model for understanding these interesting aspects of Mongolian nationalism. Formal theories of nationalism tell us about the formation of nation and state in the industrial age, facilitated by print media or division of labour that enabled people to imagine a community. Gellner (1983) heralds the arrival of nationalism in the industrial age, and Hobsbawm (1990) predicts the death of nationalism in the near future. This is a story of the birth of a community, but not about the perpetuation of the community. In the post-modern era, to use the fashionable term, if a nation envisages itself as an eternal body, then this involves national reproduction. I therefore see the concept of the nation as intrinsically related to understandings of nature. A nation on this view is not a steel product, but highly perishable; it needs to be fed and cleansed, like a human being who needs food, shelter, hygiene, sex, and reproduction. The question of sexuality and biological reproduction of the nation has been relatively ignored in studies of nationalism.

Mosse (1985) pioneered a study linking nationalism and 'respectable' sexuality. The emergence of nationalism in late eighteenth-century Europe coincided with the appearance of bourgeois sexual morality, which was to determine the manners and morals of society. 'Respectability' is thus an ideology that cannot be separated from nationalism. It provides society with an essential cohesion. Nationalism invents an ideal male and female image, and emphasizes the friendship of men. Mosse argues that 'nationalism had a special affinity for male society and together with the concept of respectability legitimized the dominance of men over women' (1985: 67). This respectability is the essence of the survival and perpetuation of a nation, and it creates a border that outsiders cannot cross. Outsiders are regarded as morally decadent, undermining and polluting the nation.

Mosse's study has found echoes in recent studies. Parker *et al.* convincingly demonstrate that nationalism and concepts of sexuality, two of the most powerful ideologies of modern times, forged notions of identity that divided the world 'along seemingly natural lines of national affiliation and sexual attachment' (1992: 2). Let us look at a few examples.

In Singapore, according to Heng and Devan (1992), the male- and Chinese-dominated Singaporian state machine waged a propaganda war to urge and encourage educated middle-class and professional Chinese women to produce more children, to counteract the 'irresponsible' high birth rate of the lower-class Malay and Indian women. The prime minister, Lee Kuan Yew, openly attacked educated Chinese women for not producing the 'genetically superior' children necessary for the prosperity of the Singaporian nation. 'The narrative behind Lee's narrative could then be read: a fantasy of self-regenerating fatherhood and patriarchal power, unmitigated, resurgent, and in endless (self-)propagation, inexhaustibly reproducing its own image through the pliant, tractable conduit of female anatomy—incidental, obedient, and sexually suborned female bodily matter' (1992: 350). The authors point out that 'the figure of threat, auguring economic and social disintegration, dismantling the foundations of culture, undermining, indeed, the very possibility of a recognizable future is always, and unerringly, feminine'. They discover a common feature of all nationalisms: 'Women, and all signs of the feminine, are by definition always and already anti-national' (1992: 356).

Holy (1993), on the other hand, writes that the Czechs culturally conceptualize the state as feminine. The Czechs expect the state to provide a motherly touch for the nation. The homeland has become the 'mother country', and members of the nation are metaphorically children of the mother country. Whether in Singapore, where the rulers are extending 'fatherly' hands to urge the women to bear more children for the nation, or in the Czech republic, where the state is expected to behave in a motherly way to its citizens, one thing is common: the nation(-state) is clearly gendered.

I suggest that we may conceptualize a nation like the contemporary Mongols of Mongolia as a bond of brotherhood which subjugates 'femininity'. But the community is, now, in the phrase of Anderson, imagined, facilitated by the media; it is based on one or a combination of several of the following features: homeland, language, race, and religion, or any elements that grip the mind as principles of an identity. I suggest that all these features are 'feminine', that is, protected and defended by men. Now we may say that men's interest in these features is that they guarantee the perpetuation of the bond by controlling the land, women, language, culture, etc. The state is the highest power enabling men to guarantee this control.

This community operates on two levels, which we may metaphorically call patrilineal exogamy and tribal endogamy. Formerly, even during the Soviet period, the Mongol community was in a sense open, accepting and absorbing features from outside, symbolically represented by seeking alliance through Manchu princesses and Russian wives. However, the recent nationalist discourse makes the nation endogamous in ideology.

It is with this complex, yet very basic, idea of clan exogamy and tribal endogamy that a modern nation such as Mongolia operates. A struggle between two nations is a struggle between two fraternities, for the control of symbolic femininity and indeed real women. A foreign man is disliked for fear of his undermining this brotherhood by marrying the women, occupying the territory, assimilating the language, etc. When we deconstruct the whole idea of nationalism to these basic ideas of kinship ideology, we discover that the goal of the Mongols today is precisely a return to the clan system, but with this new idea that clan exogamy must take place within the nation, which should be endogamous.

In my own concept of nation as a male solidarity group subjugating 'femininity', the interaction between nations is indeed an exchange of femininity, represented in feminine elements as they are desired and wanted and controlled by men. These feminine objects, whatever they are, also bear the mark of a community of origin; they are not things in the field to be picked up freely, but continue to be in some sense non-alienable objects.

The basic human interaction, as Lévi-Straussian structuralist universalist theory holds, is the way culture understands nature. The literature in this field is immense, and I do not intend to review it here, but I wish to make one point: culture is above all an abstraction from, or a reflection of, nature. It is the control of nature in all sorts of forms, and it is not accidental that it so often acquires an equivalent form in gender relations, man (seen as 'culture') versus woman (seen as 'nature'), and the former's desire to control the latter.

However, human societies used to have mechanisms for gender interaction, but modern nationalism destroys or erodes those mechanisms, producing what is now called hybridity. Let me develop this point further. Nomads and sedentary people in Inner Asia have been interacting for thousands of years, accepting and giving ideas, goods, and women. It is in this system of exchange that I find particularly interesting the notion of purity and pollution. Foreign things were always regarded as polluting, but formerly the Mongols were able to absorb the pollution. Now it is not so easy, though they are trying. Let us examine some basic mechanisms. A person by leaving home tends to be regarded as polluted. During the Mongol Empire period, arriving foreigners had to go through two fires. This idea persists today among older people, who still purify their hands and clothes by incense smoke after returning from a journey. Things walked over or stepped over by women are also purified. This ideology may be further seen in the milk and meat system. Women are 'flesh', and both women and flesh (meat) are 'consumed'; yet they could be dangerous, as can be seen from the fact that the incoming bride had to be purified between two fires in the wedding ceremony. They are polluting to the 'bone'—that is, the patrilineage, or clan. The Mongols have another system for purification: fermented mare's milk (*airag*). Although most kinds of milk are handled by women, mares used to be milked by men only (now by women!), and the symbolic consumption of *airag* was virtually entirely to do with men. The function of *airag* (men usually drink 10–20 pints a day in summer) is to detoxify the flesh (meat), which is regarded as mildly noxious when consumed in summer. The essential point is that the Mongols had a mechanism to handle the pollution, and were able to absorb it.

This is more a hypothesis than a definite conclusion. Should this hypothesis be correct, then, the Mongols are now coming back to this system, as opposed to the Communist ideology which held meat simply as prestigious and a sign of civilization. The purifying function of the traditional item (*airag*), a safety-valve in the actual or symbolic exchanges in the past, is now symbolically revived. It is a revival of purity as the essence of the nation as against all alien things and ideas.

In the past, meat and milk were not oppositional, but harmonious. In modern Mongolia, this relation has been broken. They now have an oppositional relationship: milk represents the steppe, herdsmen, and tradition, and thus 'old Mongolia', while meat represents urbanity, workers, modernity, and thus 'new Mongolia' (see Mróz 1977). This transformation shows something of a Russian influence, and indeed, during the Soviet period, we saw that the Mongols consumed a lot of Russian 'women-flesh'. The cry for tradition in Mongolia is a cry for the return of a detoxifying agent. However, the function of the sour milk has changed, from 'purify and include' to 'cleanse and exclude'. While in the past the sour milk was consumed for the purpose of purifying the stomach in summer, so as to be better able to consume meat in winter, today the required detoxifying agent is to cleanse the whole geo- and bio-body of the nation and exclude impure substances, such as *erliiz* or outsiders, which are supposed to have poisoned the nation.

Anderson suggests that nationalism might best be conceived 'as if it belonged with "kinship" or "religion"' (1983: 15). He observes that 'in the modern world everyone can, should, will "have" a nationality, as he or she "has" a gender' (1983: 14). Human thinking tends to be dichotomous, or dialectical; one can decide on friends and enemies, insiders and outsiders, but there are also *erliiz*, who are undecidables. This binary principle of nationality, or gender, also produces bastards or half-breeds, homosexuals or bi-gender identities, in all societies. In modern times, it is the all-pervasive legitimizing power of nation that creates 'national bastards'. These are people of such categories as 'can no longer be included within philosophical (binary) opposition, resisting and disorganizing it, without ever constituting a third term, without ever leaving room for a solution in the form of speculative dialectics' (Derrida 1981: 71). In the words of Bauman (1990), they are strangers:

The strangers are not, however, the 'as-yet-undecided'; they are, in principle, undecidables. They are that 'third element' which should not be. The true hybrids, the monsters: not just unclassified, but unclassifiable. They therefore do not question this one opposition here and now; they question oppositions as such, the very principle of the opposition, the plausibility of dichotomy it suggests. They unmask the brittle artificiality of division—they destroy the world. They stretch the temporary inconvenience of 'not knowing how to go on' into a terminal paralysis. They must be tabooed, disarmed, suppressed, exiled, physically or mentally—or the world may perish. (1990: 148–9)

Like all the other self-perpetuating social groupings, both territorial and non-territorial, the national states collectivize friends and enemies. In addition to this universal function, however, they also eliminate the strangers; or at least they attempt to do so. . . . *The national state is designed primarily to deal with the problems of strangers, not enemies.* It is precisely this feature that sets it apart from other supra-individual social arrangements. (1990: 153; emphasis mine)

The fraternal solidarity is now designed not to produce such strangers, or hybrid monsters, and as far as the Inner Mongols are concerned, since they are already such monsters, both Chinese and Mongolian states are targeted against them.

What Does it Mean to be a Hybrid?

I have written extensively that Inner Mongols are now increasingly defining themselves in diasporic terms. As often as not, their dream or passion for their imagined or real homeland is dashed or dampened. A small but typical example may illustrate what I mean. In Inner Mongolia, a song was composed with an Inner Mongolian tune but based on a Halh modern poem: *Bi Mongol Hün* (I am a Mongol), as mentioned in Chapter 6. It is a song vastly popular in Inner Mongolia, to the dismay of the Chinese. The song found its way into Mongolia, with a film entitled *Duguilong*, a six-part series depicting an Ordos Mongol national hero Shine Lama fighting Chinese war-lords attempting to encroach on Mongol land early this century. The film was shown in December 1991 in Ulaanbaatar, and it was favourably received. About one month later, however, I heard over the radio that the poem was being sung to a different tune. As I found out, the melody was newly composed, in the spirit of 'pluralism'. But it is more than pluralism in that, as some Halh explained to me, they needed to claim back what they have lost.

Looking at the national political landscape, centre building may be seen in the traditional landscape setting. The Mongolian *oboo* (a cosmic hill, turned into a Buddhist Mount Sumer) is linked to heaven and earth by a symbolic pole. (There can be hundreds of *oboo* in Mongolia, but they represent just one symbolic idea.) In the past the Mongols would climb up the hill and pay respect to the local deity, for rain and good fortune, but they would not allow any impurity—that is women—to approach it. Should we take such a ritual as a worship of society, as Durkheim would think, then in modern Mongolia, the *oboo* has been revived, allowing women to join in the worship. By going to the *oboo*, one

is purified and becomes more Mongol. Inner Mongols are now symbolically excluded from the worship of the national *oboo*—Mongolia. They
can go there, but only as guests. It is not important whether the national
magic mountain is the Buddhist Mount Sumer or a modern nation-state,
but it matters for what purpose it is used.

In contemporary Mongolia, the Halh have begun to rebuild the
Mongolian political landscape, as can be seen from the symbolic construction in the foundation-laying ceremony for the planned mausoleum
of Chinggis Khan in Ulaanbaatar in early 1992. Deputies of the National
Congress brought stones and *arashan* (holy water) from their homes all
over the country and formed an *oboo*. The idea was, I was told, that the
spirits of all the mountains, rivers, and springs would be gathered there
to protect Chinggis Khan. An alternative explanation is that Chinggis
Khan rules every corner of Halh Mongolia. Note that the flags displayed
at the ceremony were only from the four Halh *aimag*s in the Manchu
period. The shrinking empire of Chinggis Khan is symbolized in this
oboo and mausoleum. An Inner Mongolian whispered to me, 'But there
isn't anything about Inner Mongolia.' One may aptly compare it with the
black people's outcry in England, 'There ain't no black in the Union
Jack' (see Gilroy 1987).

Then what is the political landscape in Inner Mongolia? The shrines at
the Chinggis Khan memorial in Ordos include all the heroes and ancestors of the Mongols. The official eight white tents (*naiman tsagaan ger*)
contain shrines of Chinggis Khan, his four consorts, and his four sons,
among whom the empire was divided. There are also shrines of almost all
his generals and chiefs scattered over Ordos. According to the myth,
after Chinggis died, every 'tribe' in the Mongol Empire sent a group of
people with their emblem spirit (*süld*), and these, with their ancestor
shrines, settled in Ordos to safeguard and pay tribute to the shrine
(*onggon*) of Chinggis Khan. This political landscape tells of a particular
ethnic outlook towards all the Mongols.

It is a long journey from *Goliin Uls* (Core Nation) to *Töv Halh Uls*
(Central Halh Nation) as a representation of the Mongol homeland.
The term *Gol* essentially has two meanings, river and aorta, both of
which mean core or centre. However, river is horizontal, and aorta is
vertical. The horizontal river is a core to link numerous peoples or
nations who use the river; it is thus a lifeline to them all. The
vertical aorta links blood inside the body, to provide it with good
circulation. In the Mongol *ger* structure, the hearth is called *golomt*
(derived from *gol*), and connects the family with the ancestry and

Heaven, through fire and the vertical column of smoke. To destroy the *golomt*, or cut the aorta (*gol tasalh*), means the death of a person or a lineage. By monopolizing the *gol*, real or symbolic, the Halh Mongols have shed their 'bosom' (south), and established a nation on the 'back' (north) of the magic mountain.

It is hard for Inner Mongols to renounce their myth equivalent to the Malinowskian 'ancestor holes', and turn their horse-heads. If their horse-heads were directed forcefully to the south earlier, as was done by the Chinese to the horse statue on the roof of the Inner Mongolian Museum, they have to turn them by themselves this time. Their dream of crawling back in to their ancestor holes or climbing up the *oboo* was an attempt to purify themselves from the Chinese. But over several decades, their separation from Mongolia, a fate beyond the will of the Inner Mongols, turned them into something impure from another direction.

To be an Inner Mongolian now means having a feeling of diaspora and hybridity, but unlike immigrants, the Inner Mongols experience this in their homeland—that is, Inner Mongolia. This is a story of natives becoming strangers in their own homelands.

The Chinese Middle Kingdom is now being bombarded by two traditional sets of barbarians, the northern and the southern. The traditional peripheries have now become centres: Mongolia is an ideological centre of democracy, and South China is an economic centre. Both of these challenge the Middle Kingdom, forcing it to take the stance of what Friedman (1993) calls 'Fascist Socialism'. Chinese nationalists are blowing, in order to maintain their hegemony, a Chinese north-westerly wind, in an urge to reclaim the prestige of their own 'ancestor holes', their yellow river and yellow earth. One should perhaps recall Dikötter's (1992) study showing that eugenics, or race discourse, funda-mentally shaped a Chinese racial outlook in the early twentieth century, rejecting the animal-humans (formerly the nomads, this time the West-erners), and more recently refusing to grant them citizenship. Ironically, today, under the new nationalist rhetoric, the nation is called *zuguo—muqin* (ancestral country—mother), and everybody whose ancestry hap-pens to be mentioned in Chinese history is called *tong bao* (same-mother-born children). The state has invented a common ancestor for all fifty-six nationalities of the 'big family': namely, Yan and Huang, the ancestors of the pre-Han people. This nation-state rhetoric deprives minorities even of their own ancestry in order to secure political loyalty for the Chinese state. But despite the rhetoric, unfortunately, this 'mother' does not trust her 'children'.

The discrimination against the Inner Mongols, as discussed above, may be 'natural' as some would argue, for they are an ethnic minority. But I would argue that the system of nation-state is such that it makes everybody's life uneasy. What Myron Cohen writes of the Chinese situation is true also of the Mongols: 'for much of China's population, being Chinese is culturally much easier today than it ever was in the past, for this identification no longer involves commonly accepted cultural standards. Existentially, however, being Chinese is far more problematic, for now it is as much a quest as it is a condition' (1991: 133). In Mongolia, similarly, there used to be a Mongolian cultural pattern in the past, and Mongolness was not something imposed, as we have seen. Today, when ideas of nationalism prevail, being Mongol is associated with a demanding idea of 'purity', and also becomes 'as much a quest as it is a condition'. This creates a constant generation of uncertainty. Thus, almost any Mongol might find themselves in the situation Bauman describes below:

The strangers refused to split neatly into 'us' and 'them', friends and foes. Stubbornly, they remained hauntingly indeterminate. Their number and nuisance power seem to grow with the intensity of dichotomizing efforts. As if the strangers were an 'industrial waste' growing in bulk with every increase in the production of friends and foes; a phenomenon brought into being by the very assimilatory pressure meant to destroy it. The point blank assault on the strangers had to be from the start aided, reinforced and supplemented by a vast array of techniques meant to make a long-term, perhaps permanent, cohabitation with strangers possible. And it was. (Bauman 1990: 155)

Bauman suggests that modernity creates ambivalence despite the fact that nationalism is against this ambivalence. Modernity in Mongolia continues to create ambivalence or hybridity, despite Mongols' deep aversion to it. However, this does not remain a mere discourse, but a weapon for political use. The nationalist logic is that of the nation as a computer-like totality; if it is to function well, all the components (people) must be sure of the proper order. We have seen that the Halh (such as those of Zavhan), and even the president, have been subjected to 'genetic scanning'. What differentiates the nationalist state from the past clan is that the latter had a mechanism to allow a suspiciously born, bone-polluting person to form a separate clan (for example, the Jadaran clan as mentioned in the *Secret History*), but today there is no such mechanism. In such a context, whoever claims to be a genuine Mongol in Mongolia must face a cultural disinfectant scanner programme. The *erliiz* is perhaps not so much like national 'industrial waste' that can be dumped, as like waves of viruses to be feared and loathed. Thus, to be a Mongolian in Mongolia is no longer any easier than to be an Inner Mongolian.

We are at the crossroads of tradition or translation (see Robins 1991), pushing toward fundamentalism and its associate, hybridity. As far as I am concerned, the question remains one of Inner Mongolian identity; if they are categorized as *erliiz*, do the Inner Mongols regard themselves as such? It would perhaps take courage to admit that. I have no right to determine the road the Inner Mongols might take, but I myself am forced to join Salman Rushdie in his celebration of 'hybridity' or 'translated man':

Standing at the centre of the novel is a group of characters most of whom are British Muslims, or not particularly religious persons of Muslim background, struggling with just the sort of great problems that have arisen to surround the book, problems of hybridization and ghettoization, of reconciling the old and the new. Those who oppose the novel most vociferously today are of the opinion that intermingling with different cultures will inevitably weaken and ruin their own. I am of the opposite opinion. The Satanic Verses celebrates hybridity, impurity, intermingling, the transformation that comes of new and unexpected combinations of human beings, cultures, ideas, politics, movies, songs. It rejoices in mongrelization and fears the absolutism of the Pure. *Mélange*, hotchpotch, a bit of this and a bit of that is *how newness enters the world*. It is the great possibility that mass migration gives the world, and I have tried to embrace it. The Satanic Verses is for change-by-fusion, change-by-conjoining. It is a love-song to our mongrel selves. (Rushdie 1991: 394)

It is not clear whether this mongrel love-song would soften the hearts of the fundamentalists. And it seems that the world is now trapped in this dilemma, a dilemma created by this modern world. Let me issue a plea for an understanding of the *erliiz* phenomenon. The notion of *erliiz* in the period of the nation-state warrants the world's utmost attention. This discussion may bring out a clear message: rather than making useless attempts to dump this 'industrial waste', *erliiz* (social or biological bastards, beings or ideas) may be a bridge between nations, and may be recyclable, if 'undecidable'. After all, there are no pure human beings in the world. Nor are there pure ideas void of external influences. It is a world of 'bastards', a world of 'dirt', and a world of 'mixture'; but the people pretend otherwise and are prepared to die for this pretence. In *erliiz* exists a mixture of blood or thoughts. If he has no land in which to live on the 'nationally' owned earth, he cannot live on Mars; if he is to survive, if the world is to survive, at least let *erliiz* be a medium for dialogues between nations. As Victor Hao Li notes:

At such a juncture, those who to one degree or another straddle two cultures have a special role, and with it a special responsibility.... We are conveyers, not simply of goods and services, but of knowledge and understanding and trust. We have the skills and the interest to deal with cultural differences, linguistic barriers, and differences in values and institutions—all those problems so often lead to misunderstanding and strife. We are, or can be, the bridge linking two societies, and linking the past with the future. (Li 1994: 220)

The Future of Hybrids

In this book, I have suggested that Inner Mongols are victims of a 'purity' mode of thinking from a centre with which they want to be associated. In this sense they are not just victims of a given stereotype, but slaves to their own thought. After all, they have that notion of blood and purity in the first place. They aspire to go to Mongolia precisely because of a despairing feeling that their home is irretrievably polluted or damaged, one in which no pure Mongols can be bred. As long as this mode of thinking persists, they will continue to feel misplaced in both societies. My critique of purity and my celebration of hybridity entail not accepting our so-called inferior or polluted identity, nor struggling to cleanse ourselves so as to be accommodated in the dominant paradigm of thought. That would be no more than a vicious circle, or what Spivak calls 'reverse ethnocentrism' in the nativist critique of imperialism in reversing the opposition of colonized/colonizer. Reverse ethnocentrism, despite the ferocity of its attack on imperialism, falls into a fundamental trap: that of thinking and constructing within the frame set by the colonizer. Such a reverse ethnocentrism therefore, Spivak argues, amounts to a nostalgic assumption that '[a] critique of imperialism would restore the sovereignty for the lost self of the colonies so that Europe could, once and for all, be put in the place of the other that it always was. It...seems to me that it is this kind of revisionary impulse that is allowing the emergence of the "Third World" as a convenient signifier' (quoted in Young 1990: 168).

The role of hybridity, if there is one, must be to make a certain criticism of the dominant ideology, yet step outside the hegemonic paradigm. Failing 'to reverse an opposition of this kind is to remain caught within the very terms that are being disputed' (ibid.). For a hybrid to make a better escape, he or she has to get out of this entangling web. In this sense, a certain interpretation of the status of Indian untouchables may offer an alternative. Appadurai conveys the central message of Khare's study: namely, that the untouchables do not see themselves as being on the hierarchical ladder of Brahmanic morality, but rather see themselves as ascetics.

With this key step, instead of playing the impure foil to the Brahman, the Untouchable becomes his civilizational critic and his moral conscience. No longer a product of some sort of 'karmic' Fall, the Untouchable becomes a brutalized representative of the ascetic ideal of ordinary life. His degradation and oppression are no more regarded as just working out of the joint scheme of *dharma* (social law) and *karma* (cosmic causal law) but of the blindness of the Brahmanic social order to the axioms underlying its own existence. (Appadurai 1986: 752)

I now want to note the non-Halh Mongolian contribution. My claim is certainly controversial, but it is a little-known fact that non-Halh Mongols have played the major political roles in Mongolia in this century. While they contribute to the centrality of Halh land, by staging their action in that land, they nevertheless do not wish to be marginalized.

It is in the emergence of the interstices—the overlap and displacement of domains of difference—that the intersubjective and collective experiences of nationness, community interest, or cultural value are negotiated. How are subjects formed 'in-between', or in excess of, the sum of the 'parts' of difference (usually intoned as race/class/gender, etc.)? . . . Increasingly, 'national' cultures are being produced from the perspective of disenfranchised minorities. (Bhabha 1994: 2–6)

Non-Halh Mongols are not only contributing to the 'authentic' Mongolian culture; they (along with other ethnic minorities) are also shaping and defining the Chinese culture, equally challenging the essentialization of one majority nationality within the nation-state. Perhaps this is the power of the hybrids (including minorities and diaspora). They do not fit a nation-state. As they are tailored to befit the nation-state, the nation-state has also to reshape itself to accommodate them. In the process, the core is somewhat transformed. This is perhaps the sense of Bhabha's trans-national and translational sense of hybridity of imagined communities.

This is obviously a very optimistic view of hybridity and marginalization, but perhaps it makes sense in the long term. The real question is: What if hybrids are not allowed to contribute on the ground? I want here to register my pessimism. The irritation of Mongols in China with

Mongols in Mongolia is largely about the issue of representation. Can a sub-nation or subaltern group represent a culture in the name of the whole? Or indeed, can they represent something of their own? The very problem of the identity of Mongols is a primordial identity which in its representation overlaps that of the Mongol nation. This problem some-what resembles the relationship between Third World intellectuals in the First World and the real Third World countries. It is a question of location; the location of this essentialized 'Third World' presents a difficulty not only for academics: 'If you displace it (third world) into the third world, but on the other hand, you again reconstruct the third world as people of colour and marginalized people in the United States. These migrant communities become more real than the "original" cultures, to the great irritation of the activists as well as the intellectual elites in the "original" cultures' (Spivak 1993: 12). The irritation of colonial marginals with the master is well known, especially in the form of what Bhabha (1994) calls 'mimicry', or 'hidden transcript' as James Scott (1990) describes it. However, like the 'Third World' in the First World, the Mongolian experience in China is a signifier for opposition, resistance, or anti-imperialism, a struggle for cultural autonomy, and so on (Bulag, forthcoming). But their annoyance to the 'original' Mongol culture is that the Inner Mongolian culture is made more 'real' and is seen as more authentic, since what the Inner Mongols articulate is usually an essentialized category of culture codified in opposition to the dominant Han Chinese culture. In a nation-state, cultures enjoy the luxury of experimentation and development, as Mongols in Mongolia have done. The heightened sense of ethnic identity expects the backing of, or takes glory from, a 'motherland', imagining a united front on this particular issue. The failure on the part of the imagined motherland to deliver that united front can only cause disappointment. Unfortunately, what are now open to Inner Mongols are two fronts: they have to struggle to defend their own self-claimed authentic representation not only in the hegemonic nation-state in which they are a minority, but also to prove constantly to the imaginary homeland that their premiss of Mongolness is correct. It is the doubt of authenticity that is most devastating for Inner Mongols, as with the hybridized aboriginals whose right to represent their own culture is often dismissed on the ground of inauthenticity (see Griffiths 1994).

The real problem, or dilemma, for Inner Mongols is therefore whether their version of Mongol culture, which shares the same 'roots' as that of the Mongols in Mongolia, is legitimate. This was not a problem in the past, because socialist Mongolian nationhood was based on items and criteria of futuristic modernity, denouncing and severing links with the immediate past. Now that Mongolia has started to be narcissistic, as Inner Mongols are, clashes will be inevitable as to who represents authenticity. Inner Mongols may or may not compromise on this point. They may seriously start to resist the cultural hierarchy based on the concept of linear history which privileges Halh culture in Mongolia and Han culture in China.

Bibliography

Aberle, David F. (1953), *The Kinship System of the Kalmuk Mongols* (University of New Mexico Press: Albuquerque, N. Mex.).

Academy of Sciences MPR (1990), *Information Mongolia* (Pergamon: Oxford).

Adiya, J. (1991), 'Er hünii dotor emeel hazaartai mori' (The Fully Saddled Horse among Men), *Hotol Chuulgan*, 30 Mar.

Agudamu and Ürgen (eds.) (1987), *Mongol Hurim* (Mongol Wedding) (Inner Mongolian Cultural Publishing House: Huhhot).

Ahmad, Aijaz (1992), *In Theory: Classes, Nations, Literatures* (Verso: London).

Aikman, David Barrington Thomson (1983), 'A Comparative Study of Mongolian Political Terminology, Part I', *Journal of the Anglo-Mongolian Society*, 8/1–2: pp. v–x, 1–35.

Akim, G. (ed.) (1990), *B. Rinchan: Huuramba* (B. Rinchen: The Cheating Scholar) (n.p.: Ulaanbaatar).

Alioshin, Dmitri (1941), *Asian Odyssey* (Cassel and Company Ltd.: London).

Altantsetseg, N. (1978), 'XIX zuuni süüliin hagas—XX zuuni ehnii Övör Mongol' (Inner Mongolia in the Second Half of the Nineteenth Century and the Beginning of the Twentieth Century), *Dornodahini Sudlalin Asuudal*, 1.

Anderson, Benedict (1983), *Imagined Communities: Reflections on the Origin and Spread of Nationalism* (Verso Editions and New Left Books: London).

Andrews, P. A. (1981), 'Ejen Qoriy-a', *Journal of the Anglo-Mongolian Society*, 7/2: 1–49.

Ang, Ien (1993), 'To Be or Not to Be Chinese: Diaspora, Culture and Postmodern Ethnicity', *Southeast Asian Journal of Social Science*, 21/1: 1–17.

Anonymous (1992), 'Tüühen üzegdel: Hasagiin ih nüüdel' (A Historical Phenomenon: Kazakh Exodus), *Tusgaar Togtnol*, 10–20 Aug.

Appadurai, Arjun (1986), 'Is *homo hierarchicus*?', *American Ethnologist*, 13/4: 745–61.

Ariunchimeg, G. Amgalan (1992), 'Erüül biegüi Mongol hün' (Mongols without Healthy Bodies), *Erüül Enxiin Tölöö*, 2, 18–31 Jan.

Arvidsson, Claea, and Blomqvist, Lars Erik (eds.) (1987), *Symbols of Power* (Almquist & Wiksell: Stockholm).

Atwood, Christopher (1994), 'Revolutionary Nationalist Mobilization in Inner Mongolia, 1925–1929' (Ph.D. dissertation, Indiana University).

Baabar, B. (1990), *Buu Mart! Martval Sönönö* (Don't Forget! Or Perish) (Social-Democratic Movement Press: Ulaanbaatar).

—— (1992), 'Tsever tsusni Mongol' (Pure-blooded Mongols), *Mongoliin Zaluuchuud*, 5 and 6, Mar.

——(1996), *XX zuuni Mongol: nüüdel suudal, garz olz* (Twentieth-Century Mongolia: Nomadism and Sedentarism, Losses and Gains) (State Photographic Centre: Ulaanbaatar).

Baatar, Ts., and Gantulga, Ts. (1992), 'Altain Urianhain ugsaa garal, tüühiin asuudald' (On the Question of the Origin and History of the Altai Urianghai), *Dornodahini Sudlal*, 2: 51–62.

Bacon, Elizabeth E. (1958), *Obok: A Study of Social Structure in Eurasia* (Wenner-Gren Foundation for Anthropological Research: New York).

Badamhatan, S. (1980), 'BNMAU-in ündestnii ba ugsaatni högjliin asuudald' (On the Question of National and Ethnic Development in the MPR), *Tüühiin Sudlal*, 9.

——(1982), 'BNMAU-in ugsaatni högjliin yavts' (Ethnic Process in the MPR), in S. Badamhatan (ed.), *Orchin tsagiin ugsaatni yavts ba sotsialist ahui* (Contemporary Ethnic Process and Socialist Way of Life) (Academy of Sciences: Ulaanbaatar), 9–22.

——(ed.) (1987) *Halhiin ugsaatnii zui* (Halh Ethnography) (State Publishing House: Ulaanbaatar).

Badarchi, Sodovin (1994), 'Mongolin Buriadiig ustgasan ni' (Exterminating the Mongolian Buryats), *Il Tovchoo*, 32.

Badral, S. (1994), 'Halh, Halhai buyu gal golomt' (Halh, Halhai or Fire Hearth), *Il Tovchoo*, 30.

Barnett, S. (1977), 'Identity Choice and Caste Ideology in Contemporary South India', in K. David (ed.), *The New Wind: Changing Identities in South Asia* (Mouton: The Hague), 393–416.

Barth, F. (ed.) (1969), *Ethnic Groups and Boundaries* (Little, Brown & Co: Boston).

Batbayar, Ts. (1992), ' "Glavlit"-iin süns "Mongol Televiz"-d tenüüchilj baina' (The Spirit of 'Flash' is Haunting the 'Mongol Television'), *Bodliin Solbitsol*, 2.

——(1993), 'Mongolia in 1992: Back to One-Party Rule', *Asian Survey*, 33/1, 61–6.

Batmönh, J. (1986), 'MAXN-in XIX ih huralin shiidveriin bieleltiin yavts, namin baiguulagin zoriltin tuhai' (On the Process of Implementing the Resolution of the XIX MPRP Congress, and the Aim of the Party Organization), in *MAXN-in Töv Horooni II Bügd Hural* (State Publishing House: Ulaanbaatar).

Batnairamdal, P. (1991), 'Tsus min bulingartval yanaa aa?' (What if our Blood becomes Polluted?), *Bodliin Solbitsol*, 4.

Batsuur, J. (1987), 'BNMAU-in hün amin genetikiin sudalgaa medee VII udamshlin polimorf ABO PGM, GLO$_1$ EsD, Hp, Tf, Gc, C′3 sistemuud ba hün amin genetic togtots' (The Study of the Population Genetics in the MPR, the Seven Inheritance Polymorphous Systems: ABO PGM, GLO$_1$ EsD, Hp, Tf, Gc, C′3 and the Structure of Population Genetics), *Shinjleh Uhaani Akademiin Medee*, 3.

——(1988), 'Hünii biologiin orchin tsagiin tulgamdsan asuudluud' (Contemporary Questions Concerning Human Biology), *Ünen*, 18 May.

Battogtoh, S. (1991), *Nuuts huivaldaanaas nugalaa zavhrald* (From the Secret Plot to the Deviation) (State Publishing House: Ulaanbaatar).

Bauman, Zygmunt (1990), 'Modernity and Ambivalence', in Mike Featherstone (ed.) *Global Culture: Nationalism, Globalization and Modernity* (Sage Publications: London), 143–69.

Bawden, Charles (1958), 'Two Mongol Texts Concerning Obo-Worship', *Oriens Extremus*, 5/1: 23–41.

——(1968), *The Modern History of Mongolia* (Weidenfeld and Nicolson: London).

——(1990), 'Mongolian "Wind-Horse" Offerings', in Tadeusz Skorupski (ed.), *Indo-Tibetan Studies: Papers in Honour and Appreciation of Professor David L. Snellgrove's Contribution to Indo-Tibetan Studies*, Buddhica Brittannica, Series Continue 2 (Institute of Buddhist Studies: Tring), 29–36.

Bayasgalang, S. (1991), 'Mongol Golomt—Halh Töviin Üzel' (Mongol Hearth—The Halh-centrist Notion), *Mongolin Duu Hooloi*, 8.

Bazargur, D., Shiirevadia, C. and Chinbat, B. (1993), *Territorial Organization of Mongolian Pastoral Livestock Husbandry in the Transition to a Market Economy* (Institute of Development Studies, University of Sussex: Brighton).

Becker, Jasper (1992), *The Lost Country: Mongolia Revealed* (Hodder & Stoughton: London).

Benson, Linda (1988), 'Osman Batur: The Kazak's Golden Legend', in Linda Benson and Ingvar Svanberg (eds.), *The Kazaks of China: Essays on an Ethnic Minority* (University of Uppsala Press: Uppsala), 141–88.

Bhabha, Homi K. (ed.) (1990), *Nation and Narration* (Routledge: London and New York).

——(1994), *The Location of Culture* (Routledge: London and New York).

Bira, Sh. (1988), *Menggu shixueshi: shisan shiji–shiqi shiji* (Mongolian Historiography: Thirteenth to Seventeenth Centuries) (Chinese trans. by Chen Hongfa) (Inner Mongolian Education Press: Huhhot).

Bonavia, David (1983), 'Old Game, New Moves', *Far Eastern Economic Review*, 120/23.

Borchigud, Wurlig (1996), 'Transgressing Ethnic and National Boundaries: Contemporary "Inner Mongolian" Identities in China', in Melissa Brown (ed.), *Negotiating of Ethnicities in China and Taiwan* (Institute of East Asian Studies, University of California: Berkeley), 160–82.

Borjigin, Batu (1990), 'History of Mongolian Genetics and Eugenics', *Inner Mongolian Normal College Journal*, Spring.

Borneman, J. (1992), *Belonging in the Two Berlins: Kin, State, Nation* (Cambridge University Press: Cambridge).

Bouquet, Mary (1993), *Reclaiming English Kinship: Portuguese Refractions of British Kinship Theory* (Manchester University Press: Manchester and New York).

Bousiang (1984), *Monggul üsüg bichig-un uhagan* (Mongolian Philology) (Inner Mongolian Education Press: Huhhot).

Boyle, John Andrew (tr.) (1971), *The Successors of Genghis Khan* (translated from the Persian of Rashid al-Din) (Columbia University Press: New York and London).

Bromley, Yu. (1974), 'The Term Ethnos and its Definition', in Bromley (ed.), *Soviet Ethnography and Anthropology Today* (Mouton: The Hague), 55–72.

Brown, Lester (1995), *Who Will Feed China: Wake-up Call for a Small Planet* (Earthscan: London).

Brown, William A., and Onon, Urgunge (translation and annotation) (1976), *History of the Mongolian People's Republic* (Mongolian version editors: B. Shirendev, M. Sanjdorj) (East Asian Research Center, Harvard University: Cambridge, Mass., and London).

Brownell, Susan (1995), *Training the Body for China: Sports in the Moral Order of the People's Republic* (University of Chicago Press: Chicago).

Bruun, Ole, and Odgaard, Ole (1996), 'A Society and Economy in Transition', in Bruun and Odgaard (eds.), *Mongolia in Transition: Old Patterns, New Challenges* (Curzon: Richmond, Surrey), 23–41.

Buell, Paul D. (1990), 'Pleasing the Palate of the Qan: Changing Foodways of the Imperial Mongols', *Mongolian Studies: Journal of the Mongolian Society*, 13: 57–81.

Bulag, Uradyn E. (1994), 'Dark Quadrangle in Central Asia: Empires, Ethnogenesis, Scholars and Nation-States', *Central Asian Survey*, 13/4: 459–78.

—— (forthcoming), 'The Cult of Ulanhu in Inner Mongolia: History, Memory, and the Making of National Heroes', *Central Asian Survey*.

—— and Humphrey, Caroline (1996), 'Some Diverse Representations of the Pan-Mongolian Movement in Dauria', *Inner Asia: Occasional Papers*, 1/1: 1–23.

Butler, W. H. (ed.) (1982), *The Mongolian Legal System: Contemporary Legislation and Documentation* (Nijhoff: The Hague).

Byamba (1991), *Yapond zugtaj garsan Byamba* (Byamba who Fled to Japan), (tr. from Japanese into Mongolian by D. Almaas) (Soyombo: Ulaanbaatar).

Byambadorj, T. (1991), 'Eh oron eheldegtsegtee duusah yosgui' (There is no Reason for the End of the Motherland when she was just Born), *Bodliin solbitsol*, 7.

Byambasüren, S., Oyuntuya, D., and Dorjijadamba, Sh. (1990), 'The Social Questions of the Mentally Handicapped People', *Erüül Mend*, 6.

Cammann, Schuyler (1963), 'Mongol Dwellings—With Special Reference to Inner Mongolia', in Denis Sinor (ed.), *Aspects of Altaic Civilization* (Indiana University Press: Bloomington, Ind.), 17–22.

Campi, Alicia J. (1991), 'The Rise of Nationalism in the Mongolian People's Republic as Reflected in Language Reform, Religion, and the Cult of Chinggis Khan', *Bulletin: The IAMS News Information on Mongol Studies*, 2: 3–15.

Cao, Yongnian (1990), 'Chuanguoxi yu Ming-Meng Guanxi' (Heirloom Royal Seal and the Ming–Mongol Relationship), *Inner Mongolia Social Sciences*, 2: 60–4.

Chang, K. C. (ed.) (1977), *Food in Chinese Culture: Anthropological and Historical Perspectives* (Yale University Press: New Haven and London).

Chen, Ching-lung (1989), 'Chinese Symbolism among the Huns', in K. Sagaster and H. Eimer (eds.), *Religious and Lay Symbolism in the Altaic World and Other Papers* (Otto Harrassowitz: Wiesbaden), 62–70.

Cheney, George A. (1968), *The Pre-Revolutionary Culture of Outer Mongolia* (Indiana University Press: Bloomington, Ind.).

Chimid, R. (1992), 'Jirgalang hemeeh zurgan bichig' (An Ideogram called Happiness), *Nüüdelchin*, 2.

Chimidorjiyev, Sh. B. (1991), *Kto mi—Buryat—Mongoli?* (Who are we—Buryat—Mongol?) (The Association of the Writers: Ulan Ude).

Choibalsang, H. (1951), *Iltgel ba Ügüülel* (Reports and Essays), vol. 1 (State Publishing House: Ulaanbaatar).

Chuluun, S. (1992), ' "Seremjiltügei!" gehiin uchir' (The Reason for Saying 'Be Vigilant!'), *Ardiin Erhe*, 19 Feb.

Cleaves, Francis Woodman (tr. and ed.) (1982), *The Secret History of the Mongols* (Harvard University Press: Cambridge, Mass.).

Clifford, James (1988), *The Predicament of Culture: Twentieth-Century Ethnography, Literature, and Art* (Harvard University Press: Cambridge, Mass.).

——and Marcus, George E. (eds.) (1986), *Writing Culture: The Poetics and Politics of Ethnography* (University of California Press: Berkeley, Los Angeles, and London).

Cohen, Anthony P. (1985), *The Symbolic Construction of Community* (Routledge: London).

Cohen, Myron (1991), 'Being Chinese: The Peripheralization of Traditional Identity', *Dædalus*, 120/2: 151–70.

Connor, Walker (1984), *The National Question in Marxist–Leninist Theory and Strategy* (Princeton University Press: Princeton).

Coox, A. D. (1985), *Nomonhan: Japan against Russia, 1939* (Stanford University Press: Stanford, Calif.).

Dalai, Ch. (1991*a*), 'Hoyor ih hörshtei gedgee buu mart!' (Don't Forget we have Two Big Neighbours!), *Ünen*, 25 June.

——(1991*b*) 'Oirad Mongolchuudin tüühees ögüüleh ni' (Talking from the History of the Oirat Mongols), *Dornodahini Sudlal*, 1: 19–24.

Damdinsüren, Ts. (1982), *Monggol uran johiyal-un degeji jagun bilig orosibai* (One Hundred Treasures of Mongolian Literature), vol. 2 (Öbür Monggol-un arad-un heblel-un horiy-a: Huhhot).

Dandii, D. (1990), 'Tsagaan ideenii ulamjlal, eruul mend' (The Tradition of White Food and Health), *Shinjleh Uhaan Amidural*, 5.

Dashbalbar, O. (1995), 'Dashiin Byambasüren Tanaa' (To Dashiin Byambasüren), *Ardiin Erh*, 16 Feb.

Dashnyam, G., and Ochir, A. (1991), *Mongolchuudin ugiin bichig, tüüniig sergeen hötölöh ni* (The Genealogy of the Mongols and its Revival) (State Historical Archive: Ulaanbaatar).

Dashpurev, D., and Soni, S. K. (1992), *Reign of Terror in Mongolia 1920–1990* (South Asian Publishers: New Delhi).

Dashtseveg, B. (1976), *MAXN-aas sharin shashin, tüünii üldegdliin esreg yavuulsan temtsliin zarim asuudal* (Some Questions in Relation to the Struggles Waged by the MPRP against Yellow-Sect Buddhism and its Remnants) (State Publishing House: Ulaanbaatar).

Dawson, C. (1955), *The Mongol Mission* (Sheed and Ward: London and New York).

De Rachewiltz, Igor (1971–84), *The Secret History of the Mongols*, in *Papers on Far Eastern History* (Australian National University Press: Canberra).

Derrida, Jacques (1981), *Disseminations*, tr. Alan Bass (University of Chicago Press: Chicago).

Dikötter, F. (1992), *The Discourse of Race in Modern China* (Hurst & Company: London).

Dojoodorj (1991), *Yu Tsedenbaliin Zaluurch* (Yu. Tsedenbal's Helmsman) (n.p.: Ulaanbaatar).

Dominguez, Virginia R. (1986), *White by Definition: Social Classification in Creole Louisiana* (Rutgers University Press: New Brunswick, NJ).

——(1990), 'The Politics of Heritage in Contemporary Israel', in Richard G. Fox (ed.), *Nationalist Ideologies and the Production of National Cultures* (American Anthropological Association: Washington), 130–47.

Dorj, P. (1961), 'Ündesnii asuudlin talaar MAX Namaas bolovsruulsan programm ba uls töriin bodlogo' (MPRP's Programme and Policies on the Nationality Question), *Mongol Ulsin Ih Surguuliin Erdem Shinjlgeenii Bichig*, 6/2.

Douglas, Mary (1966), *Purity and Danger: An Analysis of Concepts of Pollution and Taboo* (Routledge & Kegan Paul: London).

——(1971), 'Deciphering a Meal', in Clifford Geertz (ed.), *Myth, Symbol, and Culture* (W. W. Norton & Company: New York), 61–81.

Dragadze, T. (1980), 'The Place of "Ethnos" Theory in Soviet Anthropology', in Ernest Gellner (ed.), *Soviet and Western Anthropology* (Duckworth: London), 160–70.

——(1993), 'Soviet Economics and Nationalism in the Gorbachev Years. Regionalism, Ethnicized Regionalism and Constitutional Regionalism', in Marco Buttino (ed.), *In a Collapsing Empire: Underdevelopment, Ethnic Conflicts and Nationalisms in the Soviet Union* (Feltrinelli: Milan), 73–82.

Duara, Prasenjit (1993), 'De-constructing the Chinese Nation', *Australian Journal of Chinese Affairs*, 30: 1–26.

Dumont, Jean-Paul (1978), *The Headman and I: Ambiguity and Ambivalence in the Fieldworking Experience* (University of Texas Press: Austin, Tex., and London).

Dupuy, Trevor N., and Blanchard, Wendell (1970), *Area Handbook for Mongolia* (US Government Printing Office: Washington).

Durkheim, E. (1965), *The Elementary Forms of the Religious Life* (Free Press: New York).

Dürven Ündes (1959), *Anagaah Uhaani Dürven Ündes* (Four Roots of Medical Science) (Nationality Publishing House: Beijing).

Eberhard, Wolfram (1982), *China's Minorities: Yesterday and Today* (Wadsworth: Belmont, Calif.).

Eidlitz Kuoljok, Kerstin (1985), *The Revolution in the North: Soviet Ethnography and Nationality Policy* (Almquist & Wiksell International: Uppsala).

Eimer, Helmut (1989), 'The Fear of Being Reborn as a Pig', in K. Sagaster and H. Eimer (eds.), *Religious and Lay Symbolism in the Altaic World and Other Papers* (Otto Harrassowitz: Wiesbaden), 109–12.

Ekvall, Robert B. (1972), 'Demographic Aspects of Tibetan Nomadic Pastoralism', in Brian Spooner (ed.), *Population Growth: Anthropological Implications* (Massachusetts Institute of Technology Press: Cambridge, Mass.), 269–85.

Elleman, Bruce A. (1994), 'Soviet Policy on Outer Mongolia and the Chinese Communist Party', *Journal of Asian History*, 28/2: 108–23.

Endicott-West, Elizabeth (1989), *Mongolian Rule in China: Local Administration in the Yuan Dynasty* (Council on East Asian Studies, Harvard University: Cambridge, Mass.).

Enhbat, B. (1991), 'Obogoo sergeej udmaa avarya' (Revive the Clan and Save our Descent), *Mongoliin Zaluuchuud*, 47–8.

Enhtungalag, D. (1990), 'Yos surtahuuni amdral: ergetsüülel, zahidal' (Morality and Life: Review and Letters), *Mongoliin Zaluuchuud*, 109.

Enhtuya, B. (1991), 'Örh tolgoilson hüühnüüd' (Household-heading Girls), *Ardiin Erh*, 27 Feb.

Enkhbat, Badarchyn, and Odgaard, Ole (1996), 'Decentralization and Local Governance', in Ole Bruun and Ole Odgaard (eds.), *Mongolia in Transition: Old Patterns, New Challenges* (Curzon: Richmond, Surrey), 165–89.

Epstein, Arnold Leonard (1978), *Ethos and Identity: Three Studies in Ethnicity* (Tavistock: London).

Erdene, Ch. (1991), 'Arga biligiin uhaan bol manai yazguur öv' (The Idea of Arga–Bilig is our Ancestral Heritage), *Il Tovchoo*, 6.

Erdenebileg, Ts. (1992), 'Requiem to Arslan—Lev Gumilev', *Mongol Messenger*, 44.

——(1994), 'Talking about the Mongol Script', *Mongol Messenger*, 48.

Fei, Xiaotong (1989), *Zhonghua minzu de duoyuan yiti geju* (Plurality and Unity in the Configuration of the Chinese Nation) (Central Nationality Institute: Beijing).

Fiddes, Nick (1991), *Meat: A Natural Symbol* (Routledge: London).

Firth, Raymond (1973), *Symbols, Public and Private* (George Allen & Unwin: London).

——Hubert, J. and Forge, A. (1969), *Families and their Relatives* (Routledge & Kegan Paul: London).

Fischer, Michael M. J. (1986), 'Ethnicity and the Post-Modern Arts of Memory', in Clifford and Marcus (eds.), 194–233.

Forbath, Ladislaus (1936), *The New Mongolia* (William Heinemann: London and Toronto).

Friedman, Edward (1993), 'A Failed Chinese Modernity', *Dædalus*, 122/2: 1–18.

——(1995), *National Identity and Democratic Prospects in Socialist China* (M. E. Sharpe: Armonk and London).

Friters, Gerand (1949), *Outer Mongolia and its International Position*, ed. E. Lattimore, intro. O. Lattimore (Johns Hopkins University Press: Baltimore).

Galdan, B. (1992), 'Nutgarhah övchin gedeg' (The Disease called Localism), *Il Tovchoo*, 20–30 Sep.

Ganbat, H. (1991), 'Hüseegüi hüühed' (Unexpected Children), *Ünen*, 17 Jan.

Ganhuyag, N. (1994), 'Resettlement of Kazakhs Has Stopped', *Mongol Messenger*, 24.

Gaunt, John (1993), 'Charismatic Warlords in Revolutionary Mongolia' (Ph.D. dissertation, University of Cambridge).

Geertz, Clifford (1973), 'After the Revolution: The Fate of Nationalism in the New States', in *The Interpretation of Cultures: Selected Essays* (Basic Books: New York), 234–54.

——(1983), ' "From the Native's Point of View": On the Nature of Anthropological Understanding', in *Local Knowledge: Further Essays in Interpretive Anthropology* (Basic Books: New York), 55–70.

Gellner, Ernest (1983), *Nations and Nationalism* (Basil Blackwell: Oxford).

——(1987), *Culture, Identity, and Politics* (Cambridge University Press: Cambridge).

——(1988), *State and Society in Soviet Thought* (Basil Blackwell: Oxford).

Gernet, Jacques (1962), *Daily Life in China on the Eve of the Mongol Invasion, 1250–75* (Stanford University Press: Stanford, Calif.).

Gilroy, P. (1987), *There Ain't no Black in the Union Jack* (Hutchinson: London).

Gladney, Dru C. (1991), *Muslim Chinese: Ethnic Nationalism in the People's Republic* (Council on East Asian Studies and Harvard University Press: Cambridge, Mass., and London).

——(1994), 'Representing Nationality in China: Refiguring Majority/Minority Identities', *Journal of Asian Studies*, 53/1: 92–123.

——(1995), 'China's Ethnic Awakening', *Asia Pacific Issues: Analysis from the East–West Center*, 18.

——(1996), 'Relational Alterity: Constructing Dungan (Hui), Uygur, and Kazakh Identities across China, Central Asia, and Turkey', *History and Anthropology*, 9/4: 445–77.

Goldstein, Melvyn C. and Beall, Cynthia M. (1994), *The Changing World of Mongolia's Nomads* (University of California Press: Berkeley and Los Angeles).

Gongor, D. (1970), *Halh Tovchoon I: Halh Mongolchuudin Övög Deedes ba Halhin Haant Uls (VII–XVII zuun)* (A Brief Halh History, I: The Ancestors of the Halh Mongols and the Halh Khanate—VII–XVII centuries) (Academy of Sciences: Ulaanbaatar).

——(1978), *Halh Tovchoon II: Halh Mongolchuudin Niigem-ediin Zasgiin Bai-guulal (XI–XVII)* (A Brief Halh History, II: The Socio-Economic Organizations of the Halh Mongols—XI–XVII centuries) (Academy of Sciences: Ulaanbaatar).

Goody, Jack (1983), *The Development of Family and Marriage in Europe* (Cambridge University Press: Cambridge).

Griffin, Keith (ed.) (1995), *Poverty and the Transition to a Market Economy in Mongolia* (Macmillan: London).

Griffiths, Gareth (1994), 'The Myth of Authenticity', in Chris Tiffin and Alan Lawson (eds.), *De-Scribing Empire* (Routledge: London), 70–85.

Grivelet, S. (1995), 'Reintroducing the Uighur-Mongolian script in Mongolia today', *Mongolian Studies: Journal of the Mongolian Society*, 18: 49–60.

Guérer, Annick Le (1993), *Scent: The Mysterious and Essential Powers of Smell*, tr. Richard Miller (Chatto & Windus: London).

Gulliver, Philip Hugh (ed.) (1969), *Tradition and Transition in East Africa: Studies of the Tribal Element in the Modern Era* (University of California Press: Berkeley).

Gungaadash, B. (1986), *BNMAU-in niigem-ediin zasgiin gazarzui* (The Socio-Economic Geography of the MPR) (State Publishing House: Ulaanbaatar).

Hahaar, O. (1992), 'Nüüdeliin tuhai shuugian' (The Noise of Emigration), *Ünen*, 25 Jan.

Hamayon, Roberte N. (forthcoming), 'Shamanism, Buddhism, and Epic Heroism: Which Supports the Identity of the Post-Soviet Buryats?', tr. C. Humphrey, *Central Asian Survey*.

Handelman, Don, and Shamgar-Handelman, Lea (1990), 'Shaping Time: The Choice of the National Emblem of Israel', in Emiko Ohnuki-Tierney (ed.), *Culture Through Time—Anthropological Approaches* (Stanford University Press: Stanford, Calif.), 193–226.

Harris, Marvin (1978), *Cannibals and Kings: The Origins of Cultures* (Collins: London).

——(1986), *Good to Eat: Riddles of Food and Culture* (Simon & Schuster: New York).

Haslund, Henning (1934), *Tents in Mongolia (Yabonah): Adventures and Experiences among the Nomads of Central Asia*, tr. Elizabeth Sprigge and Claude Napier (E. P. Dutton: New York).

Hayden, Robert M. (1992), 'Constitutional Nationalism in the Formerly Yugoslav Republics', *Slavic Review*, 51/4: 654–73.

Heaton, William (1992), 'Mongolia in 1991: The Uneasy Transition', *Asian Survey*, 32/1: 50–5.

Hechter, M. (1975), *Internal Colonialism* (Routledge: London).

Heissig, W. (1966), *A Lost Civilization, the Mongols Rediscovered*, tr. from German by D. J. S. Thomson (Thames & Hudson: London).

——(1980), *The Religions of the Mongols* (Routledge & Kegan Paul: London).

Heng, Geraldine, and Devan, Janadas (1992), 'State Fatherhood: The Politics of Nationalism, Sexuality and Race in Singapore', in Parker *et al.* (eds.), 343–64.

Herzfeld, Michael (1992), *The Social Production of Indifference: Exploring the Symbolic Roots of Western Bureaucracy* (Berg: New York and Oxford).

Hobsbawm, Eric (1983), 'Mass-Producing Traditions: Europe, 1870–1914', in Hobsbawm and Ranger (eds.), 263–307.

——(1990), *Nations and Nationalism since 1680: Programme, Myth, Reality* (Cambridge University Press: Cambridge).

——(1992), 'Ethnicity and Nationalism in Europe Today', *Anthropology Today*, 8/1: 3–13.

——and Ranger, Terence (eds.) (1983), *The Invention of Tradition* (Cambridge University Press: Cambridge).

Holy, Ladislav (1993), 'The End of Socialism in Czechoslovakia', in C. M. Hann (ed.), *Socialism: Ideals, Ideologies, and Local Practice* (Routledge: London and New York), 204–17.

——and Stuchlik, Milan (1983), *Actions, Norms and Representations: Foundations of Anthropological Inquiry* (Cambridge University Press: Cambridge).

Hopkirk, Peter (1990), *The Great Game: On Secret Service in High Asia* (Oxford University Press: Oxford).

Hroch, Miroslav (1993), 'From National Movement to the Fully-Fledged Nation', *New Left Review*, 198: 3–20.

Humphrey, Caroline (1971), 'Some Ideas of Saussure Applied to Buryat Magical Drawings', in Edwin Ardener (ed.), *Social Anthropology and Language* (Tavistock: London), 271–90.

——(1974a), 'Horse Brands of the Mongolians: A System of Signs in a Nomadic Culture', *American Ethnologist*, 1/3: 471–88.

——(1974b), 'Inside a Mongolian Tent', *New Society*, Oct., 273–5.

——(1978), 'Pastoral Nomadism in Mongolia: The Role of Herdsmen's Cooperatives in the National Economy', *Development and Change*, 9: 133–60.

——(1979), 'The Uses of Genealogy: A Historical Study of the Nomadic and Sedentarized Buryats', in L'Équipe écologie et anthropologie des sociétés pastorales (ed.), *Pastoral Production and Society* (Cambridge University Press and Maison des Sciences de l'Homme: Cambridge and Paris), 235–60.

——(1981), 'Text and Ritual for the Libation of Mare's Milk', *Journal of the Anglo-Mongolian Society*, 7/2: 78–96.

284   *Bibliography*

Humphrey, Caroline (1983), *Karl Marx Collective: Economy, Society and Religion in a Siberian Collective Farm* (Cambridge University Press: Cambridge).

—— (1990), 'Buryats', in Graham Smith (ed.), *The Nationalities Question in the Soviet Union* (Longman: London and New York), 290–303.

—— (1991), 'Icebergs, Barter and Mafia in Provincial Russia', *Anthropology Today*, 7/2: 8–13.

—— (1992*a*), 'The Moral Authority of the Past in Post-Socialist Mongolia', *Religion, State and Society*, 20/3–4: 375–89.

—— (1992*b*), 'Women and Ideology in Hierarchical Societies in East Asia', in S. Ardener (ed.), *Persons and Powers of Women in Diverse Cultures* (Berg: New York and Oxford), 178–92.

—— (1994), 'Remembering an "Enemy": The Bogd Khaan in Twentieth-Century Mongolia', in Rubie S. Watson (ed.), *Memory, History, and Opposition under State Socialism* (School of American Research Press: Santa Fe, N. Mex.), 21–41.

—— with Onon, Urunge (1996), *Shamans and Elders: Experience, Knowledge, and Power among the Daur Mongols* (Clarendon Press: Oxford).

—— Sneath, David, and Chopping, Mark (1993), 'Cambridge University MacArthur Project for Environment and Cultural Conservation in Inner Asia: Interim Report 1992' (MS).

Hün (1992), *Mongol Ulsin Hün Amin Talaar Oirin Jilüüded Avch Heregjüüleh Arga Hemjeenii 'Hün' Ündesnii Hötölbör* (National 'Man' Programme to be Implemented in the Coming Years in Relation to the Mongolian Population) (n.p.: Ulaanbaatar).

Hyer, Paul (1969), 'Ulanhu and Inner Mongolian Autonomy under the Chinese People's Republic', *Mongolia Society Bulletin*, 9/15: 24–62.

—— (1978), 'Mongolian Stereotypes and Images: Some Introductory Observations', in L. V. Clark and P. A. Draghi (eds.), *Aspects of Altaic Civilization*, vol. 2 (Asian Studies Research Institute, Indiana University: Bloomington, Ind.), 65–80.

—— and Heaton, William (1968), 'The Cultural Revolution in Inner Mongolia', *China Quarterly*, Oct.–Dec, 114–28.

Ichinnorov, S. (1990), *MAXN-in oron nutgiin ba anhan shatni baiguulagin tüühees* (History of the Regional and Basic Level Organizations of the MPRP) (State Publishing House: Ulaanbaatar).

Illingworth, Ronald S. (1987), *The Normal Child: Some Problems of the Early Years and their Treatment*, 9th edn. (Churchill Livingstone: Edinburgh, London, Melbourne, and New York).

Irinchen (1984), 'Zhungguo beifang minzu yu Mengguzu zuyuan' (Nationalities in North China and the Ethnogenesis of the Mongolian Nationality), in *Yuan shi lun ji* (People's Publishing House: Beijing).

Isaacs, Harold R. (1989), *Idols of the Tribe: Group Identity and Political Change* (Harvard University Press: Cambridge, Mass.).

Ishjamts, N. (1990), 'Chingisiin Mendelsnii 800 Jiliin Oig Temdeglesen Tuhai Durdatgal' (Reminiscences of Celebrating the 800th Anniversary of Chinggis Khan's Birth), *Dornodahinii Sudlal*, 2.

——(1991), 'Mongol, Türeg ugsaatni tüühen holbogdol' (The Historical Relations between Mongols and Turks), *Ündesnii Deveshil*, 17 Apr.

Jadambaa, R. (1990), 'Akademich Ts. Damdinsüreng heletssen ni' (Discussions on Academician Ts. Damdinsüren), *Manai Inder*, 11–12: 49–59.

Jagchid, Sechin (1988), 'Reasons for the Nondevelopment of Nomadic Power in North Asia since the Eighteenth Century', in *Essays in Mongolian Studies* (Brigham Young University Press: Salt Lake City), 173–7.

——and Hyer, Paul (1979), *Mongolia's Culture and Society* (Westview: Boulder, Colo.).

——and Symons, Van Jay (1989), *Peace, War and Trade along the Great Wall: Nomadic–Chinese Interaction through Two Millennia* (Indiana University Press: Bloomington, Ind.).

Jakubowska, Longina (1990), 'Political Drama in Poland: The Use of National Symbols', *Anthropology Today*, 6/4: 10–13.

Jameson, Fredric (1986), 'Third World Literature in the Era of Multinational Capitalism', *Social Text*, 15: 65–88.

Jamsran, L. (1992), *Mongolchuudiin Sergen Mandaltiin Ehen* (The Beginning of the Mongolian Renaissance) (Soyombo: Ulaanbaatar).

Jamtsarano, Ts. ([1934] 1979), *Ethnography and Geography of the Darkhat and Other Mongolian Minorities* (Mongolia Society: Bloomington, Ind.).

——(1961), 'Kul't chingisa v Ordose iz puteshestviya v yujnuyu Mongoliyu v 1919' (The Cult of Chinggis in Ordos, from Journeys in South Mongolia in 1919), *Central Asiatic Journal*, 7: 194–234.

Janabel, Jiger (1996), 'When National Ambition Conflicts with Reality: Studies on Kazakhstan's Ethnic Relations', *Central Asian Survey*, 15/1: 5–21.

Janhunen, Juha (1990), *Material on Manchurian Khamnigan Mongol*, Castrenianumin Toimitteita, 37 (Castrenianum Complex of the University of Helsinki Finno-Ugrian Society: Helsinki).

——(1991), *Material on Manchurian Khamnigan Evenki*, Castrenianumin Toimitteita, 40 (Castrenianum Complex of the University of Helsinki Finno-Ugrian Society: Helsinki).

——(1996), *Manchuria: An Ethnic History* (The Finno-Ugrian Society: Helsinki).

Jankowiak, William R. (1988), 'The Last Hurrah? Political Protest in Inner Mongolia', *Australian Journal of Chinese Affairs*, 19–20: 269–88.

——(1993), *Sex, Death and Hierarchy in A Chinese City: An Anthropological Account* (Columbia University Press: New York and Oxford).

Joó, Rudolf (ed.) (1994), *The Hungarian Minority's Situation in Ceauşescu's Romania* (Atlantic Research and Publications: Highland Lakes, NJ).

Juergensmeyer, Mark (1993), *The New Cold War? Religious Nationalism Confronts the Secular State* (University of California Press: Berkeley, Los Angeles, and London).

Jügder, Ch. (1987), *Mongold feudalizm togtoh üyeiin niigem-uls tör, gün uhaani setelgee* (Social, Political and Philosophical Mentalities during the Period when Feudalism was Established in Mongolia) (Academy of Sciences: Ulaanbaatar).

Kabzinska-Stawarz, Iwona (1987), 'Eriin Gurvan Naadam', *Ethnologia Polona*, 13.

Kaplonski, Christopher (1993), 'Collective Memory and Chingunjav's Rebellion', *History and Anthropology*, 6/2–3: 235–59.

——(1996), ' "For the Memory of the Hero is his Second Life": Truth, History and Politics in Late Twentieth-Century Mongolia' (Ph.D. dissertation, Rutgers University).

Kara, G. (1991), 'A Forgotten Anthem', *Mongolian Studies: Journal of the Mongolia Society*, 15: 145–54.

Kertzer, David I. (1988), *Ritual, Politics, and Power* (Yale University Press: New Haven and London).

Khan, Almaz (1995), 'Chinggis Khan: From Imperial Ancestor to Ethnic Hero', in Stevan Harrell (ed.), *Cultural Encounters on China's Ethnic Frontiers* (University of Washington Press: Seattle and London), 248–77.

Khazanov, A. M. (1984), *Nomads and the Outside World* (Cambridge University Press: Cambridge).

Krader, Lawrence (1963), *Social Organization of the Mongol Turkic Pastoral Nomads* (Mouton: The Hague).

Krueger, J. R. (tr.) (1967), *The Bejewelled Summary of the Origin of Khans—A History of the Eastern Mongols to 1662*, by Sagang Sechen (part 1) (Indiana University Press: Bloomington, Ind.).

Largey, Gale P., and Watson, David R. (1972), 'The Sociology of Odors', *American Journal of Sociology*, 77: 1021–34.

Larson, Frans August (1930), *Larson, Duke of Mongolia* (Little, Brown: Boston).

Lattimore, Owen (1941), *Mongol Journeys* (Jonathan Cape: London).

——(1950), *Pivot of Asia: Sinkiang and the Inner Asian Frontiers of China and Russia* (Little, Brown: Boston).

——(1962), *Nomads and Commissars: Mongolia Revisited* (Oxford University Press: New York).

——(1987), 'Mongolia as a Leading State', *Mongolian Studies: Journal of the Mongolia Society*, 10: 5–18.

Lauf, Detlef Ingo (1976), *Tibetan Sacred Art: The Heritage of Tantra* (Shambhala: Boston).

Leach, Edmund (1954), *Political Systems of Highland Burma* (Bell: London).

——(1961), 'The Structural Implications of Matrilateral Cross-Cousin Marriage', in *Rethinking Anthropology* (Athlone Press: London), 54–104.

——(1972), 'Anthropological Aspects of Language: Animal Categories and Verbal Abuse', in Pierre Maranda (ed.), *Mythology* (Penguin: Harmondsworth), 39–67.

Leavitt, Gregory (1989), 'Disappearance of the Incest Taboo: A Cross-Cultural Test of General Evolutionary Hypotheses', *American Anthropologist*, 91/1: 116–31.

——(1990), 'Sociobiological Explanations of Incest Avoidance: A Critical Review of Evidential Claims', *American Anthropologist*, 92/4: 971–93.

Lévi-Strauss, Claude (1966), 'The Culinary Triangle', *Partisan Review*, 33: 586–95.

——(1969), *The Elementary Structures of Kinship* (Eyre & Spottiswoode: London).

——(1978), *The Origin of Table Manners* (Jonathan Cape: London).

Lhagvadorj, O. (1991), 'Mongol hünii oyun, udamshlin sang hamgaalya' (Protect the Intelligence and Genetic Fund of the Mongols), *Erdeniin Erh*, 1–15 Feb.

Li, Victor Hao (1994), 'From Qiao to Qiao', in Tu Wei-ming (ed.), *The Living Tree: The Changing Meaning of Being Chinese Today* (Stanford University Press: Stanford, Calif.), 213–20.

Lin, Gan (1979), *Zhaojun yu Zhaojunfen* (Zhao Jun and Zhaojun's Tomb) (Neimenggu Renmin Chubanshe: Huhhot).

Löfgren, O. (1985), 'Our Friends in Nature: Class and Animal Symbolism', *Ethnos*, 8: 184–213.

Louden, J. B. (1977), 'On Body Products', in J. Blacking (ed.), *The Anthropology of the Body* (Academy Press: London), 161–78.

Lovely Ordos (1985), *Keai de Eerduosi* (Lovely Ordos) (Inner Mongolian Publishing House: Huhhot).

Lubsandanjin (1990), *Altan Tovch* (Golden Summary) (Ulsiin Hevleliin Gazar: Ulaanbaatar).

Lubsanjab, Choi (1980), 'Milk in the Mongol Customs: Some Remarks on its Symbolic Significance', *Etnografia Polska*, 24: 41–3.

Mach, Zdzislaw (1985), 'National Symbols in the Context of Ritual: The Polish Example', *Journal of the Anthropological Society of Oxford*, 1: 19–34.

Maidar, Ts. (1990), *Honhnii duun, Önöögiin Bidnii 'nen shine' tüüh* (The Songs of the Bell, the More Recent History of our Time) (n.p.: Ulaanbaatar).

Maiskii, I. (1921), *Sovrennaya Mongoliya* (Contemporary Mongolia) (n.p.: Irkutsk).

Major, John S. (1990), *The Land and People of Mongolia* (J. B. Lippincott: New York).

Mao Zedong (1991), 'Zhonghua suweiai zhongyang zhengfu dui neimenggu renmin xuanyan' (Declaration to the Inner Mongolian People from the Chinese Soviet Government, 20 Dec. 1935), in Zhonggong zhongyang tongzhanbu (compiler), *Minzu wenti wenxian huibian: 1921, 7–1949, 9* (Zhonggong Zhongyang Dangxiao Chubanshe: Beijing).

Mauss, Marcel ([1925] 1954), *The Gift: Forms and Functions of Exchange in Archaic Societies* (Cohen & West: London).

Milivojevic, M. (1991*a*), 'The Mongolian People's Army: Military Auxiliary and Political Guardian', in Shirin Akiner (ed.), *Mongolia Today* (Kegan Paul International: London and New York), 136–54.

——(1991*b*), *The Mongolian Revolution of 1990: Stability or Conflict in Inner Asia?* (Research Institute for the Study of Conflict and Terrorism: London).

Minis, A., and A. Sarai, (1960), *BNMAU Bayan Ölgii Aimgiin Kazah Ard Tümnii Tüühees* (From the History of the Kazakh People in Bayan Ölgii Province of the MPR) (The State Publishing House: Ulaanbaatar).

Mongush, Mergen (1993), 'The Annexation of Tannu-Tuva and the Formation of the Tuva ASSR', *Central Asian Survey*, 12/1: 81–6.

Morgan, David (1987), *The Mongols* (Basil Blackwell: New York).

Moses, Larry W. (1967), 'Soviet–Japanese Confrontation in Outer Mongolia: The Battle of Nomonkhan-Khalkhin Gol', *Journal of Asian History*, 1: 64–85.

——(1977), *The Political Role of Mongol Buddhism* (Indiana University Press: Bloomington, Ind.).

Mosse, George L. (1985), *Nationalism and Sexuality: Respectability and Abnormal Sexuality in Modern Europe* (H. Fertig: New York).

Mróz, Lech (1977), 'Milk/Meat = Tradition/Modernity', *Ethnologia Polona*, 30: 61–6.

Murphy, G. (1966), *Soviet Mongolia: A Study of the Oldest Political Satellite* (University of California Press: Berkeley).

Murphy, R. F. and Kasdan, L. (1959), 'The Structure of Parallel Cousin Marriage', *American Anthropologist*, 61: 17–29.

Nagaanbuu, N. (1995), 'Eleg negtei l um bol eh ornoo deedleh ni "huul" ' (It is the 'Law' for all those who Think of Being of One Liver to respect the Motherland), *Hün Erdene*, 2.

Naran Bilik (1989), 'Guanyu Xingmin De Yuyan Bianxi Yanjiu' (Linguistic Analysis of Names) (Ph.D. dissertation, Central Nationality Institute, China).

Narangerel, S. (1990), *R. Choinomd Tulgasan Yal* (Crime Charged against R. Choinom) (Mongol Uran Zohiol Press: Ulaanbaatar).

Narayan, Kirin (1993), 'How Native is a "Native" Anthropologist?', *American Anthropologist*, 95/3: 671–86.

National Security Council of Mongolia (1995), 'Concept of National Security of Mongolia (Article 9: Security of the Population and its Gene Pool)', *Mongol Messenger*, 14.

Natsagdorj, Sh. (1962), *Halhiin Tüüh* (History of the Halh) (Ulsiin Hevleliin Hereg Erhleh Horoo: Ulaanbaatar).

——(1968), *To Wang ba tüünii surgaal* (To Wang and his Teachings) (State Publishing House: Ulaanbaatar).

——(1972), *Sum, hamjlaga shav' ard* (Arrow [district], Serf, Disciple, and Commoner) (State Publishing House: Ulaanbaatar).

Nergui, O. (1991), 'Harid odson hairan ch saihan büsgüichuud' (The Wasted Beautiful Ladies who have gone to Foreign Land), *Zohist Ayalguu*, 21.

Nomin, L. (1992), 'A New National Problem?', *Mongol Messenger*, 37.

Norovsambuu, S., and Dashjamts, D. (eds.) (1988), *Öngörsnii üldegdel, önöögiin sörög üzegdel, tüüniig davan tuulah asuudal* (The Past Remnants, their Contemporary Negative Phenomena, and the Question of Eliminating Them) (Academy of Sciences: Ulaanbaatar).

Norovsambuu, S. *et al.* (eds.) (1989), *Mongoliin Örnöd Nutgiin Hün Amin Aj Töröh Yosni Högjil* (The Development of the Life-style amongst the Populations in the Western Zone of Mongolia) (State Publishing House: Ulaanbaatar).

Nyambuu, Ch. (1976), *BNMAU-in hün amiin nöhön üildverleliin baidal* (The Situation of Demographic Development in the MPR) (State Publishing House: Ulaanbaatar).

Nyambuu, H. (1979), *Mongolin Belegdel* (Mongolian Symbols) (State Publishing House: Ulaanbaatar).

——(1992), *Mongolin Ugsaatani Zuin Udirtgal: Ugsaatni Büreldhuun Garval Zui* (An introduction to the Ethnography of Mongolia: Ethnic Composition and Ethnogenesis) (Surah Bichig Hüühdiin Nomin Hevleliin Gazar: Ulaanbaatar).

Ochir, A. (1993), *Mongolin Oiraduudin Tüühiin Tovch* (A Brief History of the Oirats in Mongolia) (Oirad Mongolin Soyol Irgemshil Niigemleg: Ulaanbaatar).

Ochirbat, Punsalmaagiin (1996), *Tengriin Tsag* (The Heavenly Hour) (Nomin Impex: Ulaanbaatar).

Ohnuki-Tierney, Emiko (1987), *The Monkey as Mirror: Symbolic Transformations in Japanese History and Ritual* (Princeton University Press: Princeton).

Okada, Hidehiro (1989), 'Dayan Khan in the Battle of Dalan Terigün', in Walther Heissig and Klaus Sagaster (eds.), *Gedanke und Wirking: Festschrift zum 90. Geburtstag von Nikolus Poppe* (Otto Harrassowitz: Wiesbaden), 262–70.

——(1991), 'Origin of the Caqar Mongols', *Mongolian Studies: Journal of the Mongolian Society*, 14: 155–79.

——(1993), 'The Khan as the Sun, the Jinong as the Moon', in Barbara Kellner-Heinkele (ed.), *Altaica Berolinensia: The Concept of Sovereignty in the Altaic World* (Otto Harrassowitz: Wiesbaden), 185–90.

Onon, Urgunge (translation and annotation) (1990), *The History and the Life of Chinggis Khan* (E. J. Brill: Leiden).

——and Pritchatt, Derrick (1989), *Asia's First Modern Revolution: Mongolia Proclaims its Independence in 1911* (E. J. Brill: Leiden).

Otgonbaatar, R. (1986), 'Soyombo Üseg Süld Temdgiin Holboo' (The Connection between the Soyombo Script and the Emblem Symbol), *Dornodahini Sudlalin Asuudal*, 2.

Oyunbilig (1987), 'Guanyu Zhuoketu Taiji' (On Tsogt Taiji), *Neimenggu daxue xuebao*, 3.

Paine, Robert (1989), 'Israel: Jewish Identity and Competition over "Tradition"', in E. Tonkin, M. McDonald, and M. Chapman (eds.), *History and Ethnicity* (Routledge: London and New York), 121–36.

Panoff, F. (1970), 'Food and Faeces: A Melanesian Rite', *Man*, 5/2: 237–52.

Pao, Kuo-yi (1964), 'Family and Kinship Structure of the Khorichin Mongols', *Central Asiatic Journal*, 9/4: 277–311.

Parker, A., Russo, M., Sommer, D., and Yaeger, P. (eds.) (1992), *Nationalisms and Sexualities* (Routledge: New York and London).

Pegg, Carole (1991), 'The Revival of Ethnic and Cultural Identity in West Mongolia: The Altai Urianghai Tsuur, the Tuvan Shuur and the Kazak Sybyzgy', *Journal of the Anglo-Mongolian Society*, 13/1–2: 71–84.

——— (1998), Performing Identities in Mongolia: Music, Dance and Oral Narrative (Washington University Press: Seattle).

Perlee, H. (1975), *Mongol Tümnii Garliig Tamgaar Haij Sudlah ni* (Tracing the Origin of the Mongols by Seals) (State Publishing House: Ulaanbaatar).

Polo, Marco (1931), *The Travels of Marco Polo* (George Routledge: London).

Poppe, Nicholas (1978), *Tsongol Folklore* (Otto Harrassowitz: Wiesbaden).

Potkanski, T., and Szynkiewicz, S. (1993), *The Social Context of Liberalization of the Mongolian Pastoral Economy: Report of Anthropological Fieldwork* (Institute of Development Studies, University of Sussex: Brighton).

Potter, Jack M. (1993), 'Socialism and the Chinese Peasant', in C. M. Hann (ed.), *Socialism: Ideals, Ideologies, and Local Practice* (Routledge: London), 157–71.

Potter, Sulamith Heins, and Potter, Jack M. (1990), *China's Peasants: The Anthropology of a Revolution* (Cambridge University Press: Cambridge).

Pozdneyev, A. M. (1971), *Mongolia and Mongols*, tr. John Roger Show and Dale Plank (Indiana University Press: Bloomington, Ind.).

——— (1978), *Ritual and Religion in Society: Lamaist Buddhism in Late 19th-Century Mongolia* (Indiana University Press: Bloomington, Ind.).

Pürev, J. (1990), 'An Open Letter to the Soviet President Gorbachev: Is Mongolia Really so much Indebted to the Soviet Union?', *Mengu Xiaoxi Bao*, 38.

Pürev, O. (1990), 'B. Rinchen—ugsaatni zuich, utga sudlaltan' (B. Rinchen—Ethnographer, Etymologist), in G. Akim (ed.), *Bilguun Nomch Byambin Rinchen* (Mongol Uran Zohiol: Ulaanbaatar).

Radnaabazar, J. (1991), *Ugiin Bichig* (Genealogy) (n.p.: Ulaanbaatar).

Ranger, Terence (1983), 'The Invention of Tradition in Colonial Africa', in Hobsbawn and Ranger (eds.), 211–62.

Rechung Rinpoche (1973), *Tibetan Medicine* (Wellcome Institute of the History of Medicine: London).

Rinchen, B. (1958), 'Soemba—emblema svobodi i nezavisimosti mongol'skogo naroda' (Freedom and Independence of the Mongolian People), in *Iz Nashego Kul'turanogo Nasledia* (From Our Cultural Heritage) (n.p.: Ulaanbaatar), 12–16.

—— (1968), 'Urag Törliin Uchir' (On Kinship), *Zaluu Üye*, 4.

—— (1969), *Mongol Ard Ulsin Hamnigan Ayalgu* (The Hamnigan Dialect in People's Mongolia) (Academy of Sciences: Ulaanbaatar).

—— (1977), 'Everlasting Bodies of the Ancestral Spirits in Mongolian Shamanism', *Studia Orientalia*, 47: 175–80.

—— (ed.) (1979), *Mongol Ard Ulsin Ugsaatni Sudlal Helnii Shinjleliin Atlas* (Ethnographic and Linguistic Atlas of the Mongolian People's Republic) (Academy of Sciences: Ulaanbaatar).

Robins, K. (1991), 'Tradition and Translation: National Culture in its Global Context', in J. Corner and S. Harvey (eds.), *Enterprises and Heritage: Crosscurrents of National Culture* (Routledge: London), 21–44.

Rosaldo, Renato (1993), *Culture and Truth: The Remaking of Social Analysis* (Routledge: London).

Rosenberg, Daniel (1982), 'Leaders and Leadership Roles in a Mongolian Collective: Two Cases', *Mongolian Studies: Journal of the Mongolian Society*, 7: 17–51.

Rossabi, Morris (1988), *Khubilai Khan: His Life and Times* (University of California Press: Berkeley).

Rupen, Robert (1964), *Mongols of the Twentieth Century* (Indiana University Press: Bloomington, Ind.).

—— (1979), *How Mongolia is Really Ruled: A Political History of the Mongolian People's Republic, 1900–1978* (Hoover Institution Press: Stanford, Calif.).

Rushdie, S. (1991), *Imaginary Homelands* (Granta Books: London).

Saha, N., and Tay, J. S. H. (1992), 'Origins of the Koreans', *American Journal of Physical Anthropology*, 88: 27–36.

Sainjirgal and Sharaldai (1983), *Altan Ordun-u Tayilg-a* (The Ritual of the Golden Palace) (Nationality Publishing House: Beijing).

Samand, U. (1991), 'Obog gedeg etsgiin ner uu?' (Is Obog Patronymic?), *Üg*, 11–20 Oct.

Sambuu, B. (1983), *Nüigem Sudlaliin Ündsen Oilgoltin Tovch Toli* (A Concise Dictionary for Basic Understanding of Social Research) (State Publishing House: Ulaanbaatar).

Sanders, Alan J. K. (1987), *Mongolia: Politics, Economics and Society* (Frances Printer: London).

—— (1991), 'Restructuring and "Openness" ', in Shirin Akiner (ed.), *Mongolia Today* (Kegan Paul: London), 57–78.

—— (1992), 'Mongolia's New Constitution: Blueprint for Democracy', *Asian Survey*, 32/6: 506–20.

—— (1993), 'The Turkic Peoples of Mongolia', in Margaret Bainbridge (ed.), *The Turkic Peoples of the World* (Kegan Paul International: London and New York), 179–200.

—— (1996), *Historical Dictionary of Mongolia* (Scarecrow Press: Lanham, Md., and London).

Sanjdorj, M. (1980), *Manchu Chinese Rule in Northern Mongolia*, tr. U. Onon (C. Hurst & Co.: London).

Sanjmyatav, Bazariin (1991), *Gurvan ulsiin Hiagtiin gereenii tuhai tüühen ünen* (The Historical Truth of the Khiagt Tripartite Treaty) (n.p.: Ulaanbaatar).

Scott, James (1990), *Domination and the Arts of Resistance: Hidden Transcripts* (Yale University Press: New Haven and London).

Serruys, Henry (tr.) (1971), 'A Field Trip to Ordos: A Newspaper Report from 1936', *Mongolia Society Bulletin*, 9/1.

—— (1974), *Kumiss Ceremonies and Horse Races* (Otto Harrassowitz: Wiesbaden).

—— (1987), *The Mongols and Ming China: Customs and History*, ed. Françoise Aubin (Variorum Reprints: London).

Sharab, N. (1991), 'Udmiin san ariun baig' (May the Genetic Fund be Pure), *Ünen*, 10 Apr.

Shelear and Stuart, Kevin (1989), 'The Tungus Evenk', *Journal of the Anglo-Mongolian Society*, 12/1–2.

Shi, Fu (1993), *Wai Menggu duli neimu* (The Inside Story of the Independence of Outer Mongolia) (Renmin Zhongguo Chubanshe: Beijing).

Shirendyv, B. (1968), *By-Passing Capitalism* (State Publishers: Ulaanbaatar).

—— (1972), '(BNMAU)-1921 oni ardin huv'sgalin ündesen shinj chanar, gol ür düng' (The Basic Nature and Consequence of the (1921) People's Revolution), in *Mongol ardiin huvsgaliin 50 jiliin oid zoriulsan erdem shinjilgeenii chuulgani material* (State Publishing House: Ulaanbaatar).

—— and Natsagdorj, Sh. (eds.) (1968), *Bügd Nairamdah Mongol Ard Ulsiin Tüüh* (History of the Mongolian People's Republic) vol. 2 (Academy of Sciences: Ulaanbaatar).

Shnirelman, Victor A. (1996), *Who Gets the Past: Competition for Ancestors among Non-Russian Intellectuals in Russia* (The Woodrow Wilson Center Press: Washington).

Skapa, Barbara, and Benwell, Ann Fenger (1996), 'Women and Poverty during the Transition', in Ole Bruun and Ole Odgaard (eds.), *Mongolia in Transition: Old Patterns, New Challenges* (Curzon: Richmond, Surrey), 135–46.

Smith, Anthony D. (1986), *The Ethnic Origins of Nations* (Basil Blackwell: Oxford).

—— (ed.) (1992), *Ethnicity and Nationalism* (E. J. Brill: Leiden).

Sneath, David (1991), 'The Oboo Ceremony among the Barga Pastoralists of Kholon Buir, Inner Mongolia', *Journal of the Anglo-Mongolian Society*, 13/1–2: 56–65.

—— (1994), 'The Impact of the Cultural Revolution in China on the Mongolians of Inner Mongolia', *Modern Asian Studies*, 18/2: 409–30.

—— (1996), 'Power Centres and Élite Cultures: Notes Towards a Dualistic Cultural Model of Mongolian History', *Inner Asia: Occasional Papers*, 1/1: 101–7.

Snelling, John (1993), *Buddhism in Russia: The Story of Agvan Dorzhiev, Lhasa's Emissary to the Tsar* (Element: Shaftesbury).

Sokolewicz, Zofia (1982), 'Traditional Worldview in Contemporary Mongolia', *Studies in Third World Societies*, 18: 125–39.

Solongo, D. (1992), 'Man in the Focus of Attention', *Mongol Messenger*, 15.

Spivak, Gayatri Chakravorty (1992), 'Women in Difference: Mahasweta Devi's "Douloti the Beautiful" ', in Parker *et al.* (eds.), 96–120.

——(1993), *Outside the Teaching Machine* (Routledge: New York and London).

Sprinker, Michael (1993), 'The Nation Question: Said, Ahmad, Jameson', *Public Culture*, 6.

Stalin, J. V. (1953), *Works, 1907–1913*, vol. 11 (Foreign Languages Publishing House: Moscow).

State Statistical Office (1991), *National Economy of the MPR for 70 Years: (1921–1991)* (State Statistical Office of the MPR: Ulaanbaatar).

Stein, Sir Aurel (1928), *Innermost Asia: Detailed Reports of Explorations in Central Asia, Kan-su and Eastern Iran: Carried Out and Described under the Orders of H.M. Indian Government*, vol. 2 (Clarendon Press: Oxford).

Stites, Richard (1984), 'Adorning the Revolution: The primary symbols of Bolshevism 1917–1918', *Sbornik*, 10: 38–42.

Stuart, Kevin (1996), 'Blue Spots, Idiots, Barbarians, and Tiffin in the Deep Dark Heart of Asia: Mongols in Western Consciousness' (Ph.D. diss., University of Hawaii).

Sugita, Kurumi (1980), 'Some Materials for the Study of Mongolian Women', *Etnografia Polska*, 24: 53–63.

Sumyabaatar (1966), *Buriadin Ugiin Bichigees* (From the Buryat Genealogy) (Academy of Sciences: Ulaanbaatar).

Surmaajav, B. (1991), 'Butachid töröö bitgii hötlüüleerei' (Don't Let a Bastard Take the Helm of the State), *Il Tobchoo*, 1.

Szynkiewicz, Slawoj (1975), 'Kin Groups in Medieval Mongolia', *Ethnologia Polona*, 1: 113–33.

——(1977), 'Kinship Groups in Modern Mongolia', *Ethnologia Polona*, 3: 31–45.

——(1986), 'The Khoshuts of the Mongol Altai: Vicissitudes of Self-Identification', *Ethnologia Polona*, 12: 37–50.

——(1987a), 'Ethnic Boundaries in Western Mongolia: A Case Study of a Somon in the Mongol Altai Region', *Journal of the Anglo-Mongolian Society*, 10/1: 11–16.

——(1987b), 'Settlement and Community among the Mongolian Nomads', *East Asian Civilizations*, 1: 10–44.

——(1988), 'Ethnicity in Western Mongolia: Its Sources and Transition', in *Poland at the Twelfth Congress of Anthropological and Ethnological Sciences* (Ossolineum).

Takahasi, K., and Suvd, D. (1993), 'Adult Lactose Absorption in Mongolia', *Anthropological Science*, 101/3: 301–6.

Tangad, Dan-Aajavyn (1989), 'Dried Dung, the Traditional Mongolian Fuel', tr. and ed. K. Chabros, *Journal of the Anglo-Mongolian Society*, 12/1–2.

Tatar, M. (1976), 'Two Mongol Texts Concerning the Cult of the Mountains', *Acta Orientalia Academiae Scientiarum Hungaricae*, 30: 1–58.

Thierry, François (1989), 'Empire and Minority in China', tr. Tony Berrett, in Gérard Chaliand (ed.), *Minority Peoples in the Age of Nation-States* (Pluto Press: London), 76–99.

Tishkov, V. A. (1989) 'Glasnost and Nationalities within the Soviet Union', *Third World Quarterly*, 11/4: 191–207.

—— (1992), 'The Crisis in Soviet Ethnography', *Current Anthropology*, 33/4: 371–94.

Tod, D. (1991), 'Buriadiin ard tümnii emgenelt huvi zaya' (The Tragic Fate of the Buryats), *Hödölmör*, 14–15.

Tölölyan, Khachig (1991), 'The Nation-State and its Others', *Diaspora*, 1/1: 3–7.

Tsedev, Dojoogyn (ed. and introduction) (1989), *Modern Mongolian Poetry: Modern Mongolian Poetry (1921–1986)*, trans. D. Altangerel (State Publishing House: Ulaanbaatar).

Tsenddoo, B. (1994), *Uls Töriin 333 Onigoo: 1921–1994* (333 Political Jokes: 1921–1994) (Mongol Press: Ulaanbaatar).

Tserenhand, G. (1987), 'Buriadiin garal üüseld holbogdoh temdeglel' (Records Related to the Buryat Ethnogenesis), *Ethnografiin Sudlal*, 10.

Tserinpilov, V. B. (1996), 'Virazhenie "pyat tsevetnih i chetire chujih" v Mongol'ski letnopusyah XIII–XIV vv', (The Expression 'The Five Coloured and Four Foreign' in Mongolian Manuscripts of the 13th–14th Centuries), *Mongolovegnie Issledovaniya*, 1: 49–58.

Tsevel, Ya. (1963), *Mongol tailvar toli* (A Mongolian Explanatory Dictionary) (Academy of Sciences: Ulaanbaatar).

Tu Men and Zhu, Dongli (1995), *Kang Sheng yu 'Neirendang' Yuanan* (Kang Sheng and the Framed-up Case of 'the Inner Mongolian People's Revolutionary Party') (Zhonggong Zhongyang Dangxiao Chubanshe: Beijing).

Turner, Victor W. (1967), *The Forest of Symbols* (Cornell University Press: Ithaca, NY).

—— (1979), 'Betwixt and Between: The Liminal Period in the Rites de Passage', in William Lessa and Evon Vogt (eds.), *Reader in Comparative Religion: An Anthropological Approach*, 4th edn. (Harper and Row: New York and London), 234–42.

Tuyabaatar, Lh. (1990), 'Örgöö ger dotroo öör ger barih hereg baina uu?' (Is it Necessary to Build Another House inside the Palace?), *Hödölmör* 28/7.

Van Amersfoort, Hans (1995), 'Institutional Plurality: Problem or Solution for the Multi-Ethnic State?', in Sukumar Periwal (ed.), *Notions of Nationalism* (Central European University Press: Budapest, London, and New York), 162–81.

Vanchigdorj (1991), 'Süslen Zütgeye' (Let's Endeavour with Faith), *Utga Zohiol*, 11 Jan.

Van den Berghe, Pierre L. (1980), 'Incest and Exogamy: A Sociobiological Reconsideration', *Ethology and Sociobiology*, 1: 151–62.

Verdery, Katherine (1991), *National Ideology under Socialism: Identity and Cultural Politics in Ceauşescu's Romania* (University of California Press: Berkeley).

——(1992), 'Comment: Hobsbawm in the East', *Anthropology Today*, 8/1.

——(1993), 'Ethnic Relations, Economies of Shortage, and the Transition in Eastern Europe', in C. M. Hann (ed.), *Socialism: Ideals, Ideologies, and Local Practice* (Routledge: London), 172–86.

——(1996), *What Was Socialism, and What Comes Next?* (Princeton University Press: Princeton).

Vladimirtsov, B. Y. ([1934] 1980), *Menggu Shehui Zhidu* (Social Organization of the Mongols), tr. from Russian into Chinese by Liu Rongjun (China Social Sciences Publishing House: Beijing).

Vlcek, Emanuel (1965), 'A Contribution to the Anthropology of the Khalkha-Mongols', *Anthropologia*, 9/6–7: 285–367.

Vreeland, H. H. (1957), *Mongol Community and Kinship Structure* (HRAF Press: New Haven).

Walby, S. (1992), 'Women and Nation', in Smith (ed.) (1992).

Waldron, Arthur (1990), *The Great Wall of China: From History to Myth* (Cambridge University Press: Cambridge).

Wasilewski, J. S. (1975), 'Space in Nomadic Culture: A Spatial Analysis of the Mongol Yurts', in Walther Heissig (ed.), *Altaica Collecta. Berichte und Vortrager der XVII Permanent International Altaistic Conference 1974* (Otto Harrassowitz: Wiesbaden), 345–60.

Watson, Peggy (1993), 'The Rise of Masculinism in Eastern Europe', *New Left Review*, 198: 71–82.

Wei, Jingsheng (1992), 'Wei Jingsheng's Letter to Deng Xiaoping in 1992' (MS, 3 Oct. 1992).

Winichakul, Thongchai (1994), *Siam Mapped: A History of the Geo-Body of a Nation* (University of Hawaii Press: Honolulu).

Winrow, Gareth M. (1992), 'Turkey and Former Soviet Central Asia: National and Ethnic Identity', *Central Asian Survey*, 11/3: 101–12.

Wolfram, Sybil (1987), *In-laws and Outlaws: Kinship and Marriage in England, 1800–1980* (St Martin's Press: New York).

Woody, W. (1993), *The Cultural Revolution in Inner Mongolia: Extracts from an Unpublished History*, ed. and tr. Michael Schoenhals (Centre for Pacific Asia Studies at Stockholm University: Stockholm).

Worden, Robert L., and Savada, Andrea Matles (eds.) (1991), *Mongolia: A Country Study* (Federal Research Division, Library of Congress: Washington).

Xie, Zaishan (1985), *History of Yeke Zhu League* (in Chinese) (Yimeng wenshi ziliao: Dongsheng).

Yoshino, Kosaku (1992), *Cultural Nationalism in Contemporary Japan* (Routledge: London and New York).

Young, Robert (1990), *White Mythologies: Writing History and the West* (Routledge: London and New York).

Yu, Zenghe (editor-in-chief) (1994), *Zhongguo Zhoubian Guojia Gaikuang* (Information on Countries Surrounding China) (Zhongyang Minzu Daxue Chubanshe: Beijing).

Zardihan, K., and Chuluunbaatar, G. (1991), *Sotsializm uu? Esvel högjliin gajiluu?* (Socialism? Or Deviation in Development?) (Nuuts Tovchoo: Ulaanbaatar).

Zayabaatar, J. (1990), 'Butach hüüheded buruu bii gejüü uu?' (What is Wrong with Bastard Children?), *Setgüülch*, 4.

Zenee, M. (1992), 'Mongol dah' ardchilal Fashist Shinjtei' (Democracy in Mongolia is Fascist in Nature), *Üg*, 4 May.

Zhukovskaya, Natalia L. (1991), 'Buddhism in the History of Mongols and Buriats: Political and Cultural Aspects', in Gary Seaman and Daniel Marks (eds.), *Rulers from the Steppe: State Formation on the Eurasian Periphery* (Ethnographics Press: Los Angeles), 242–54.

INDEX